Religion &
Classical Warfare

Religion &
Classical Warfare

Archaic and Classical Greece

Edited by
Matthew Dillon, Christopher Matthew
and Michael Schmitz

Pen & Sword
MILITARY

First published in Great Britain in 2020 by
Pen & Sword Military
An imprint of
Pen & Sword Books Ltd
Yorkshire – Philadelphia

ISBN 978 1 47383 429 3

A CIP catalogue record for this book is
available from the British Library.

Typeset by Mac Style
Printed and bound in the UK by TJ International Ltd,
Padstow, Cornwall.

MIX
Paper from
responsible sources
FSC® C013056

Pen & Sword Books Limited incorporates the imprints of Atlas,
Archaeology, Aviation, Discovery, Family History, Fiction, History,
Maritime, Military, Military Classics, Politics, Select, Transport,
True Crime, Air World, Frontline Publishing, Leo Cooper, Remember
When, Seaforth Publishing, The Praetorian Press, Wharncliffe
Local History, Wharncliffe Transport, Wharncliffe True Crime
and White Owl.

For a complete list of Pen & Sword titles please contact

PEN & SWORD BOOKS LIMITED
47 Church Street, Barnsley, South Yorkshire, S70 2AS, England
E-mail: enquiries@pen-and-sword.co.uk
Website: www.pen-and-sword.co.uk

Or

PEN AND SWORD BOOKS
1950 Lawrence Rd, Havertown, PA 19083, USA
E-mail: Uspen-and-sword@casematepublishers.com
Website: www.penandswordbooks.com

Contents

Abbreviations of Ancient Sources

c.	circa (about or approximately, used for dates)
sv, svv	*sub vide*, see under
Ach. Tat.	Achilles Tatius *Leucippe and Clitophon* (early second century AD)
Ael.	Aelian (AD 165/170–230/235)
Nat. An.	*On the Nature of Animals*
Var. Hist.	*Various Histories*
Ael. Tact.	Aelian the Tactician (fourth century BC)
Aesch.	Aeschylus (525? – 456 BC)
Agam.	*Agamemnon*
Eum.	*Eumenides*
Persai	*Persians*
Prom. Bound	*Prometheus Bound*
Seven	*Seven Against Thebes*
Supp.	*Suppliant Women*
Aeschin.	Aeschines *Orations* (*c.* 397–322 BC)
Andoc. *Myst.*	Andocides *On the Mysteries* (399 BC)
Apollod.	*Apollodorus* (first or second century AD)
Bibl.	*Bibliotheke* (*The Library*)
Epit.	*Epitome* (of *The Library*)
Ap. Rhod. *Argon.*	Apollonius of Rhodes *Argonautica* (third century BC)
Ar.	Aristophanes (*c.* 460/450–386 BC)
Arist.	Aristotle (384–322 BC)
Cael.	*de Caelo* (*On the Heavens*)
Prob.	*Problems*
[Arist.]	Pseudo-Aristotle
Ath. Pol.	*Athenaion Politeia* (written 330s BC)
Mir. ausc.	*de Mirabilibus Auscultationibus* (*On Marvellous Things Heard*) (late fourth-third century BC?)
Aristid.	Aristides [AD 117–c. 181]
Or.	*Orations*
Panath.	*Panathenaic Oration*
Arr	Arrian (AD 85–145)

Anab.	Anabasis
Tact.	Tactica
Asclep. *Strat.*	Asclepiodotus *Stratagems* (first century AD)
Athen. *Deip.*	Athenaeus *Deipnosophistae* (*Wise Men at Dinner*) (*c.* AD 200)
Aul. Gell.	Aulus Gellius *Attic Nights* (*c.* AD 180)
Bacchyl.	Bacchylides (*c.* 520–450 BC)
Callim.	Callimachus (third century BC)
Cic.	Cicero (106–43 BC)
Div.	*de Divinatione* (*On Divination*)
Inv.	*de Inventione* (*On Invention*)
Leg.	*de Legibus (On the Laws)*
Nat. Deor.	*de Natura Deorum (On the Nature of the Gods)*
Dem.	Demosthenes *Orations* (384–322 BC)
Ep.	*Epistles*
Dio Chrys. *Or.*	Dio Chrysostom *Orations* (*c.* AD 40–120)
Diod.	Diodorus Siculus *Universal History* (first century BC)
Diog. Laert.	Diogenes Laertius *Lives and Opinions of Eminent Philosophers* (first half of the third century AD)
Dion. Hal.	Dionysius of Halicarnassus (Augustan era)
On Thuc.	*On Thucydides*
Rom. Ant.	*Roman Antiquities*
Diosc.	Dioscorides *de Materia Medica* (*Concerning Medical Material*) (first century AD)
Eur.	Euripides (480s – 407/6 BC)
Andr.	*Andromache*
Bacch.	*Bacchae*
El.	*Electra*
Erech.	*Erechtheus*
Hec.	*Hecabe*
Heracl.	*Heracles*
Hipp.	*Hippolytus*
Iph. Aul.	*Iphigenea at Aulis*
Iph. Taur.	*Iphigenea at Tauris*
Med.	*Medea*
Phoen.	*Phoenician Women*
Rhes.	*Rhesus*
Suppl.	*Suppliant Women*
Troj.	*Trojan Women*
Eustathius *Il.*	*Commentary on the Iliad* (*c.* AD 1115–1195)

Front. *Strat.*	Frontinus *Stratagems* (died AD 103/4)
Gorg. *Hel.*	Gorgias *Helen* (first century BC)
Hdt.	Herodotus *Histories* (second half of the fifth century BC)
Hes.	Hesiod (writing around 700 BC)
Shield Her.	*Shield of Heracles*
Theog.	*Theogony*
Hesych.	Hesychius *Lexicon* (fifth century AD)
Hippoc.	Hippocrates (late fifth to mid-fourth century BC)
Morb. sacr.	*de Morbo Sacro* (*On the Sacred Disease*)
Aer.	*de Aere Aquis et Locis* (*Concerning Air, Water, and Places*)
Hom.	Homer (eighth century BC)
Il.	*Iliad*
Od.	*Odyssey*
Hom. Hymn	*Homeric Hymn* (seventh century BC)
Isoc.	Isocrates *Orations* (436–338 BC)
Jul. Afric. *Kest.*	Julius Africanus *Kestoi* (*c.* AD 160–240)
Justin *Epit.*	Justin *Epitome of 'The History of Philip' of Pompeius Trogus* (second or third century AD)
Livy	Livy *History of Rome* (59 BC–AD 17)
Luc.	Lucian (born *c.* AD 120)
Deor. Dial.	*Deorum Dialogi* (*Dialogues of the Gods*)
Icar.	*Icaromenippus*
Philopseud.	*Philopseudes* (*Lover of Lies*)
Lycoph. *Alex.*	Lycophron *Alexandra* (third or second century BC)
Lycurg. *Leocr.*	Lycurgus *Oration Against Leocrates* (delivered 330 BC)
Macrob. *Sat.*	Macrobius *Saturnalia* (fifth century AD)
Nonnus *Dion.*	*Dionysiaca* (written *c.* AD 450–470)
Onas. *Strat.*	Onasander *Strategikos* (*On Generalship*) (first century AD)
Ov.	Ovid (43 BC–AD 17)
Met.	*Metamorphoses*
Tr.	*Tristia*
Pal. Anth.	*Palatine Anthology* (compiled *c.* AD 940)
Paus.	Pausanias *Description of Greece* (wrote *c.* AD 150)
Philost.	Philostratus (third century AD)
Gymnast.	*Gymnasticus*
Imag.	*Imagines* (*Images*)
Phot. *Lex.*	Photius *Lexicon* (*c.* AD 810–893)
Pin.	Pindar (born 518 BC?)
Isth.	*Isthmian Odes*
Nem.	*Nemean Odes*

Olym.	*Olympian Odes*
Pyth.	*Pythian Odes*
Plat.	Plato (*c.* 429–347 BC)
Apol.	*Apology*
Charm.	*Charmides*
Crit.	*Crito*
Menex.	*Menexenus*
Pol.	*Politics*
Rep.	*Republic*
Pliny *Nat. Hist.*	*Natural History* (AD 23/24–79)
Plut.	Plutarch (second century AD)
Ages.	*Agesilaus*
Alc.	*Alcibiades*
Alex.	*Alexander*
Arat.	*Aratus*
Arist.	*Aristides*
Cat. Min.	*Cato Minor* (*The Younger*)
Cim.	*Cimon*
Cleom.	*Cleomenes*
Luc.	*Lucullus*
Lyc.	*Lycurgus*
Lys.	*Lysander*
Marc.	*Marcellus*
Mor.	*Moralia*
Nic.	*Nicias*
Pel.	*Pelopidas*
Per.	*Pericles*
Pyrr.	*Pyrrhus*
Sol.	*Solon*
Them.	*Themistocles*
Thes.	*Theseus*
Polemon	Polemon the Sophist (second century AD)
Call.	*Declamation 1: Callimachus*
Cyn.	*Declamation 2: Cynegirus*
Poll.	Pollux *Onamasticum* (second century AD)
Polyaen. *Strat.*	Polyaenus *Stratagems* (second century AD)
Polyb.	Polybius *The Histories* (*c.* 200–118 BC)
Porph. *Abst.*	Porphyry *On Abstinence* (AD 234 – *c.* 305)
Quint. Smyrn.	Quintus Smyrnaeus *Fall of Troy* (fourth century AD)

schol.	scholiast (an ancient commentator on a passage in a literary work)
Soph.	Sophocles (496/5 – *c.* 406 BC)]
Ant.	*Antigone*
El.	*Electra*
Oed. Col.	*Oedipus at Colonus*
Phil.	*Philoctetes*
Trach.	*Women of Trachis*
Stat. *Theb.*	Statius *Thebaid* (*c.* AD 45/early 50s–96)
Steph. Byz.	Stephanus of Byzantium *Ethnica* (sixth century AD)
Stob. *Flor.*	Stobaeus *Florilegium* (written in early fifth century AD)
Strabo	Strabo *Geography* (born *c.* 64 BC, writing in Augustus' reign)
Suda	Suda *Lexicon* (end of the tenth century AD)
Tac.	Tacitus (born between AD 56–58)
Germ.	*Germania*
Hist.	*Histories*
Theophr. *Hist. Pl.*	Theophrastus *Enquiry* (*Historia*) *into Plants* (*c.* 350–287 BC)
Timaeus *Lex Plat.*	Timaeus *Lexicon Platonicum* (*Lexicon of Plato's Works*) (*c.* AD 250)
Thuc.	Thucydides *History of the Peloponnesian War* (second half of the fifth century BC)
Virg. *Aen.*	Virgil *Aeneid* (written between 29–20 BC)
Vitruv.	Vitruvius *Architecture* (written in the second half of the first century BC)
Xen.	Xenophon (430–*c.* 355 BC)
Ages.	*Agesilaus*
Anab.	*Anabasis*
Cav. Comm.	*The Cavalry Commander*
Cyr.	*Cyropaedia* (*The Education of Cyrus*)
Hell.	*Hellenica* (*Greek Affairs*)
Lac. Pol.	*Lacedaemonian Politeia* (*Constitution of the Spartans*)
Mem.	*Memorabilia*

Abbreviations of Modern Works

ABV	Beazley, J.D., 1956, *Attic Black-Figure Vase-Painters*, Oxford.
AC	*L'Antiquité Classique*
Aegaeum	*Annales d'Archéologie Égéenne de l'Université de Liège et UT-PASP*
AJA	*American Journal of Archaeology*
AJAH	*American Journal of Ancient History*
AJPh	*American Journal of Philology*
AN	*Ancient Narrative*
AncW	*The Ancient World: A Scholarly Journal for the Study of Antiquity*
Antichthon	*Antichthon: Journal of the Australasian Society for Classical Studies*
ARV²	Beazley, J.D., 1963, *Attic Red-Figure Vase-Painters*, vols i–iii, 2nd edn, Oxford.
Athenaeum	*Athenaeum. Studi di Letteratura e Storia dell'Antichità*
BCH	*Bulletin de Correspondance Hellénique. Athènes: École Française d'Athènes*
BICS	*Bulletin of the Institute of Classical Studies*
CID	Rougemont, G., 1977, *Corpus des Incriptiones de Delphes*, vol. 1, Paris.
ClAnt	*Classical Antiquity*
CPh	*Classical Philology*
CQ	*Classical Quarterly*
CR	*Classical Review*
CRAI	*Comptes Rendus. Académie des Inscriptions et Belles-Lettres*
CSCA	*Californian Studies in Classical Antiquity*
CSCPh	*Cornell Studies in Classical Philology*
CW	*The Classical World*
Digressus	*Digressus. The Internet Journal for the Classical World*
EA	*Epigraphica Anatolica: Zeitschrift für Epigraphik und Historische Geographie Anatoliens*
Ethnos	*Ethnos. Journal of Anthropology*
FD	*Fouilles de Delphes*

FGrH	Jacoby, F., 1923–58, *Die Fragmente der Griechischen Historiker*, Berlin; Fornara, C.W., 1994, Leiden.
Geology	*Geology. The Geological Society of America*
G&R	*Greece & Rome*
GHI	Tod, M.N. (ed.), 1946 (vol. i, 2nd edn), 1948 (vol. ii), *A Selection of Greek Historical Inscriptions*, Oxford.
GIF	*Giornale Italiano di Filologia*
GRBS	*Greek, Roman and Byzantine Studies*
Hermathena	*Hermathena: A Trinity College Dublin Review*
Hesperia	*Hesperia: The Journal of the American School of Classical Studies at Athens*
Historia	*Historia: Zeitschrift für Alte Geschichte/Revue d'Histoire Ancienne*
HR	*History of Religions*
HSPh	*Harvard Studies in Classical Philology*
HThR	*The Harvard Theological Review*
ICret.	Guarducci, M., 1935–50, *Inscriptiones Creticae*, vols 1–4, Rome.
ICS	*Illinois Classical Studies*
IG	*Inscriptiones Graecae*
I.Gonnoi	Helly, B., 1973, *Gonnoi, vol. 2: Inscriptions*, Amsterdam.
I.Knidos	Blumel, W. (ed.), 1992, *Die Inschriften von Knidos I*, Bonn.
I.Lindos	Blinkenberg, C. (ed.), 1941, *Lindos. Fouilles et recherches, 1902–1914, Vol. 2: Inscriptions*, Berlin.
IMT Kyz Kapu Dağ	Barth, M., and Stauber, J. (eds), *Inschriften Mysia und Troas. Kyzikene, Kapu Dağ, nos. 1401–1856*, Leopold Wenger Institut, Universität Munchen; version of 25.8.1993 (Ibycus); Packard Humanities Institute CD #7, 1996.
I.Stratonikeia	Sahin, S. (ed.), 1981, *Die Inschriften von Stratonikeia 1: Panamara*, Bonn.
JAH	*Journal of Ancient History*
JHS	*The Journal of Hellenic Studies*
JMH	*Journal of Military History. The Society for Military History*
Klio	*Klio. Beiträge zur Alten Geschichte*
Ktema	*Ktema: Civilisations de l'Orient, de la Grèce et de Rome Antiques*
LHR	*Law and History Review. American Society for Legal History*
LIMC	*Lexicon Iconographicum Mythologiae Classicae* i–viii, 1981– 1997, Zurich & Munich.

LSAG	Jeffery, L.H., 1990 (1963), *The Local Scripts of Archaic Greece*, revised edition and supplement by Johnston, A.W., Oxford.
LSCG Suppl.	Sokolowski, F., 1962, *Lois Sacrées des Cités Grecques: Supplément*, Paris.
LSJ[9]	Liddell, H.G., Scott, R., Jones, H.S., *et al.*, 1996, *A Greek-English Lexicon, 9th edn with a Revised Supplement*, Oxford.
Meiggs and Lewis	Meiggs, R., and Lewis, D., 1988, *A Selection of Greek Historical Inscriptions to the End of the Fifth Century* BC, 2nd edn, Oxford.
Military Review	*Military Review. The Professional Journal of the U.S. Army*
Mnemosyne	*Mnemosyne: bibliotheca classica Batava*
Mouseion	*Mouseion: Journal of the Classical Association of Canada / Revue de la Société Canadienne des Études Classiques*
NC	*Numismatic Chronicle*
Numen	*Numen: International Review for the History of Religions*
OlBer	1937–1999, *Bericht über die Ausgrabungen in Olympia*, vols 1–12, Berlin.
PCG	Kassel, R., and Austin, C., 1983–1998, *Poetae Comici Graeci*, vols 1–8, Berlin.
PCPhS	*Proceedings of the Cambridge Philological Society*
Phoenix	*Phoenix: Journal of the Classical Association of Canada / Revue de la Société Canadienne des Études Classiques*
P&P	*Past and Present: A Journal of Historical Studies*
RE	*Realencyclopädie der Classischen Altertumswissenschaft*
REA	*Revue des Études Anciennes*
REG	*Revue des Études Grecques*
RhM	*Rheinisches Museum für Philologie*
RHR	*Revue de l'Histoire des Religions*
SCI	*Scripta Classica Israelica: Yearbook of the Israel Society for the Promotion of Classical Studies*
SEG	*Supplementum Epigraphicum Graecum*
SH	Lloyd-Jones, H., 1983, *Supplementum Hellenisticum*, Berlin.
SIG[3]	Dittenberger, W. (ed.), 1915–1924, *Sylloge Inscriptionum Graecarum*, vols 1–4, third edition, Leipzig.
TAPhA	*Transactions of the American Philological Association*
ThesCRA	*Thesaurus Cultus et Rituum Antiquorum*, 2004–2014, 10 vols, Los Angeles.

TrGF	Snell, B., Kannicht, R., and Radt, S. (eds), 1971–2004, *Tragicorum Graecorum Fragmenta*, vols 1 (2nd edn), 2–5, Göttingen.
ZA	*Ziva Antika / Antiquité Vivante*
ZPE	*Zeitschrift für Papyrologie und Epigraphik*

Spelling of Ancient Names and Terms

On the whole, the familiar Latin form of spelling Greek names and terms has been employed in this volume, except when the Greek form would in fact be more familiar and neater, such as *Phobos* for fear (and not *Phobus*). Transliteration of the Greek letter *kappa* with a *k* has generally been avoided, but rather a *c* is usually employed, as, for example, Hector, the spelling of which is more familiar to readers than is Hektor. Strict transliterations, such as Achilleus rather than the Latin Achilles, have also been avoided so that the names will be immediately clear to the reader. A long vowel in Greek is indicated by a circumflex, as in *chrêsmos* (oracle).

Notes on Contributors

Matthew Dillon (University of New England)
Matthew Dillon is the Professor of Classics and Ancient History at the University of New England, Australia, and gained his BA Hons and MA at the University of Queensland. His research interests include ancient Greek and Roman religion and how religious beliefs intersected with the workings of these ancient societies. He has written several articles and books on Greek religion, including *Girls and Women in Classical Greek Religion* (Routledge, 2002), and Omens and Oracles. Divination in Ancient Greece (Routledge, 2017), as well as textbooks and sourcebooks on ancient Greece and Rome. He is currently working on a monograph project concerning brutality and discipline in the ancient Greek world, with a major focus on Greek warfare. He has also published on Greek epigraphy and society.

Matthew Gonzales (St Anselm College)
Matthew Gonzales was born and raised in Central Texas. He received his BA in Classics from The University of Texas at Austin. He pursued his doctoral studies at the American School of Classical Studies at Athens and The University of California, Berkeley. He is Professor of Classics at Saint Anselm College in Manchester, New Hampshire. His recent publications include: 'The Shrine of Asprachoma Near Mycenae and its Dedications from the Persian Wars', *Zeitschrift für Papyrologie und Epigraphik* 184 (2013), 131–38, and 'Lost Dedications Commemorating Rhodian Victory Over Antiochus III', *Zeitschrift für Papyrologie und Epigraphik* 184 (2013), 172–74.

Bruce LaForse (Wright State University)
Bruce LaForse received a PhD in Classics from the University of Texas at Austin. He has also studied at the American School of Classical Studies in Athens and the American Numismatic Society in New York. He is an Associate Professor of Classics at Wright State University in Dayton, Ohio, where he is also a faculty advisor for the university's Veteran and Military Center and teaches courses for the Veteran Services Minor. His research has focused on perceptions of ethnicity, and on warfare, especially as depicted in the works of Xenophon. Recent publications include 'Praising Agesilaus: the

Limits of Panhellenic Rhetoric', *Ancient History Bulletin* 27 (2013), 29–48, and a chapter entitled 'Fighting the Other, Part 1: Greeks and Achaemenid Persians' in *The Oxford Handbook of Warfare in the Classical World* (Oxford, 2013), edited by L. Tritle and B. Campbell.

Christopher Matthew (Australian Catholic University)

Christopher Matthew completed his undergraduate degree in ancient history at the University of New England, Australia, in 2005 before moving to Macquarie University to complete a doctorate examining ancient Greek warfare in 2009. The author of several books and numerous articles on ancient warfare, he was awarded the title of Honorary Associate by Macquarie University in 2015 in recognition of his position as a leading professional with expertise in his field and for his 'demonstrated commitment to excellence, education, and research'. His work has formed the basis of several documentaries and radio interviews, and has resulted in him acting as a historical and creative consultant for museum exhibitions and film projects. He has taught at a number of universities across Australia and has given more than twenty public lectures at various universities, museums and other institutions across the country in recent years. In 2010, he took up the position of Lecturer in Ancient History at the Australian Catholic University, where he teaches units on the Greek City-States, the Fall of the Roman Republic, Pompeii, Ancient Greek Drama, the Ancient Near East, and the History and Geography of Ancient and Modern Rome.

Sonya Nevin (University of Roehampton)

Sonya Nevin is a Researcher at the University of Roehampton in London, where she has lectured in ancient Greek religion and ancient warfare. Her research focuses on historiography, religion in ancient warfare, and Classical reception. She is the author of *Military Leaders and Sacred Space in Classical Greek Warfare: Temples, Sanctuaries and Conflict in Antiquity* (I.B. Tauris, 2017). Her other publications include 'Animating Ancient Warfare: The Spectacle of War in the Panoply Vase Animations' in *War as Spectacle: Ancient and Modern Perspectives on the Display of Armed Combat* (Bloomsbury) and 'Negative Comparison: Agamemnon and Alexander in Plutarch's *Agesilaus-Pompey*' (*GRBS* 54). She completed her doctorate at University College Dublin on the historiography of military interaction with sacred space, holding the John Henry Newman Scholarship and the Arts and Celtic Studies Doctoral Fellowship. She is the co-director of The Panoply Vase Animation Project (www.panoply.org.uk), which creates animations from the scenes on ancient Greek vases, including projects for the Ashmolean

Museum, the Ure Museum, the UCD Classical Museum and the National Museum in Warsaw.

Lara O'Sullivan (University of Western Australia)

Lara O'Sullivan is a lecturer at the University of Western Australia. She completed a PhD under the supervision of Professor Brian Bosworth in 1999, and subsequently held a Re-Entry Postdoctoral Fellowship at the University of Western Australia from 2008–2010. She has given classes as a visiting academic at Edith Cowan University in Perth and at the University of Tasmania. In 2011, she was appointed to her current teaching and research position at the University of Western Australia, where she teaches courses predominantly in Greek history and the Classical languages and supervises research projects in Athenian history and cult. She has served on the editorial committee of *Antichthon*, the journal of the Australasian Society for Classical Studies. At present, she is enjoying the administrative challenges of serving as Chair of the Discipline Group of Classics and Ancient History at her institution.

Her main research interests are in the field of Hellenistic Athens. These interests are reflected in her 2009 monograph, *The Regime of Demetrius of Phalerum in Athens, 317–307 BCE: A Philosopher in Politics* (Leiden, Brill). She has published numerous articles and book chapters on aspects of Greek history, culture and politics, with an occasional foray into cross-disciplinary fields. (A survey of the impacts of deforestation on malaria in ancient Roman times and in present-day Australia is a notable example of the latter; this co-authored paper appeared in the 2008 volume of the prestigious American journal *Bioscience*.) She is currently co-editing a volume on the experiences and representations of violence in the Hellenistic period.

Ian Plant (Macquarie University)

Dr Ian Plant is the Head of the Department of Ancient History, Macquarie University. He studied Classics (including Ancient Greek and Latin) and Ancient History at the University of Canterbury, where he completed his doctoral studies under the supervision of Dr Katherine Adshead and Professor Kevin Lee. He taught at the University of Western Australia before taking up the post at Macquarie. His fields of research are Greek history and historiography, especially the study of Thucydides. He has published two books: *Women Writers of Ancient Greece and Rome* (Equinox, London, 2004) and *Myth in the Ancient World* (Palgrave Macmillan, South Yarra, 2012).

Ian Rutherford (University of Reading)

Ian Rutherford is Professor of Classics at the University of Reading. His major research interests are in ancient Greek literature and connections between early Greece and other ancient cultures, especially Anatolia and Egypt. His major publications are *Pindar's Paeans: A Reading of Fragments with a Survey of the Genre* (2001) and *State Pilgrims and Sacred Observers in Ancient Greece: A Study of* Theôriâ and Theôriâ (2013). Volumes he has edited or helped to edit include *Anatolian Interfaces: Hittites, Greeks and their Neighbours* (2007), *Wandering Poets in Ancient Greece Culture* (2009) and *Greco-Egyptian Interactions: Literature, Translation, and Culture, 500 BC–AD 300* (2016). His next book will be on the Anatolian, especially Hittite, background of Greek religion. He was a Visiting Research Fellow at the Institute for the Study of the Ancient World in New York (2013–2014) and is a Residential Fellow at the Research Center for Anatolian Civilizations at Koç University in Istanbul (2017).

Michael 'Maxx' Schmitz (University of Melbourne)

Maxx Schmitz is an academic specialist at the University of Melbourne, Australia. He gained his BA Hons and PhD in Ancient History from the University of New England where he taught ancient warfare as well as Greek and Roman history. His research interests include ancient warfare and military technology. He has written several articles, encyclopaedia entries, and books, including: *Roman Annexation, Costs and Benefits of Trajan's Dacian Conquest* (2010) and *Dacian Military Equipment and Technology* (2011), and his next book examines the Roman conquest of the Danube.

Matthew Trundle (University of Auckland)

Matthew Trundle studied in the UK (BA Joint Honours) at the University of Nottingham and in Canada (MA in Roman History, PhD in Greek History) at McMaster University, before teaching in Toronto at Glendon College, York University, and researching with the University of Chicago excavations at Corinth and Isthmia in Greece, where he worked for two years. He came to New Zealand in 1999 as Lecturer in Classics at Victoria University of Wellington, becoming Senior Lecturer (2005) and Associate Professor (2011), before moving to the University of Auckland to become Chair and Professor of Classics and Ancient History in 2012. His research interests are primarily in ancient Greek history, and his publications focus on the social and economic aspects of the Classical Greek world. He is the author of *Greek Mercenaries from the Late Archaic Period to Alexander* (London and New York, 2004), and has edited volumes entitled *New Perspectives on Ancient*

Warfare (Leiden, 2010) and *Beyond the Gates of Fire: New Perspectives on the Battle of Thermopylae* (Bradford, 2013). He has also published numerous articles, most recently 'Mercenaries', in *The Oxford Handbook of Classical Warfare* (Oxford, 2013), 330–51; 'Greek Athletes and Warfare in the Classical Period' in *Nikephoros* 25 (2012 [2014]), 221–37; 'Coinage and the Economics of the Athenian Empire' in *Circum Mare* (Leiden, 2016) 65–79; and 'The Spartan Krypteia' in *The Topography of Violence in the Greco-Roman World* (Ann Arbor, 2016), 60–76. He is currently completing the publication of the inscriptions from Isthmia in the Roman period, as well as a monograph on the impact of coinage on the Greek cities in the Classical period along with several projects related to war and money in Greek antiquity.

List of Figures

Preface

We editors hope that readers will find this volume useful in understanding the relationship which the ancient Greeks believed they had with the divine when conducting war. This volume is one of a three-part series, and will be followed by *Religion and Classical Warfare II: The Roman Republic*, and *Religion and Classical Warfare III: The Roman Empire*. The editors would like to thank most sincerely the Pen & Sword editor Philip Sindell for encouraging this three-volume project. His support and patience have been most appreciated; without him, this multi-volume project would not have proceeded.

Introduction:
New Perspectives on Classical Greek Religion and Warfare

Matthew Dillon

Ancient Greek religious beliefs and practices greatly influenced or interacted with Greek warfare, generals and the individual combatants in battles. Yet in the modern scholarship of Greek warfare, such religious factors are a relatively neglected topic. This volume is written by ten international experts in Greek history, and seeks to draw attention to the role which the ancient Greeks of the Archaic and Classical periods believed their gods played in warfare – both wars between Greek states, and against *barbaroi* (barbarians), especially the Persians. Without an understanding of the Greek ideology of divine assistance prior to and during battle, the religious rituals surrounding Greek warfare are inexplicable. Only by coming to a realization that the ancient Greek attitude to the gods involved their unequivocal popular belief in a divine interest in human affairs, particularly in one of the most important spheres of Greek activity, warfare, can Greek warfare – as a system of cultural values working within a ritual context and framework – be understood. The attention paid to the appearance of the entrails of a beast sacrificed before battle, the abandoning of long-planned military campaigns due to earthquakes, the special devotion to deities of battle and war, and other ritual (in the religious sense) features of Greek warfare only make sense if the sacred acts and beliefs surrounding Greek warfare are examined in detail.

W. Kendrick Pritchett was the first scholar in English to undertake a comprehensive treatment of the intersection of Greek religion and warfare in his third volume of *The Greek State at War* (Berkeley, 1979), subtitled *Religion*. He surveyed the state of scholarship in the German language, noting that Ulrich von Wilamowitz commented in 1893 that it was belief in divine assistance from Artemis that was a major factor in motivating the Athenians to victory at Marathon in 490 BC.[1] While debate emerged about this position, Wilamowitz was clearly correct, but despite this early start to studies of Greek religion and Greek warfare, it was Pritchett's volume many decades and a few generations of scholars later which established as a tenet in international ancient history scholarship that war and religion were fundamentally and intrinsically interwoven in the ancient Greek world. Religion and war went unequivocally 'hand in hand'. No war was waged in ancient Greece without reference to the divine. Pritchett surveyed and collected numerous pieces of literary and epigraphic (the evidence of inscriptions) evidence on many themes relating to religion and war, revealing the depth of evidence about the Greek gods in military conflict. In particular, he listed and discussed individually many pieces of evidence to create an exhaustive source of information. Yet his emphasis was mainly on description, and the reader is often left to draw their own conclusions, or more appropriately, to think about what all this evidence might mean. His focus, too, was actually narrow, with his main interest being in the interplay of divination and Greek warfare, in vows made before and during battle and their fulfillment, in the appearance of gods and semi-divine figures during battle, as well as war-festivals. As the current volume indicates, there are many more fields to explore, and this volume addresses many of these. But it is easy to criticize this scholar, who laid down the path for future studies in this field; it must be recognized that he wrote a work which all scholars and students alike interested in Greek religion and warfare are indebted to and have read for several decades, and will need to do so for many years to come.

Following Pritchett's pioneering work, various articles emerged dealing with Greek beliefs and warfare, with a focus on the historiography of the main Classical authors dealing with war. Thucydides in particular came in for special attention, with varying scholarly views arguing a spectrum of positions, ranging from him being an atheist (an idea now thoroughly discredited on the basis of the evidence he himself supplies in his work) to his being a firm believer in oracles. Simon Hornblower argued that Thucydides should have written much more about religion and its role in the Peloponnesian War, an argument which has merits but perhaps underestimates the attention which Thucydides did pay to religious aspects of the conflict.[2] Borimir Jordan was more concerned with what he does tell the reader about Greek religion,[3] while Nanno Marinatos clearly demonstrated that Thucydides did believe in one aspect of divine involvement in particular: oracular pronouncements – particularly the Delphic – and clearly derived intellectual pleasure from being able to interpret oracles correctly,[4] but also that he was very interested in intersections between religious beliefs and individuals, armies and states within the Peloponnesian War period.[5]

While there is a clear contrast between Herodotus and Thucydides, it is not as marked as sometimes assumed – Herodotus, like Thucydides, does not have the gods in Homeric style interfering in the battle, but does have them interested in the Greek victory, and the gods clearly have a role, if only in a collective sense, with a distant involvement, of ensuring the defeat of the Persians. Divine heroes put in an appearance on several occasions. Moreover, the Persian Wars were momentous, an epic worthy of divine intervention, whereas the Peloponnesian War, despite being a 'great war and more deserving of writing about than any previous conflict' according to Thucydides,[6] was a parochial power struggle amongst two Greek states and their respective allies.

Other scholars have touched on particular aspects of religion and war. M.D. Goodman and A.J. Holladay discussed in broad terms the importance of divination and how religious festivals impinged on warfare.[7] Louis Rawlings similarly offered some over-arching observations, but importantly proving that in a survey of Greek warfare such as his, a chapter on gods and war is now *de rigeur*.[8] Proving that this topic is not simply Anglophone, Raoul Lonis' 1979 classic focussed on the relationship between religion and victory, while Anne Jacquemin's 2000 monograph treatment of religion and war in the Greek world covered a wide range of topics, including the gods and heroes of war, rituals associated with battle, prayer and sacrifice, divination and post-war dedications of booty to sanctuaries of the gods, and is to date the most detailed monograph treatment of various aspects of religion and Greek warfare.[9]

The gods even rate topic headings in treatments of the rules of war, as in Peter Krentz's article, which includes sacred truces and the erection of trophies,[10] and in the treatment of sacred places by Adriaan Lanni.[11] Angelos Chaniotis, too, examines sanctuaries in times of war, divine involvement in battle and war rituals, usefully in the Hellenistic period.[12] Individual aspects of religion and Greek warfare have attracted attention. Most notable of these is the *sphagia*, the final sacrifice made by diviners immediately prior to a battle commencing, which Jean-Pierre Vernant, Michael Jameson, Robert Parker and Matthew Dillon, amongst others, have examined.[13] The purpose of this sacrifice – at the very moment prior to battle – and how it related to military divination and its ideology (both sides make the sacrifice so that they win: but how did they view the gods if they lost?) have made it one of the more important aspects in ascertaining and comprehending the religious mentality of the Greeks in battle.

Coming to more recent scholarship, Sonya Nevin (with a book chapter in this volume) has published *Military Leaders and Sacred Space in Classical*

Greek Warfare: Temples, Sanctuaries and Conflict in Antiquity (London, 2017), which examines and analyses the belief that ancient Greek armies showed respect for sacred places. It asks what that respect meant in the context of ancient Greek warfare and how military leaders balanced the demands of war and religion, particularly with regard to the use of sanctuaries as fortresses, the fate of sacred places and objects after a state's defeat, responses to the presence of temples near battle sites, sanctuaries as places of asylum, and the dynamics of the Sacred Wars. These questions are approached primarily through an analysis of the ancient discourse of war, demonstrating the values that are revealed in the ways that military interaction with the sacred is used to characterize individual leaders and their states, and to explore and articulate moral themes. Quite recently, *The Religious Aspects of War in the Ancient Near East, Greece and Rome* (Leiden, 2016), edited by Krzysztof Ulanowski, has appeared, while this volume itself was in its final stages of production. In it, Robert Parker introduces Greek religion and warfare, and six specialist papers follow: the fate of the defeated in war; the burning of Greek temples by the Persians; weather, luck and the divine in Thucydides; piety in Xenophon's *Hipparchikos*; the torch race at the Bendideai; and Alexander the Great's use of religion and mythology while on campaign. Nevertheless, despite this scholarship, some works on Greek warfare do not even mention the gods.

War and the gods in ancient Greece will no doubt continue to attract scholarly attention. The ten authors in this volume have approached a variety of topics which will hopefully lead to a comprehensive understanding of crucial intersections and interactions between religious belief and the practices of warfare. A rigorous source methodology is employed. All varieties of evidence are utilized: those of the written sources, which assume the most significance, especially given that the written histories of the Archaic and Classical worlds are histories of warfare above all else. The first work of Greek literature, Homer's *Iliad*, is, after all, a military history of part of the tenth year of the Trojan War, and reveals rich detail on how the gods and mortals interacted on the battlefield and off it, and provides a conceptual framework within which Greek attitudes towards the divine in the context of armed activity can be understood, both in the Heroic period and in the Classical.

Such written sources are supported and augmented by other evidence. The Greek epigraphic habit saw important political decrees inscribed by the state, especially at Athens, where the fourth-century BC *Ephebic Oath* represents the contractual relationship between the defenders of this city and its gods, setting out the parameters of a military ideology in which mortals alone cannot defend a city and its territory.[14] Other states also inscribed decrees, such as that dealing with compulsory dedications to be made to the cult of the war-god Enyalios on the island of Rhodes.[15] Inscriptions are particularly important, as whereas it could be argued that the military historians did reflect the views of the society in which they lived, inscriptions record what a community *as a whole* had discussed and decided upon, and hence believed, providing a unique insight into state and communal ideology of the gods' role in war. Inscriptions from throughout the Greek world are discussed in this volume, and in particular provide information on states other than Sparta and especially Athens, whose concerns occupy so much of the written source material available to the modern scholar.

Iconography relating to military themes largely takes the form of vase scenes, carved marble reliefs, bronze artefacts and coins. These do not simply illustrate the written evidence, but also show where the emphasis lay when art was employed to depict martial themes. Scenes of warriors departing for war and pouring libations are common on Athenian vases, but so too are scenes of the hoplite performing a divinatory sacrifice while members of his family look on (Figure 3.1). These scenes are for the private viewer, reflecting the concerns of this individual hoplite and his family – but then in turn therefore the concerns of all hoplites, and so demonstrate the religious commitment to ascertaining the will of the gods and hopefully their approval before setting out to war.

Athena gazes sadly at an engraved list of the Athenian war dead on a fifth-century BC marble relief, reflecting the ideology of state commemoration of those who died to defend Athens, and the goddess' sadness stands as metonymous for the grief both the state and individual felt for the loss of its soldiers (Figure 6.1), just as Zeus himself grieved for the death of his son Sarpedon in battle.[16] Coins in particular show repeatedly, over several centuries and across the entire Greek world, the *tropaion* – battle trophy monument – made of a full complement (panoply) of weapons and armour captured from the enemy, with the goddess Nikê present (Figure 9.1). Such coins acknowledge the assistance of this goddess, and the gods as a whole, in granting the victory which allowed armour and weapons to be captured from the enemy and erected at the site of the victory. Iconography therefore recognizes the symbiotic relationship in war between mortals and gods, and presents particular themes which the ancient viewer considered to be important. A Greek ruler who issued a coin showing Athena at a *tropaion* was not merely advertising his victory but thanking the goddess; those who organized the erecting of the statue of the goddess Nikê on the prow of a stone ship at Samothrace were publicly acknowledging her role in their victory (Figure 9.5). Utilizing these wide-ranging literary, epigraphic and artistic sources of information, the contributors have written seminal submissions to the study of Greek religion and warfare.

This volume itself opens with a discussion of the attitudes of the three major Greek historians of the Classical period, and thereby establishes the nature of the historical record concerning religious beliefs and their impact. Bruce LaForse, in *Religion and Warfare in Herodotus, Thucydides and Xenophon*, considers the role the gods and religion played in war in the three major historians of the Classical Greek era, Herodotus, Thucydides and Xenophon. Divination, prophecy and portents of various kinds appear in all three writers, though far more frequently in Herodotus and Xenophon, who also accept that the gods could intervene in human affairs, at least indirectly. Thucydides, by contrast, never depicts the gods affecting human affairs, although he considers that human belief in them and in divination can influence the outcome of military events. All three historians assign responsibility for what happens chiefly to mortals. Portents and divination often appear at key historical junctures in Herodotus, such as at the commencement of a battle. For Xenophon, consultation of the gods was often the act of a practical commander seeking guidance with how to deal with the unforeseeable. Thucydides consistently respects prophecies from the oracle at Delphi. All three historians are witness to the influence of religious belief on practices of warfare and the behaviour of combatants.

According to Greek belief, the gods and semi-divine heroes took an active interest in all mortal affairs, and as warfare was certainly one of the ancient Greeks' main activities, the role which combatants and their cities believed the gods played in individual battles came to the attention of the historians of the day. In *The Role of Religion in Declarations of War in Archaic and Classical Greece*, Matthew Trundle examines the part played by the gods in declarations of war, and also religious factors as contributing to the origins of a war. It seems, however, that the gods played little or often no role in a state declaring war or commencing war on another state. More important was that once a campaign or conflict commenced, the gods were *then* invoked, to assist in defeating the enemy, and were particularly seen as important through divination. Hence Sonya Nevin, in *Omens, Oracles and Portents*, considers the crucial impact on warfare practices of the Classical Greek belief that the gods were thought to have knowledge that humans were not privy to. If they were fortunate, mortals might come to share some of those insights through divinely sent signs. In matters of war, every advantage was important and could mean the difference between success and disaster. Reading divine signs was therefore an essential part of military life, and this chapter looks at what forms these signs took, how and when they might be obtained, and how states and generals incorporated them into their military decisions.

With the gods so actively interested in the outcome of battles, Ian Plant, in *Oaths and Vows: Binding the Gods to One's Military Success*, explores examples of oaths and vows to divinities as attested in military contexts. A shared belief in the gods' interest in such promises was held by the community as a whole, and this was a key factor in enabling both individuals and *poleis* (city states) to make and respect their promises. While anecdotes report circumvention of oaths, the public nature of oaths ensured the widespread respect for them in the Greek world. In a similar way, the gods were thought to provide a sanctioning mechanism when Greek states holding festivals proclaimed sacred truces, which applied to both local and Panhellenic ('all the Greeks') religious festivals and were announced months in advance. Ian Rutherford, in *Sacred Truces and Festivals Interrupting War: Piety or Manipulation?*, explores these. Such truces did not mean the cessation of war as such throughout the Greek world: rather, the intention was that the sacred site of the festival and the state hosting it would be sacrosanct during the period of the sacred truce, and truces aimed to provide security and safety for the pilgrim worshippers making their way to the festival in question. In addition, it compelled the army of the state celebrating a festival to cease warfare and to honour the god or gods of the festival in question. Yet the sacred calendar could also be manipulated for military reasons, so that festivals were not celebrated when they ought to have been, but later.

While there were many gods associated with military activity, the virgin goddess Athena was the primary deity of battle, combat and warfare, as Matthew Dillon demonstrates in *Militarising the Divine: the Bellicosity of the Greek Gods*, through discussing the Homeric and Classical evidence. Yet Ares has been rather underestimated as a god of war due to Homer's negative portrayal of him, and similarly Aphrodite, as pictured by Homer as a goddess of love, has suffered to an even greater degree. She was, after all, the goddess who was credited by the Corinthians as keeping the Persians at bay in 480 BC, and was also worshipped as a warrior goddess at Sparta. Yet she was depicted by Homer as a weakling, attacked by the Greek mortal hero Diomedes at the instigation of and with the encouragement of Athena. Enyalios is shown to be a major deity of war, while various battlefield emotions, such as panic and fear, were accorded semi-divine status. The Greek gods and semi-divine heroes were in fact an active presence not only in the battlefields of Homeric epic, but in historical clashes as well. In *Epiphanies in Classical and Hellenistic Warfare*, Lara O'Sullivan traces the trajectory of such wartime epiphanies, whether experienced as anthropomorphic manifestations or as demonstrations of divine power, across the Classical and Hellenistic periods. The contexts in which divine aid was elicited is explored, and the impact that a perceived epiphany had on the mortal combatants is examined. Further, this contribution seeks to situate epiphanic episodes within the broader dynamic of the prestige that attended upon military victory in the ancient world.

Hoplites and sailors alike believed that the gods and heroes were present in the battle, and in *Fate, Predestination and the Mindset of the Greek Hoplite in Battle*, Christopher Matthew argues that a system of belief – either in a deity or in some other quasi-divine functionary – has played a regular part in the psyche of the warrior throughout history and is often used as a coping mechanism to allow a combatant to accept (and possibly understand) the seemingly random chaos that is unfolding around them on the battlefield. Such beliefs have influenced soldiers in ancient Greece and in modern times, and, despite the changing nature of religion over the centuries, one element of the divine which has endured in the mindset of warriors is an acceptance in the concept of the workings of Fate.

Having accepted divine assistance, and been victorious in war, the gods had to be thanked for the role they were believed to have played. Michael Schmitz, in *Thanking the Gods and Declaring Victory: Trophies and Dedication in Ancient Greek Warfare*, discusses a significant change in the material way in which the gods were thanked for victory. Prior to the Persian Wars, dedications made by individuals of armour, and especially of helmets at Zeus' sanctuary at Olympia, were very common. After the Persian Wars, a *tropaion* would be erected by the victor on the battlefield: a panoply (set) of armour captured from the enemy would be put up on a tree or wooden stake. Such a trophy was by its nature impermanent, and in 371 BC the Thebans were the first Greeks to erect a permanent stone monument to commemorate their victory over other Greeks. A wounded soldier who survived battle with the assistance of the gods could also call on divine assistance to heal him, and in this situation the non-combatant deity Asklepios was worshipped, as well as an array of magical practices. In *Magic and Religion in Military Medicine in Classical Greece*, Matthew Gonzales explores how magico–religious belief and ritual suffused the human experience in the ancient Greek world, and the 'empirical' realm of military medicine was no exception. A wide range of sources clearly document an early, thorough and lasting melding of magic and religion with the 'rational' practice of military medicine. Beginning with a discussion of the healing power of the gods in the epic tradition, the ministrations of heroes, everyday soldiers, doctors and priests are explored, illustrating the blending of magical and practical knowledge and technique that prevailed in the practice of military medicine in the Classical world.

The chapters in this volume do not of course cover every single aspect of how the gods were perceived to act in the lead-up to war and throughout it, and how they were viewed by individuals and states after a conflict ceased. Yet the book provides a reasonably holistic discussion, starting with the attitudes of three historians to the divine role in warfare, before moving on to the declaration of war, through to thanking the gods for victory – and requesting their help to cure battle-wounds. No doubt interest will continue to grow in the relationship between warfare and religion in the ancient Greek world. The ten papers in this volume aim to provide an accessible approach and introduction to the topic. In the hard-headed tradition of all things military, this volume deliberately eschews obscurantism (writing so that no-one other than the author understands what the article is about), jargon and academic elitism. Rather than being a series of specialist papers on narrow topics, each of the chapters has been specifically commissioned to provide a solid survey and interpretation of a particular theme concerning the matrix between belief in the divine, and the theory and practice of ancient Greek warfare. Alongside seasoned academics, many of the papers are contributed by young scholars who have already established an international reputation and written monographs in their areas of expertise. Hopefully the volume will realize something of what the three editors set out to achieve: a readable, accessible book on the beliefs surrounding the Greek gods in the context of battles and warfare.

Notes

1. Pritchett, 1979, 1–3.
2. Hornblower, 1992; and see more recently Rawles, 2015, with respect to the Sicilian Expedition (415–413 BC).
3. Jordan, 1986.
4. Marinatos, 1981.
5. Marinatos, 1981a.
6. Thuc. 1.1.
7. Goodman and Holladay, 1986, 152–60.
8. Rawlings, 2007, 177–202.
9. Lonis, 1979; Jacquemin, 2000.
10. Krentz, 2002, 26–27, 32.
11. Lanni, 2008, 477–78.
12. Chaniotis, 2005, 143–64.
13. Vernant, 1988; Jameson, 1991 (2014); Parker, 2000; Dillon, 2008; see also Sonya Nevin's discussion in this volume.

14. *IG* ii², 204; see Ian Plant's discussion in this volume.
15. Gonzales, 2008.
16. Hom. *Il.* 16.419–58, with Figure 6.3.

Bibliography

Chaniotis, A., 2005, *War in the Hellenistic World: A Social and Cultural History*, Oxford.

Dillon, M.P.J., 2008, '"Xenophon sacrificed on account of an expedition" (Xenophon *Anabasis* 6.5.2): Divination and the Sphagia Before Ancient Greek Battles', in Brulè, P., and Mehl, V. (eds), *Le sacrifice antique. Vestiges, procédures et stratégies*, Rennes, 235–51.

Gonzales, M., 2008, 'New Observations on the Lindian Cult-Tax for Enyalios ("SEG" 4.171)', *ZPE* 166, 121–34.

Goodman, M.D., and Holladay, A.J., 1986, 'Religious Scruples in Ancient Warfare', *CQ* 36.1, 151–71.

Hornblower, S., 1992, 'The Religious Dimension to the Peloponnesian War, or, What Thucydides Does Not Tell Us' *HSPh* 94, 169–97.

Jacquemin, A,. 2000, *Guerre et religion dans le monde grec (490–322 av. J.-C.)*, Paris.

Jameson, M.H., 1991, 'Sacrifice Before Battle', in Hanson, V.D. (ed.), *Hoplites: The Classical Greek Battle Experience*, London, 197–227 (republished in Jameson, M.H., 2014, *Cults and Rites in Ancient Greece. Essays on Religion and Society*, edited by A.B. Stallsmith, Cambridge, 98–126).

Jordan, B., 1986, 'Religion in Thucydides', *TAPhA* 116, 119–47.

Krentz, P., 2002, 'Fighting by the Rules: the Invention of the Hoplite Agon', *Hesperia* 71, 23–39.

Lanni, A., 2008, 'The Laws of War in Ancient Greece', *LHR* 26.3, 469–89.

Lonis, R., 1979, *Guerre et religion en Grece a l'epoque classique. Recherches sur les rites, les dieux, l'ideologie de Ia victoire*, Paris.

Marinatos, N., 1981, 'Thucydides and Oracles', *JHS* 101, 138–40.

—— 1981a, *Thucydides and Religion*, Konigstein.

Nevin, S,. 2017, *Military Leaders and Sacred Space in Classical Greek Warfare: Temples, Sanctuaries and Conflict in Antiquity*, London.

Parker, R., 2000, 'Sacrifice and Battle', in Wees, H. van (ed.), *War and Violence in Ancient Greece*, London, 299–314.

Pritchett, W.K., 1979, *The Greek State at War. Part III: Religion*, Berkeley.

Rawles, R., 2015, 'Lysimeleia (Thucydides 7.53, Theocritus 16.84): What Thucydides Does Not Tell Us About the Sicilian Expedition', *JHS* 135, 1–15.

Rawlings, L., 2007, *The Ancient Greeks at War*, Manchester.

Spalinger, A., and Nadali, D. (eds), 2016, *Greece and Rome. Ancient Warfare* 1, Leiden.

Ulanowski, K., 2016, *The Religious Aspects of War in the Ancient Near East, Greece, and Rome*, Leiden.

Vernant, J.-P., 1988, 'Artémis et le sacrifice préliminaire au combat', *REG* 101, 221–39.

Chapter 1

Religion and Warfare in Herodotus, Thucydides and Xenophon

Bruce LaForse

Introduction

This chapter examines how the three major historians of the Classical Greek era, Herodotus, Thucydides and Xenophon, incorporate religion and its place in warfare into their works, and what role, if any, in influencing human affairs they assign to the gods. It was war, and the desire to record its events and deeds, which inspired these men to write pioneering works of history. All three historians were, no doubt, steeped in the poetry of Homer, whose *Iliad* depicts religious rituals, practices and the gods themselves playing an important role in warfare. They each include portents and divination in their accounts, but by no means in the same way or with the same frequency, nor do they all agree on the extent to which divine power, in whatever form, affects human events.

None of the three portray major deities, as Homer does, appearing on the battlefield or acting directly to alter the course of events. All three assign a broad range of responsibility for what happens among men to the human actors themselves. Herodotus and Xenophon, however, believed both that the gods shaped human events indirectly and that they might share information with humans about the future, or matters otherwise unknowable, through their oracular shrines or prophecies, for example in the form of dreams, or portents such as earthquakes, eclipses and other natural phenomena. Thus divination, seers, the consultation of oracles and the appearance of various omens figure prominently in their narratives. These also appear in Thucydides, but much less frequently, and while Herodotus and Xenophon state explicitly their belief in the gods and the mechanism of prophecy, Thucydides makes no such statement. He records instances where men's belief in gods and prophecies alters the course of events, and he recognized that religious rituals and values helped keep a society stable, but it is not easy to determine if Thucydides himself believed in the gods and prophecy.

Herodotus

Herodotus (*c.* 480s–420s BC) was from Halicarnassus (modern Bodrum) on the west coast of modern Turkey, a cosmopolitan port city that was then part of the Persian Empire. He seems to have travelled widely, perhaps as an exile or for commercial reasons, spent time in Athens and likely eventually settled at the Athenian-sponsored Panhellenic colony of Thurii in Italy. His history of the Persian Wars (499–479 BC) includes extensive ethnographic and anthropological information about the peoples and states comprising the two sides in the conflict. He pays particular attention to religious beliefs, customs and practices.

According to Herodotus, the gods were intimately involved in the events of the Persian Wars and dramatically affected the outcome. While the gods themselves do not appear on the battlefield, they indirectly influence events, for example, by providing a timely windstorm or flood tide.[1] They communicate frequently with humans through oracles, omens and other prophetic signs; they also answer prayers and can punish impiety. Not only does Herodotus assume that the gods exist, but he also believes that each culture devises its own view of them as well as its own rituals and rites: 'Everyone without exception believes his own customs, and the religion he was brought up in, to be the best; and that being so, it is unlikely that anyone but a madman would mock at such things.'[2] Wars do not arise between worshippers of conflicting pantheons, one group trying to impose its gods on the other. The gods, both Greek and foreign, all belong to the same category, regardless of the titles or rituals various humans may assign to them. Indeed, instead of citing a particular deity, Herodotus often refers simply to the divine, the god or the gods, usually interchangeably. The vagueness may also reflect Herodotus' characteristic care to avoid offending anyone, human or divine.[3]

Despite his respect for what moderns might call diversity, there are limits to what Herodotus accepts. Still, he includes stories that he does not believe, though he gives his readers fair warning: 'My business is to record what people say, but I am by no means bound to believe it.'[4] Thus, though he records supernatural elements, he often rejects them. For example, he presents a rationalizing alternative explanation for an account he had heard for the origin of the oracle of Zeus at Dodona that involved 'the obvious impossibility of a dove using the language of men.'[5] Similarly, he does not think a human is likely to encounter a god face to face, though that might have been possible in the far remote past in Egypt.[6] A notable exception to this is the story of Pheidippides, the long-distance runner Athens sent to seek help from Sparta when the Persians had landed at Marathon in 490. He reported that while crossing Mount Parthenium near Sparta, the god Pan called to him by name and asked why the Athenians had not returned his friendliness to them in the past, though he had been and would be useful to them. That Pan appears to one person on a remote mountain (near the end of a very long run), and not to a packed meeting of the Athenian Assembly on the Pynx in downtown Athens, may have made the story more acceptable, though Herodotus does not indicate whether or not he believes it. He does note that the Athenians accepted Pheidippides' story, that they immediately instituted an annual ceremony in honour of Pan with a torch race and sacrifices, and that after the war they built a shrine to Pan on the slopes of the Acropolis.[7]

There are several instances in which divine figures may have appeared among humans, but they all involve minor deities or heroes.[8] Herodotus usually does not explicitly vouch for the authenticity of the stories, but rather introduces them with a phrase that distances them, such as that he heard them by report. He calls them marvels (*thômata*), which in the proem or introduction to his work he promises to include in his narrative along with the great deeds by both Greeks and barbarians. In concluding his description of the fighting at Marathon, Herodotus gives the figures for those killed on both sides and then appends a story about a 'marvellous thing' (*thôma*) that occurred during the battle. While fighting, an Athenian soldier named Epizelus, though not physically wounded, suddenly went blind and remained so for the rest of his life: he claimed that he saw a large, bearded hoplite coming at him who turned aside and killed the man next to him.[9] Herodotus refers to the giant hoplite as a 'phantom' (*phasma*). He uses this same word in one of the three versions he gives for how the sea battle at Salamis began. The Athenians and Aeginetans, rivals afterwards for top honours as best fighters in the battle, each offer a version which credits one of their own vessels for overcoming an initial hesitation to engage on the part of the Greek fleet and launching an attack. Herodotus adds that there was a popular belief that a phantom woman (*phasma*) appeared and cried out in a voice that the whole fleet could hear, 'Strange men, how much farther do you propose to go astern?'[10] Herodotus does not explicitly endorse or reject any of the three alternatives. By ascribing the story of the phantom woman to popular belief, he may undercut its authenticity, yet the other two stories come from obviously biased sources. It is impossible to determine if Herodotus included the phantom woman because he thought that version might be true, and thus a marvellous thing (*thôma*), or for the sake of thoroughness, since many people at the time apparently did believe the story.

There are instances, however, where Herodotus does state unequivocally that he believes that the gods affect human events, if not directly in person.

These fall into two general, if not always mutually exclusive, categories: his belief, first, in oracles, omens and other such prophecies, and second, in divine punishment for impieties such as violating the sanctuaries of the gods. In his account of the Greek victory at Salamis, Herodotus pauses when he reaches the eve of the battle to quote a prophecy that said, in sum, that the gods will bring freedom to Greece, and he cites it to support his belief in prophecies: 'Now I cannot deny that there is truth in prophecies, and I have no wish to discredit them when they are expressed in unambiguous language [he here quotes the prophecy]. With that utterance of Bacis in mind … I do not venture to say anything against prophecies, nor will I listen to criticism from others.'[11] The proviso about ambiguous language would seem to leave Herodotus a useful way out, but in fact oracles and prophecies in *The Histories* are almost always fulfilled, even if humans often struggle to interpret them correctly and cannot be sure they have done so until after the fact. For example, all of the seers and diviners at the Battle of Plataea, where the Persians also employed a Greek seer, were accurate, though the Persian commander Mardonius in the end ignored his.[12]

Mardonius' failure to heed his seer's advice highlights the central role that humans play in the process of divination. In consulting an oracle, they have to know which question to ask, and when. When a divine sign appears, be it in the form of a bird or a dream or any other medium, the enormous responsibility of correct interpretation rests entirely on the humans involved.

Two examples illustrate the challenge of interpreting prophecies from Delphi, the most influential oracle in Herodotus' world. When contemplating a campaign against the growing power of Persia to his east, the mid-sixth-century Lydian King Croesus consulted Greek oracles for advice. He first tested their accuracy by sending trial questions. Having decided Delphi was reliable, he flooded the sanctuary with fabulously rich offerings, hoping to win the god's favour before asking if he should attack Persia. Blinded by his utter confidence in his own good fortune, Croesus fails to see the obvious ambiguity in the oracle's reply that if he does attack Persia he will destroy a great empire. It never occurs to him that he might destroy his own.[13]

In contrast, when the Athenians consult Delphi about the impending invasion of Xerxes, the oracle responds with rare clarity that the invaders will occupy all Attica and destroy its shrines.[14] In despair, the Athenians approach the oracle again, this time bearing olive boughs as suppliants, and ask for a better prophecy. The reply reaffirms that Attica will be taken, but with the important exception that 'the wooden wall shall not fall'.[15] Back in Athens, interpretation of the oracle gave rise to public debate. The professional interpreters (*chrêsmologoi*) maintained that the 'wooden wall' referred to a thorn hedge which once surrounded the Acropolis that alone, therefore, would escape destruction. As a consequence, they argued that the Athenians should abandon any idea of resisting Xerxes and seek a new home elsewhere. Themistocles, however, arguing that the powerful Athenian fleet constituted the 'wooden wall', persuaded the Athenians to continue to oppose Xerxes, even if it meant evacuating their homeland.[16] The Athenians draw exceptional praise from Herodotus because 'not even the terrifying warnings of the oracle at Delphi could persuade them to abandon Greece'.[17]

As the example of the 'wooden walls' prophecy shows, even professionals could make mistakes. A further complicating factor is that, as Herodotus notes, some interpreters, not to mention oracular shrines, took bribes. For example, at the behest of the Pisistratidae, who were hoping to return to power in Athens with Persian help, Onomacritus, a *chrêsmologos* (collector of oracles), revealed to Xerxes only those prophecies that would encourage him to invade Greece, omitting those that did not.[18] Though these two accounts portray the *chrêsmologoi* in a bad light, Herodotus clearly especially esteems the oracles attributed to Bacis, who must have been a similar sort of, perhaps even archetypal, oracle-collector.[19]

Further proof, in Herodotus' eyes, that oracles were true comes from those that can scarcely be understood and seem even nonsensical, until they are fulfilled. Long before the Persian Wars, an Athenian seer had predicted that the women living in a coastal region of Attica called Colias would 'cook their food with oars'. After the sea fight at Salamis, many of the disabled ships and other wreckage washed ashore at Colias, providing ample firewood for cooking.[20]

Another example of a prophecy fulfilled in an unexpected fashion includes a prophecy within a prophecy. After the battles of Thermopylae and Salamis, the oracle at Delphi told the Spartans to go to Xerxes, ask him for reparations for the death of Leonidas and to accept whatever he gave them. The Spartan envoy confronted Xerxes in Thessaly as he was handing over his army to his chief general Mardonius, and demanded satisfaction for the blood of Leonidas. Xerxes pointed to Mardonius and told the Spartans they would get all the satisfaction they deserved from him. When Mardonius dies fighting the Spartans at Plataea, Herodotus pauses briefly to note that his death paid them back for Leonidas, and that Xerxes' unwitting prophecy, induced by the Delphic command to Sparta, had been fulfilled.[21]

It was also crucial to recognize when a prophecy had been fulfilled. The Spartan King Cleomenes, buoyed by an oracle that he would capture Argos, invaded Argive territory and managed to trap much of the Argive army in a forest, which he then burned. Upon discovering that the forest was named after the local hero Argos, Cleomenes returned to Sparta and disbanded his army, believing that he had inadvertently, as it were, fulfilled the oracle without taking the city of Argos. The Spartans tried him for treason, accusing him of taking a bribe to leave the city of Argos unharmed. When he explained the oracle, they acquitted him.[22]

On the other hand, the lack of a specified time for some oracles provided leeway for interpretation. In the period after Salamis, the Spartans were worried that the Athenians might accept an offer of alliance from Persia. Herodotus says that the existence of a prophecy that the Persians and Athenians were fated one day to drive the Dorians (i.e., the Spartans) from the Peloponnese exacerbated these fears.[23] Spartan concern about such an alliance faded, however, once the wall the Peloponnesians were building across the Isthmus at Corinth was nearly completed. Apparently, the immediate applicability of the prophecy seemed less likely and no longer frightened the Spartans, who may have reasoned that the Athenian–Persian alliance would instead come in the distant future.[24] Even when facing a prophecy that has to come true, mortals may not know exactly when, or in what circumstances it will be fulfilled, but they still bear responsibility for their actions regardless.

Besides communicating through oracles and other prophetic signs, the gods in Herodotus answer prayers. Men who have been respectful of the gods generally get what they seek; the impious are ignored, or worse.[25] A good example of the former is the Greek prayers to the Winds. As Xerxes' massive fleet approached Artemisium (and his army Thermopylae), the Delphians sought advice from the oracle and received this reply: 'Pray to the Winds, for they will be allies to Greece.' They reported this to the rest of the Greek alliance, and Herodotus says that it boosted morale at a critical moment. The Delphians later consecrated an altar to the Winds and offered sacrifices on it, which, Herodotus says, they continued to do down to his own time.[26]

In fact, windstorms played a critical role in the Greek victory. A severe storm destroyed at least 400 Persian ships near Artemisium before the fleet could engage with the Greeks. Herodotus reports a story that the Athenians had sought the assistance of Boreas, the North Wind, on the advice of an oracle, and that when they had seen the storm approaching – or possibly sooner – they had offered sacrifice to Boreas and his wife Orithyia, pleading that they destroy the Persian fleet as they had in 492 at Athos. Herodotus notes that he cannot say if this is why the storm hit Xerxes' fleet, but he affirms that the Athenians were sure of it, and that they subsequently built Boreas a shrine in Athens. Meanwhile, the Persian Magi also offered sacrifices to the Winds and put spells on them, attempting to halt the storm. They even offered sacrifices to Thetis (mother of Achilles) and the Sea Nymphs, which finally ended the storm after three days, or, Herodotus adds, it may be that the wind simply abated on its own.[27] When another storm shortly afterwards destroyed the entire 200-ship contingent the Persians had sent around the outside of the island of Euboea, hoping to trap the Greek fleet in the Euripus, Herodotus had no doubt that 'God was indeed doing everything possible to reduce the superiority of the Persian fleet and bring it down to the size of the Greek'.[28]

At Plataea, the gods answered a Greek prayer in dramatic fashion. The Spartans refused to engage while their pre-battle sacrifices kept returning unfavourable omens, even though many of them were being killed and even more wounded by Persian archery. Their commander Pausanias, in desperation, looked to the nearby temple of Hera and prayed to the goddess that she not let the Greeks lose their hope of victory. As he spoke, the sacrificial victims were favourable and the Greeks leapt to the attack.[29]

The majority of Herodotus' statements expressing his own view of the gods and how they affect human affairs concern divine punishment for impious behaviour. The Trojans' defeat at the hands of the Greeks, for example, came about through 'divine volition in order that their destruction might plainly prove to mankind that great offences meet with great punishments at the hands of god. This, then, is my own interpretation.' The Trojans suffered because Paris violated the laws of hospitality by stealing Helen from his host Menelaus. Interestingly, Herodotus argues at length that Helen never got to Troy, that a storm forced Paris' ship to Egypt, where King Proteus confiscated Helen and the property Paris had stolen from Menelaus. The Trojans, Herodotus argues, surely would have returned Helen to the besieging Greeks if they had her. For Herodotus, that the Greeks destroyed Troy anyway emphasizes the enormity of Paris' crime and the justice of the severe punishment.[30]

The mistreatment or killing of heralds was a grave offence in the ancient world. Both the Athenians and Spartans murdered the envoys Darius sent when he was seeking submission from the Greek cities. Herodotus says that it is unclear how the Athenians were punished, but he finds fascinating what happened to the Spartans. For a long time they were unable to obtain favourable sacrifices. They decided, therefore, to send two full-citizen volunteers to Xerxes for him to kill as atonement for the dead Persian envoys. Xerxes, however, spared the two men and sent them back to Sparta. Decades later, in the early stages of the Peloponnesian War, the Athenians captured and executed two Spartan ambassadors who were on their way to Persia. The two happened to be the sons of the very men Xerxes had spared. For Herodotus, this was no coincidence but 'clear evidence of divine intervention'.[31]

Individuals in the *Histories* who regularly commit brazenly impious acts all suffer punishment that, even if he does not say so explicitly, Herodotus nonetheless manages to make clear comes from the gods. For example, Artaÿctes, the Persian governor in the Chersonese, stole the treasure from the shrine of the hero Protesilaus, farmed the sacred precinct and had sexual intercourse with women in the sanctuary. The Athenians took him prisoner, stoned his son to death before his eyes and then crucified him. Instead of a statement in his own voice about divine justice, Herodotus includes a story he says was current in that region. One of Artaÿctes' Athenian guards was cooking fish which suddenly started leaping about on the coals. Artaÿctes himself interpreted the sign as Protesilaus telling him that even though the hero was dead, he still had the power from the gods to punish.[32]

Herodotus relates what he regards as a marvel (*thôma*) at the Battle of Plataea, the fact that though the fighting took place close to the sanctuary of Demeter, no Persian soldier appears to have set foot on the sacred ground, nor were there any dead Persians found there, though lying all around the precinct there were great numbers of their dead. Herodotus offers his explanation of what happened, with a typically cautious proviso: 'My own view is – if one may have views at all about divine matters – that the Goddess herself would not let them in, because they had burnt her sanctuary at Eleusis.'[33]

Much the most dramatic account Herodotus gives of divine protection of a shrine is Apollo's defence of Delphi. As the Persians were drawing near, the Delphians asked the oracle if they should hide the sacred treasures or evacuate them. The god replied that he could guard his own property. The Delphians fled, all but sixty men and the priest of the oracle. As the Persians approached the sanctuary, the priest noticed the sacred weapons had somehow moved from inside the temple and were now lying on the ground in front of the shrine.[34] This is the first marvel (*thôma*). Even more amazing in Herodotus' eyes is what happened when the Persians came to the Temple of Athena Pronaos. Thunderbolts struck them and two peaks of Mount Parnassus crashed down, killing many of them. At the same time, there was a battle cry from inside the shrine. The Persians fled, with the Delphians pursuing and slaughtering a large number of them. Herodotus later interviewed Persian survivors and heard of yet another marvel. Among those pursuing the Persians were two giant hoplites whom the Delphians claimed were the local heroes Phylacus and Autonous, whose enclosures were near the temple of Apollo. The rocks that fell from Parnassus, Herodotus notes, were still there in his time.[35] In this instance, Apollo defended his shrine but did not make an actual appearance. He worked indirectly, in much the same way Demeter did in the example cited above. Unlike at Potidaea or Plataea, where the act itself was proof of divine intervention, at Delphi there were marvels: the miraculous transpositioning of the sacred weapons, the battle cry from the temple and the two giant heroes. Herodotus seems to believe that these marvels took place.

Two similar marvels that occurred just before the Greek force engaged the Persians at Mycale elicit an explicit statement from Herodotus. A herald's staff (see Figure 2.1) turned up on the beach as the Greeks were advancing, and at the same time a rumour ran through the ranks that the Greeks had defeated Mardonius at Plataea, a battle that was taking place on the same day:

> Many things make it plain to me that the hand of God is active in human affairs – for how else could it be, when the Persian defeat at Mycale was about to take place on the same day as his defeat at Plataea, that a rumour of that kind should reach the Greek army, giving every man greater courage for the coming battle and a fiercer determination to risk his life for his country?

The rumour, Herodotus points out, turned out to be true – the fighting at Plataea had taken place that morning. Moreover, he adds, both battles took place near a precinct of Demeter of Eleusis.[36]

Xerxes exhibits many of the impious and outrageous behaviours of his predecessors, though usually to a more extreme degree. Like Croesus and Cyrus, Xerxes believed that his success must be inevitable. Like Cambyses, he freely violated numerous religious rules and taboos, such as burning sanctuaries and temples.[37] He also mutilated the body of the Spartan King Leonidas, recalling Cambyses' burning of the corpse of the Egyptian King Amasis. He fell in love with and took women he should not have. He branded, scourged and yoked the Hellespont. Unlike the earlier kings, however, at the critical moment, Xerxes did try to heed the words of a wise advisor before disaster could overtake him. Just as Xerxes was about to accept the advice of his uncle Artabanus that he not invade Greece, a dream tells him that he must. The dream subsequently appeared to Artabanus as well, whose counsel to Xerxes had comprised in essence the lessons Solon had tried to teach Croesus, that the gods tend to knock down the tall, overturn the prosperous and are envious of human good fortune. The dream insisted that Xerxes must invade Greece: 'it must happen (*to chrêon genesthai*).'[38]

It must happen, it was fated – Herodotus uses several formulations of this phrase to describe an event or outcome that seems to be beyond human or divine control. For example, it was fated that Candaules and Miltiades end badly (Candaules was betrayed by his wife and killed by Gyges after bragging about her beauty, whilst Miltiades, victor of Marathon, died in prison of gangrene after his failed expedition to Paros).[39] Herodotus does not elaborate why something must happen, nor does he name the power behind this fate, necessity, or destiny. Moreover, prayers, sacrifices, dedications and other forms of supplication have no effect on it. Even the gods cannot overturn it, as the priestess at Delphi states, explaining to Croesus that Apollo could not change his fate: 'Not god himself could escape destiny.'[40] The working-out of this fate sometimes takes the form of divine punishment for an impiety. Miltiades, for example, violated a sanctuary of Demeter. This force may also at times be behind the principle of reversals in fortune, as Solon outlines to Croesus, that Herodotus sees operating in human affairs. Croesus, Cyrus and Xerxes, among others, all suffer catastrophic falls from great heights of success. Thus a variety of factors may be at work in an individual's downfall. Croesus' extraordinary success led him to misinterpret an oracle and invade Persia. Attempting to add Persia to his string of unbroken victories offended the gods. In addition, his ancestor Gyges had offended the gods by overthrowing Candaules and founding a dynasty that, as a result, was fated to end in the fifth generation afterwards – so that Croesus was fated to pay for his ancestor's offence with his own defeat. Xerxes' dream, which leads him to his defeat, ensures that he could not escape his fate. Herodotus has Themistocles explain Xerxes' defeat in a way that sums up many of the historian's own views:

> Indeed it was not we who performed this exploit; it was the gods and the heroes, who were jealous that one man in his godless pride should be king of Asia and of Europe too – a man who does not know the difference between sacred and profane, who burns and destroys statues of the gods, and dared to lash the sea with whips and bind it with fetters.[41]

Thucydides

Thucydides (*c.* 460–400 BC) came from a wealthy aristocratic Athenian family. He served as one of the annually elected ten generals in 424 during the Peloponnesian War (431–404 BC) and was exiled shortly afterwards when the Athenians blamed him for the loss of the important northern Aegean city of Amphipolis.[42] He probably spent much of his exile at Corinth, a key Spartan ally. His historical scope is much narrower than that of Herodotus, focusing almost exclusively on politics and warfare, devoting little space to ethnography or anthropology. His history of the Peloponnesian War is unfinished, breaking off abruptly in 411 BC.

Unlike Herodotus, Thucydides never says that he sees divine power or the hand of the gods at work in human affairs. He does not record reports of heroes, phantoms or other semi-divine figures appearing on the battlefield. Nor does he express a positive belief in oracles, as Herodotus explicitly does. This does not mean, as has often been assumed, that Thucydides was an atheist or a sceptic, and entirely pragmatic. He certainly was interested in religion and recognized its central role in virtually every aspect of daily life in the ancient Greek world, including warfare.[43] At the very least, respect for the gods and their rituals helped reinforce the stability and prosperity of the community, and not just by keeping the gods propitiated.

Like Herodotus, Thucydides notes instances where adherence to ritual, or impious behaviour, affects the course of human events; unlike his predecessor, he does not attribute consequences or outcomes to divine intervention. Human belief in the gods, however, can influence what happens. He relates the following incident, for example, without comment. In 412 BC, the Corinthians spoiled an expedition they had planned along with the Spartans and other allies to help the Chians rebel from Athens when they refused to postpone celebrating the Festival of Poseidon at Isthmia, despite the pleadings of the Spartan King Agis, thereby losing the crucial element of surprise and allowing the Athenians time to prepare.[44] Thucydides can also use religion to comment indirectly on human behaviour. When the Athenians occupy the precinct and temple of Apollo during the Delion campaign in 424 BC, he clearly depicts them as blatantly violating standard Greek norms of piety. He does not say, however, that the Athenian defeat is a divine punishment. But his portrait of the Athenians' disregard for the god and his property, including the highly sophistical speech they give justifying their actions, highlights their arrogance.[45]

The various gods oversaw and protected all manner of human interactions. Thus, breaking an oath, for example, offended not only the party to whom it was sworn, but also Zeus Horkios, and therefore was a religious offence in addition to a social, economic or legal one. In the debate at Sparta in 432 BC about whether to declare war on Athens, both sides invoked the oaths sworn to confirm treaties, and the gods who witnessed them, as a rhetorical tool in attempting to sway the Spartans, whom Thucydides (and Herodotus) often portray as especially sensitive to religious concerns. The Corinthians argued that if the Spartans failed to help their allies in the face of Athenian aggression, it is Sparta that would have broken the treaty of alliance and that would incur the disfavour of the gods. In response, the Athenians warned the Spartans not to break their treaty with them, calling on the gods who witnessed the oaths.[46] Ultimately, the Spartans decided that the Athenians had violated the treaty. As Thucydides says, however, even though they had made up their own minds, they nonetheless sent to Delphi to ask the god if they would fare well in the coming war. Apollo answered emphatically that they would win if they put their whole strength into the war and that he would support them whether they asked him to or not.[47] Nonetheless, when the Spartans suffered serious setbacks in the first phase of the war, they attributed their misfortunes to having been the first to break the treaty. In 414 BC, however, when the Syracusans and Corinthians asked for help against Athens during the Peace of Nicias, they readily supplied it in the belief that this time the Athenians had clearly been the first to violate the treaty.[48]

In describing the bloody factionalism at Corcyra, Thucydides says that at the height of the violence the bond that held members of a given party together was not adherence to divine law or custom but rather their complicity in crime.[49] Some have seen in this passage evidence that Thucydides accepted a role for the divine, however indirectly, in the human realm, that he must not have been a sceptic or atheist.[50] Regardless of what Thucydides' personal views of the gods may have been, the episode does show that he saw the key role that belief in the gods, or at least respect for their rituals and other such conventions, played in maintaining community and political relations. Indeed, properly performing religious rituals on behalf of the state for Thucydides is one of the hallmarks of good government. He praises the rule of the Peisistratid tyrants at Athens because they 'cultivated wisdom and virtue as much as any, and without exacting from the Athenians more than a twentieth of their income, splendidly adorned their city, and carried on their wars, and provided sacrifices for the temples'.[51]

So it is clear that Thucydides believed that even the performance of conventional ritual was important. But it is just these regular rituals that he often does not describe. He rarely mentions those that accompanied most military activities, in particular the sacrifices before battle, although (or perhaps because) he served as a general and must have overseen the performance of such rites many times. On the other hand, Thucydides can illustrate implicitly the kind of breakdown of moral standards he explicitly describes happening at Corcyra simply by contrasting the words of those professing to act in accordance with the gods with their actions.[52]

Oracles and other forms of prophecy do appear in Thucydides' narrative, though much less frequently than in Herodotus. Individuals and states take them seriously and can alter their behaviour or actions in response. For example, the Spartans on occasion abandoned a military enterprise when the sacrifices (*diabateria*) they traditionally made before crossing their border were not favourable.[53] Similarly, commanders had to take into account and explain to their troops the significance of natural phenomena, such as earthquakes, eclipses, thunder and lightning, which typically were viewed as divine signs.[54]

Thucydides' views of prophecy are much harder to discern than those of Herodotus, who states outright that he accepts the validity of prophecy and will not hear others speak against it.[55] Despite that statement, Herodotus' narrative depicts a range of reasons to be wary of prophecies, and in particular to take great care interpreting them. At the very least Thucydides agrees with the last point. In his digression on Cylon's attempt to become tyrant of Athens in the seventh century, he suggests that Cylon failed to interpret correctly an oracular response from Delphi urging him to seize the Athenian acropolis during the great festival of Zeus. Cylon assumed this meant the festival at Olympia – he had been an Olympic victor. But Thucydides adds that the Athenians had a local festival with the same name, which they celebrated outside the city. Cylon, Thucydides says, never thought to ask Delphi for clarification, nor did the oracle offer it. Here, and in one or two other passages, Thucydides seems to be in what Hornblower terms a Herodotean vein: Cylon fails to interpret an oracle in much the same way that Croesus and other figures in Herodotus do.[56] There is no criticism of consulting oracles, or of acting on their advice, as a process.

Indeed, it is significant that Thucydides shows nothing but respect for the Delphic oracle throughout his work.[57] By contrast, he often describes other forms of prophecy and their purveyors with what many commentators see as irony, sarcasm and disapproval. He targets the *chrêsmologos* (oracle collector or reciter) and the *mantis* (seer), terms that fit a wide range of practitioners employing a variety of prophetic methods. They were not attached officially to an oracular shrine such as Delphi, but operated independently, often for whatever profit they could earn. A *chrêsmologos* kept a library of oracles and prophecies on which he could draw to address nearly any occasion or contingency. A seer could perform whatever his specialty was – reading entrails, interpreting dreams or bird omens – on the spot for a customer. Seers could achieve high status; there was at least one on the staff of every general. But most probably did not.[58]

Thucydides shows these diviners thriving, particularly in periods of high emotion, uncertainty and excitement, implying that they exploited such conditions to ply their trade. For example, when it became increasingly apparent that Athens and Sparta would go to war, he observes that:

Zeal is always at its height at the commencement of an undertaking; and on this particular occasion the Peloponnesus and Athens were both full of young men whose inexperience made them eager to take up arms, while the rest of Hellas stood straining with excitement at the conflict of its leading cities. Everywhere predictions were being recited and oracles being chanted by such persons as collect them.[59]

Likewise, when the Spartans first invaded Attica and were pillaging Acharnae, many Athenians were eager to march out while others just as emphatically were not. Thucydides says that groups of people formed in the streets, and that when the debate grew hot the *chrêsmologoi* did not miss this opportunity: 'Oracles of the most various import were recited by the collectors, and found eager listeners in one or the other of the disputants.'[60] These same practitioners were active in the period when the Athenians decided to send their ill-fated force to Sicily, though Thucydides does not reveal this until after the expedition ends in disaster. At that point, he reports that the Athenians were angry with the *chrêsmologoi*, *manteis* (seers) and all other diviners who had encouraged them to hope to conquer Sicily.[61] Interestingly, the *chrêsmologoi* seem to disappear from the record after this. For example, three of Aristophanes' earlier plays contain scenes spoofing the *chrêsmologoi*,[62] but none of his plays dating to after the Sicilian expedition do.[63]

Those consulting *chrêsmologoi* and *manteis* do not come off well either. Like Cylon (and Croesus in Herodotus), they often fail to scrutinize adequately the prophecies they receive. In another passage, Thucydides points out the tendency of people consulting an oracle while in a crisis to hear what they want to hear. At the height of the plague in its first year, the Athenians recalled an old prophecy which stated that: 'A Dorian (i.e., Spartan) war shall come and with it pestilence. So a dispute arose as to whether dearth (Greek *limos*: famine) and not death (Greek *loimos*: plague, pestilence) had been the word in the verse; but at the present juncture, it was of course decided in favour of the latter, for the people made their recollection fit in with their sufferings. I suppose, however, that if another Dorian war should ever afterwards come upon us, and a famine should happen to accompany it, the verse will probably be read accordingly.'[64]

This prophecy most likely came from the collection of a *chrêsmologos*; Thucydides reports that old men claimed it had been uttered long ago. At any rate, it did not result from a consultation at a shrine such as Delphi, which alone was probably enough to elicit his critical tone. But it is the way people interpreted the prophecy – to 'fit in with their sufferings' – that chiefly draws his criticism. Thucydides himself offers a counter example in interpreting a fragmentary and presumably old oracle about a plot of land below the Athenian acropolis called the *Pelargikon*, the occupation of which was prohibited by a curse. It read, 'Better that the *Pelargikon* be unworked.' Of course, as with many other sacred enclosures and temples in Athens, people whom the war forced to move inside the city walls for safety built shelters on the *Pelargikon*. Thucydides says that the prophecy came true in a way that was the opposite from what was expected. Occupation of the plot did not cause the misfortunes suffered, but rather the oracle simply said that when the *Pelargikon* was occupied it would be on a day that was evil for Athens. Here again, Thucydides does not question the content of the prophecy, which, significantly, he identifies as Pythian (from Delphi), but corrects the interpretation.[65]

Thucydides comments on oracles in the so-called second preface, saying that the fact that the war lasted twenty-seven years provides 'an instance of faith in oracles being for once justified by the event. I certainly remember that all along from the beginning to the end of the war it was commonly declared that it would last thrice nine years.' This sounds like a wholesale dismissal of prophecy, even though on other occasions Thucydides seems to accept oracles, as pointed out above. Note, though, that the Greek word for oracles in this passage is *chrêsmos*, which Thucydides uses for prophecies from *chrêsmologoi* and similar diviners, but never for an oracle from Delphi.[66]

Herodotus often sees the will of the gods at work in natural phenomena such as windstorms, floods and earthquakes. Thucydides never explicitly assigns divine responsibility for such events. Instead, he may offer reasonably accurate speculation, for example, about when solar eclipses occur and how earthquakes can cause tsunami flooding.[67] He does, however, describe how these events influence the actions of men who believe they are divine signs, usually without criticism or comment. When the war was about to break out and in the excitement *chrêsmologoi* and *manteis* were in great demand (as discussed above), he says that people were also highly attuned to any natural phenomenon, such as a recent major earthquake on Delos, and were quick to assume they were 'ominous of the events impending; indeed, nothing of the kind was allowed to pass without remark'.[68]

Yet in several passages Thucydides himself seems to suggest that there might be a connection between human events and these natural occurrences. In introducing his work, he argues that the Peloponnesian War far outstripped any predecessor in its violence, scope and duration, with 'disasters of a kind and number that no other similar period of time could match'. He cites not just the widespread destruction of cities and vast numbers of people killed or banished; there was also an unparalleled number of violent earthquakes and solar eclipses, devastating droughts which caused famines, and worst of all the plague at Athens.[69] He does not seem to regard the large number of earthquakes and the like during the war as a coincidence, but does not explicitly say there is a connection, as Herodotus might have done. Thucydides' vivid language may simply serve to strengthen his case for the pre-eminent significance of his account of the war. Note that he nowhere includes any droughts or resulting famines, so there is some exaggeration in the passage. In another passage, however, in which he reports the terrible casualties of the second outbreak of the plague (4,400 hoplites, 300 cavalry and an unascertainable number of the general populace), he adds that at this time there were also numerous earthquakes in Athens, Euboea and Boeotia.[70] In neither of these passages is there anything more than the slightest hint that Thucydides saw some sort of connection, presumably divine, between the human disasters and the natural phenomena. But the hint is there nonetheless.

When others interpret an earthquake as an omen and adjust their actions in response, Thucydides does not criticize them for doing so, though neither does he confirm that he too believes the omens; he merely reports without comment. On one occasion, a meeting of the Athenian assembly adjourned before making a key decision about a controversial alliance when there was an earthquake. Similarly, when the Argives and Spartans were at Corinth, each trying to persuade the Corinthians to join their alliance, an earthquake brought a long meeting to an end without a Corinthian decision.[71] Thucydides makes no comment, but it seems clear that in each case the earthquake was minor and that the parties involved were not in danger but took it as a sign to stop what they were doing. He gives no indication that he disapproved or thought it foolish to end the meetings without settling an important issue. He records several other similar occasions on which earthquakes, regarded as omens, put an end to or altered significantly a major military undertaking, all of them involving the Spartans. When the Spartans were on their way to invade Argos, an earthquake at Cleonae made them return home. In the first phase of the war, the Spartans and their allies were preparing to invade Attica when a series of earthquakes at the Isthmus made them turn back. Finally, in 411 BC, the Spartans were readying an allied fleet of forty ships, ten of which they themselves were to supply, to send to Ionia under the command of Melanchridas. Before the fleet could sail, there was an earthquake that, Thucydides implies, prompted the Spartans to send Chalceus as commander instead of Melanchridas, and only five of their own ships instead of ten.[72] Again, Thucydides reports these incidents without comment, as though he and his readers regard them as perfectly normal and expected behaviour.

The best-known and most dramatic instance in Thucydides' work of humans reacting to a natural phenomenon involves a lunar eclipse instead of an earthquake. At perhaps the most critical moment for the fate of their expedition to Sicily, when even the general Nicias, who had been reluctant to give up the siege of Syracuse after a series of setbacks, had at last agreed that the Athenians should depart for home and they were on the point of sailing away, there was an eclipse of the moon. This awed most of the Athenians, and even though beforehand they had been eager to depart, they now pressed their generals to wait. Nicias was also deeply affected by the eclipse and refused even to consider leaving until the 'thrice nine days' prescribed by the seers had passed. Here, in a highly scrutinized and analyzed passage, Thucydides comments on Nicias' decision, characterizing him as 'somewhat overaddicted to divination and practices of that sort'.[73] Looking to pin down Thucydides' views, scholars understandably have focused on this passage, in which he comments in his own voice on divination. Some argue that Thucydides criticizes both divination and Nicias for believing in it; they conclude that he was at the very least a sceptic. Others see his criticism aimed, however gently, solely at Nicias; that is, the phrasing seems to allow for some recourse to divination, just not too much. The Greek noun for divination in this passage, *theiasmos*, occurs only here in Thucydides. He uses, however, the closely related verb form (*theiasantes*, a participle from *theiazein*: to prophesy, divine) in the passage (discussed above) in which he reports the anger Athenians felt after the Sicilian debacle at *chrêsmologoi*, *manteis* and as many others as had prophesied (*theiasantes*) that they would take Sicily.[74] Like many Athenians, Nicias, it seems, regularly consulted oracle-mongers, seers and the like, practitioners whose work Thucydides for the most part rejects. Since Thucydides seems to accept, tacitly, that natural phenomena such as eclipses may not always occur randomly, his criticism of Nicias' penchant for divination may refer not to his taking the eclipse as a sign but to Nicias' too-ready acceptance of the seers' recommendation that he delay the Athenians' departure for 'thrice nine days'. Thucydides' epitaph for Nicias, whom the Syracusans executed, suggests that he did not consider this facet of Nicias' character a major flaw: Nicias was 'a man who, of all the Hellenes in my time, least deserved such a fate, seeing that the course of his life had been regulated with strict attention to virtue'.[75]

Xenophon

In his *Hellenica* (*Greek Affairs*), the Athenian Xenophon picks up the narrative of the Peloponnesian War where Thucydides' unfinished account abruptly leaves off in 411 BC, carries it through the end of the war in 404 BC and down to the second Battle of Mantineia in 362 BC. Like his two predecessors, Xenophon was an exile. The Athenians banished him sometime in the 390s BC, perhaps for his involvement in the Younger Cyrus' failed attempt to overthrow his brother as Great King of Persia, his subsequent close ties to Sparta, or both. As a young man, he was a follower of Socrates. He was deeply interested in politics, military tactics and practices, and perhaps above all in the principles of leadership. He wrote Socratic dialogues, treatises on economics, hunting, horsemanship and the duties of a cavalry commander, as well as an encomium of the Spartan King Agesilaus. His *Cyropaedia* (*The Education of Cyrus*), a fictional account of Cyrus the Great's rise to power, remained the handbook for princes until supplanted by Machiavelli. The *Anabasis* (*The Trip Upcountry*) is a memoir-like account (albeit written in the third person) of his experiences helping lead a contingent of Greek mercenaries, the famous Ten Thousand, back from the heart of the Persian Empire after the Younger Cyrus' failed coup in 401 BC. While still in Asia Minor, Xenophon and the remnants of the Ten Thousand took service with the Spartans when they went to war with Persia in 399 BC. He became close friends with the Spartan King Agesilaus (ruled *c.* 400–360 BC), and through that connection, along with the ties he undoubtedly still had in Athens, was at the centre of Greek affairs for most of the first half of the fourth century. His works offer a broad range of perspectives from which to derive his views on the gods, religion and their role in warfare. Not surprisingly, the generals he clearly admires in his *Hellenica* display traits similar not only to those of his fictional Cyrus the Great, but also to those he depicts himself as having as a general in the *Anabasis*.

In several of his works, he states explicitly his view on both the importance and the proper scope of divination. The gods know the past, the present and the future – everything that is important. But humans should consult them only concerning that which they have no ability to know. This would include, for example, whether or not it would be advantageous for a skilled general to accept the command of a particular army at a given time. On the other hand, humans should not ask the questions which their own learning, experience and common sense can answer. Socrates, Xenophon says, believed that 'what the gods have granted us to do by help of learning, we must learn; what is hidden from mortals we should try to find out from the gods by divination: for they give signs to those whom they favour.'[76] Just as in Herodotus, it is important to perform sacrifices correctly at the right time to maintain the favour of the gods; the human relationship with the gods plays out largely through divination and the correct interpretation of omens and oracles.

Xenophon depicts himself in the *Anabasis* frequently consulting the gods for help in making key decisions. Since he did not have regular access to an established oracular shrine, he typically had a seer examine the liver of a sacrificed animal, a process that required a professional's trained eye.[77] So, for example, when the army offered him sole command, Xenophon sacrificed and when the results were unfavourable he rejected the offer.[78]

Modern readers have occasionally suspected that ancient figures used sacrifices and omens to further their own agendas.[79] In the *Anabasis*, though, there are several instances when unfavourable omens prevented the Greeks from pursuing a course of action that they all desired or even desperately needed to take. A dramatic example of this took place at Calpe Harbour on the Black Sea. Surrounded by hostile forces, the Greeks were safely, if reluctantly, ensconced in a strong defensive position on a natural harbour. But provisions were running out and the sacrifices for battle were unfavourable. Shifting the focus of the sacrifices to obtaining supplies failed to get favourable results. At length, though the men were out of food, Xenophon refused to lead the army out for any reason until the sacrifices were positive. Many of the Greeks suspected, at least initially, that Xenophon was delaying because he hoped to found a city with them on the harbour. To counter that, Xenophon invited not only all seers who might be present, but also anyone else to witness the sacrifices. Nearly the entire army showed up, but the results were still inauspicious. In desperation, one of the other generals led 2,000 volunteers on a foraging expedition. Persian cavalry routed them, killing over 500 men. Finally, after a ship laden with grain (and additional animals for sacrifice) arrived, the sacrifices turned positive and the Greeks fought their way out of the predicament. As is often the case in the *Anabasis*, the results of divination support Xenophon's view of the situation and the stance he takes. The fate of the foraging party does suggest that it would have been disastrous to have led out the entire army at that time, despite the lack of food.[80]

Another instance of divination preventing the Greeks from doing what they wanted, but in which Xenophon does not have a personal stake, occurred when the Greeks reached the territory of the Tibarenians. The land of the latter was flat, well suited for a hoplite army such as the Ten Thousand, and its fortresses not formidable. Having decided to plunder the country so the men could enrich themselves, the Greek generals initially rejected the gifts of friendship the Tibarenians offered. But after many failed sacrifices, all the seers declared that the gods were not in favour of a war. This forced the generals to accept the Tibarenians' gifts and refrain from ravaging their land.[81]

Interpreting an oracular response requires great care; so too does formulating the question one asks an oracle, or when making a sacrifice. Note that in the episode at Calpe Harbour when the sacrifices forbade attacking the enemy, Xenophon changed to sacrificing about obtaining provisions. Humans have plenty of scope to influence the outcome of a particular crisis or puzzle, and thus bear considerable responsibility for it. Xenophon himself provides a good illustration of this. When invited to join Cyrus the Younger's expedition, he sought the advice of Socrates about whether to accept, and Socrates told him to consult the oracle at Delphi. But at Delphi, Xenophon asked not whether he should join Cyrus but rather to what god he should sacrifice in order best to make the journey he had in mind, meet with good fortune and return home safely. Apollo, Xenophon reports, told him which gods. Back in Athens, Socrates criticized Xenophon for not asking the key question and for deciding on his own to join Cyrus, but noted that since he had asked as he did, to do as the god directed.[82]

In the first part of his *Hellenica* (through to 2.3.10), Xenophon, to some degree, follows the tone and structure of Thucydides; for example, he never mentions sacrifices before battles. In the rest of the work, however, he frequently includes them and other religious practices. An episode in 388 BC illustrates in unusual detail a commander consulting oracles, sacrificing, and interpreting omens during a military campaign. Interestingly, the focus is not Xenophon's close friend and patron Agesilaus, but rather Agesipolis, the other of Sparta's two kings at the time, who had received the command when the Spartans decided to invade Argos. In response to this threat, the Argives had proclaimed the sacred months, essentially a religious treaty that all states had to observe, even though it was not the usual time for them. After obtaining favourable omens at the border sacrifices that Spartan forces typically made before leaving their own territory, Agesipolis went to Olympia to consult the oracle of Zeus about the propriety of rejecting the Argives' claim of a sacred truce. The oracle replied that it was not impious to reject an unjustly declared holy truce. Agesipolis then travelled to Delphi and got the same response. Joining his army, Agesipolis marched to Argos, where he turned away garlanded Argive heralds and, much to their surprise, rejected the holy truce they tried to proclaim. He then invaded Argive territory, but on his first night there as the men were dining, the god Poseidon, Xenophon says, sent an earthquake. With Agesipolis leading, the Spartans sang a paean to Poseidon. The men assumed they would head home, because Agesilaus' predecessor, Agis, had led the army back from an invasion of Elis when there was an earthquake.[83] But Agesipolis interpreted the omen differently, saying that if the earthquake had struck before the Spartans had entered Argive territory, he would have turned back, but since the god had sent it after they had already invaded, he thought it was divine encouragement to continue the campaign. The next day, then, he sacrificed to Poseidon and led his men deeper into Argive territory, all the way to the walls of the city itself, striving to advance further and do more damage than Agesilaus had achieved in an earlier invasion. He advanced so rapidly that the Argives closed their gates before their allied Boeotian cavalry were safely inside. The troopers could only cling closely to the walls 'like bats'. Xenophon says that many men and horses would have been killed if it had not happened that the Spartans' contingent of Cretan archers had not been off ravaging another Argive town. A little later, however, when they were encamped near the city walls, a thunderbolt struck the Spartans, killing several men. Then when Agesipolis sacrificed with a view to building a fort at the entrance to Argive territory, the victim's liver lacked a lobe, and Agesipolis led the army away and disbanded it. But Xenophon notes that the Spartan had done a great deal of damage to the Argives because he had attacked them unexpectedly.

Xenophon concludes his description of the campaign on this seemingly positive note, but there is reason to think that he regarded Agesipolis' decision to interpret the earthquake as a sign to advance as a mistake. Although the Spartans' rapid advance caught the enemy cavalrymen in a highly vulnerable position, the very men who could have finished them off happened to be elsewhere. This is exactly the kind of bad luck that Xenophon believes befalls those who fail to act properly towards the gods.[84]

For Xenophon, the greatest evidence of a man's reverence for the gods is his ability to keep an oath. In the encomium he wrote of Agesilaus, for example, he cites as proof of the Spartan king's respect for the gods the fact that his enemies considered his oaths and treaties to be more reliable than even their friendship with each other.[85] Similarly, Xenophon's laudatory summary of Cyrus the Younger's character in the *Anabasis* emphasizes that the Persian considered it of the utmost importance never to break his word or a sworn treaty.[86] Conversely, anyone who breaks an oath can expect the gods to support his enemies. The Persian Satrap Tissaphernes, who appears in the *Anabasis* and *Hellenica*, offers a stark example. He broke a truce with the Ten Thousand after the death of Cyrus, murdering their generals at a conference. Then, a few years later, he broke a truce with Agesilaus, which he had already flagrantly flouted to double the size of his army, but to no avail. A year later, Agesilaus defeated him in battle and the Persian king had him beheaded.[87]

This principle helps explain, in Xenophon's eyes, the downfall of Sparta in the 370s. After Sparta defeated Olynthus in 379, he observes that Sparta had reached the pinnacle of its power. It controlled Thebes and Boeotia, had brought to heel and punished other rebellious allies, and had isolated Athens: 'It seemed that Sparta had at length established its empire most excellently and securely.' But he then adds the following observation:

> Now one could mention many other incidents, both among Greeks and barbarians, to prove that the gods do not fail to take heed of the impious and those who do wicked things; but at present I will speak of the case which is before me. The Spartans, namely, who had sworn that they would allow the cities to be autonomous, after seizing possession of the acropolis of Thebes, were punished by the very men, unaided, who had been thus wronged, although before that time they had not been conquered by any single one of all the peoples that ever existed.[88]

With unexpected ease, the Thebans did evict the Spartans from the Cadmea, their acropolis, and executed the traitorous Thebans who had helped them seize it. But surely the statement also looks ahead to the surprising and landmark Theban defeat of Sparta at Leuktra some eight years later. Indeed, Xenophon issues a similar judgment regarding Sparta in the wake of the failed peace conference of the major Greek states in 371 BC that led to that humiliating Spartan defeat. Eager to punish the Thebans after at least a decade of increasing hostilities, the Spartan Assembly ordered an invasion of Boeotia, rejecting as foolish a counter-proposal that they first follow the terms of the recent treaty so that 'the gods would be most favourably inclined to them'. When the Spartans scorn what he clearly believes was the correct course of action, Xenophon notes that 'the divinity (*to daimonion*) was leading them on', i.e., to their downfall. In the battle that follows, Xenophon says that everything went against the Spartans, while for their opponents everything went right, even what happened by chance.[89] To be sure, it is clear that good Theban planning played a role, though Xenophon mentions neither Epaminondas nor Pelopidas, possibly because in his view they served chiefly to carry out a divine punishment of Sparta. Perhaps further evidence of the Spartans' failure to respect the gods properly is that they undertook the campaign even though it was during one of their most important religious festivals, the Gymnopaidiai. Previously, the Spartans had famously refrained from campaigning for religious reasons on several occasions.[90]

In general, though, Xenophon champions a fairly conventional set of moral standards and only rarely explicitly attributes even an indirect role for the gods in human events on a grand scale. In a few instances, Xenophon suggests that a piece of good luck might be evidence for divine favour,[91] but as a rule, humans bear the responsibility for their actions. As Xenophon has the Thessalian strongman Jason of Pherae observe, in a sentiment reminiscent of Herodotus, god often delights in making the small great and the great small.[92] In punishing the impious, however, the gods themselves do not intervene but rather work through other mortals. In the case of the Spartans, it is the Thebans, for whom everything goes right at Leuktra, who bring them down.

Xenophon portrays himself voicing this view in the *Anabasis*. In a dispute over leadership at one point, the Greeks split into several groups, one of which a Thracian force had trapped on a nearby hilltop. In rallying his troops to aid their erstwhile comrades, Xenophon says, 'and it may be that the god is guiding events in this way, he who wills that those who talked boastfully, as though possessed of superior wisdom, should be brought low, and that we, who always begin with the gods, should be set in a place of higher honour than those boasters.'[93]

Conclusion

As intimate and omnipresent as religious ritual, portents and divination were in Greek life, and in particular in most aspects of Greek warfare, it is striking how much responsibility all three historians assign for what happens among men to humans themselves. Of the three, Herodotus demonstrates the broadest interest in omens, portents and prophecies in any form, regardless of whether they originated from a prestigious oracular shrine such as Delphi, or had been passed down over the years from an unknown or forgotten source. In his narrative, it is incumbent upon humans to recognize and interpret an omen or prophecy correctly, a process that is rarely simple or straightforward. In addition, a prophecy or portent often occurs at a key historical juncture and can highlight a crucial decision or action, such as the Delphic admonition to the Athenians to rely on a wooden wall for safety against Xerxes.[94] Herodotus also delights in prophecies that are fulfilled in an unexpected way, even if they have no major impact on history, and he sometimes cites them as proof that the gods have a hand in human affairs.[95]

Portents, prophecy and especially divination figure prominently in Xenophon's historical narratives, though they only rarely have the same global impact that they often can in Herodotus. Instead, Xenophon emphasizes what might be called the practical aspect of divination as a means of finding out about the future and getting advice on matters outside the scope of human learning and skill.[96] Included in this category are sacrifices

to obtain the goodwill of the gods and to make sure that a planned course
of action will not be impious or otherwise offensive to the gods. Xenophon
often depicts prophecy, divination and religious matters from the viewpoint
of a general who deals with them on a daily basis.

Both Herodotus and Xenophon believe that the gods punish impiety.
Damaging a temple or sanctuary, harming or killing a suppliant or a person
under the protection of the gods such as a herald or ambassador, are
especially serious offences. Both historians depict the breaking of an oath as
highly offensive to the gods. For Xenophon, keeping one's word is perhaps
the chief defining characteristic of a man's reverence towards the gods.[97]
This is true for states as well as individuals. Thus the Spartans' breaking of
oaths led to their defeat at Leuktra.

For Herodotus, divine punishment for impiety often is a factor in the
catastrophic downfall of powerful figures such as Cyrus and Xerxes. He has
the Athenian sage Solon trying to warn the Lydian King Croesus that his
seemingly unending good fortune may not be enduring, that men are subject
to chance and that the gods are particularly jealous of human prosperity.[98]
This motif of a divinely caused reversal of fortune also appears in Xenophon,
though far less frequently than in Herodotus. For example, the powerful
Thessalian ruler Jason of Pherae remarks – not long before his assassination
– that the gods delight in making the great small and the small great.[99]

In contrast to his predecessor and successor, Thucydides never depicts
divine power in any form affecting human affairs. But he does recognize
that human respect for religious rituals, customs and sanctuaries, or the
lack thereof, and belief in the gods, can have a dramatic impact on historical
events. Individuals and states can change their actions or policies depending
on the outcome of a sacrifice, an earthquake can put an end to a campaign
or a religious festival might prevent the timely participation in a military
expedition.[100] In general, though, Thucydides omits almost entirely the
kinds of everyday divination and other religious rituals that Xenophon
makes an integral part of his narratives, as well as the dramatic prophecies
that Herodotus often portrays occurring in a crisis. From the handful of
instances in which Thucydides discusses a prophecy, divination or oracle,
it is possible to discern a rough taxonomy. He is contemptuous of oracle-
collectors (*chrêsmologoi*) and seers (*manteis*), and usually does not present
those who consult them in a positive light. On the other hand, he is never
disrespectful of prophecies from Delphi. In the so-called second preface,
Thucydides disdainfully states that the only prophecy concerning the war
that came true was the one that predicted it would last thrice nine years.[101]
Yet in a digression on the Athenian Cylon's attempt to seize control of the

city in about 630 BC, Thucydides sounds almost Herodotean, critiquing Cylon's failure both to interpret correctly a prophecy from Delphi and to ask for greater clarity with a follow-up question.[102] Unlike Herodotus and Xenophon, Thucydides does not attribute natural phenomena, such as earthquakes and eclipses, to divine intervention or see them as portents, though in a couple of instances he seems to suggest tacitly that they can occur in conjunction with important or disastrous human events.[103]

Notes

1. Hdt. 8.13, 129.
2. Hdt. 3.38. All translations of Herodotus are from the Penguin edition by A. de Selincourt, revised by J. Marincola (1996).
3. Hdt. 2.3, 65; Mikalson, 2003, 131.
4. Hdt. 7.152, see also 2.123.
5. Hdt. 2.57.
6. Hdt. 2.144. For other examples, see 1.181–82, 4.105.2, 5.86.3, 8.8.2–3. Cf. Mikalson, 2003, 145–46.
7. Hdt. 6.105; Harrison, 2000, 91; see aso Lara O'Sullivan in this volume.
8. Harrison, 2000, 84–85.
9. Hdt. 6.117. Ael. *Var. Hist.* 7.38 writes that Epizelus appears in the famous painting of Marathon in the Painted Stoa in the Athenian Agora; thus he was probably a well-known figure.
10. Hdt. 8.84. See Tritle, 2000, 63–65, who suggests that Epizelus may have suffered from a form of post-traumatic stress disorder.
11. Hdt. 8.77. Note that the Euboeans ignore Bacis' prophecy about the coming Persian invasion and consequently lose all their livestock: 8.26.1–3.
12. Hdt. 9.37–38; Mikalson, 2003, 140–41; Dillery, 2005, 206–09.
13. Hdt. 1.53, cf. 1.91 where the oracle points out this failing later when Croesus complains that it had misled him.
14. Hdt. 7.140.
15. Hdt. 7.141.
16. Hdt. 7.142–143.
17. Hdt. 7.139. See also Mikalson, 2003, 56–57.
18. Hdt. 7.6.
19. Hdt. 8.29, 77, 96; 9.43. On Bacis, see Harrison, 2000, 122–24; Mikalson, 2003, 85–86; Dillery, 2005, 168–72, 179–81, 224. For *chrêsmologoi*, see Sonya Nevin in this volume.
20. Hdt. 8.96.
21. Hdt. 8.114, 9.63–64.
22. Hdt. 6.79–82. Other examples include Hippias at Marathon, 6.107, and Cambyses at Egyptian Ecbatana, 3.64.
23. Hdt. 8.141.
24. Hdt. 9.8. Harrison, 2000, 150, sees this as an oracle with an implied condition, that is, *if* the Athenians and Persians ally, the Dorians would be evicted from the Peloponnese. Mikalson, 2003, 148 rightly classifies this among prophecies that Herodotus describes as inescapable, that must happen.

25. Mikalson, 2003, 48.
26. Hdt. 7.178.
27. Hdt. 7.188–91; Athos storm, 6.44.
28. Hdt. 8.13.
29. Hdt. 9.61–62. Pritchett, 1979, 78, 83; Jameson, 1991, 207.
30. Hdt. 2.120.
31. Hdt. 7.133–37; see also Thuc. 2.67. For Thucydides, there is no religious element to this story. Instead he focuses on the Athenians' summary execution of the envoys, en masse and without letting them speak, and ignores the coincidence of their fathers having been spared by Xerxes. See Gomme, 1956, 199–200; Hornblower, 1991, 350–51, 1992a, 152.
32. Hdt. 9.121.
33. Hdt. 9.65. See also 8.129, where a tidal wave drowns Persians who had desecrated a sanctuary of Poseidon.
34. For other examples of weapons moving mysteriously outside of temples, see Xen. *Hell.* 6.4.7; Diod. 15.53; Polyaen. *Strat.* 2.3.8.
35. Hdt. 8.37–39.
36. Hdt. 9.100–01.
37. Note that the Athenians and Ionians accidentally burnt the temples at Sardis in the opening stages of the Ionian Revolt in 498 BC. Xerxes later claimed that he was invading Greece in order to conquer Athens and to set it on fire to punish the Athenians for the temples, sanctuaries and groves they destroyed at Sardis; Hdt. 5.100–03, 7.8b, 8.53.2.
38. Hdt. 8.51–55. Other examples include: 3.1, 7.17, 7.35, 7.238, 9.108.
39. Hdt. 1.8, 6.135.
40. Hdt. 1.91; Mikalson, 2003, 149.
41. Hdt. 8.109.3.
42. Thuc. 4.106.3, 5.26.5.
43. Scholars who see in Thucydides some measure of acceptance of a role for the gods and religion in general include: Oost, 1975; A. Powell, 1979; C.A. Powell, 1979; Marinatos, 1981, 1981a; Jordan, 1986; Badian, 1989, 98. Hornblower, 1992, believes he was at best a sceptic. Dover, 1970, 394, argued that Thucydides 'may well have been an atheist', a view he later modified (Dover, 1987, 65, 72) in the light of the articles by Oost and Marinatos, accepting that Thucydides for many years had been open to the possibility of a role for the divine in human affairs but near the end of his life adopted a more cynical view.
44. Thuc. 8.7–10.
45. Thuc. 4.89–101. Jordan, 1986, 130.
46. Thuc. 1.72.5, 1.78.4. On attitudes towards breaking oaths generally, see Dover, 1974, 246–50, and on these passages, 165–66, 184–85; Pearson,1962, 116; Flower, 2012, 205–06; Hirsch, 1985, 19, 29, 41, 161. Xenophon is particularly attuned to the consequences of breaking an oath, for example, *Hell.* 3.4.11, 5.4.1, 6.4.3, *Anab.* 3.1.19–23, 3.2.7–10. Thucydides notes that the Spartans attributed the setbacks of the Archidamian phase of the war to their not adhering to the terms of treaty with Athens, 7.18.2. See Dover, 1970, 394; Hornblower, 2008, 573–75.
47. Thuc. 1.118.3.
48. Thuc. 7.18.1–3.
49. Thuc. 3.82.6; Oost, 1975, 187.
50. Oost, 1975, 189; Marinatos, 1981, 31–34; Jordan, 1986, 133–34.

51. Thuc. 6.54.5. All translations of Thucydides are from Strassler, 1996, which uses a lightly modified version of Richard Crawley's 1874 translation.
52. For example, the speeches preceding the Spartans' execution of the Plataeans; the speeches and actions of Brasidas; the contrasting lives and fates of Alcibiades and Nicias.
53. Thuc. 5.54.1–2, 5.116.1.
54. For example, Thuc. 6.95.1 (earthquake), 7.50.4 (eclipse), 6.70.1, 7.79.3 (thunder and lightning).
55. Hdt. 8.77.1–2.
56. Thuc. 1.126 (see also Hornblower, 1991, 206–08); see Thuc. 2.102.5 on Alcmaeon.
57. Jordan, 1986, 129 n.23.
58. For an excellent recent treatment, see Flower, 2008, 132–52.
59. Thuc. 2.8.1–3.
60. Thuc. 2.21.3.
61. Thuc. 8.1.1.
62. For example, *Knights*, 109–49, *Peace*, 1052–119, with Flower, 2008, 63; *Birds*, 593–97, 959–91, with Flower, 2008, 103; see also Bowden, 2004, 234.
63. Flower, 2008, 139. He speculates that either their profession was so discredited that it died out, or that their role in the whole episode was simply too painful to satirize. He notes that Aristophanes does not joke about the plague.
64. Thuc. 2.54.2–3. See Oost, 1975, 189; Marinatos, 1981, 48–49; Dover, 1987, 69–70; Furley, 2006, 419.
65. For discussions of this passage, see Oost, 1975, 188; Powell, 1979, 46; Marinatos, 1981, 232–40; Jordan, 1986, 130–31; Dover, 1987, 67–69; Hornblower, 1991, 270.
66. Thuc. 5.26.3. See Flower, 2008, 145 on why oracular centres may have inspired greater trust than *chrêsmologoi*. Other oracular responses from Delphi in Thucydides, 2.21.3, 3.104.1, 5.103.2.
67. Thuc. 2.28.1, 3.89.5.
68. Thuc. 2.8.3.
69. Thuc. 1.23.1–3.
70. Thuc. 3.87.3–4. See also Hornblower, 1991, 495 on this passage, and on a similar passage, 4.52.1, see Hornblower, 1996, 211.
71. Thuc. 5.45.4, 5.50.5. See Pritchett, 1979, 108–24 on eclipses, earthquakes, lightning and weather-related phenomena as portents.
72. Thuc. 6.95.1 (Cleonae), 3.89.1 (Isthmus), 8.6.5 (incident in 411 BC).
73. Thuc. 7.50.4. A sampling of scholarship on what Pritchett calls the most famous eclipse in antiquity includes Dover, 1970, 428–29; Oost, 1975, 192–93; A. Powell, 1979, 47; C.A. Powell, 1979, 23–28; Pritchett, 1979, 109–11; Marinatos, 1981, 63; Jordan, 1986, 134–35; Parker, 2000, 305; Furley, 2006, 436–37; Flower, 2008, 114–19; Hornblower, 2008, 642–44.
74. Thuc. 8.1.1.
75. Thuc. 7.86.5.
76. Xen. *Mem.* 1.1.9. The translation is from the Loeb Classical Library edition of Xenophon's *Memorabilia* by E.C. Marchant, 1923 (with minor modifications Henderson by 2013), London and New York. There are similar statements at *Cyr.* 1.6.23, 1.6.44–46, *Cav. Comm.* 9.8–9. See Parker, 2004, 133–34.
77. Xenophon himself clearly had picked up some skill at this. He notes at *Anabasis* 5.6.29 that by always attending the sacrifices he had learned enough so that a seer would be unlikely to be able to deceive him. In the *Cyropaedia*, Cyrus' father

recommends that his son learn the rudiments of divination so as not to be at the mercy of an unscrupulous seer, or to avoid being at a loss if he found himself without a seer (1.6.2). Elsewhere in the *Anabasis*, Xenophon interprets his own dreams (3.1.11–13; 4.3.8) and in an assembly proclaims a timely sneeze by one of the men propitious (3.2.9).

78. Xen. *Anab.* 6.1.22–24 and 31; see also 6.2.15 and 7.6.43–44 for similar instances.
79. Parker, 2004, 143–44; Flower, 2008, 153–87.
80. Xen. *Anab.* 6.4.12–6.5.21. On how Xenophon depicts himself using divination, see Flower, 2012, 204.
81. Xen. *Anab.* 5.5.2–4. Other examples where unfavourable sacrifices prevent an army or individual from proceeding in a desired course of action include, for example, *Anab.* 6.6.36, *Hell.* 3.1.16–19.
82. Xen. *Anab.* 3.1.4–7.
83. Xen. *Hell.* 3.2.22–29. Agis invaded Elis in 402 or 401 BC – the chronology is controversial. He invaded Elis a second time either at the end of the same year or the beginning of the next. See Pritchett, 1979, 117–18; Hamilton, 1982, 286–90; Cartledge, 1987, 249.
84. Xen. *Hell.* 4.7.2–7. Tuplin, 1993, 75, for Xenophon believing Agesipolis misinterpreted the earthquake. On the other hand, Bowden, 2004, 236–37, argues that Xenophon portrays Agesipolis as 'a leader who knows exactly how to use divination, and who goes as far as he is permitted, but no further'.
85. Xen. *Ages.* 2.2. This reverence includes fulfilling vows made to the gods and dedicating a portion of the spoils of victory at their shrines. For example, Agesilaus dedicated a tenth of the booty from his expedition to Asia at Delphi in 394 BC: Xen. *Hell.* 4.3.21. Similarly, Xenophon made dedications to Apollo at Delphi and Artemis at Ephesus: *Anab.* 5.3.5–6.
86. Xen. *Anab.* 1.9.7–8.
87. Xen. *Anab.* 3.1.21–22, *Hell.* 3.4.11, *Ages.* 1.13.
88. Xen. *Hell.* 5.3.27, 5.4.1; modified translation of Brownson, 1921.
89. *Hell.* 6.4.1–3, 8.
90. *Hell.* 6.4.12 and 16. See Tuplin, 1993, 138–39 on the Thebans as the instruments of divine punishment and on the 'striking irony' of Leuktra occurring during a religious festival. For the Spartans refraining from warfare for religious reasons, see Hdt. 6.106, 7.206; Thuc. 5.54.1, 5.55.3, 5.116.1. On the Spartans as especially circumspect in observing religious rites, omens and the like, see Holladay, 1986, 152–60; Jordan, 1986, 124, 136–37; Parker, 1989, 154–62; Furley, 2006, 427–30. Kagan, 1981, 84–88 believes the Spartans used unfavourable omens to avoid fighting.
91. For example, Xen. *Anab.* 1.4.18, where the Euphrates is unexpectedly fordable; 4.5.4, when the wind dies down suddenly immediately after a sacrifice to it; 5.2.24, when a chance fire inspires Xenophon to engineer an escape for Greeks trapped in a village.
92. Xen. *Hell.* 6.4.24, cf. *Anab.* 3.2.10.
93. Xen. *Anab.* 6.3.18. The translation is from the Loeb Classical Library translation of Xenophon's *Anabasis* by Brownson, 1922, revised by J. Dillery, 2001, London and Cambridge MA.
94. Hdt. 7.141.3.
95. Hdt. 8.96.
96. For example, *Cyr.* 1.6.23, 1.44–46.

97. Xen. *Ages.* 2.2, *Anab.* 1.9.7–8.
98. Hdt. 1.30–33.
99. Xen. *Hell.* 6.4.24.
100. Thuc. 5.54.1–4, 7.18.1–3.
101. Thuc. 5.26.3.
102. Thuc. 1.126.
103. Thuc. 3.87.3–4.

Bibliography

Badian, E., 1989, 'Plataea Between Athens and Sparta' in Beister, H., and Buckler, J. (eds), *Boiotika*, Volume 5, Munich, 95–111.

Bowden, H., 2004, 'Xenophon and the Scientific Study of Religion', in Tuplin, C.J. (ed.), *Xenophon and His World: Papers from a Conference Held in Liverpool in July 1999*, Stuttgart, 229–46.

—— 2005, *Classical Athens and the Delphic Oracle: Divination and Democracy*, Cambridge.

Brownson, C., 1921, *Xenophon*, vol. i, London and Cambridge MA.

Burkert, W., 1985, *Greek Religion* (trans. Raffan, J.), Cambridge MA.

Cartledge, P., 1987, *Agesilaos and the Crisis of Sparta*, Baltimore.

Dillery, J., 1995, *Xenophon and the History of His Times*, London and New York.

—— 2001, *Xenophon*, vol. iii, Cambridge MA.

—— 2005, 'Chresmologues and Manteis: Independent Diviners and the Problem of Authority', in Johnston, S.I., and Struck, P.T. (eds), *Mantikê: Studies in Ancient Divination*, Leiden, 168–231.

Dover, K.J,. 1970, *A Historical Commentary on Thucydides*, vol. iv, Oxford.

—— 1974, *Greek Popular Morality in the Time of Plato and Aristotle*, Oxford (corrected reprint 1994, Indianapolis).

—— 1987, 'Thucydides on Oracles', in Dover, K.J., *The Greeks and their Legacy*, Oxford, 65–73.

Edmunds, L., 1984, 'Thucydides on Monosandalism (3.22.2)', in Rigsby, K.J. (ed.), *Studies Presented to Sterling Dow*, Durham, NC (*GRBS* Monograph 10), 71–75.

Flower, M., 2008, *The Seer in Ancient Greece*, Berkeley.

—— 2012, *Xenophon's 'Anabasis' or 'The Expedition of Cyrus'*, Oxford.

Furley, W.D., 2006, 'Thucydides and Religion', in Rengakos, A., and Tsakmakis, A. (eds), *Brill's Companion to Thucydides*, Leiden and Boston, 415–38.

Gomme, A.W., 1956, *A Historical Commentary on Thucydides*, vol. ii, Oxford.

—— 1962, *A Historical Commentary on Thucydides*, vol. iii, Oxford.

Gould, J., 1989, *Herodotus*, New York.

Hamilton, C., 1982, 'Étude chronologique sur le règne d'Agésilas', *Ktema* 7, 281–96.

Harrison, T., 2000, *Divinity and History: The Religion of Herodotus*, Oxford.

Henderson, J., 2013, *Xenophon*, vol. iv, Cambridge MA.

Hirsch, S., 1985, *The Friendship of the Barbarians*, London and Hanover.

Holladay, A., 1986, 'Religious Scruples in Ancient Warfare', *CQ* 36, 151–60.

Hornblower, S., 1991, *A Commentary on Thucydides. Volume i: Books i–iii*, Oxford.

—— 1992, 'The Religious Dimension to the Peloponnesian War, or, What Thucydides Does Not Tell Us', *HSPh* 94, 169–97.

—— 1992a, 'Thucydides' Use of Herodotus', in Sanders, J.M. (ed.), *ΦΙΛΟΛΑΚΩΝ: Lakonian Studies in Honour of Hector Catling*, London, 141–54.

—— 1996, *A Commentary on Thucydides, Volume ii: Books iv–v.24*, Oxford.

—— 2008, *A Commentary on Thucydides, Volume iii: Books v.25–viii.109*, Oxford.

Jameson, M., 1991, 'Sacrifice Before Battle', in Hanson, V.D. (ed.), *Hoplites: The Classical Greek Battle Experience*, London and New York, 197–227.

Jordan, B., 1986, 'Religion in Thucydides', *TAPhA* 116, 119–47.

Kagan, D., 1981, *The Peace of Nicias and the Sicilian Expedition*, Ithaca and London.

Marinatos, N., 1981, *Thucydides and Religion*, Konigstein.

—— 1981a, 'Thucydides and Oracles', *JHS* 101, 138–40.

Marincola, J., 1996, *Herodotus: The Histories*, Harmondsworth.

Mikalson, J., 1984, 'Religion and the Plague in Athens, 431–423 B.C.', in Rigsby, K.J. (ed.), *Studies Presented to Sterling Dow*, Durham NC (*GRBS* Monograph 10), 217–25.

—— 2003, *Herodotus and Religion in the Persian Wars*, Chapel Hill and London.

—— 2005, *Ancient Greek Religion*, Malden MA and Oxford.

Oost, S., 1975, 'Thucydides and the Irrational: Sundry Passages', *CPh* 70, 186–96.

Parker, R., 1989, 'Spartan Religion', in Powell, A. (ed.) *Classical Sparta: The Techniques Behind Her Success*, Norman and London, 142–72.

—— 2004, 'One Man's Piety', in Lane Fox, R. (ed.), *The Long March: Xenophon and The Ten Thousand*, New Haven and London, 131–53.

—— 2011, *On Greek Religion*, Ithaca and London.

Pearson, L., 1962, *Popular Ethics in Ancient Greece*, Stanford.

Powell, A., 1979, 'Thucydides and Divination', *BICS* 26, 45–50.

Powell, C.A., 1979, 'Religion and the Sicilian Expedition', *Historia* 28, 15–31.

Pritchett, W.K., 1979, *The Greek State at War. Part III: Religion*, Berkeley.

Strassler, R., 1996, *The Landmark Thucydides*, New York.

Strauss, L., 1974, 'Preliminary Observations on the Gods in Thucydides' Work', *Interpretation* 4, 89–104.

Tritle, L., 2000, *From Melos to My Lai: War and Survival*, London and New York.

Tuplin, C.J., 1993, *The Failings of Empire*, Stuttgart.

Chapter 2

The Role of Religion in Declarations of War in Archaic and Classical Greece

Matthew Trundle

Religion played a central role in every aspect of Greek life, with the importance of warfare and religion meaning that religious rites and rituals accompanied military action from start to finish for all Greek communities. Due to Thucydides' pragmatic and cynical approach to his history, the role of religion appears less significant than it ought to have been for the ancient Greeks at war. Thus, Thucydides made no direct mention of the role of the gods or of sacred invocation in the causes of the war in 432 BC that resulted in the Spartan declaration against Athens. He focused entirely and in detail on the pragmatic causes of the war and the *casi belli* (causes of the war) relating to Athenian infractions against Sparta's allies and thus against the thirty-year truce of 446/445 BC.[1]

Even Thucydides, however, indirectly recognized that religion played some role in the opening moments of the Peloponnesian War. He relates that the Athenians responded to Sparta's first ultimatum in 432 BC with one of their own. The Spartans were to drive out the curse of Taenarum and the curse of the goddess of the Bronze House.[2] Thucydides explains that these demands related to the murder of helots at the start of the helot revolt *c.* 465 BC, and the forced death of Pausanias, the son of Cleombrotus, who had effectively been starved to death in the Temple of Athena Chalkios. He also explains that the Athenian demands were in response to the perpetual Spartan calls that the Athenians 'drive out' the Alcmaeonidae, whose ancestors had brought pollution on their family (*genos*) and the city through the sacrilegious murder of the followers of Cylon in 632 BC.[3] Readers will immediately recall that the attempted Spartan invasion of Athens in 508 BC in response to the Cleisthenic revolution, that came in the wake of the overthrow of tyranny and of the elected Archon Isagoras, had followed on the heels of the same request. Cleisthenes was himself a well-known member of the Alcmaeonid clan. In 432 BC, however, Pericles stood as the most prominent Alcmaeonid, connected to the family through his mother Agariste, a niece of Cleisthenes.[4]

Thus, even the Peloponnesian War, with its well-charted origins through the growth of Athenian power and the fear this caused at Sparta, alongside the various complaints of Sparta's allies and regional conflicts between Corinth and Athens over Corcyra and Potidea, had a religious dimension.

The omnipresence of religious rites, sacrifice and ritual more generally in every aspect of Greek warfare should make unpicking the role of religion as a *casus belli* or in declaring war in Greek contexts, therefore, relatively simple or even obvious. This, however, is not the case. This chapter explores the enigma of religion in declarations of war, and what is known about the role of the gods in such declarations and in the origins of war more generally in the Greek world. Peter Krentz wrote an important preliminary study of the role of ritual and convention in Greek military actions.[5] He first focused on the formalized nature of Greek declarations of war, citing Herodotus and Polybius.[6] Krentz's Herodotean example focuses on Mardonius' speech before the Battle of Thermopylae, concerning the way in which the Greek states wage wars against one another. According to Mardonius, the Greeks begin offensives by declaring war openly and proceed to find an open space in which to fight, where due to the openness of the encounter the winners come off almost as badly as the losers. This passage is clearly designed to juxtapose the more sophisticated, and dare one suggest more sneaky, means of fighting employed by the Persians with those of the 'above board' and honourable Greeks. In similar fashion, and in Krentz's second example, Polybius notes how in the past, war was never conducted fraudulently, but that in an imaginary 'good old days', Greeks declared war on each other and gave each other advanced notice of battle (*tous polemous allêlois proulegon*). Both of these Greek writers thus present a view of war gilded by their own prejudices and conventions. Krentz notes that the earliest instance of a herald declaring war in any Greek context is the Corinthian herald who announced to the Corcyraeans that Corinth intended to sail against Corcyra.[7] He seems to argue that this was exceptional, and that the normal path for Greek states on the brink of war was to seek reparation through negotiation prior to military action. He cites Homeric examples, such as Odysseus seeking retribution from the Messenians for 300 stolen sheep, and of course most famously the Greeks seeking the return of Helen from Troy prior to the great siege.[8] Krentz does not go further than this to explode any myths around Greek declarations of war as a central part of a ritualized or agonistic aspect of military engagements. He suggests that arbitration and negotiation were regular means in solving interstate disputes.[9] As just noted, the first known formal declaration of war occurred on the eve of the Peloponnesian War, the Corinthians against the Corcyraeans, and this perhaps should not surprise observers. Scholars have long suggested that the period of the later fifth century BC and the Peloponnesian War itself saw enormous changes in the nature of Greek warfare. The fact that this period displays the first known instance of a declared military action proves this.

Some Greek wars certainly had religious origins, the most famous of these being the Sacred Wars (*hieroi polemoi*) fought for the control of important religious sanctuaries. These wars saw coalitions of Greek communities vie with one another for control of the major Panhellenic sanctuaries, such as Delphi and Olympia, and management of their festivals and oracles. Thus, Delphi witnessed four major sacred wars declared specifically for control of its sacred *temenos* (sanctuary), but equally importantly for control of the rich store of sacred dedications within it. These wars were always connected to wider geo-political struggles within the Greek world. The first of these, though largely mythical in its historicity and reception, was declared on the original holders of the land of Delphi, the Cyrrhaeans.[10] The story of this war played a largely aetiological role in explaining the origins of the community of Delphian priests, which administered the sanctuary in the Classical Period, as well as the emergence of the Amphyctionic Council and League that oversaw and protected the site. The historical Second (460/459–446/445 BC) and Third (356–346 BC) Sacred Wars lay far more in the real Classical world of inter-state rivalries that included struggles for control of the sanctuary.[11] The former war paralleled the First Peloponnesian War and thus saw Athens, as an enemy of Thebes, excluded from the sanctuary, while the latter saw Phocis briefly lay claim to and hold the site, supported by Athens and Sparta, against a coalition of Thebes, Locris, Thessalian cities and ultimately Philip of Macedon. Olympia also witnessed wars for its control. One aetiological myth for the games at Olympia had Pheidon of Argos reorganize the festival after conquering the northern Peloponnese and capturing the site.[12] Later myths suggested that the local villagers of Pisa had once presided over the Olympic festival and lost control of it to the larger polis of Elis at some time in the distant past. In 403–401 BC, Sparta wrested control of the site from Elis and considered re-establishing management by Pisa.[13] In 365 BC, the recently united Arcadians seized the sanctuary and hosted the festival competitions of 364 BC, during which the Eleians attempted to reclaim control of the sacred area by military force.[14] Spectators of the contests witnessed the battle unfold before their eyes. Control of Olympia and its contests clearly led to envy, political interest and ultimately to military pressure. The same was true of both Isthmia and Nemea. Argos and Corinth regularly clashed for control of each of these sites in the Classical period. Even Athens had increasing interests at Isthmia as its power grew through the fifth century BC.

Other wars between Greek states certainly had religious origins. By the fifth century, Athens and Aegina had a long history of enmity. Herodotus details how the Athenians and Aeginetans found themselves enemies in the first place in a very peculiar manner.[15] The crops of the Epidaurians in the north-eastern Peloponnese failed, so they sought advice from Delphi. The oracle advised setting up olive-wood statues to two goddesses. The Epidaurians asked the Athenians for olive trees from which to carve the statues. These they received in return for an annual tithe. When Aegina rebelled from Epidaurus and war followed, the Aeginetans carried off the two statues and established them elsewhere. The Epidaurians ceased to pay the annual tithe on account that they no longer possessed the wooden images. The Athenians sought redress, attempted to snatch away the statues themselves from the Aeginetans, and violence and enmity naturally followed between the two states. Needless to say, Herodotus sees this story as explaining the longstanding enmity between Athens and Aegina. The whole affair weaves together seamlessly religious fervor with political and economic interests.

In regard specifically to declarations of war, the Greeks seem to have distinguished between 'announced' wars as opposed to 'unannounced' ones. In the former, the role of the herald (*keryx*) was central to announcing and declaring military action. The notion of the war without a herald (*polemos akeryktos*), or an unproclaimed war, suggested a conflict without rules in which surprise attacks and sacrilegious behaviour were the norm – often associated with wars without truces in which the dead went unreturned and unburied and the usual rules of ritualized engagement did not apply.[16] The herald and the rules associated with his activity and the wars that followed were, in theory, sacrosanct.

Drew Griffith explains that heralds became involved in state negotiations only after negotiation had actually broken down.[17] A part of his argument suggests that heralds were inviolable and identified themselves as such through accoutrements like the herald's staff. Others, therefore, would be at risk from potential enemies. The staff was significant. A scholiast to Thucydides 1.146, in which the Corinthians and the Corcyraeans conducted exchanges without heralds, describes this herald-staff in *caduceus*-like terms. In other words, the Greek herald-staff was associable with Roman traditions and Roman Fetial priests (*fetiales*) who acted as heralds in the prelude to war in Roman contexts. The scholiast describes the staff as 'a straight piece of wood having on each side two snakes entwined and placed face to face', and as central to a herald's identity.[18] Perhaps the scholiast wrote in the knowledge of Roman traditions. The Greek herald thus carried an upright piece of wood similar to the Roman *caduceus* (Figure 2.1).[19] Some Greek

Figure 2.1: A Greek bronze finial (end-piece) of a herald's wooden staff, the *kerykeion*, dating to the late sixth or early fifth century BC. Height: 18.7cm. The Metropolitan Museum of Art New York, inv. 1989.281.57. (© *The Metropolitan Museum of Art; image source: Art Resource (526418)*)

evidence suggests that wars against non-Greek opponents required none of the niceties of wars in which the rules applied. All such wars were wars with neither truce nor herald. The Greek states fought such wars without a herald announcing them (*akeryktos*) or without truce to enable burial of dead with proper rites (*aspondos*).

Occasionally, however, local wars, especially those that had a religious flavour, might lead Greek states to set aside religious and other protocols against fellow Greeks. As seen above, Herodotus details the origins of hostilities between Athens and Aegina as the result of a dispute over the ownership and value of two wooden religious statues that originally had little to do with Aegina itself.[20] In typical Herodotean fashion, he begins the discussion of the various disputes with a war fought between Thebes and Athens that then dragged the Aeginetans into further conflict with Athens with its own teleology.[21] Athenian attempts to retrieve the wooden statues laid the foundations for Aeginetan-Athenian hostility. Subsequently, after the Boeotians and Chalcidians failed to defeat Athens in the wake of the Athenian democratic revolution in 507/506 BC, the Thebans sent to Delphi for advice on how they might gain retribution against Athens. Delphi advised them to seek help from the 'nearest' (*anchistos*), interpreted as the island of Aegina, whose eponymous goddess was sister of Thebe.[22] To cut a long story short, when the symbolic gesture of sending a statue of the Aeginetan goddess to Thebes failed, the Aeginetans agreed to assist the Thebans with real force and attacked Athens without first a declaration of war by a herald. Their decision to act so pragmatically, not to mention impiously, was explained by the former outrages of the Athenians in trying to recapture the lost wooden statues in the earlier conflict. This whole cycle of stories appears neatly circular and self-explanatory, if somewhat grubby.

Such wars without heralds pronouncing their beginning appear several times in Greek historical sources. Thus, Epidamnus and Corcyra waged such a war about 435 BC;[23] the Athenians passed a decree to wage a war with neither herald nor truce against the Megarians after the murder of their herald in the lead-up to the Peloponnesian War;[24] after the death of Cyrus the Younger and during the *Anabasis* of Xenophon, the isolated Greek army agreed to wage such a war with the Persians after the betrayal and murder of their generals by Tissaphernes;[25] and Jason of Pherae engaged similarly against the Phocians at the time of the Battle of Leuktra (371 BC).[26] Allusions to wars without truces and heralds appear elsewhere in Greek literature, strengthening the case that some wars may well have had some religious and ritualized conventions attached to their commencement.[27] It is, however, not easy to gauge the norm. Our sources tend to highlight bad behaviour, and often bad behaviour that resulted in punishment (by the gods). It is probably not the case that such exceptions prove the rule.

Some historical Greek wars seem divinely inspired. Xenophon describes how a divine power (*daimonion*), translated by some English commentators as 'Fate', directed the Lacedaemonian Assembly not to disband the Spartan army nor to deal diplomatically with the various cities of Boeotia, but to invade Boeotia and attack the Thebans.[28] This course of action ultimately played out in the Spartan defeat at Leuktra in 371 BC. This is a clear illustration of Xenophon's bias toward divine power directing human action and human failings.

The role of Delphi in the beginnings of Greek wars also appears significant at times, but only in specific instances, and not as often as might be expected. There is perhaps some suggestion that the use of Delphi as a *casus belli* or even as a point of justification for war through its oracular function between two Greek states was frowned upon in Greek thinking, even though it does feature in some intra-Greek war origin stories. Delphi was after all a Panhellenic sanctuary to which all Greek communities had access and respected. Our most famous instance of states or rulers using Delphi to justify warfare comes from powers outside of the Greek world, and the case of Croesus of Lydia, who asked the oracle what would happen if he invaded the emerging empire of Cyrus the Great, only to be told that a great empire would fall if he did so, with the inevitable and well-known consequences, remains a paradigm.[29]

For some Greek states, Delphi was the first port of call when considering action against Greek opponents (rather than non-Greek enemies) seeking retribution, or advice on how they might achieve victory. But, tellingly, several of the stories told in Herodotus regarding Delphi's role in the origins of wars have little to do with righting wrongs or seeking retribution. Croesus' attack on Cyrus has provided one example. For example, the Spartans sent to Delphi simply for their own ambition and with no religious justification, seeking to conquer the whole of Arcadia, only to be confounded by an ambiguous oracle 'granting' them Tegea, resulting in a Spartan defeat.[30] The Spartans who survived the battle ended up enslaved upon and cultivating the very land they had come to enslave, in a classic twist of Delphic oracular fate. The Spartans returned to Delphi to seek answers, and thus Delphi assisted Sparta in finding the bones of Orestes and the means for the defeat of the Tegeans.[31] The Thebans, as seen, sent to Delphi seeking advice on retribution against the Athenians after the defeat of Chalcis and the Boeotians about 506 BC, only to be told to seek the assistance of Aegina.[32] Perhaps more significantly, Delphic consultation concerned various matters in addition to and not only concerning military actions. The Delphic oracle cannot be viewed as a regular and normal avenue for states seeking reasons or justification for declarations of war.

The Romans, famously, had an elaborate ritual for declaring war, outlined in detail by Livy[33] and Dionysius of Halicarnassus.[34] A Fetial priest crossed over the border and into the territory of the people from whom retribution was sought. Four times (at the border, to the first person he met, the first person he met at the gate of the chief city and finally to the magistrates of the people) he invoked Jupiter, citing the justice of the Roman cause and detailing what crime required redress. If no redress came forth within a month, he went out once again and cast a spear tipped with iron and blood into enemy territory, and simultaneously declared war.

As we have already noted, Drew Griffith finds parallels between Greek heralds and aspects of Roman Fetial priests. The staff carried by the Fetial priest was a *caduceus*. He points out, following Lewis and Short, that the *caduceus* is a stylized version of the *hiketêria*, the staff or olive branch wreathed in woolen fillets, which is the mark of the suppliant (*hiketês*) identified in Homer's *Iliad*.[35] Drew Griffith also notes that despite obvious differences, both rituals conferred immunity on the bearer, and the importance of the staff as a mark of office identified the herald to potential opponents. He goes on to cite Gomme, in his note on Thucydides 1.53.1, who calls the *hiketêria* a 'flag of truce' (for the Romans, a *velamentum*), which is a stick wrapped in fillets (Roman *infulae*) used to surrender. As mentioned already, the scholiast to Thucydides 1.143 noted the similarity between the *caduceus* and the wooden staff of the Greek herald.[36] By way of further association with Roman practice, and in this instance with the god Jupiter, Hikesios is a well-known epithet of Zeus in Greek tradition, though used in different contexts than diplomacy.[37]

In the historical accounts of wars, the Spartans appear to have had something close to the Roman Fetial practice, except one connected more closely to the launching of a campaign across the borders of Lacedaemon, rather than a priest invoking divine power and seeking vengeance from the enemy. This Spartan practice of sacrifice at the border remains the closest that we come to such a religious rite of war declaration. Ancient sources refer to it as the *epitheiasmos*,[38] which appears only in Spartan contexts. Thus, and for example, Thucydides describes how the Spartan King Archidamus invoked the gods and local heroes as he prepared to cross the Spartan border on campaign. The king first made a protestation to the gods and heroes of the country, saying thus:

All you Gods and Heroes, protectors of Plataea, be witnesses that we neither invade this territory (wherein our fathers after their vows unto you overcame the Medes, and which you made propitious for the Greeks to fight in) unjustly (*adikôs*) now in the beginning because they have first broken the league they had sworn, nor what we shall further do will be any injury because, though we have offered many and reasonable conditions, they have yet been all refused; assent you also to the punishment of the beginners of injury and to the revenge of those that bear lawful arms.[39]

This declaration invokes the gods as witness of injustice that will be rectified through military action. On three other occasions, Thucydides refers to Spartans sacrificing before crossing the frontier.[40] Significantly, in each of these instances, the Spartans abandoned plans to cross into enemy territory as the sacrifices proved unfavourable. Presumably this was the reason Thucydides mentions the role of the sacrifice at the border, because it explained the cause of Sparta's decision not to continue with the campaign. Xenophon confirms the Spartan practice of sacrifice at the beginning of a campaign and at the Spartan frontier. He also refers more than once to required sacrifices as Spartan kings crossed from their country into another. The term that both Thucydides and Xenophon used for such offerings at the frontier is *diabateria*. This term literally means sacred things (*hiera*) for that which must be crossed over. Indeed, it seems that Spartan commanders always offered such sacrifices to Zeus and Athena before crossing the frontier. Xenophon explicitly states that such sacrifices were 'necessary'. This was equally the case for crossing rivers,[41] with Xenophon recording the holding of such sacrifices at the frontier seven times in his *Hellenica*.[42] Careful reading of the text demonstrates that these sacrifices took place at the limits of Spartan territory, as on several of these occasions the Spartan sacrifice preceded their departure from Spartan territory and their arrival at Tegea, their closest neighbour and ally, even though the target of their campaign lay further afield, sometimes beyond the Peloponnese.

The role of heralds in arbitration and that of the Fetial priesthood should not be overlooked as another point of comparison. Wiedemann argued that the Roman *fetiales* had more in common with peacemakers seeking compromise than war-makers seeking violence.[43] In this sense, the Greek heralds, Fetial equivalents if they might be termed as such, sought out arbitration themselves instead of war; otherwise, why would war without heralds be considered so anathema?[44] Here, Krentz's point regarding Greek interest in arbitration to solve disputes with which this discussion began can be returned to. One aspect of Roman Fetial procedure, however, may have roots in common with the Greeks, and that is the casting of a spear into enemy territory. This appears in several Greek traditions, most famously when Alexander began his campaign in Asia by casting his spear into the sand as he landed in Anatolia.[45] The idea of spear-won property, including territory, has a long tradition.[46] It is difficult to know whether spear-won land or property had any religious connections in a Greek context, or even any association with Roman Fetial law and notions of a spear-cast prior to war.

All campaigns of course began with a sacrifice. Best-known of all the accounts connected to sacrifice prior to military adventures abroad must be Agamemnon's legendary sacrifice of his daughter Iphigeneia at Aulis.[47] In the historical period, the Spartan King Agesilaus sacrificed at Aulis as he embarked on his campaign in Asia in 396 BC.[48] Xenophon states clearly that Agesilaus had sacrificed everything necessary before departing Spartan lands.

War, as we know, pollutes all. Murder, in whatever form, challenges human sensibilities. Plutarch recalls that the Spartans annually declared war on their helot population.[49] He adds that the purpose of this declaration freed the Spartans from religious pollution (*euagês*) if they killed a helot at any time.[50] War became not only a ritualized form of violence, but also a legalized one. This ritual no doubt had its roots in the Messenian Wars and possibly even earlier hostilities within Laconia that produced the original helot populations. But the fact that it aimed to absolve the *Spartiatai* from divine retribution provides an important insight into its purpose and the role of religious ritual in absolving guilt for murder as opposed to random killing. The murder of helots, no matter how unjustified or connected to the power imbalance between servile and free men, in and of itself, remained a challenge for elite Spartans, which explains the existence of the religious basis of the declaration of war. More broadly, it suggests that Greeks felt uncomfortable about killing other Greeks.

Underpinning declarations of war, therefore, lay divine forces. Thanks as always to Thucydides, many Greek scholars follow his lead and identify the role of Honour (*timê*), Profit (*ôphelia*) and Fear (*deos*) in the origins of wars.[51] Each of these phenomena had a divine manifestation, but Fear in particular enjoyed special worship in Sparta as a singularly important deity. Notably of course, according to Thucydides, Spartan fear of Athens played the central role in Sparta's decision to declare war in 432 BC and thus to commence the Great Peloponnesian War. The Spartan cult to Phobos is well known.[52] Plutarch notes that Spartans revered Fear so greatly as they considered it to be the main support for the *politeia* of no less than the Spartan state, community and constitution itself. Alongside Fear, Honour and Profit, Greeks fought wars for justice (*Dikê*). Significantly, *Dikê*, a daughter of Zeus, sister of peace (*Eirene*) and good government (*Eunomia*), oversaw cases of retribution. In Herodotus, the Persian Wars have *Dikê*, or the transgression of *Dikê*, at the basis of the conflict between mainland Greeks and Persians. Thus, the first theft of women from both Asian and European coasts contravened *Dikê*. The Persians sought *Dikê* (redress) from the Greeks for the theft of women, and this ultimately led to Xerxes' great invasion of Greece.[53]

Finally, the role of the war god Ares in the origins of wars is not well attested. The image of Ares, of course, remained ambivalent to most Greeks. He was the most hateful (*echthistos*) of all Zeus' children.[54] There are very few shrines and temples to his name. That stated, he is often invoked on the battlefield, both in war cries and pre-battle sacrifices, often with his alternative epithet of Enyalios.[55] There is little evidence to show his invocation in actual declarations of war.

In concluding this chapter, what remains intriguing is the lack of information in the ancient sources for the role of religion in the declarations of ancient wars. For a people who clearly invoked the gods and performed religious rites at every significant moment, the lack of the use of religion in declarations of war appears striking. Sacrifice clearly played significant roles at the start of deliberations concerning military action, the initiation of campaigns and prior to battle. Yet, the invocation of the gods and of religious transgression in the actual declaration of wars appears almost absent from the historical record. There is little to suggest that the Greeks had something directly parallel with the Roman Fetial procedure, for example, despite some similarity in the use of heralds and their paraphernalia, specifically the wooden staff with wooden fillets. In sum, then, we are left to ponder whether the Greeks saw war so pragmatically that the gods played no role in its declaration, but were called upon to assist in the outcome once war had begun. Or perhaps Plato's statement that peace is a state of undeclared war between *poleis* meant that the gods were unnecessary to declare war, but essential to both the decision to fight and determining its outcome.[56]

Notes

1. Cf. Hornblower, 1992.
2. Thuc. 1.128–34; for a good discussion, see Marr, 1998, 120–24.
3. Thuc. 1.126.
4. See Hdt. 6.131.
5. Krentz, 1982, esp. 25–26.
6. Hdt. 7.98.1; Polyb. 13.3.2–6.
7. Thuc. 1.29.
8. Krentz, 1982, 26; Hom. *Od.* 21.16–21, *Il.* 3.205–24, 11.138–42.
9. Most recently, however, Cozzo, 2014, argued that mediation in Greek disputes often resulted in a 'zero sum game' that often led to increased cycles of enmity and violence.
10. For the best recent discussion of the historicity of the First Sacred War, see Hall, 2013, 312–17; at 317, he states regarding any kernel of truth to the war, 'if there is a kernel it is so minute as to be practically insignificant'; for a good initial discussion concerning the war's historicity, see Robertson, 1978, 38–73.
11. For the Second Sacred War, see Thuc. 1.112, and brief discussion in Hornblower, 2011, 28–35; for the origins of the Third Sacred War, see Diod. 15.14.3–4, 16.23–24.2, 16.29.2–4; Justin *Epit.* 8.1.4–7; Paus. 10.2.3; for a general introduction to the conflict, see Buckler, 1989.
12. Hdt. 6.127.3; Ephorus *FGrH* 70 F115; see Hall, 2013, 54–56.
13. Xen. *Hell.* 2.2.21–31; Diod. 14.17.4–12, 34.1.
14. Xen. *Hell.* 7.4.12–32; Diod. 15.77.1–4, 78.2–3, 82.1.

15. Hdt. 5.82–89.
16. For brief discussion, see Wees, 2004; the main evidence is Hdt. 5.81 and Thuc. 1.146, but see also Soph. *Trach.* 45; Eur. *Heracl.* 89. For discussion of the latter references, see Myres, 1943.
17. Griffith, 2008, 182–84.
18. Griffith, 2008, 182, citing the scholiast and noting Charles Ducker's *Fragments*, 1.105–07.
19. Griffith, 2008, 182.
20. Hdt. 5.81–89.
21. Hdt. 5.79–81.
22. Hdt. 5.79.1.
23. Thuc. 1.146.
24. Plut. *Per.* 30.3.
25. Xen. *Anab.* 3.3.5.
26. Xen. *Hell.* 6.4.21.
27. Dem. 18.262; Plut. *Arist.* 1.5.
28. Xen. *Hell.* 6.4.3; see for example the Brownson 1921 translation.
29. Hdt. 1.53.1–3.
30. Hdt. 1.66.
31. Hdt. 1.67–68.
32. Hdt. 5.79.
33. Livy 1.32, see also 1.36.3.
34. Dion. Hal. *Rom. Ant.* 2.72.
35. Hom. *Il.* 1.14–15; Lewis and Short, 1879, 260; Griffith, 2008, 183.
36. Gomme, 1945, 190; see Tac. *Hist.* 1.66.
37. See Aeschyl. *Supp.* 616; Soph. *Phil.* 484; Eur. *Hec.* 345.
38. The most detailed discussion of the *epitheiasmos* appears in Pritchett, 1979, 322–23.
39. Thuc. 2.74, see also 7.75.
40. Thuc. 5.54, 5.55, 5.116.
41. Xen. *Hell.* 3.4.3.
42. Xen. *Hell.* 3.2.22 (against Elis), 3.5.7 (against Thebes), 4.7.2 (against Argos), 5.1.33 (against Thebes), 5.3.14 (against Phlius), 5.4.37 (against Thebes), 5.4.47 (against Thebes).
43. Wiedemann, 1986, 478–90.
44. See Göttling, 1840, 196, who connects the Fetiales with the Doric form of κῆρυξ and κηρύκειον.
45. Diod. 17.17.2.
46. Hom. *Il.* 9.343; cf. Eur. *Andr.* 155; Hdt. 8.74, 9.4; cf. Soph. *Ajax* 211.
47. Hom. *Il.* 2.305–07.
48. Xen. *Hell.* 3.4.3–4.
49. Plut. *Lyc.* 28.4; Aristotle in Rose, 1886, F538, and now Gigon, 1987, F543.
50. Plut. *Lyc.* 28.4.
51. Thuc. 1.76.
52. Plut. *Cleom.* 8.3, 9.7; Mactoux, 1993, 210–13, 259–304; Richer, 2005, 111–22.
53. Benardete, 2017, 1–12, argues that *Dikê* is not used of Athenian complaints and underpinning military actions, but only of the Persians.
54. Hom. *Il.* 5.890; on Ares, see Burkert, 1985, 169–70, 415 n.13.
55. Xen. *Anab.* 1.8.18.
56. Plat. *Laws* 626a.

Bibliography

Benardete, S., 2007, 'Freedom, Grace and Necessity', in Velkley, R. (ed.), *Freedom and the Human Person*, Washington, 1–12.

Brownson, C.L., 1921, *Xenophon. Hellenica. Books v–vii*, vol. ii, Cambridge MA.

Buckler, J., 1989, *Philip II and the Sacred War*, Leiden.

Burkert, W., 1985, *Greek Religion: Archaic and Classical*, Oxford.

Cozzo, A., 2014, '*Nel mezzo.' Microfisica della mediazione nel mondo greco antico*, Pisa.

Crawly, R. 1874, *The History of the Peloponesian War*, London.

Crowley, J., 2012, *The Psychology of the Athenian Hoplite*, Cambridge.

Dewald, C., 2013, 'Justice and Justifications: War Theory Among the Greeks', in Neusner, J., Chilton, B.D., and Tully, R.E. (eds), *Just War in Religion and Politics*, Lanham, 27–50.

Ducrey, P., 1986, *Warfare in Ancient Greece*, New York.

Fauquier, M., and Villette, J.-L., 2000, *La vie religieuse dans les cités grecques aux VIe, Ve et IVe siècles*, Paris.

Gigon, O., 1987, *Aristotle: Librorum deperditorum fragmenta*, Berlin.

Gomme, A.W., 1945, *A Historical Commentary on Thucydides*, vol. i, Oxford.

Göttling, K.W. von, 1840, *Geschichte der römischen Staatsverfassung bis zu C. Cäsar's Tod*, Halle.

Griffith, R. Drew, 2008, 'Heralds and the Beginning of the Peloponnesian War (Thuc. 2.1)', *CPh* 103.2, 182–84.

Hall, J., 2013, *A History of the Archaic Greek World: 1200–479 BC*, 2nd edn, Oxford.

Hanson, V.D., 1995, *The Other Greeks: The Family Farm and the Agrarian Roots of Western Civilization*, Los Angeles.

Hornblower, S., 1992, 'The Religious Dimension to the Peloponnesian War, or, What Thucydides Does Not Tell Us', *HSPh* 94, 169–97.

—— 2011, *The Greek World 479–323 BC*, 4th edn, Florence KY.

Jacquemin, A., 2000, *Guerre et religion dans le monde grec (490–322 av. J.-C.)*, Paris.

Krentz, P., 1982, 'Fighting by the Rules: The Invention of the Hoplite Agôn', *Hesperia* 71, 23–39.

—— 1985, 'The Nature of Hoplite Battle', *ClAnt* 4, 50–61.

—— 2007, 'War', in Sabin, P., Wees, H. van, and Whitby, M. (eds), *The Cambridge History of Greek and Roman Warfare*, vols 1–2, Cambridge, 147–85.

Lendon, J.E., 2005, *Soldiers and Ghosts. A History of Battle in Classical Antiquity*, New Haven.

Lewis, C.T., and Short, C., 1879, *A Latin Dictionary*, Oxford.

Mactoux, M.-M., 1993, 'Phobos a Sparte', *Revue de l'histoire des religions* 210.3, 259–304.

Marr, J., 1998, 'What Did the Athenians Demand in 432 B.C.?', *Phoenix* 52.1/2, 120–24.

Myres, J.L., 1943, 'AKHRUKTOS POLEMOS (Herodotus, V.81)', *CR* 57, 66–67.

Ober, J., 1994, 'Classical Greek Times', in Howard, M., Andreopoulos, G., and Shulman, M. (eds), *Constraints on Warfare in the Western World: The Laws of War*, New Haven, 13–26.

Pritchard, D. (ed.), 2010, *War, Culture and Democracy in Classical Athens*, Cambridge.

Pritchett, W.K., 1979, *The Greek State at War. Part iii: Religion*, Berkeley.

—— 1985, *The Greek State at War. Part iv*, Berkeley.

Rawlings, L., 2007, *The Ancient Greeks at War*, Manchester.

Richer, N., 2005, 'Personified Abstractions in Laconia: Suggestions on the Origins of Phobos', in Stafford, E., and Herrin, J. (eds), *Personification in the Greek World: From Antiquity to Byzantium*, Aldershot, 111–22.

Robertson, N., 1978, 'The Myth of the First Sacred War', *CQ* 28.1, 38–73.

Rose, V., 1886, *Aristotelis qui ferebantur librorum fragmenta*, Leipzig.

Runciman, W.G., 1998, 'Greek Hoplites, Warrior Culture, and Indirect Bias', *The Journal of the Royal Anthropological Institute* 4, 731–51.

Sabin, P., Wees, H. van, and Whitby, M. (eds), 2007, *The Cambridge History of Greek and Roman Warfare*, vols 1–2, Cambridge.

Schwartz, A. 2009, *Reinstating the Hoplite: Arms, Armour and Phalanx Fighting in Archaic and Classical Greece*, Stuttgart.

Wees, H. van, 2004, *Greek Warfare: Myths and Realities*, London.

Wiedemenn, T., 1986, '*Fetiales*: A Reconsideration', *CQ* 36.2, 478–90.

Chapter 3

Omens, Oracles and Portents: Divine Guidance in Warfare

Sonya Nevin

When Xenophon wrote his treatise offering advice on being a cavalry commander, he drew to a close with the observation that:

> If anyone is surprised at my frequent repetition of the exhortation to work with god, I can assure him that his surprise will diminish if he is often in danger, and if he considers that in war enemies plot against each other, but seldom know what will come of their plans.[1]

In Classical antiquity, divination, the art of reading signs from the gods, accompanied all major decisions and many other occasions. It was all the more important in warfare, where good decisions and intelligence were vital in the face of danger, uncertainty and awful responsibility for the well-being of others. Xenophon's long career as a military leader and as a writer reflecting on recent history and good leadership make him an important source of knowledge about warfare and religious practice.[2] In the passage above, he talks with the voice of experience to stress that for those in danger, 'working with god' is the sensible recourse. This chapter will explore the omens, oracles and portents through which gods might guide those involved in conflict. It will examine what forms divination took, the circumstances in which it was carried out, and how its results were interpreted and made meaningful.

Xenophon's emphasis is upon the guidance that gods can offer. He continues and closes with:

> There is none that can give counsel in such a case but the gods. They know all things, and warn whomsoever they will in sacrifices, in omens, in voices, and in dreams. And we may suppose that they are more ready to counsel those who not only ask what they ought to do when they are in need, but who serve the gods with all their might in good fortune.[3]

Human knowledge is limited; divine knowledge is all-encompassing. There is no certainty about who the gods will help, but for those who are favoured, that preference manifests in the provision of counsel through signs. In *Prometheus Bound*, the immortal Titan Prometheus lists the benefits he bestowed on humankind. These include the knowledge of numbers, astronomy, medicine, carpentry, metals, sailing and how to yoke animals. Amongst these essentials of civilization is the art of divination:

> I distinguished the different forms of prophecy, and among dreams I first discerned which are destined to come true; and voices baffling interpretation I explained to them, and signs from chance meetings. The flight of crook-taloned birds I distinguished clearly – which by nature are auspicious, which sinister – their various modes of life, their mutual feuds and loves, and their interactions; and the smoothness of their entrails, and what colour the gall must have to please the gods, also the speckled symmetry of the liver-lobe; and the thigh-bones, wrapped in fat, and the long chine I burned and initiated mankind into an occult art. Also I cleared their vision to discern signs from flames, which were obscure before this.[4]

To Xenophon's 'sacrifices, omens, voices, and dreams', we can add guidance that comes through birds and fire. Back in the *Homeric Hymns* of the seventh to sixth century BC, Apollo had said that he would have a temple built at Delphi and that humans who offered him sacrifice there would receive his counsel: oracles.[5] As with most things in Greek religion, there is a dynamic of reciprocity, but this is still a favour and as such it is guidance that should be heeded. This was a society in which gods and other supernaturals controlled and might live in the natural environment, and in which people were familiar with stories of gods walking amongst humans in disguise and helping their favourites. In that context, there was nothing out of the ordinary in the idea that divine guidance could be sent in many forms, whether it was deliberately sought or spontaneously bestowed. The ability to read these signs was, as *Prometheus Bound* expresses, a fundamental aspect of civilized knowledge. Without this knowledge, humans groped like other animals, blindly making choices without ever having the complete picture. With it, humans were distinguished from other animals and brought closer to the gods. For this reason, ancient literature contains the assumption that it is good to follow omens and oracles, and reckless to ignore them. How they were to be followed, however, was harder to ascertain.

With no distinct priestly class or overarching religious authority, everyday ancient Greeks could and did venture their own interpretations of omens and oracles. On the other hand, experts were available to assist, such as seers (*manteis*) and specialists in oracles (*chrêsmologoi*).[6] Their skills were frequently associated with coming from a particular place, such as Elis, the territory containing the sanctuary of Zeus at Olympia, or descent from a famous family of seers. The tradition of using diviners in warfare was very ancient. All the mythical wars had their seers: Amphiaraus and Tiresias were on opposing sides at Thebes, while Calchas, Helenus and Polydamus worked their art at Troy.[7] The skill of a good seer continued to be valued in the wars of the Classical period, and on some occasions states seem to have gone to considerable effort to secure the services of particular individuals.[8] Nonetheless, the art of divination (*mantikê*) could be learned by anyone.[9] Xenophon learned the art through observing others, and recommends it as something military leaders should pick-up to make them more independent and efficient.[10] A professional seer was not thought to create good omens; they could only offer the best chance of reading them correctly. Even then, they could only advise on what should be done, not on what would definitely happen, and the final decision was always the general's.[11]

Religious practices have to be useful in some way, or they do not survive. From a modern perspective, it is not always easy to see how divination was useful to the ancient Greeks, but it was considered so useful that it enjoyed high cultural prestige for over 1,000 years. Part of the enduring appeal of divination came from its flexibility. It did not tell people what would happen next week, or next year. It offered people something that would help them to make or confirm decisions about the things that were weighing on them. Some forms of divination selected a 'yes' or 'no' answer to a question, providing an authoritative answer where a decision was needed.[12] Most forms offered more ambiguous responses that invited debate as to their meaning, with the act of interpretation helping individuals or communities to arrive at decisions. In either mode, systems of divination tended (and still tend in the modern era) to enable their participants to receive the sort of result they desired.[13] By deciding what question to ask at a pre-arranged divination, what to interpret as a spontaneous omen, how to interpret these special messages, and whether or not to seek further confirmation, questioners retained control of the process to a considerable degree, even while divination offered them something extra to consider. As such, this was not so much conscious manipulation but an interplay of conscious and subconscious factors combined.

It was accepted that oracles and omens were always right, but that fallible humans might easily misunderstand them. Hindsight was always an essential ingredient in the process; only then could mortals make sense of the whole.

Calchas, at Troy, knew the past as well as the future;[14] that is, he could make sense of what had formerly been unclear. Again, this emphasis on hindsight is not indicative of conscious manipulation but of the flexibility inherent in all divination. This factor is reflected in our sources. Even Thucydides engaged in this pursuit, interpreting an old oracle that the Peloponnesian War had made sense of although it was too late to do anything about it.[15] Historians necessarily operated with hindsight, and hindsight has an ability to tidy up stories of anticipation and outcome in a way that reflects both the origin of the stories – in some cases communities which may have been shaping and passing on stories for generations – and the authors' own need to shape and connect events into narratives that reflect religious and social expectations. Stories about oracles and omens are something like a game of whispers, but one in which the story gets more rather than less cohesive with each transmission. The majority of occasions on which omens were received are never mentioned; when they occur in histories they are there as a means of marking decisions and turning points, and guiding our interpretation of the decisions that were made and the people who made them.

Situations and Interpretations: Going to War

Numerous situations called for divination in ancient warfare, from the decision to go to war, departure for campaign, frontier crossing and regular sacrifices at the start of the day, to any number of decisions such as whether to break camp, form an alliance, change direction or retreat. Going into battle always called for divination. For practical reasons, visiting an oracle tended to relate to the outbreak of war rather than the day-to-day of campaign life. Whether or not to go to war was always a major decision, so it was natural for the gods to be consulted. The most prestigious site was the oracle at the sanctuary of Apollo at Delphi, while there were others, such as the sanctuaries of Zeus at Olympia and Dodona, and more local sites such as the sanctuaries of Apollo at Argos and at Calapodhi in Phocis. Private individuals and state representatives travelled a long way to consult Delphi on what must often have been expensive and difficult journeys. This is a testament to the value that was placed on the responses. People were not obliged to consult oracles; they did so because the answers they received were considered worth the trouble to obtain.

At Delphi, the Pythia spoke Apollo's words in response to enquiries put forward by visiting delegates. The answers to queries were frequently obscure and ambiguous. The Pythia spoke to them in a trance-like state, probably self-induced.[16] Delegates would return home with the response and begin the challenging process of interpreting it. Other questions invited the oracle to choose from a range of pre-conceived options: should I do *x* or *y*? To whom should I sacrifice in order to do *z*?[17] Xenophon, as an individual, faced a major decision when he was invited to join Cyrus' expedition to Asia. He relates how Socrates was concerned for him and advised him to visit Delphi about the matter. Xenophon made the journey and asked the oracle which god he should sacrifice to for success. Socrates took him to task for asking this question rather than whether or not he should go at all. Through his choice of question, Xenophon demonstrates one of the 'stratagems by which believers avoid surrendering their autonomy of action'.[18]

The Spartans consulted Delphi at the opening of the Peloponnesian War. Thucydides relates:

> And though the Lacedaemonians had made up their own minds on the fact of the breach of the treaty and the guilt of the Athenians, yet they sent to Delphi and inquired of the god whether it would be well with them if they went to war; and, as it is reported, received from him the answer that if they put their whole strength into the war, victory would be theirs, and the promise that he himself would be with them, whether they invoked him or not.[19]

Thucydides represents the oracle being used as a final check on a decision that had essentially been made. The framing of the question left room for manoeuvre; they sought advice on the outcome, not permission to fight. The visit by state officials (the *Pythioi*) offered time for further reflection and access to Apollo's wide-spanning vision. With no warning from the oracle, and no decision to change course, the oracle's response offered validation at a stressful time. The response is nonetheless equivocal; the Spartans will win 'if they try their hardest'. Such a clause provides both encouragement to strive hard and the flexibility to ensure that the oracle remained relevant no matter what happened.

The Athenians also consulted oracles about conflict. One of the most famous wars, that between the Greeks and Persians, drew forth one of the most famous oracles – the 'wooden wall' oracle delivered before the evacuation of Athens and the Battle of Salamis. Herodotus provides an extensive narrative of this consultation which, while it should not be regarded as literally true in all respects, offers an essentially reliable depiction of the process of consulting and responding to an oracle.[20] With the Persian army already in Europe, the Athenians sent delegates to Delphi for advice. Herodotus does not relate the question put to the Pythia, but the preceding narrative had set up the Athenians' options of abandoning their country or submitting to Xerxes.[21] The oracle advised flight, with terrifying reference to fire and blood. The disconcerted delegates requested a second oracle and received one which foretold that Athena would intercede with Zeus on the Athenians' behalf, that 'the wooden wall' would not fall, and that 'divine Salamis' would bring death to women's sons. The delegates returned to Athens, where the oracles were debated by the citizen body. The intention was to follow the oracles' guidance, but, as always, the oracles were ambiguous. What follows is a debate that replays the discussion that the Athenians must already have been having: should they stay or go? Some interpreted the 'wooden wall' as reference to the acropolis, others connected it to the navy. The fleet option won out and the city was evacuated, indirectly fulfilling the oracle that recommended flight, but in a more optimistic spirit. They sought the correct interpretation, and they did so with reference to the situation they were in and to the majority's desire to oppose the Persians.[22]

That, at least, is how Herodotus represented the episode. The process of receiving and debating the oracle had to be recognizable to his readership. There had, however, been around fifty years for the story to be refined in oral culture, inevitably influenced by hindsight, before Herodotus himself worked the story to meet the needs of his *Histories*. He used it to emphasize the point he had been making, namely, the Athenians' brave determination to fight in a frightening situation.[23] His narrative also provides a spectacular introduction to the strategist of Salamis, Themistocles, who appears brave, intelligent, pious and persuasive in his campaign to push the 'navy' interpretation.[24] Had the Athenians been essentially wiped out, the story would have been told quite differently (if at all), and it would have been different again if they had joined the Persian Empire. Reshaping through hindsight plays a role in all the oracle-stories that we have. We cannot see clearly what happened in these situations, although we can see that oracles, particularly oracles from Delphi, were valued within debates about going to war and that they might play a prominent role in the social memory of how those conflicts unfolded.

Private individuals or those conducting state matters might consult collections of oracles as an alternative (or, more likely, addition) to oracular sites. These collections were often owned by *chrēsmologoi*; they had been (or were claimed to have been) delivered earlier, written down, and collated for reference.[25] Herodotus refers to 'an Athenian named Onomacritus, a *chrēsmologos*, who had arranged and edited the oracles of Musaeus ['He of the Muses']'.[26] If what was written seemed pertinent to the current situation, it made sense to factor it into decision-making. Onomacritus is said to have used his command of the oracles to influence decisions at the court of the Peisistratids and, later, with Xerxes. The Spartans were said to have consulted this collection (or one like it) when they considered war with Athens.[27] The Athenians consulted *chrêsmologoi* rather than Delphi when they weighed up the prospect of the Sicilian Expedition. When news arrived that the expedition had been destroyed, the Athenians, Thucydides tells us, became angry with the *chrêsmologoi* for having encouraged them.[28] On one hand this suggests the influence of the *chrêsmologoi*, but Thucydides himself undermines this by ridiculing the people's self-delusion in being so angry with the *chrêsmologoi* and those who spoke in favour of the expedition 'as though they themselves had not voted for it'. Thucydides' reader has by this point been through an enormous twenty-seven chapters on the decision to launch the expedition,[29] in which greed rather than omens persuaded the Athenians. Indeed, the only omen mentioned is an apparently discouraging one, the destruction of the herms.[30] Thucydides acknowledges that the *chrêsmologoi* participated in the decision, but rejects the Athenians' complaint that the *chrêsmologoi* made them act as they did. There were plenty of other factors in the decision-making process; they only emphasized the role of the *chrêsmologoi* when they wanted someone to blame.

When important decisions were being made, unusual occurrences were readily interpreted as omens. They could play a role in decisions about going to war and in how those wars were remembered. When Pausanias described the Spartan campaign against Asia under King Agesilaus, he contrasted two parties' differing responses to the omens they received. The Corinthians, he explains, reluctantly declined the Spartans' invitation to send troops because their temple of Zeus had just burned down, which was taken as an ill omen for the campaign.[31] A temple fire would be an unusual and significant enough event to prompt reflection on its meaning, but it did not automatically oblige the Corinthians to act in one way or another. It is likely that some in Corinth supported the campaign and some did not (there would soon be a *stasis* [civic conflict] over the issue of loyalty to Sparta). For those disinclined towards war, the fire would appear to be confirmation of their concerns. Their view might not be unanimous, but if enough of the decision-makers considered the fire a negative omen and the war, coincidentally and/or consequently, a bad idea, it would not go ahead. The omen would be an acceptable explanation to give to the Spartans.

As for the Spartans, they took the opportunity to carry out an extra sacrifice before departing at Aulis in Boeotia. Sacrifice was the most common way of seeking omens. The practice seems to have arrived in Greece from Mesopotamia in the eighth–seventh centuries BC.[32] A military leader might carry out the sacrifice himself or, probably more often, have a seer do it on his behalf.[33] All aspects of sacrifice could be significant, including the behaviour of the animal and any strange occurrences, but the most important factor, as we heard from Prometheus, was the condition of the victim's insides. These were examined, and factors such as the smoothness of the entrails and the shape and colour of the organs, especially the liver, indicated encouragement or discouragement. These signs offered guidance on the sort of questions put to oracles: is it advisable to do *x* or is it advisable to do *y* now?[34] A misshapen liver (missing the *processus pyramidalis*) was always regarded as a discouraging sign, but the reading of other blemishes or features of physiognomy were a matter of more subtle interpretation. If a positive result was not forthcoming, it was acceptable to sacrifice again. An episode in Xenophon's *Anabasis* suggests that three sacrifices about the same question was the upper limit for one day,[35] although this limit may not have been universal. On campaign, there might be more than one seer working with the general, which gave him further options about which interpretation to go with.[36]

Xenophon describes the Spartans' departure sacrifices:

I will explain how the king sets out with an army. First he offers up sacrifice at home to Zeus the Leader and those associated with him [the Dioskouroi]. If the sacrifice appears propitious, the fire-bearer takes fire from the altar and leads the way to the borders of the land. There the king offers sacrifice again to Zeus and Athena. Only when the sacrifice proves acceptable to both these deities does he cross the borders of the land. And the fire from these sacrifices leads the way and is never quenched and animals for sacrifice of every sort follow.[37]

After these usual sacrifices, Agesilaus, leader of the Spartan expedition to Asia, went into Boeotian territory and sacrificed at Aulis, imitating Agamemnon's sacrifice before the Trojan War.[38] The Thebans objected to this unsanctioned use of the sanctuary, sending riders who swept the sacrifice from the altar to the floor. Agesilaus, 'although annoyed that the sacrifice was not completed, nevertheless crossed into Asia'.[39] With this emphasis on the aborted sacrifice and Agesilaus' response, Pausanias stresses that this was a bad omen and that Agesilaus might have been expected to cancel. He did not. Much as the Athenians ignored the smashed herms, the Spartans ignored the ruined sacrifice. On both occasions, someone presumably argued that these events were not the bad omens they might appear, but with hindsight such confidence appeared arrogant or foolhardy. Pausanias describes how the campaign suffered a premature end, caused by 'the malevolence of some gods'.[40]

Pausanias had no cause to deny that the campaign fell short of its designs, and the story of the omens expresses the idea that this was always going to happen. Its failure is made meaningful through the moralizing contrast between the Corinthians' correct interpretation of and obedience to their omen (despite their disappointment!) and Agesilaus' decision to ignore his. The account of the Corinthians' behaviour should not be taken as reliable evidence that Greeks would cancel an expedition they were keen to go on exclusively because of an event such as a temple fire. It *does* constitute evidence, however, that such an action was presentable as both plausible and laudable.

Things look different in an earlier account of the campaign. Xenophon describes the spoiled sacrifice:

> The Boeotarchs, learning that he was sacrificing, sent horsemen to tell him not to sacrifice, and the victims, already sacrificed, they swept from the altar. Furious and calling the gods to witness, Agesilaus embarked on his trireme and sailed away.[41]

Although there are subtle differences, this account, like Pausanias', uses the bad omen of the spoiled sacrifice to anticipate the campaign's disappointing outcome.[42] To a greater extent, however, the story is used to foreshadow (and, in part, explain) the deterioration of the relationship between Sparta (especially Agesilaus) and Thebes in the future; the sacrifice is mentioned multiple times in this respect.[43] Xenophon waits until after the expedition to mention the Corinthians' refusal. Describing the intensification of conflict between the two states, he cites Sparta's grievances against Thebes: that they had spoiled Agesilaus' sacrifice and persuaded the Corinthians not to go to Asia.[44] There is no mention of the fire, and we have instead a story of Theban influence that Pausanias chose not to repeat. The accusation of Theban influence suits a list of complaints where we would not expect to find reference to a pious decision to heed an omen. Xenophon does contrast different responses to omens on other occasions (see below), but with this episode the Corinthians' decision has more effect as a factor in the Spartan-Theban rivalry than it would serving as a moral example. Was there a fire? Perhaps. There seems little cause to doubt that the temple was burned by Pausanias' day, as he reports, but there has been no confirmation that it took place at the relevant time and there is even some confusion regarding its identification.[45] Did Thebes influence Corinth? Perhaps. Perhaps not.

Neither Xenophon nor Pausanias had the capacity or inclination to give the entire picture. Working with the material available, they both shaped their narratives to express different ideas.

According to Plutarch, part of the reason for the anger against Agesilaus was that he went against custom to use his own seer to perform the sacrifice instead of the person appointed by the sanctuary.[46] The close relationship typical of military leaders and their seers (and difficulties in Sparta's relationship with Boeotia) explains Agesilaus' recklessly undiplomatic behaviour in this matter. The omens in a sacrificial victim would be read with consideration for the situation in hand and the plans of those involved. Understanding between the military leader and the seer was therefore vital to a thorough reading. Amongst the Spartans, there was a culture of closeness between the kings, seers, and *Pythioi*; many plans will have been discussed and military decisions taken together, with the result that the seers had a good knowledge of the circumstances in which they were performing and of what was hoped for.[47] Seers often fought as well as divining, another factor that encouraged mutual interest.[48] This does not mean that they would simply invent responses altogether, but with an appreciation of the situation and interests of those involved, they would be expected to read the signs accordingly; 'sensitized' (as Robert Parker has put it) to imperfections where caution was necessary and 'desensitized' in contrary situations.[49] References to the skill of particular seers demonstrates that it was not all a matter of subjective interpretation, yet subjectivity was relevant enough that it was usually possible for people to get the endorsement or discouragement that they were looking for. Sparta had invested a great deal in the preparations for departure; a minor blemish upon a liver might be counted insignificant, and the sacrifice therefore a success.[50] A seer who was a friend and confidant could be expected to be sympathetic to these needs and to read relevance in the broader positivity of successful preparations. A Boeotian seer was an unstable variable. The Boeotians' shock intervention could not be seen as a positive sign. Agesilaus' friendly seer might have said that it was not so significant that they need cancel, but, particularly with hindsight, less sympathetic observers inevitably saw this as a mistake and a sign of further troubles to come between the two states.

Individuals also sacrificed before war. Between the late Archaic and early Classical periods, scenes of hoplites examining livers or entrails before leaving home enjoyed a brief popularity on Athenian vases.[51] For example, an Attic red-figure amphora depicts an Athenian hoplite examining part of the entrails of a sacrificed animal before setting out for war, while a slave holds the main organ of divination, the liver (Figure 3.1). A woman (probably

Figure 3.1: An Athenian hoplite examines the entrails of a sacrificed animal before setting out for war. Athenian red-figure amphora by the Kleophrades Painter, dating to about 500–475 BC. Martin von Wagner Museum der Universität Würzburg L507. (*Courtesy of Granger Historical Picture Archive/Alamy*)

his wife) and a Scythian raise their arms, indicting acceptance of positive omens. It is typical for the hoplites in scenes of this sort to be accompanied by a youth and sometimes by an older man (or men) and women. While these onlookers channel the viewer's gaze, encouraging them to esteem the hoplite, they probably also reflect the reality of departure sacrifices as a communal act.[52] The individual had limited flexibility about postponing if the results of repeated sacrifices were unequivocally bad but, as with state scenarios, domestic sacrifices were read by individuals sensitized to the needs of the moment. It would be extraordinary odds to get three badly deformed livers in a row and in face of lesser blemishes the dynamic of group interpretation must frequently have ensured that a positive reading was viable from some quarter. The scenes often present the onlookers making encouraging gestures, particularly the older men, who can be interpreted as professional *manteis* or older relatives.[53] If a nervous soldier was disquieted by what he saw, another member of the party might be able to offer a more positive reading to send him off in good spirits.

Divination on Campaign

Once a campaign was underway, divination continued to be important. Part of the reason for the frequency of divination through sacrifice was that most victims would then be eaten. Armies travelled with flocks for the purpose of sacrifice and consumption.[54] Xenophon describes the Spartan kings getting up early on campaign in order to sacrifice before the enemy and so increase the chances of winning divine favour. The leaders of all sections of the army participated in this rite before receiving their daily orders.[55] Crucial decisions would be accompanied by sacrifice and hepatoscopy, and these were times to be on the look-out for further guidance.

The *Anabasis* provides a famous example of the role of divination in military decision-making with a decision about breaking camp.[56] By this stage in Xenophon's account, the Greek mercenaries had worked their way back from Asia to Thrace, where hostile forces continued to assail them. Xenophon had used sacrificial divination to help him decide whether or not to stay with the others.[57] At Calpe, they all prepared to leave but found the sacrifices discouraging and delayed. Some soldiers suggested that Xenophon was obliging the seer to report bad omens in order to persuade them to stay and found a colony. Xenophon's response was to invite anyone who chose to attend the next day's sacrifices so that they might see that they were conducted correctly. Three lots of sacrifices proved discouraging, so they remained where they were despite unrest over the shortage of food. News of a ship arriving with provisions seemed to provide an explanation for the bad omens, but they remained discouraging even when they sacrificed three times about going foraging. Eventually, the impetuous leader, Neon, led out troops despite the sacrifices. Five hundred of them were promptly killed. Xenophon offered up one of the few remaining animals and led a successful recovery operation. Finally, following an attack on their camp, the sacrifices proved favourable and an eagle was seen in an auspicious area; they set off on the next stage of their journey.

As Xenophon describes it, the army speculated about why the sacrifices discouraged departure, considering a dishonest collusion between general and seer and the imminent arrival of provisions. Accusations of dishonesty in seers are a consistent feature of cultures which practice divination, without this reflecting an overall rejection of the practice. It is a rejection of the individual, not the concept.[58] The reason for the delay then seems to be confirmed by the enemies' attacks.[59] This appears to be a case of what Xenophon described in the *Cavalry Commander*, of the gods knowing more than humans and helpfully sending warnings. Xenophon's idealized representation of this episode tells us that an ancient readership would be expected to consider it a good thing to hold a difficult position in obedience to sacrificial omens without knowing why the omens were that way; but it does not provide unequivocal evidence of people actually doing that, nor of how frequently others did it. There is a lot more that we cannot know about the situation. Xenophon is both the star and the author of a story that had been shaped by piety and posterity. As Xenophon remembers, or at least as he relates it, this is a story in which piety is rewarded and impiety – Neon's impetuous advance – is swiftly rebuked. The episode therefore offers a guide on how a good commander should behave, how the gods aid them, and how reckless it is to ignore them. But we cannot know how keen Xenophon was to move the army, whether he wanted to stay and found a colony as some suspected, whether he did have knowledge of the enemy's proximity or whether he was desperate to go and resisted anyway.[60] Was the seer 'sensitized' to approve staying or going? Either is possible. The invitation to the army to watch the sacrifices indicates the extent to which divination was an art that any soldier might have learned.[61] But while they may all have been able to see that the essentials of the rites were carried out properly, the seer's professional prestige may still have carried a particular interpretation. We cannot escape the fact that the story is set up to contrast Xenophon's good leadership and Neon's bad, and while the gist of the story may represent what happened, we cannot know how strongly it has been shaped by this imperative.[62]

Commanders faced serious decisions about whether or not to form alliances and whether to push on with their advances.[63] These situations called for divination; they were also times when the participants probably had a fair idea of the outcome they desired, and looked to the sacrifice for ratification or extreme contradiction. During his Asian campaign, Agesilaus had the option of advancing in Phrygia or returning to the sea. This decision came directly after his cavalry had suffered a loss at the hands of an equal number of Phrygians:[64]

> After this cavalry battle had taken place and Agesilaus on the next day was offering sacrifices with regard to advancing, the livers of the victims were found to be lacking a lobe. This sign having presented itself, he turned and marched to the sea. And perceiving that, unless he obtained an adequate cavalry force, he would not be able to campaign in the plains, he resolved that this must be provided.[65]

Xenophon is open here about Agesilaus' reading of the strategic situation: the king could see that it was unsafe to advance. The sacrifice was still conducted, because this was a major decision, but it is not surprising that the sacrifices reflected the hostile situation and discouraged advance. Xenophon is comfortable expressing this symmetry because omens were expected to present a reading of the strategic situation, which was dire. This is not the sort of circumstance where the leader insists that the seer sacrifice again and again; instead, the slightest blemish confirms the inclination to depart.[66] This was a turning point in Agesilaus' career. After returning to the sea, he was called back to Greece and never made the inland campaigns he had desired. This is perhaps the reason for Xenophon's reference to the emphatic omen – the entrails were not just mildly off, the liver showed as bad a warning as could be. Agesilaus would have been both foolhardy and impious to advance in the face of such clear guidance and strategic weakness. The retreat was disappointing, but it was nothing to criticize.

Crossing natural barriers such as rivers or sea called for sacrificial offerings to the deities of those places. These seem to have been *sphagia* sacrifices rather than the more usual form of sacrifice (*hiera*).[67] As such, the animal's throat was pierced and divination was done by watching the flow of its blood, probably from observing its colour and coagulation. The animal in this form of sacrifice would not be eaten. Herodotus offers an interesting example of a water-border sacrifice in his account of a campaign against Argos shortly before the Persian Wars.[68] According to this story, King Cleomenes of Sparta failed to get positive omens when sacrificing to cross a river near Argos. In response, Cleomenes praised the river for its commitment to the Argives, suggesting that by refusing to give good omens, the river was warning Cleomenes away and thereby protecting them. Cleomenes abided by the warning, but this does not mean that he abandoned his attack. The Spartans withdrew and headed to the sea, where they sacrificed a bull (another *sphagia* – and an expensive offering). With good results, they proceeded. They crossed into Argive territory by this alternative route and enjoyed wild success in the battle that followed. As with similar cases, it is not possible to recover the literal truth of what happened, but it is clear that this aspect of the story rests on the reader's acceptance of the idea that an army would pause for sacrifices at crossing points of this sort, and that it would be good military practice to follow omens, even if there is no information on why they are indicating what they do. The story does not suggest that the whole campaign should be abandoned in the face of discouraging omens. It remains for the seers and leader to judge the extent of the omen's warning and decide whether the army should return home or simply find a new route. Whether or not they have judged correctly could not be ascertained until the completion of the campaign, and could still be open to debate even later.

The behaviour of birds featured in military decisions. Divination in the Homeric epics often takes this form;[69] the reading of bird movements (augury) was very ancient in Indo-European culture, more so than the reading of livers (hepatoscopy). It is thought to have developed from early human knowledge, gained through observation of animals, which could promote survival by indicating things such as the presence of water or something to scavenge.[70] Euripides has Theseus refer to three main techniques for obtaining omens: 'Where sight fails us and our knowledge is not sure, the seer foretells by gazing on the flame, by reading signs in folds of entrails, or by divination from the flight of birds.'[71] In augury, broadly speaking, bird activity to one's right was a positive omen, on the left negative, while it was advisable to consult a specialist for guidance on further details of their behaviour. When Xenophon had doubts about accepting a command he was tempted to take, he sacrificed for guidance, but also recalled an episode some time before when he asked a seer about a screeching eagle he had seen and received cautioning words in response. This, and the memory of a strange dream, combined to persuade him to decline the post.[72] When crucial decisions were being made, striking avian behaviour, or even the memory of it, could indicate the right course, while the flexibility of the model left participants scope to decide which birds they found significant and what their actions meant.

The coincidence of unusual events and important decisions helped to indicate the difference between omens and everyday occurrences. This distinction was also important in divination through dreams. As early as the Homeric epics, there is reference to dreams' varying significance. Some show intimations of the future, others only delusions;[73] it is not always easy to tell the difference. When they were significant, dreams offered outstanding access to the divine.[74] With the spirit loosened from the body through unconsciousness, it was closer to the divine realm and therefore well placed to witness insights denied to waking mortals. Xenophon expressed the significance of his dream by telling us that it contained striking features (lightning – Zeus' sign – striking his father's house) and that it came at a crucial time. Plutarch presents many scenarios in which generals experienced oracular dreams before major events. He is most positive about those who consult with others about their meaning rather than ignoring them or deciding their meaning alone.[75] If a dream was striking, consultation was the best way to establish if the dream was an omen, and if so, how to act on it.[76]

Any strange malformations in living organisms might be assessed as a type of omen (a practice of divination called 'teratology'). Chance events and coincidences were also potential omens. Herodotus, for example, implies that the coincidence of more than one Persian War battle taking place beside a sanctuary of Demeter was indicative of divine involvement.[77] Sneezes at opportune moments might be regarded as confirmation of a suggestion. Plutarch includes one in a story about Themistocles, and although the story is apocryphal, his observation that a sneeze on the right is a good thing is delivered matter-of-factly as a commonplace.[78]

Chance words spoken might also be considered as a divine sign in response to the immediate circumstances (cledonomancy). Names could be regarded as indicators of something significant too, by chance or design. The Spartans, for example, seem to have made Alcidas their colony-founder for Heracleia partly because 'Alcidas' was an alternative name for Heracles and the coincidence boded well.[79] The chance arrival or presence of someone with a pertinent name might be taken as confirmation of a decision or as an indicator of things to come.[80] Herodotus relates an intriguing episode from the naval campaigns of the Persian Wars.[81] King Leotychidas showed reluctance to lead the fleet beyond Delos. Samian envoys arrived, adding pressure to move by announcing that the Samians were ready to revolt. Leotychidas asked the speaker his name. The reply was 'Hegesistratos' (Army Leader). The king took this as a good sign and advanced the fleet to success. The identification of the name as an omen serves several functions in this example. First and foremost, it could have been genuinely reassuring to Leotychidas as evidence confirming the right time. It could also facilitate a change of opinion (from reluctant to willing) without loss of face; no subject or ally had obliged Leotychidas to advance – he changed his mind of his own volition following the gods' guidance. This need not be a conscious manipulation, but rather something that 'felt' right. The omen also serves a narrative function by expressing the Spartans' reluctance and the tension surrounding their decisions and leadership. It communicates the piety of the Greek cause by providing another example of their adherence to omens.[82] The first group of factors indicates how useful and flexible divination by spontaneous omen was for military leaders. The second group indicates how stories about omens and major historical events helped to provide tension, express turning points, and communicate the values of those involved. Distinguishing exact literal reality from ideological tweaks or inventions is scarcely possible; but it is still valuable that we can be confident that an omen of this sort was remembered as having played a role in this episode and that this was represented as a positive thing.

When the Earth Shakes or the Sky Changes

Natural disturbances such as geological or meteorological events could urge commanders to review the status of their campaigns. Earthquakes are still relatively common in the Peloponnese, and there is no need to doubt that they occasionally coincided with military activities. They were quite consistently, although not exclusively, regarded as warnings, although it was not always certain which side was being warned. Thucydides relates that when the Spartans and their allies headed north under King Agis to invade Attica, they turned back at the Isthmus in response to a series of violent earthquakes.[83] They returned and ravaged Attica a year or so later,[84] so it is unwise to assume that the earthquakes were used as an excuse to turn back. It is possible that Agis and the other leaders had misgivings that the earthquakes encouraged, but as there are always dangers and unknowns in warfare, misgivings are reasonable, and the other Spartans accepted that this response to the earthquakes was also reasonable. Later on in the Peloponnesian War, the Spartans marched against Argos via Cleonae, near the site of the Panhellenic Nemean Games. When an earthquake occurred, they retreated home.[85] As with the previous occurrence, this did not prompt them to abandon their plan altogether, only to delay it. They returned within the year.[86] Xenophon also describes Agis abandoning a campaign in response to earthquakes, in this case during an invasion of Elis, a territory containing the sanctuary at Olympia.[87] Agis disbanded the army, but returned the following year to great success.[88] The Spartans were walking a public-image tightrope by attacking the organizers of the Olympic Games. Obedience to an omen – and reports of that obedience amongst the allies, the wider population, and from a relatively sympathetic author such as Xenophon – was important for retaining the moral high-ground, as well as being militarily prudent.

Alternative interpretations of earthquakes were possible. In Herodotus' account of the Battle of Salamis, the Greek allies, under Spartan leadership, respond to an earthquake with a resolution to pray and seek divine aid from local heroes.[89] They were famously victorious, so their response to the earthquake would seem to have been correct. It should be noted that they are not described as having ignored it, which would typically be regarded as impiety, but the response was not automatic retreat. On another occasion, in Argive territory, the Spartans reacted differently to an earthquake. Agesipolis led this campaign, having first consulted Delphi and Olympia for approval.[90] Xenophon relates that the earthquake struck just when the after-dinner libations had been made. The king's companions struck up the paean (hymn) to Poseidon, the earth-shaker, and the army expected to withdraw, following Agis' example in Elis:

> But Agesipolis said that if the god had sent an earthquake when he was about to invade, he should have thought that he was forbidding the

invasion; but since he sent it after he had invaded, he believed that he was urging him on.[91]

Because Agesipolis ended up retreating following lightning strikes on his camp, it might easily be assumed that Xenophon was questioning Agesipolis' response to the earthquake. This would be over-hasty. Xenophon stresses that before the storm, the army achieved considerable success; the warning lightning is more associated with a plan to fortify a position in Argive territory than it is with the earlier decision about whether to cancel the campaign. On deciding about the fortification, the victim's liver looked inauspicious, and the Spartans went home 'having inflicted very great harm on the Argives'.[92] His response to the earthquake was bold, but it turned out to be right. When the signs were less ambiguously negative – the lightning strikes and bad liver – he obediently departed. This is a positive example in which the leader resists pushing their luck. The question of timing and intent is significant. Agis experienced earthquakes 'when they had just arrived in the enemy's country'[93] and just as he went to cross a natural border.[94] The fact that Agesipolis was safely into Argive territory apparently influenced his perception of what was being communicated through the earthquake. The Greek allies' situation was different again. They were fighting a defensive battle, and it is likely that this discouraged them from regarding the earthquake as a sign to leave, although the option was still there and could have been taken had they felt less resolute.

Agesipolis' behaviour could be represented rather differently. While Xenophon emphasized Agesipolis' consultation of the oracles and provided direct speech to explain his response to the earthquake, Pausanias has Agesipolis ravaging the Argolid against custom and without oracular sanction, and when 'there was an earthquake, not even so would Agesipolis consent to take away his forces. And yet more than any other Greeks were the Lacedaemonians (in this respect like the Athenians) frightened by signs from heaven.'[95] Pausanias writes that Agesipolis withdrew only after deaths and madness induced by the storm, and seems to link this campaign to his sudden death afterwards, although this was in fact some eight years later.[96] The lack of emphasis on any success, the focus on flouting custom and ignoring omens, and the link to premature death, evidently comes from a tradition with a more hostile view of the invasion. That hostility is expressed in part through an alternative representation of the king's response to omens. In literature, as in life, an unusual interpretation of an omen is possible, but an explanation and good outcome have to be there to avoid the suggestion of poor leadership and bad character.

Celestial activity such as eclipses or the appearance of celestial bodies or shooting stars could be considered signs from the divine. Some military leaders and seers would have enough astronomical knowledge to predict or explain some of these celestial events, but that did not mean that their occurrence lacked other meanings.[97] Yet the Greeks were not as systematic or proscriptive about the meaning of celestial activity as some ancient peoples. Pindar, for example, suggests that the occurrence of a solar eclipse means something, but he puzzles as to whether it anticipates war, famine, cold, heat, flooding or something else altogether.[98] There was no pre-established rule of what it meant, nor a code for interpreting similar phenomena.[99]

One of the more famous examples of misinterpreted omens concerns a celestial event – the eclipse that occurred at Syracuse as the Athenians prepared to leave. Stories of misinterpretations are just as important to divining cultures as those of successful interpretations or problems arising from ignoring them. Identifying the right time to leave Syracuse was a major decision, and as such it would be usual for sacrificial omens to be taken. The eclipse was an additional unsought omen that became the focus of the decision-making process. As Thucydides tells it:

> After all was made ready and when they were about to make their departure, the moon, which happened then to be full, was eclipsed. And most of the Athenians, taking this event seriously, urged the generals to wait. Nicias, who was somewhat too given to divination and the like, refused even to discuss further the question of their removal until they should have waited three times nine days, as the seers prescribed.[100]

There is here a familiar pattern, with the omen occurring and the observers debating its implications for their situation. The response of army, generals and seers is to follow the omen's guidance, although there is uncertainty about how to do that. Most see it as a sign to delay, but the question of how long to wait was still open. Nicias, in overall charge, appears to be criticized for closing down the debate after hearing from the seers. The decision to remain so long was disastrous, resulting in massive loss of life and equipment. Plutarch's biography of Nicias was written after some 500 years of debate about this fatal decision. As is appropriate to biography, Plutarch recounts the events with more focus on his protagonist's response. Nicias is 'terrified' by the eclipse, as are the ignorant and superstitious amongst those around him.[101] Plutarch explains that while the cause of solar eclipses was widely understood, lunar eclipses had only recently been explained and they remained mysterious and frightening. Plutarch adds that Nicias lacked a good seer at this point, with Stilbides, his former seer, having died. Had this not been the case, a safer interpretation might have been forthcoming. Philochorus, for example, had since written that an eclipse should have been regarded as a good omen for escapees, since they needed to act undetected.[102] Autoclides, meanwhile, had taken issue with the seers' recommendations, arguing that it was only necessary to delay by three days following a lunar eclipse, not twenty-seven.[103] Plutarch's criticism of Nicias is not that he followed an omen, but that he followed it incorrectly because his character fault – timidity – blinded him to other possibilities.

In Herodotus, there is something of a motif of military leaders who groan in realization that they have wrongly interpreted oracles or omens. The most famous of these is Croesus, who arrogantly tested the Greek oracles and received Delphi's advice that if he attacked Cyrus, a great empire would fall. He did attack, and his own empire fell. The oracle was typically ambiguous, and Croesus' character fault was the cause of his misunderstanding.[104] We saw how Cleomenes came off well after responding to negative omens during his attack on Argive territory. This came following Delphi's announcement that he would capture Argos. He followed up the battle by burning the survivors to death in a sacred grove, only to be disappointed when he learned that the grove was dedicated to Argos. This was the only Argos he would capture. What would have happened had he not killed the suppliants is not examined, but the reader is left with the sense that Cleomenes got what he deserved.[105] The story of this whole campaign plays back and forth with the idea of how an individual's nature affects the way they respond to omens and the character traits this reveals. If people suffered for doing reckless things after divination, it was their own fault for interpreting the guidance recklessly. Likewise, people were not entitled to do immoral things just because an oracle or omen appeared to encourage it. In one Herodotean story, some Cymeans who asked an oracle about expelling a suppliant were surprised to be encouraged to do it. When further enquiries were made, the oracle declared that as the original question was despicable, the answer was designed to ensure the questioner's quick demise.[106] 'Gods easily give men the wrong idea,' Semonides the poet complained.[107]

Conclusion

Throughout the Classical period, the reading of omens and oracles was a constant part of military life. It would have had its place in most Greeks' memories of being at war, as part of the rhythm of campaign life in day-to-day periods and as the focus of intense speculation during times of crisis.

Warfare is dangerous and unpredictable. Omens and oracles did not change that, but they seemed to alleviate its worst extremes by offering some hope of avoiding otherwise unpredictable disaster. Disasters still afflicted people, but then some might be considered deserved or fated, and others the product of limited human insight into the mysteries of divine warnings. None of this challenged the idea that the gods know more than humans and might share glimpses of that knowledge. When we look at evidence of military decisions influenced by omens and oracles, we do well to assume neither total cynicism nor irrational dependence; these decisions required intelligence and intuition, even when divination was part of the mix. We should also remain alert to what an ancient author might be expressing through stories of omens and oracles. What turning point are they exploring? How are they encouraging us to regard the decision being made? And how has this been brought to reflect upon the character and judgement of those involved in making it? The sign is one thing, but interpreting it correctly is the key to meaning.

Notes

1. Xen. *Cav. Comm.* 9.8–9; trans. Marchant, 1925.
2. A benefit explored particularly in Parker, 2004a, 131–53, and Bowden, 2004, 229–46.
3. Xen. *Cav. Comm.* 9.9; trans. Marchant, 1925.
4. Aesch. *Prom. Bound* 484–99; trans. Smyth, 1926.
5. *Hom. Hymn* 3 *Pythian Apollo* 287–93.
6. For the distinction, see esp. Dillery, 2005, 167–232, and Bowden, 2003, 256–74.
7. Bremmer, 1996, 97–98; Dillery, 2005, 172–78; Johnston, 2008, 113.
8. See for example, Hdt. 9.33–36.
9. See for example, Isoc. 19.5.44–45.
10. Xen. *Anab.* 5.6.29; *Cyr.* 1.6.2; Dover, 1973, 64; Bowden, 2003, 258–59, and 2004, 234; Johnston, 2008, 110–16.
11. Dover, 1973, 64; Burkert, 1985, 113–14; Bremmer, 1996, 99; Flower, 2008.
12. Burkert, 2005, 35, notes that decision by lot for example is 'absolutely rational and effective' as a means of making a choice. Even the gods were thought to practise it: *Il.* 15.188–93.
13. Whittaker, 1965, 27; Pritchett, 1979, 78–81; Parker, 2000, esp. 79–80; Bradford, 1992, 31–33; Burkert, 2005, 167–232.
14. Hom. *Il.* 1.70.
15. Thuc. 2.17.
16. There have been suggestions of toxic fumes befuddling the Pythia (esp. Boer, Hale and Chanton, 2001, 707–10, summarized in Johnston, 2008, 47–50); these, however, have been soundly refuted: Lehoux, 2007, 41–56. On the Pythia's experience, see Whittaker, 1965, 22–24; Maurizio, 1995, 69–86.
17. Fontenrose, 1978, 11–57.
18. Xen. *Anab.* 3.1.5–8; quotation: Parker, 2004a, 147; Burkert, 2005, 39, agrees that this sort of careful question selection was 'common practice'.

19. Thuc. 1.118.3; trans. Smith, 1919; see Hornblower, 1991, 196–95 for discussion.
20. Hdt. 7.140–41; Bowden, 2003, 272–74, notes that while the wooden wall debate is probably ahistorical in its detail, it illustrates the kinds of debate that went on.
21. Hdt. 7.139.
22. Harrison, 2000, 149–52; Nevin, 2017.
23. Hdt. 7.138–39; see esp. Maurizio, 1997, 316–18.
24. Struck, 2003, 183, notes that divination debates are a 'contest of manly virtues, embedded in the give and take of public speaking'.
25. Johnston, 2008, 137–39. Dillery, 2005, 218 is sceptical about the oracle-collections in Herodotus, noting that they belong to a world of the written word, not to an oral one. They belong more to the late Classical period, but it is not entirely clear when they began appearing.
26. Hdt 7.6.3.
27. Hdt. 5.90–94; Nevin, 2017.
28. Thuc. 8.1.1.
29. Thuc. 6.6–6.32.
30. Thuc. 6.27.
31. Paus. 3.9.2.
32. Burkert, 1985, 112–13.
33. Flower, 2008, 162, notes that the seer's role is frequently overlooked. He refers to Xen. *Anab.* 2.1.9, which describes the leader, Clearchus, sacrificing, although it transpires that the sacrifice was taking place elsewhere without him. As the results were remarkable, someone called Clearchus from a meeting to see the results of *his* sacrifice.
34. Parker, 2004a, 150.
35. Xen. *Anab.* 6.4.16.
36. The general, Nicias, still had seers to consult after the death of his main seer, Stilbides (Thuc. 7.50.4, see below).
37. Xen. *Lac. Pol.* 13.2–3; trans. Marchant, 1923.
38. For which see: Aesch. *Agam.* 1520–59; Soph. *El.* 516–609; Eur. *El.* 1018–30; Eur. *Iph. Aul.* 1540–1612, *Iph. Taur.*; Apollod. *Epit.* 3.21–22; Paus. 1.43.1.
39. Paus. 3.9.4–5.
40. Paus. 3.9.7.
41. Xen. *Hell.* 3.4.3; trans. Brownson, 1918.
42. On Xenophon's view of the campaign, see esp. Dillery, 1995, esp. 116; Tuplin, 1993, 56–60; with Gray, 1979, 183–200.
43. Xen. *Hell.* 3.5.5, 7.1.34.
44. Xen. *Hell.* 3.5.5.
45. At 2.5.5, Pausanias had said that there were two stories about the temple (apparently the same temple mentioned at 3.9.2), namely that Achilles' son Pyrrhus had torched this temple of Apollo, and that it was a temple of Olympian Zeus which burned inexplicably. Archaeology has suggested that the burned temple beyond the city was probably the Olympieum, as the main temple of Apollo has been identified elsewhere (Bookidis and Stroud, 2004, 401–26), but the exact history of the temple is unclear.
46. Plut. *Ages.* 6.4–6; Nevin, 2014, 45–68, and 2017; with Parker, 2004b, 57–70, on sacred law.
47. Bremmer, 1996, 104; Flower, 2008, 176–83.

48. Hom. *Il.* 13.45; Pin. *Olym.* 6.17; Hdt. 7.228; Xen. *Hell.* 2.4.18–19; *LIMC* i.1 cited by Bremmer, 1996, 99; *SEG* 16.193, 29.361; Meiggs and Lewis no. 33 (*GHI* i: no. 26).
49. Parker, 2004a, 144–46.
50. Flower, 2008, 173, notes this coupling of technical skill and personal reading.
51. *ARV²* 181.1 (Wurzburg, Museum der Universitat L507, with Straten, 1995, 156–57, V297). Other similar examples are, for example, British Museum BM B171; Bonn Akademisches Kunstmuseum 464.39 (Straten, 1995, V242).
52. Onlookers as focalisers, see Stansbury-O'Donnell, 2006.
53. Gestures as defined in Stansbury-O'Donnell, 2006, 128–229; figures in departure scenes: Straten, 1995, 157. Susan B. Matheson, 'A Farewell with Arms. Departing Warriors on Athenian Vases', in Judith M. Barringer and Jeffrey M. Hurwit (eds) *Periklean Athens and its Legacy: Problems and Perspectives*, (University of Texas Press, 2005).
54. See for example, Paus. 9.13.4.
55. Xen. *Lac. Pol.* 13.3–5.
56. Xen. *Anab.* 6.4.12–6.5.2.
57. Xen. *Anab.* 6.2.15.
58. Whittaker, 1965, 34, 45–46; Parker, 2004a, 143–44.
59. Flower, 2008, 170, notes Xenophon's handling of contrasting explanations.
60. Flower, 2008, 188; Bowden, 2003, 233.
61. Bowden, 2003, 258–59.
62. Parker, 2004a, 135–36, 144 with n.37 and refs, emphasizes the influence of narrative shaping. See also for example, Xen. *Hell.* 3.1.17–19, in which Xenophon contrasts the positive experiences of a commander who follows omens, and the disaster for one who does the opposite.
63. See for example, Xen. *Anab.* 7.6.44.
64. Xen. *Hell.* 3.4.13–14.
65. Xen. *Hell.* 3.4.15; trans. Brownson, 1918.
66. Flower, 2008, 173–74; Johnston, 2008, 127, on the flexibility provided by the option to repeat or not.
67. Jameson, 1991, 202, noted this practice, with examples of the use of *sphagia* rather than *thusia* for water crossings at Aesch. *Seven* 377–79; Hdt. 6.76; Xen. *Anab.* 4.3.17.
68. Hdt. 6.76.
69. Hom. *Il.* 8.247–52; 24.315–21, *Od.* 15.525–34.
70. Burkert, 1985, 111–12, and 2005, 31–32; Johnston, 2008, 129–30.
71. Eur. *Suppl.* 211–13; cf. Soph. *Ant.* 998–1005.
72. Xen. *Anab.* 6.1.22–24, cf. 3.1.11–12. He tells the army these were signs so clear that even a non-specialist could understand them (Xen. *Anab.* 6.1.31). This has a rhetorical purpose, but relies on the assumption that anyone could read signs, even though specialists had greater insight; see Bowden, 2004, 235–36.
73. *Od.* 19.559–69.
74. Plutarch depicted his brother arguing that interpreted dreams offered the most accurate form of divination (Plut. *Mor.* 431–33). See Harris, 2009, for dreams in antiquity.
75. Plut. *Arist.* 11.5–6, *Pel.* 21.1–2.
76. Nevin, 2014, 55–56; Johnston, 2008, 134–37; Harris, 2009. For further examples, see Pritchett, 1979, 96.

77. Hdt. 9.101.
78. Plut. *Them.* 13. The story relates the human sacrifice of Persian prisoners at Salamis. Xenophon relates how a sneeze was heard at a critical moment during a speech he delivered during the march of the 10,000. Those around him reacted as if it were an omen; by acknowledging it as a positive sign from Zeus the Saviour, Xenophon secured the agreement of his audience (*Anab.* 3.2.8–9). The sneeze, its timing and the witnesses' responses made the everyday significant.
79. Hornblower, 1992, 189.
80. See for example, Hdt. 6.50.
81. Hdt. 9.91.
82. Greek armies in Herodotus do not fight without good omens, and they are always successful when they act morally in obedience to divine guidance. For more on this correlation, see Hollmann, 2005, 303 with n.53.
83. Thuc. 3.89.
84. Thuc. 4.2.
85. Thuc. 6.95.
86. Thuc. 6.105.
87. Xen. *Hell.* 3.2.24; Nevin, 2017.
88. Xen. *Hell.* 3.2.26.
89. Hdt. 8.64.
90. Xen. *Hell.* 4.7.2–3. On the consultation of the oracles, see Ian Rutherford in this volume; on this episode more broadly, Bowden, 2004, 237–38, 243.
91. Xen. *Hell.* 4.7.4; trans. Brownson, 1918, 351.
92. Xen. *Hell.* 4.7.7.
93. Xen. *Hell.* 3.2.24.
94. Thuc. 3.89.
95. Paus. 3.5.8.
96. Xen. *Hell.* 3.5.9.
97. Burkert, 1985, 112 refers to the 'quasi-rational' aspect of reading celestial phenomena, which shifted 'almost imperceptibly' to scientific meteorology and astronomy. See for further examples, Pritchett, 1979, 108–13.
98. Pin. *Paean* 9.13–20.
99. Johnston, 2008, 132, suggests that the lack of a sophisticated palace scribal system worked against the development of established official interpretations.
100. Thuc. 7.50.4; trans. Smith, 1935.
101. Plut. *Nic.* 23.
102. Plut. *Nic.* 23; Philochorus *FGrH* 328 F135.
103. Plut. *Nic.* 23; Autokleides *FGrH* 353 F7.
104. Hdt. 1.46–56, esp. 1.53, and 1.86–87; Kindt, 2006, 34–51.
105. Hdt. 6.75–84; Hollmann, 2011; Nevin, 2017.
106. Hdt. 1.158–59; Harrison, 2000, 147–48.
107. Semonides F42 (West, 1993, 20).

Bibliography

Boer, J.Z. de, Hale, J.R., and Chanton, J.P., 2001, 'New Evidence of the Geological Origins of the Ancient Delphic Oracle (Greece)', *Geology* 29, 707–10.

Bookidis, N., and Stroud, R.S., 2004, 'Apollo and the Archaic Temple at Corinth', *Hesperia* 73.3, 401–26.

Bowden, H., 2003, 'Oracles for Sale', in Derow, P., and Parker, R. (eds), *Herodotus and His World. Essays from a Conference in Memory of George Forrest*, Oxford, 256–74.

—— 2004, 'Religion and Politics. Xenophon and the Scientific Study of Religion', in Tuplin, C. (ed.), *Xenophon and His World. Papers from a Conference Held in Liverpool in July 1999*, Stuttgart, 229–46.

Bradford, A.S., 1992, 'Plataea and the Soothsayer', *AncW* 23.1, 27–33.

Bremmer, J.N., 1996, 'The Status and Symbolic Capital of the Seer', in Hägg, R. (ed.), *The Role of Religion in the Early Greek Polis*, Stockholm, 97–109.

Brownson, C.L., 1918, *Xenophon Hellenica*, vol. i, Cambridge MA.

—— 1921, *Xenophon Hellenica*, vol. ii, Cambridge MA.

Burkert, W., 1985, *Greek Religion. Archaic and Classical*, Oxford.

—— 2005, 'Signs, Commands, and Knowledge: Ancient Divination Between Enigma and Epiphany', in Johnston, S.I., and Struck, P.T. (eds), *Mantikê. Studies in Ancient Divination*, Leiden, 29–50.

Dillery, J., 1995, *Xenophon and the History of His Times*, London and New York.

—— 2005, 'Chresmologues and Manteis: Independent Diviners and the Problem of Authority', in Johnston, S.I., and Struck, P.T. (eds), *Mantike: Studies in Ancient Divination*, Leiden, 167–231.

Dover, K.J., 1973, 'Some Neglected Aspects of Agamemnon's Dilemma', *JHS* 93, 58–69.

Flower, M.A., 2008, *The Seer in Ancient Greece*, Berkeley, Los Angeles and London.

Fontenrose, J., 1978, *The Delphic Oracle. Its Responses and Operations*, Berkeley.

Gray, V. 1979, 'Two Different Approaches to the Battle of Sardis in 395 BC. Xenophon *Hellenica* 3.4.20–24 and *Hellenica Oxyrhynchia* 11.6: 4–6', *CSCA* 12, 183–200.

Harris, W.V., 2009, *Dreams and Experience in Classical Antiquity*, Washington DC and Cambridge MA.

Harrison, T., 2000, *Divinity and History. The Religion of Herodotus*, Oxford.

Hollmann, A., 2005, 'The Manipulation of Signs in Herodotus' Histories', *TAPhA* 135.2, 279–327.

—— 2011, *The Master of Signs: Signs and the Interpretation of Signs in Herodotus' Histories*, Washington DC and Cambridge MA.

Hornblower, S., 1991, *A Commentary on Thucydides. Volume i: Books i–iii*, Oxford.

—— 1992, 'The Religious Dimension to the Peloponnesian War, or, What Thucydides Does Not Tell Us', *HSPh* 94, 169–97.

Jameson, M.H,. 1991, 'Sacrifice Before Battle', in Hanson, V.D. (ed.), *Hoplites. The Classical Greek Battle Experience*, London and New York, 197–227.

Johnston, S.I., 2008, *Ancient Greek Divination*, Oxford.

Kindt, J., 2006, 'Delphic Oracle Stories and the Beginning of Historiography: Herodotus' Croesus Logos', *CPh* 101, 34–51.

Lehoux, D., 2007, 'Drugs and the Delphic Oracle', *CW* 101.1, 41–56.

Marchant, E.C. 1925, *Xenophon Scripta Minora*, Cambridge MA.

Matheson, Susan B. 'A Farewell with Arms. Departing Warriors on Athenian Vases', in Judith M. Barringer and Jeffrey M. Hurwit (eds) Periklean Athens and its Legacy: Problems and Perspectives, (University of Texas Press, 2005).

Maurizio, L., 1995, 'Anthropology and Spirit Possession: A Reconsideration of the Pythia's Role at Delphi', *JHS* 115, 69–86.

—— 1997, 'Delphic Oracles as Oral Performances: Authenticity and Historical Evidence', *ClAnt* 16.2, 308–34.

Nevin, S., 2014, 'Negative Comparison: Agamemnon and Alexander in Plutarch's Agesilaus-Pompey', *GRBS* 54, 45–68.

—— 2017, *Military Leaders and Sacred Space in Classical Greek Warfare: Temples, Sanctuaries and Conflict in Antiquity*, London.

Parker, R., 2000, 'Greek States and Greek Oracles', in Buxton, R. (ed.), *Oxford Readings in Greek Religion*, Oxford, 76–108.

—— 2004a, 'One Man's Piety: The Religious Dimension of the *Anabasis*', in Lane Fox, R. (ed.), *The Long March. Xenophon and the Ten Thousand*, New Haven and London, 131–53.

—— 2004b, 'What are Sacred Laws?', in Harris, E.M., and Rubinstein, L. (eds), *The Law and the Courts in Ancient Greece*, London, 57–70.

Pritchett, W.K., 1979, *The Greek State at War, Part iii: Religion*, Berkeley, Los Angeles and London.

Smith, C.F., 1935, *Thucydides History of the Peloponnesian War* vol. i, Cambridge MA.

Smyth, H.W., 1926, *Aeschylus*, vol. i, London.

Stansbury-O'Donnell, M.D., 2006, *Vase Painting, Gender, and Social Identity in Archaic Athens*, Cambridge.

Straten, F.T. van, 1995, *Hiera Kala: Images of Animal Sacrifice in Archaic and Classical Greece*, Leiden.

Struck, P.T., 2003, 'The Ordeal of the Divine Sign: Divination and Manliness in Archaic and Classical Greece', in Rosen, R.M., and Sluiter, I. (eds), *Andreia. Studies in Manliness and Courage in Classical Antiquity*, Leiden, 167–86.

Tuplin, C.J., 1993, *The Failings Of Empire. A Reading of Xenophon's Hellenica 2.3.11– 7.5.27*, Stuttgart.

West, M.L., 1993, *Greek Lyric Poetry*, Oxford.

Whittaker, C.R., 1965, 'The Delphic Oracle: Belief and Behaviour in Ancient Greece and Africa', *HThR* 58.1, 21–47.

Chapter 4

Oaths and Vows: Binding the Gods to One's Military Success

Ian Plant

Oaths were a vital part of the social conventions that underpinned the conduct of war in ancient Greece. In making an oath, a person called upon gods and goddesses as witnesses to oversee the fulfilment of the promise that was being made. The oath included an explicit or implicit punishment enforced by a god if the promise were not kept.[1] Fundamental to the making of such an oath was a ritual sacrifice that included acknowledgement of the gods in the act being undertaken, as well as the gift of the sacrifice itself. A vow was also a type of promise, one made to a god or a number of gods. In a military context, vows were made by individuals, armies or city-states. Like the oath, the vow was predicated on belief in the gods, and the ubiquity of the vow demonstrates a widespread belief in the efficacy of such a prayer accompanied by a gift to be given to a god to gain his or her good will.[2]

The military context provided life and death situations in which the oath played a vital role both in securing the agreement of men to go into battle and to put their lives on the line. Oaths also provided the trust necessary between antagonists to allow hostilities to cease. This chapter will review examples of oaths and vows sworn in such military contexts, identifying who took the oath, the process that was followed and the respect with which oaths were treated.

Imaginary Oaths

Greek literature pictures the gods present on the battlefield and recognizes their personal intervention in human conflict. In the *Iliad*, gods frequently intervene in fighting. Aphrodite rescues Alexandros from his single combat with Menelaus; Aphrodite herself is wounded by Diomedes as she rescues her son from the battlefield; Ares fights with Diomedes and Athena helps Diomedes drive his spear into Ares.[3] In Book 20, Zeus allows the gods to join the conflict, and Athena, Poseidon, Hermes, Hephaestus, Ares, Apollo,

Artemis, Leto, Aphrodite and the river Xanthus enter the battlefield. In the final combat between Hector and Achilles, Athena intervenes to persuade Hector to stand and fight, then she returns Achilles' spear to him so that he can deliver the killing blow.[4]

The Greeks believed strongly in the participation of their gods and heroes in their battles.[5] Hence deities were credited with supporting the Athenians in the victory at Marathon: the god Pan and the heroes Theseus, Echetlaus and a giant hoplite.[6] Two local heroes, Phylacus and Autonous, supposedly defended Delphi from the Persians in 480 BC.[7] The destruction of the Persian attack on Potidaea was put down to a divine response to sacrilege, an explanation personally endorsed by Herodotus,[8] who also relates that the Greeks called upon Ajax, his father Telamon and other heroes to come to Salamis before the battle in 480 BC. After the battle, Ajax shared in the 'first fruit' offering of three warships with Poseidon. This gift shows that the Greeks credited Ajax and Poseidon with primary responsibility for their victory and rewarded them appropriately.[9]

Examples of oaths appear in fictional military contexts as well as in accounts of historical military actions. It is worth looking at both types of texts to understand the concepts that underpinned the representation of such oaths. In Aeschylus' tragedy *The Seven Against Thebes*, the scout reports to Eteocles inside Thebes:

> Seven men, impetuous captains, slaughtered a bull in a black shield and then they swore an oath by Ares, by Enyo, and by bloodthirsty Rout, touching the bull's blood with their hands: that either they would take the city by force and sack the Cadmeans' town or they would die and mix with this earth their blood.[10]

The verb *horkômoteô* is used to denote the action of swearing of an oath by these comrades in arms. This is a compound verb, combining the simple verb swear, *omnumi*, with the cognate noun for an oath, *horkos*. The verb *omnumi* itself may be used with the cognate noun *horkon*, or an infinitive expressing the action that was being sworn. With these verbs, a god or gods, named individually or as a group, may also be cited in the accusative.[11] The oath is being sworn before these gods. As witnesses, the gods affirm the oath and it is implied that they may punish any failure to keep it.[12]

The oath sworn together by Aeschylus' seven warriors is to destroy Thebes or die: victory or death. They make their promise together and bind themselves in the presence of three gods relevant to the purpose of the action: Ares, god of war, along with Enyo, a war goddess,[13] and Phobos, a personification of panic fear.[14] Aeschylus' dramatic description of the performance of an oath illustrates that it may be given in a public religious rite,[15] the confirmation of a promise that is made through a ritual: there is a sacrifice over a shield made by the warriors,[16] the men touch the animal's blood with their hands and they call upon gods relevant to their purpose in making their promise. They bring down a curse upon themselves (their own death) if they fail. Each warrior has sworn the oath personally and they are bound together in their action by the joint oath.

This fictional account of the oath sworn by the heroes in Aeschylus can be compared with an oath that is attested from a fourth-century BC inscription found at Acharnae in Attica. This text purports to record an oath taken by the Athenians before the Battle of Plataea in 479 BC (the Oath of Plataea).[17] This inscription states that the Athenians swore to fight to the death, to stand their ground and obey their leaders. They also promised to bury their dead, not to harm their allies and to tithe the Thebans after the victory. As early as Theopompus, this oath was recognized as a forgery.[18] It looks to be a fourth-century invention written to bring together and inspire Athenians to fight Philip of Macedon with the same spirit they had displayed when they had defeated Xerxes.[19] Nevertheless, it does present the idea of a battlefield oath that Athenians in the fourth century could accept on some level as historical as well as inspirational.

The text of the Oath of Plataea includes a description of some of the ritual that accompanied the taking of an oath. It was a given fact that sacrifices would have been made to accompany the swearing, but that part of the ritual is not described in the text. Yet the inscription does indicate that after the oath was sworn, the sacrifices were covered with shields, and at a given signal from a trumpet those taking the oath called down a curse upon themselves if they should violate the oath. The text implies that all the Athenians who were about to fight took the oath together, bonding through religious ritual just as the warriors in Aeschylus' *Seven Against Thebes* did. The text includes promises that its readers might expect to see in such an oath: the commitment by the men taking the oath to fight to the death if necessary, to obey the military leaders and to bury comrades in arms who die. The oath also specifies a wish for specific benefits to come to the city and the individual if the oath is kept, and conversely the harm that will come to them both if it is violated. This self-curse is not normally stipulated in the examples of oaths that are found in historical texts, and so should be seen as part of the fabric of the rhetorical fiction of this text. Nevertheless, for an oath to have strength there had to be consequences for violation. Such consequences were underpinned by a fear of the gods.[20] In examples of historical oaths, this is something that is implied by the presence of the witnessing deities. In the Plataean oath inscription, the consequences are spelt out in dramatic fashion. As a text, the inscription may owe more to a literary ancestor such as the oath of the Seven in Aeschylus as it does to any real oath. Indeed, the text is actually missing the invocation of named or unnamed deities to witness the oath.[21] The absence of this fundamental requirement of an oath demonstrates that the narrative is at the very least not a full account of the oath and its accompanying religious ritual.

In the Oath of Plataea there is mention of *enômotarchai*, Spartan military officers who each commanded an *enômotia*. This was the military unit around which the structure of the Spartan military force was built.[22] The term is derived from the verb *omnumi*, to swear an oath. Hesychius the lexicographer attests to the fact that membership of the Spartan *enômotiai* was defined by the swearing of an oath in a religious ritual:[23]

> *Enômotiai*: a military unit bound by oath through sacrifices.

The term for this military unit substantiates the importance of oaths in the bonding of a group of men to fight together as a military unit. There is another general reference to the oath that the Spartans swore to their unit in another lexicographer, Timaeus:

> *Enômotiai*: A unit of infantry. It has been established that this comes from them swearing an oath not to abandon their formation.[24]

Van Wees has argued that the text of the Athenian oath at Plataea is actually based on the oath sworn by the Spartans on joining their *enômotiai*,[25] and that some of the promises sworn by the Spartans can be reconstructed from the Athenian oath.[26] The call for the Athenians to obey the *enômotarchai* does suggest that the text of the oath at Plataea may be partly based on a Spartan source; there is, however, insufficient evidence to determine the text of the Spartan oath of the *enômotiai* from what is in effect a rhetorical text, a re-imagining of a fictional Athenian oath.[27]

Oath of Service and Loyalty

Young Athenian men used to swear a military oath of loyalty and service, and we do have evidence for the content of their oath and the gods they called upon. They did this as an *ephêbos*, either before or after their two years of military training and service, or possibly both before and after.[28]

This training qualified a young Athenian to serve as a citizen hoplite. The taking of this oath was an essential step in recognition by the state of the *ephêboi* as citizens. There are accounts of the oath from the fourth century BC in Lycurgus[29] and from a stele found at Acharnae.[30] While such training may have had antecedents in the Archaic Period and the fifth century,[31] the more formalized period of training and the oath itself can only be securely dated to the fourth century and may have been instituted under Lycurgus.[32] The oath was sworn in the sanctuary of Aglaurus in Athens, and possibly in the boy's local deme.[33] This gave the oath local validity, with a local heroine, Aglaurus, as a witness, *histôr*, along with other gods suitable for the occasion:

> Witnesses to this shall be the gods Agraulus,[34] Hestia, Enyo, Enyalios, Ares, Athena the Warrior, Zeus, Thallo, Auxo, Hêgêmonê, Heracles, and the Boundaries of my fatherland, Wheat, Barley, Vines, Olive-trees, Fig-trees.[35]

Specific gods are called upon to witness the oath. The witnesses included martial gods (Enyo, Enyalios, Ares and Athena Areia) who were appropriate overseers of the oaths of young men taking up their role as citizen warriors for their city. While Zeus was the king of the gods and upholder of justice and power, he also had a role as the god of oaths, Zeus Horkios,[36] and is often included in oaths. Hestia (the goddess of the hearth) and the personification of boundaries of Attica represent the homes and territory that the young men would protect. Local crops are invoked as gods too,[37] as are the personifications Bloom (*Thallo*), which was worshipped as a season, Growth (*Auxo*) and Leader (*Hêgêmonê*), which were worshipped in Athens as Graces.[38] There is a strong local identity to the oath where the Athenian fruit of the earth, along with its flowering and growth, look on as the young Athenians take up their responsibility to protect that land.

This oath was taken in the shrine of the Athenian local heroine, Aglaurus. According to myth, she had been entrusted with the care of Erichthonius but killed herself after disobeying the instructions of Athena not to look in the box where Erichthonius was hidden.[39] It is not clear why Aglaurus' shrine was chosen for the taking of the oath. Another form of her name, Agraulus,[40] suggests a possible role as a local rural deity. She was credited with being the mother of Ceryx (by Hermes), the progenitor of an important *genos* (family), the Ceryci.[41] Perhaps it was as the wife of Cecrops (in myth, the second king of Athens) and daughter of Actaeus (in myth, its first king) that she had a significant place in this ceremony.[42] A later patriotic version of the myth reinvented her through syncretisation with other myths of self-sacrifice by young heroines to save Athens. This created a charter myth for her role in overseeing the moment when young Athenian men pledged to offer up their lives, if necessary, to save their *polis*.[43]

In the Ephebic Oath, the gods are called *histores*. A *histôr* (singular) is a judge as well as a witness.[44] The use of this term makes it clear that the gods are being called upon to do more than witness the oath, but are also serving to guarantee the fulfilment of the oath and judge whether or not the promises made have been kept.

In addition to personal oaths sworn by warriors, city-states swore oaths with each other that regulated their military actions. Such oaths were made to end conflict (by truces and peace treaties) or to form an alliance and pledge support for each other against a common enemy. Such oaths may even define who the common enemy was. Herodotus mentions that the Greek allies took such an oath at Pieria in 480 BC:

> The Greeks who had taken up war against the Persians swore an oath against those [who had submitted to the Persians]. This was the oath: when they had settled matters successfully they would tithe for the god in Delphi those Greeks who had given in to Persia without compulsion.[45]

There is doubt about the historicity of the account of this oath: it is not known if, where and when such an oath took place. If such an oath had been made, it is not known for certain what its actual provisions were.[46] Nevertheless, it can be accepted that Herodotus' Greek audience would have expected there to have been such an oath. The Greek allies would have needed to make an oath to bind themselves to stand together against the Persians, and such an oath would have been solemnised in a religious act. The verb used here, 'cut' (*etamon*), is typical of the act of making an oath,[47] and a reference to the accompanying practice of religious sacrifice.[48]

Oaths in Treaties and Alliances

Oaths sworn between city-states were an essential mechanism to create the trust needed to conclude hostilities and make alliances. The treaty between Athens and Halieis, made most probably in 424/423 BC, provides one such example.[49] The ambassadors from Halieis who swear to keep the provisions of the treaty of alliance with the Athenians call down a curse of utter destruction upon themselves if the people of Halieis do not keep the treaty. The gods in general are requested to witness this document, rather than any specific god, though it is to be erected both on the acropolis in Athens, home of Athena, and in the sanctuary of Apollo at Halieis. The public space in which it was to be displayed and the provision for it to be written in a permanent material (on stone) made the record of the oath permanent and public, and thus permanently binding upon those who had sworn to keep it.[50] The sacred space in which the text was to be displayed reinforces and makes public the call upon the gods to witness it.

Oaths of alliance that were sworn in the fifth century BC often had, in addition to the articles of the treaty itself, a phrase specifying that the oath had to be made in good faith and sworn without deceit: *hapanta pista kai adola*.[51] The sixth-century BC treaty between the Sybarites and the Serdaeoi is perhaps the earliest extant text of an alliance, and it contains this very provision.[52] The cities swear to be 'good friends forever, faithful and without deceit' (lines 3–5). The gods Zeus and Apollo are named as *proxenoi* for this agreement, along with the other gods and the city of Poseidonia. This is an unusual sense of the word *proxenos*, which usually means the local representatives of a foreign city. The term is perhaps explained by a gloss (exegesis) in Hesychius which states that *proxenos* also had a more general meaning of *prostatês*, meaning 'champion' or 'guardian'.[53] Yet the word implies more than just champion or guardian here: the gods are called upon as *residents* who champion the foreign state, looking after the state's interests as its human *proxenos* might do. The gods become in a sense guarantors of the agreement, their role specified here one that goes beyond merely witnessing the agreement and probably one that is assumed in the oversight of all oaths. The formulaic nature of the wording of decisions made by the *boulê* (council) and *dêmos* (people) of Athens does not lessen the importance of the call upon the gods as witness to such resolutions.

In the case of the decree made by the Athenians in 446/445 BC after the revolt of Euboea,[54] the Athenians swear not to destroy or depopulate Chalcis, nor act against individuals without proper trial. The decree specifies that the Athenian *boulê* and the jurors (*dikastai*) are to make the oath on behalf of the Athenians. Logistically, this was quite an undertaking: the *boulê* was 500 strong, and there were 6,000 *dikastai*.[55] In the decree there was provision made for the management of the process of the swearing of the oath too. The Athenian generals were to ensure that everyone took the oath, and ambassadors from Chalcis and local officials called oath-commissioners (*horkôtai*) were to administer it and record the name of everyone who took the oath:

An embassy from Chalcis together with the oath-commissioners will administer the oath taken by the Athenians, and inscribe the names of those who took the oath. The generals are to ensure that everyone takes the oath.[56]

The Chalcidians were to swear their own oath: undertaking not to rebel against Athens, to pay the tribute set, to support Athens and obey the Athenians. Every Chalcidian adult male had to swear this oath personally. Harsh penalties are specified for any Chalcidian who refuses to take the oath (he would lose his citizenship and property). This oath was to be supervised by Athenian ambassadors sent for that purpose, together with the Chalcidian oath-commissioners.[57] Later in the text, we find that the Athenian oath-commissioners numbered five on this occasion and were to be elected by the *dêmos* (lines 46–47). Representatives rather than every single citizen were to take this oath for the Athenians.[58] Nevertheless, the representative body was a very large one, perhaps as large as was logistically possible at Athens for a process such as this. Andocides does say that the whole city swore an oath as part of the reconciliation in Athens after the internal conflict of 403 BC, and perhaps he did mean that every citizen had to take the oath personally.[59] In the case of the oath about the Chalcidians, copies of the oaths were to be set up on the acropolis in Athens and in the sanctuary of Zeus Olympius at Chalcis, and were to include the names of the men who had sworn the oath (lines 57–58). So the men who took the oath had to take personal responsibility for their promise. This can be compared with the requirement for all the Chalcidians to swear, with a similar requirement imposed upon the Samians: 'All the adult male Samians swore the same oath.'[60]

The Samians were asked to swear the same oath of loyalty to the democracy that the Athenian soldiers on Samos had been asked to swear. This bound them to the Athenian democracy as well as to the fight against the Peloponnesians.[61] So examples such as these, an oath sworn between the Athenians and the Chalcidians or Samians, are indeed that. In the case of such important agreements, every citizen, or at least a large representative body of them, might have to make a personal and public pledge.

When looking at examples of treaties and alliances in historical texts, the oaths that confirm agreements are not always included. This is not because there were no oaths or that the necessary accompanying religious rite did not take place. The historian has made a literary choice to exclude such detail in the construction of his narrative. Thucydides, for example, sometimes provides such detail, but sometimes does not. He gives a fairly full account in Book 5 of the treaty and alliance between Athens and Sparta.[62] His text of the agreements here looks to be authentic: the wording is similar to that found in extant treaties and the detail he includes in the text forces us to conclude that he saw a copy of treaty itself. After the provision of the terms of the treaty, Thucydides includes a record of a specific provision for the swearing of the oath. The words of the oath that is to be sworn are given:

> Let this be the oath: 'I will keep the agreement and truce honestly and without deceit.'[63]

The text of the agreement includes other details, such as where the oath is to be sworn and where copies of the treaty are to be publicly erected on stone. The sites specified were sacred spaces in Athens and Sparta, as well as in the major Panhellenic sacred sites of Olympia, Delphi and the Isthmus.[64] In such sacred places, the oaths would be in the personal space of a deity who could watch over the compliance.[65] This stipulation also made the oaths public. When the Athenians made a treaty with the Argives, Mantineians and Eleans, shortly after making the treaty with the Spartans, they erected a copy of the new treaty at Olympia as well, and erected it during the Olympic festival.[66] This ensured that the oath was well publicized. Should a treaty be broken, the stele would, it seems, normally remain standing on public display and so attest to the failure of those who had sworn to keep their oath. There was one occasion when the Athenians formally added to the text of an important treaty that was on public display, the Peace of Nicias, that the Spartans had broken their oaths, so that the breach of faith also became part of the permanent public record.[67]

There is a further interesting provision that Thucydides includes regarding the oath in the Athens-Sparta treaty of 421 BC: seventeen men from each city are to take the oath.[68] The seventeen who took the oath from Athens and Sparta are named, and so were presumably listed on the stele as part of the public record too. The oath was to be made between Athens and Sparta, and between Athens and each of Sparta's allies individually. The Spartans were unable to swear the oath on behalf of their allies, although Athens, it appears, could and did. This reflects a difference in the power relationship between Athens, Sparta and their respective allies at that time.[69] As representatives of their *polis*, Athenian representatives could swear oaths that had currency not just for all the citizens of Athens, but also of the citizens of the cities in their empire (*archê*). The situation was reversed in 371 BC: at that time, the Spartans were able to take an oath on behalf of themselves and their allies, while the Athenians and their allies took the oath separately.[70] The assumption of the right to swear an oath that is binding on other people may come with a political office assigned to a person within a *polis*, but when exercised by one *polis* over another *polis*, is a mark of political dominance.

There is another significant provision in the treaty of 421 BC: it takes account of differences in the relative importance of different deities in each of the Greek states that are to be a party to the oath. Each man is to swear the oath that has the strongest force in his particular city – 'Let each man swear the strongest local oath.'[71] There is an identical provision in the treaty between Athens, Argos, Mantineia and Elis,[72] and a similar provision in the oath of the Samians: 'They made all the soldiers swear their strongest oath.'[73] In different states, oaths may have more solemnity when made to a particular god or group of gods. Each state had its own oath sworn upon a specific deity or group of deities considered to be the most solemn to that *polis*. This oath specifies that it has to be the strongest possible, an implication that other oaths – such as those sworn by men from another *polis* – were considered to be locally less solemn but were nevertheless recognized for their solemnity in the other *polis*.

Thucydides takes great care in recording the alliance between Athens, Argos, Mantineia and Elis.[74] Here too he gives specific details: the provisions of the alliance, the text of the oath to be sworn and specification of who must swear the oath from each city. In this case, this is the officials; the oaths are to be sworn by office holders *ex officio* (by virtue of their position), and individuals are not named. The text also specifies where the record of the alliance is to be published. There is an inscription extant in which there is a similar specification of who *ex officio* is to swear the oath. In concluding a treaty between Athens and Dionysius, the tyrant of Syracuse, the *polis* is represented in the swearing of the oath by the Athenian *boulê*, along with the generals and commanders of the infantry and cavalry: 'The *boulê*, the generals, the *hipparchs* and the *taxiarchs* shall swear the oath.'[75] On Dionysius' side, military leaders were to take the oath as well as political leaders. This treaty was a military alliance; by making the military commanders swear the alliance oath personally, the political leaders ensured that the men who had to put into effect any military action were bound by personal responsibility to ensure compliance with the treaty.

These examples can be compared with the texts of other treaties recorded less fully by Thucydides in which the oath is not included in the narrative. In Book 5, he narrates that the Spartans and Argives made a treaty to avoid further war, and then an alliance.[76] On this occasion, he records the terms of the treaty and alliance, but not the oath, the process by which it was sworn, the names of the men or the titles of the officials who took the oath, nor where copies were to be erected. In Book 8, Thucydides records two treaties between the Spartans and the Persians in which the terms of the agreement are given, but again these are not full records of the texts of the treaties. They lack the text of the oaths sworn and the names of the men who swore them.[77] Scholars have seen these examples from Book 8 as draft agreements or evidence that Thucydides' text is itself a draft.[78] While another treaty at 8.58 is formally dated, unlike the other two in Book 8 and the records of treaties in 5.77 and 5.79, a full text is still not given. There is no mention of the oaths sworn, the names of the men or officials who took the oath for each party nor the provision for the publication of the treaty.[79] The oaths, the sacrifices, and calling upon the gods as witnesses to the oaths, were essential parts of the treaty; they are what would bind the parties to the agreement and enforce compliance with its terms. Thucydides seems to have seen it as largely unnecessary to include these details in his work, perhaps because they were a constant in treaties or he saw them as part of the process of the making of the treaty. The focus of his work was not the processes that were to be followed in the making of the treaty, nor the safeguards in the treaty to ensure compliance. It was the politics reflected in the treaty and the terms of the agreement itself that interested this historian. Elsewhere, where the agreement process itself was an issue, Thucydides does give more detail. For example, in 5.38, the Boeotarchs agreed to swear an oath of alliance with the Corinthians, Megarians and Thracians, but the four Boeotian federal councils rejected the proposal and so the Boeotarchs could not take the oath. Oaths were an essential part of agreements, and without them, as in this case, the carefully negotiated alliance could not come into effect.[80]

Honouring an Oath

Poleis bound themselves to agreements through oaths, a system that made it technically difficult to repudiate an agreement. Nevertheless, a change in policy may lead to a *polis* wanting to break a sworn agreement. One strategy to enable this to happen was to deny the original authority of the men who had taken the oath to represent the *polis*. Ambassadors needed authority to conclude a treaty delegated to them if they were to swear an oath on behalf of their city; the lack of such an authority could therefore be used as an excuse for a city to repudiate an agreement. This seems to have happened when Athens sent ambassadors to conclude an alliance with the king of Persia. Herodotus carefully calls these men 'messengers', not 'ambassadors', which suggests a tradition Herodotus has followed that they did not have authority to conclude an agreement. Herodotus, however, also reveals that the men had been sent in order to conclude an agreement, which presupposes the delegation of authority. Instead, Herodotus records that they concluded the agreement *on their own authority*, absolving the Athenians themselves for any responsibility to honour the agreement they made; this seems to reflect a later Athenian embarrassment at an agreement which they did not want to honour.[81] In another example, the Thebans swore an oath in 371 BC to conclude a peace treaty with the Spartans and the Athenians (and their allies); on the following day, the Theban ambassadors tried to have the written record of the oath changed to recognize them officially as the Boeotians, and thereby acknowledge their political authority as representatives of all Boeotia, not just Thebes. The Spartan king, however, would not allow the official record of the oath to be altered.[82] Ambassadors may be sent with full powers (*hôs autokrates*) to make an agreement on behalf of their city, but this was not automatic and would need to be revealed in any negotiations that were taking place. Failure to do so, or to be equivocal as the Spartan ambassadors were in 420 BC, could be exploited by a political opportunist like Alcibiades to discredit the proposed agreement.[83]

Another reason given for not honouring an oath was that a conflicting oath prevented compliance. Thucydides notes that the Corinthians refused to be a party to a treaty agreed between the Athenians and Spartans, and that there were strong political reasons for this.[84] The Corinthians, however, gave religious reasons for their actions, arguing that they were not bound to abide by a majority vote under the terms of their alliance with Sparta and the other Peloponnesian states if there were any religious obstacle to the action, and in this case there was.[85] The text suggests that such a clause may not have been unusual in interstate agreements, and the Corinthians choose on this occasion to take full advantage of it. The Corinthians claim to have sworn prior oaths with the Potidaeans.[86] Compliance with these oaths was not negotiable: they note that they had to stay true to these oaths because they had been sworn before the gods.[87] Thucydides seems quite cynical in his report. He says that the Corinthians were only using the other oath as an excuse (*proschêma*). Yet their argument must have had some legitimacy in other eyes for it to have been presented. The respect shown to the divine in the provision of the Peloponnesian alliance reported here shows that religious sentiments were important and treated seriously in such agreements between states.[88]

Oaths were also sworn in the field as a way of securing the trust of allies or ending conflict. Xenophon narrates that the Greeks swore solemn oaths to make an alliance in the field with Ariaeus, a Persian general who had fought for Cyrus at the Battle of Cynaxa:

The Greeks and Ariaeus, along with the most important of the men with him, swore on oath that they would be allies and not betray each other. The non-Greeks also swore that they would guide them without any treachery.[89]

Xenophon has the '*barbaroi*' (barbarians) swear specific provisions that (with hindsight) the author knew Ariaeus would break, giving the use of the term 'without treachery' (*adolôs*) in the record of the oath particular poignancy. He describes a sacrifice made to accompany the oath which is reminiscent of the scene described in Aeschylus' *Seven Against Thebes*:

> They swore this and sacrificed a boar, a bull, a wolf and a ram into a shield, the Greeks dipping a sword, the barbarians a lance.[90]

The sacrifice of a wolf is unusual in a Greek religious rite and is omitted in some manuscripts (and modern editions). It may have been added by Xenophon to mark the foreignness of Ariaeus, if it was not actually historical.[91] Whereas the warriors in Aeschylus' scene touch the blood of the slaughtered animal with their hands, the oath-makers here (the Greeks and Persians; we are not told how many took the oath personally) dipped their weapons in the blood. Herodotus reports a similar (though not identical) practice among the Scythians: when making an agreement, the Scythians draw their own blood and drink it as part of the ceremony:

> Scythians make their oaths with each other like this: into a large ceramic bowl they pour wine which they mix with the blood of those who are swearing the oath, after making a small cut in the body with a drill or a knife; then they dip a sword, arrows, battle-axe and a spear into the bowl. When they have done this they say many prayers and then those who are swearing the oath and their highest ranked followers drink down the mixture.[92]

Herodotus describes the Lydians and Medes as also tasting each other's blood when making an oath, but as otherwise performing the rite in a manner similar to the Greeks.[93] Plato invents a similar custom of the drinking of blood and wine for his fictional kings of Atlantis.[94] The Scythians drink the wine with the blood, whereas the Greeks pour a libation on the ground instead of drinking it. Nevertheless, the ritual aspect of the oath is conceived as fundamentally similar to the Greek practice. The reflection of the Greek custom here may be just that, an imaginary representation of a 'barbarian' way to perform this rite.[95] Interestingly, the religious nature of the oath is maintained even in what is pictured as the practice in a foreign culture.

Agreements made in the field have as a literary precedent the truce sworn between the Trojans and Achaeans in the *Iliad*.[96] Agamemnon swears an oath by Zeus, the Sun, the Rivers, the Earth and the Dead, sacrificing to them and calling upon them to take vengeance on anyone who swears falsely. A specific curse is called down upon anyone who breaks the oath: Zeus and the other gods are asked to pour their brains on the ground (like the pouring out of the offering of wine);[97] their children are to suffer the same fate and their wives are to be taken by other men:

> Zeus, most glorious and great, and the other immortal gods: whoever are first to break their oaths, may their brains be poured onto the ground just as this wine is – theirs and their children's, and may their wives become other men's women.[98]

The gods are called upon to witness the oath and by implication to enforce the penalty for non-compliance. Zeus, as the greatest of the gods, is named, but the other gods are also included in this. The knowledge of the outcome of the war that the audience has gives real power to the threat imposed by the oath. The belief in real consequences stemming from failure to abide by such an oath is also illustrated by Homer in the narrative not long after this passage. In *Iliad* 4, the Trojans do break their oath, albeit only after the gods intervene. Athena is sent by Zeus in order to persuade them to break their oath and return to battle.[99] Zeus himself has been persuaded by Hera (against his own wishes) to make this happen so that Troy will be destroyed: the breaking of this oath dooms the Trojans. Hera's request to Zeus is for him to engineer the situation so that the Trojans break their oath:

> And you, tell Athena to go straight to the dread din of battle of the Trojans and Achaeans and test out the Trojans to see how they can be the first to harm the glorious Achaeans in violation of their oaths.[100]

When Athena successfully persuades Pandarus to shoot Menelaus and so break the oaths, Agamemnon is horrified. He points out that there are repercussions from the breaking of an oath:

> But an oath is not without consequences, and the blood of the lambs and the libations of unmixed wine and the right hands which we trust.[101]

Agamemnon expects Zeus to act; Zeus will bring about fulfilment of the ultimate consequences of the breaking of the oath, even if he does not do so at once:

> For even if the Olympian did not fulfil the consequences immediately, he will fulfil them in time.

Those who have broken the oath 'will pay a very heavy price' that will fall not just on their own heads, but also 'on their wives and children'.[102] In pronouncing, from his heart, what he knows the outcome will be, Agamemnon pictures Zeus personally overseeing the destruction of Troy:

> For I know deep in my heart and soul this fact: there will be a day when sacred Ilion will be destroyed – and Priam and the people of Priam who holds a good ash spear. And Zeus, son of Cronus, living in heaven on his high bench, will shake his dark aegis over them all in anger at their treachery. This will be fulfilled.[103]

This passage illustrates the Greek understanding of the repercussions that arise from the breaking of an oath. Agamemnon professes certainty that the breaking of the oath will mean the destruction of Troy. The audience listening to the epic being sung to them know the outcome of the war, and so know that Agamemnon is correct. This belief in the gods' interest in upholding oaths is also attested in the historical record. Important political decisions about whether to go to war may be framed as a debate about whether the other party has broken its oaths or not. In the debate at Sparta held in 432 BC which led to the Spartan decision to go to war, the Athenians tell the Spartans 'not to break the treaty and transgress their oaths'. The Athenians remind the Spartans that if they do break their oaths, the Athenians can 'call upon the gods as witnesses to the oaths' and defend themselves.[104] Subsequently, the actual decision on which the Spartans were asked to vote was not whether or not they should go to war, but whether or not the Athenians had broken the treaty and were in the wrong.[105]

The decision by the Spartans in 432 BC to go to war could only be made after the issue of whether or not the oaths had been broken had been determined.[106] According to Thucydides, in 414/413 BC the Spartans regretted their earlier determination. They attributed their failure in the Archidamian War to their fault in not fulfilling the terms of the oaths they had sworn in the Thirty Year Peace. Indeed, Thucydides has the Spartans accepting that the misfortunes they had suffered in the Archidamian War were well deserved.[107] Thucydides adds that the Spartans were particularly zealous for war in 414/413 BC because they determined the Athenians had by then been guilty of breaking their oaths, in the same way they themselves had in the Archidamian War. The transgression of the oath would now harm the Athenians as it had previously harmed them.[108]

Elsewhere, it is seen how the power of the gods to punish those who break an oath was respected and presented as a reason why military oaths should be trusted. The Greek general Clearchus elucidates the consequences of the failure to keep an oath:

> For, in the first place and most importantly, our oaths made by the gods prevent us from being enemies of each other. I would never consider happy anyone who knows full well that he is in violation of his oaths. For in a war with the gods I do not know how nor to where some fugitive might escape by quickness of foot, nor into what shadows he might slip away nor how he might establish himself in a secure place. For everything everywhere is subject to the gods and the gods rule everything equally.[109]

Xenophon puts these words in the mouth of a man whom he admired as a professional soldier.[110] Oaths, Clearchus is made to say, cannot be broken because the gods hold supreme power everywhere. In breaking an oath, he characterizes the perjurer as bringing on what amounts to a war with the gods. Such a war would be unwinnable – the gods have supreme power – and the perjurer would have nowhere to go to escape them. The Persian Tissaphernes responds by adding that the breaking of an oath is both impious and shameful, and only fools would do such a thing:

> So, as we have many different ways of waging war on you, none of which are particularly dangerous to us, why would we choose this way? Of all of them, this is the only one which is impious before the gods and the only one which is shameful before people. Only people who have no other means at all, no way at all, who are forced into something and are bad people, they are the ones who are willing to get something done through perjury before the gods and by breaking faith with people. We, Clearchus, are not like that at all. We are neither so unreasonable nor so foolish.[111]

The response by Tissaphernes is deeply ironic. Xenophon shows him breaking his oath and treacherously capturing the Greek leaders, including Clearchus, who were subsequently executed.[112] Xenophon makes Tissaphernes a hypocrite: he is the one to point out to the reader that the breaking of an oath is 'shameful on a human level' (*pros anthrôpôn aischros*) as well as 'sacrilegious in the eyes of the gods' (*pros theôn asebês*). He allows that men may be forced into perjury if they have no other options, but only then if they are 'bad people'; nevertheless, such an action is the act of the 'irrational and foolish'. The values which Tissaphernes is made to express are Greek, and thus in the eyes of his Greek readers he is made to condemn his own actions.[113] An Athenian was expected to be *hosios* (pious) and *euorkos* (oath-keeping), to be respectful to the gods and keep his oath.[114]

Official oaths were generally trusted, and because of this they had great value in military conflicts. For example, in the mid-fifth century, the Spartans and Messenians reached an agreement that allowed the Messenians safe conduct from Ithôme, where they had been besieged for ten years.[115] At the end of the century, the Spartans made a similar agreement with the helots who were holding Pylos/Coryphasium.[116] The dire consequences that were believed to befall the person who had failed to keep his oath meant that agreements could be trusted. This is not to say that individuals or states would not try to circumvent the conditions of an agreement. In 425 BC, the Athenian generals at Pylos agreed to a truce with the Spartans.[117] The Athenians did not keep a provision of their truce to return sixty or so Spartan ships which had been surrendered to them. They claimed that the Spartans had broken the terms of the truce, so keeping the ships was fully justified. Claiming that the one party had already broken their oath allowed the other party to feel justified in not keeping its promise either. The fault was with the first party to break faith.

Trust in an oath was normally sufficiently strong for it to hold, even under the pressure brought by war. For the Greeks normally fought according to accepted rules of war.[118] Using a trick, however, to avoid the obligations of an oath does appear as a story motif in fictional anecdotes. An oath with ambiguous wording could be used as a key narrative device. For example, Cleomenes was said to have attacked the Argives at night after swearing to a truce of seven days.[119] In another fictional anecdote, Anaximander came to Alexander to beg for mercy for Lampsacus; before Anaximander had asked for anything, Alexander swore by all the gods of Greece to do the very opposite of what he was asked to do. The quick-thinking Anaximander promptly asked the king to make slaves of the women and children and destroy the city.[120] In the first example, Cleomenes swore an oath that he knew he could circumvent by interpreting it in an unexpected way; in the second, Alexander was bound to do the opposite of what he wanted to do as he was unable to break the oath he had just sworn.[121]

Another story illustrating the circumvention rather than breaking of an oath was told about the Athenian general Paches. According to Thucydides, Paches invited the enemy commander at Notium, Hippias, to meet with him, promising to return him safely to his fort. Hippias agreed, but Paches took him prisoner, made a surprise attack on the fort and captured it. He then returned Hippias safely to his fort – as he had sworn to do – where he executed him.[122] A similar anecdote was told about two Spartan commanders, Thibron[123] and Dercylidas.[124] Such examples suggest that respect for the oaths sworn was expected, but that, at least in anecdotes, the words sworn rather than the spirit of the agreement was what mattered. In genuine historical examples, the parties agree to keep the oaths *dikaiôs kai adolôs* (rightly and without deceit) and to guard against such tricks, and provision is made for the settlement of disputes.[125]

Vows

A vow was a type of promissory oath. It was an oath made to the gods that was a specific promise to give a deity or deities a gift in return for specified assistance. The widespread practice of dedicating arms to a god as an act of thanksgiving implies a prior request for help made to that god, though not necessarily a vow.[126] The vow predicated provision of the promised gift on the successful outcome of the prayer, and so attempted to tie the god's goodwill towards the planned action.

In Homer, there are many examples of heroes promising gifts to a god in return for a favour expressed or implied on the battlefield. For example, before he shoots Menelaus, Pandarus prays to Apollo:[127]

> He made a vow to Apollo, Lycian-born, famous for his bow, that he would offer a glorious hecatomb of first-born lambs, when he returned home to the city of sacred Zeleia.[128]

The verb used here, *euchomai*, means both to pray and to vow. A vow is thus first and foremost a prayer, one in which a promise of a gift is made. In this case a request of the god is implied but not voiced: the bowman prays to the god who is famous for his archery before he shoots. Indeed, it was another god, Athena, who reminded Pandarus to make such a vow before he shot.[129] What Pandarus was about to do was folly – he was breaking the oath made in the treaty – but it was folly engineered by the gods.[130] Calls upon divine assistance in the heat of battle or before a military expedition were presumably not unusual, just as they were common before travel.[131]

Vows, like all prayers, were not necessarily successful. Vows may be heard but refused by the god. In the *Iliad*, such an example is seen when the hero Hector requests that a vow be made on his behalf. Hector asks his mother to gather together the older women and take them with her to vow an offering to Athena if she would help the Trojans in battle against Diomedes. Hekabe does this, makes the vow and gives Athena a fine offering, but the goddess denies her request.[132] For even when the gods listen, they may refuse a prayer.[133]

In the historical record, many occasions are found in which specific vows were made before battle. There are examples of vows made by individuals, by forces in the field and by cities as a whole.[134] Xenophon reports that the Athenians made a particular vow before Marathon:

> They vowed to Artemis that they would sacrifice as many she-goats to her as enemies they killed. They were not able to find enough goats so they decided to sacrifice 500 a year, and they are still making this sacrifice even today.[135]

Xenophon sets this comment in 401 BC; so at least until then, nearly ninety years after the battle, the Athenians had kept up the ritual sacrifice pledged in their vow. It is interesting to see that in this case, the original vow could not be met immediately, as it seems was the original intent (the total Persian dead was officially 6,400),[136] and so the practical solution of an annual sacrifice was decided upon instead.[137]

Another example of a vow made in the field also comes from Xenophon. He narrates that the Ten Thousand made a vow to sacrifice to Zeus as saviour when they reached safety.[138] Xenophon himself proposed the sacrifice to an assembly of the men. The men voted on the proposal and the outcome was unanimous assent. This vow also made a promise to sacrifice to the other gods, reflecting a common Greek practice of not wanting to exclude a possible divine ally. Unlike the earlier Athenian pledge, which they found they could not immediately fulfil exactly as pledged, this vow had a practical limitation clause: the Greeks are to sacrifice as much 'as they could'. Xenophon says that all the men took the vow after their vote.[139] The public prayer taken together and joint pledge testifies to this as a public and communal action by the soldiers, uniting them in a religious act which they later dutifully fulfilled with sacrifices and games when they reached safety.[140]

A letter attributed to Demosthenes suggests that when a city like Athens determined on military action, it would vow to dedicate victory spoils to the gods.[141] Elsewhere, Demosthenes records that the Athenians dedicated

10 per cent of all spoils to Athena and gave the other gods a further 2 per cent.[142] Such a tithe of the war booty is attested widely, and has been identified as a major source of money for the building of a good proportion of the Greeks' temples.[143] The tithe presupposes the sort of vow mentioned in Demosthenes. Another example of a vow of spoils before military action comes in the oath of the Greek allies set in the Persian Wars: the allies, as Herodotus notes, swore an oath to punish Greeks who gave in to the Persians without compulsion and to dedicate a tithe from their property to Apollo at Delphi.[144] Diodorus indicates that the allies also vowed to hold an annual festival at Plataea (the Eleutheria) in honour of freedom if they were victorious.[145]

The size of any thanks-offering promised was considered significant. Indeed, the Delphic oracle is reported to have said that an enemy must be defeated in terms of the size of the vow before it can be defeated in battle.[146] So winning a god to your side may have entailed promising more offerings in victory than your enemy did. A state might make a vow conditional on a favourable outcome. An inscription dated to 362/361 BC records a formal resolution in the form of a vow made by the Athenian *dêmos*. If a proposed alliance turns out to be beneficial for the Athenians, they promise by the resolution to make a sacrifice to Zeus Olympius, Athena Polias, Demeter and Core and the twelve gods and dread goddesses.[147] A state political action such as a treaty is thus an act that may be supported by a collective religious action, but one that could be made conditional on success where the favour of the gods could be assumed.

Conclusion: Shame and Piety

The human response to the failure to keep an oath was significant. As Xenophon puts it in the mouth of Tissaphernes, shame as well as piety was a major motivation in the keeping of an oath. Oaths were sworn in public and, where they were made on behalf of a city state, set up on stone in a permanent record. This record was published in a prominent place in the cities that were parties to the agreement. The breaking of such public promises brought shame upon those who had sworn the oath, as well as their cities.[148] On a human level, an oath was guaranteed by the good character of the man who had sworn it. Aeschylus comments that 'oaths are not a guarantee of a man, but a man is a guarantee of oaths'.[149] For Plutarch, Alexander's killing of some Indian mercenaries, with whom he had poured libations in making a truce, was contrary to the acceptable way of conducting war and was a stain on his character.[150]

It is true that not all Greeks believed in the gods, and this might be seen as undermining the authority of an oath. Plato comments that by the fourth century, views about the gods had changed and this had indeed removed the barrier to perjury, making oaths no longer secure.[151] Even earlier, Thucydides, in interpreting the military alliance that underpinned the Greek force under Agamemnon, disputes the primacy of an open-ended oath made between the suitors and the father of Helen to bind the Greek heroes to support Menelaus and fight for her return.[152] The idea that such an oath may be taken by men to force them together in a military action, even to die in the attempt, is very much a part of the Greek tradition. Yet in addressing the motivation of the suitors in this myth, while apparently accepting the general historicity of the story of the oaths themselves,[153] Thucydides analyses the political situation as he understood it in Homeric Greece, finding the power of Agamemnon the decisive factor:

> I think that Agamemnon raised his fleet because he was more powerful than anyone else in his day and not because he was simply the leader of Helen's suitors who were bound by their oaths to Tyndareus.[154]

Thucydides evaluates the account of the oaths made by the suitors of Helen against his understanding of the way that the world actually worked. For him, power was the decisive factor in political decision-making and, to put it simply, the strong ruled the weak.[155] Yet the continuity of religious practice suggests that the community as a whole continued to hold strong religious beliefs. Thucydides' contemporaries were evidently far more religious than he was: their relationship with the gods was important and underpinned their respect for oaths and vows.[156] Dionysius of Halicarnassus firmly rejects Thucydides' characterization of the Athenians, arguing that the *polis* followed divine guidance in every decision it made.[157] It is this which gave the oath its validity: a firm belief by the state, by the community as a whole if not by every individual, in their gods and the interest the gods took in their lives and the success of their *polis*.

The act of swearing an oath in a military context was in itself a political action. Oaths were sworn by individual citizens and bound those citizens to fight for their *polis* or committed the *polis* itself to a particular political action. The public nature of such promises, for which individuals had to take personal responsibility, allowed the wider Greek community a role in judging whether the action had been carried out as promised. When oaths and vows were made by representatives of one *polis* on behalf of another, as well as securing the political outcome desired, the very act of the swearing of the oath was a public assertion of the political power of one *polis* over another.

Notes

1. For a definition of an oath, see Sommerstein, 2013, 1–4, and 2014, 1–5. Sommerstein *et al.*, 2007, 2013, 2014 are now the standard works on the oath in the Greek world; on Greek alliances and treaties in general, see Baltrusch, 1994.
2. On reciprocity in Greek religious thought, see Bremmer, 1998, 127–37; Parker, 1998, 105–25.
3. Hom. *Il.* 3.373–82, 5.330–417, 846–63, 855–59.
4. Hom. *Il.* 20.23–40, 22.225–31, 22.276–77. On the Greek belief in the participation of all their gods in war, not just Ares and Athena, see Kostuch, 2011, 41–48.
5. Goodman and Holladay, 1986, 151–60; Mikalson, 2003, 169; Kostuch, 2011, 43–44.
6. Hdt. 6.105, 117; Paus. 1.15.3, 32.5; 8.54.6; Plut. *Thes.* 35, *Mor.* 305c; Ael. *Var. Hist.* 7.38; Suda *sv* Hippias, Polyzelus. See Pritchett, 1979, 11–46; Kearns 1989: 44–46; and Lara O'Sullivan's chapter on epiphanies in this volume.
7. Hdt. 8.38–39.
8. Hdt. 8.129.3.
9. Hdt. 8.64.2, 8.83.2, 8.121.1; the other two ships went to the Isthmus and Sunium, where Poseidon was worshipped. Apollo received the first fruits offering from the war booty, from which an 18ft high statue of him was made: Hdt. 8.121.2; Paus. 10.14.5.
10. Aesch. *Seven* 42–48.
11. See for example, Xen. *Anab.* 6.1.31, 6.17. Other cognate verbs were also used, such as ὁρκίζω, ὁρκόω.
12. Sommerstein, 2014a, 76, suggests that in such contexts the phrase ἵστορα ποιούμενος (making [the god] my witness) would be understood. This is perhaps unnecessary: gods could also be called upon to affirm general statements as oaths in the accusative with νή or μά, or with the μά omitted: Soph. *Ant.* 758.
13. In Homer, she is mentioned with Athena and Ares: Hom. *Il.* 5.333, 592; she was depicted in the temple of Ares in Athens: Paus. 1.8.4.
14. Phobos was listed as a god in his own right in the Selinus victory inscription: *IG* xiv 268 (mid-fifth century BC); *GHI* i, no. 37; Fornara 1983, no. 91. For the cult to Phobos at Sparta, see Plut. *Cleom.* 8.2, 9; Mactoux, 1993, 259–304.
15. The sacrifice is described but by convention not actually performed on stage; see Fletcher, 2012, 10–11.
16. For a possible significance of the use of the shield to contain blood or cut-up flesh in such a ceremony and its connection to sympathetic magic, see Faraone, 1993, 68.
17. Rhodes and Osborne, 2003, no. 88; *GHI* ii, no. 204; Fornara 1983, no. 57; Lycurg. *Leocr.* 1.80–81; Diod. 11.29.2–3.
18. Theopompus *FGrH* 88 F153.
19. For a full discussion of this oath, and the implications for our understanding of its historical context, see Cartledge, 2013, 12–40, 169–71. See also Krentz, 2007; Wees, 2006, 125–64; Siewert, 1972; Raubitschek, 1960, 178–83. For the fourth-century invention of historical inscriptions: Davies, 1996, 29–39.
20. As Burkert, 1985, 252.
21. Cf. for example, Lycurg. *Leocr.* 77 (discussed below).
22. There were thirty-two men in each *enômotia* (Thuc. 5.68.3); for the traditional belief that Lycurgus invented the *enômotiai*, see Hdt. 1.65.5. Their commander was called an *enômotarchês*: Thuc. 5.66.3; see further Lazenby, 1985.

23. Hesych. *sv enômotiai.*
24. Timaeus *Lex. Plat. sv enômotia*; also Phot. *Lex. sv enômotia*. See Bayliss, 2013, 23.
25. Wees, 2006, 125–64.
26. Hdt. 1.65.5; Thuc. 5.66.3.
27. The Athenians did use the cognate term *enômotos* ('bound by an oath') in literary texts: for example, Soph. *Ant.* 1111–13.
28. On the conflict in the sources over whether the oath was sworn on registration in the deme or on completion of the services, see Bayliss, 2013, 15.
29. Lycurg. *Leocr.* 77; see also Dem. 19.303; Stob. *Flor.* 4.1.48; Poll. 8.105; Plut. *Alc.* 15.7.
30. This is the same stele on which the 'Oath of Plataea' was inscribed. For its publication, see Robert, 1938, 293–316; Daux, 1965; Siewert, 1972, 5–7; Siewert, 1977; Rhodes and Osborne, 2003, 440–49; *GHI* ii, no. 204; Kellogg, 2008.
31. Thucydides mentions the 'youngest' as a military unit: Thuc. 1.105.4; 2.13.7. For possible echoes in fifth-century BC authors, see Siewert, 1977, 102–11.
32. See Lycurg. F5.3; [Arist.] *Ath. Pol.* 42.3–5. On this argument, see Kellogg, 2013, 265; Rhodes, 1993, 494–95.
33. See Bayliss, 2013, 15, on Lycurg. *Leocr.* 76.
34. There are alternative spellings of her name. For the spelling 'Aglauros', see for example Munich 2345 (Oreithyia Painter).
35. Lycurg. *Leocr.* 77. For the context in which the oath of the ephebes is cited by Lycurgus, see Steinbock, 2011, 279–317.
36. Mikalson, 2003, 142–43. See for example, Hom. *Il.* 19.258; Soph. *Phil.* 1324; Eur. *Hipp.* 1025; Paus. 5.24.9–11; cf. Soph. *Oed. Col.* 1767.
37. For Alcibiades' interpretation of the crops as the boundaries of Athens, see Plut. *Alc.* 15.
38. Paus. 9.35.2.
39. Eur. *Erech.* F360 (Lycurg. *Leocr.* 98–100); Philoch. *FGrH* 328 F105; Paus. 1.2.6, 1.18.2; Apollod. *Bibl.* 3.14.6; cf. Ovid *Met.* 2.737–832.
40. Hellanicus *FGrH* 4 F38; cf. Phot. *Lex. sv* agrauloi; Hom. *Il.* 18.162.
41. Paus. 1.38.3.
42. This Aglaurus is the mother of the second Aglaurus: Apollod. *Bibl.* 3.14.2.
43. Philochorus *FGrH* 328 FF105–06; Bayliss, 2013, 17–18; Boedeker, 1984, 107.
44. Hom. *Il.* 18.501, 23.486.
45. Hdt. 7.132.2.
46. For the historical problems raised by this oath in Herodotus, see How and Wells, 1912, 177–78; Siewert, 1972; Kellogg, 2013, 273–74.
47. For example, the phrase 'cutting trustworthy oaths' (*horkia pista tamontes*) in Hom. *Il.* 2.124, 3.73, 3.256, 24.483.
48. See further Bayliss, 2013a, 151. On the Near Eastern parallels to the practice, see Faraone, 1993, 65–66.
49. *IG* i³ 75. For the date, see Mattingly, 1996, 470–71.
50. See especially *IG* i³ 75.1, 25–27, 30–34.
51. *IG* i³ 53.11, see also 13–14. For the provision in other decrees, see for example *IG* i³ 54.23, 26–27, *IG* i³ 75.25.
52. *SEG* 22.336; Woodhead, 1967; Meiggs and Lewis, pp.18–19; Giangiulio, 1992, 31–44; Lombardo, 2008, 49–60.
53. Hesych. *sv* proxenos; see further Meiggs and Lewis, p.19.

54. *IG* i³ 40; see *SEG* 10.36, 42.10. For the historical context, see Ostwald, 2002, 134–43; for a revision of the dating, to the 420s BC, Mattingly, 1976 and 1992.
55. [Arist.] *Ath. Pol.* 24.3.
56. *IG* i³ 40.16–20.
57. *IG* i³ 40.32–39. Compare with the provisions for the receipt of the oath of the Eretrians: Athens will send to represent the city five ambassadors from members of the *boulé* and five private citizens: *IG* ii² 117.19–21.
58. On the practice of Athenian treaties specifying who must swear the oath, see Andrewes and Lewis, 1957.
59. Andoc. *Myst.* 90. For the historical context and discussion, see Joyce, 2015, 24–45.
60. Thuc. 8.75.3.
61. Hornblower (2008, 976–77) suggests that Thucydides may have had in mind the later enfranchisement of the Samians when he recorded this oath of loyalty.
62. Thuc. 5.17.2–19, 5.22.3–24. On the Peace of Nicias, see Kagan, 1981, 19–32; Hornblower, 1996, 467–98.
63. Thuc. 5.18.9.
64. On the process for publishing and erecting public decrees, see Henry, 2002.
65. For the choice of the acropolis in Athens for the erection of treaties, see Liddel, 2003, 80–81.
66. Thuc. 5.47.10, cf. 18.10.
67. Thuc. 5.56.3. For discussion of the preservation of stele even after the treaties they recorded became invalid, see Bolmarcich, 2007a.
68. Thuc. 5.19.
69. Mosley, 1961, 59–63. For discussion of the oaths sworn to bind together the members of the Peloponnesian League, see Bolmarcich, 2008.
70. Xen. *Hell.* 6.3.19.
71. Thuc. 5.18.9.
72. Thuc. 5.47.8.
73. Thuc. 8.75.2.
74. Thuc. 5.47.
75. *IG* ii² 105.32–34 (*GHI* i: no. 136).
76. Thuc. 5.77, 79.
77. Thuc. 8.17.4–18.3, 8.37.
78. See Gomme, 1981, 40, 143–45; Cawkwell, 2005, 149–51.
79. For scholarship on this treaty, see Hornblower, 2008, 800–01, 924–25. For sources for the treaties, see Gomme, 1981, 144–45.
80. For the political context, see Buck, 1994, 20–22.
81. Hdt. 5.73.3. For the political context, see Raubitschek, 1964.
82. Xen. *Hell.* 6.3.19. For discussion of the Theban diplomacy here, see Mosley, 1972.
83. Thuc. 5.45.2–4. The anecdote may not be a true account of events: see Gomme, 1970, 51–53; Hornblower, 2008, 105–07.
84. Thuc. 5.30.2, cf. 5.17.2.
85. Thuc. 5.30.3.
86. Thuc. 5.30.2.
87. Thuc. 5.30.3.
88. On the alliance, see Ste Croix, 1972, 101–05; for discussion of the religious impediment clause in the treaty, see Hornblower, 2008, 68–69.
89. Xen. *Anab.* 2.2.8.
90. Xen. *Anab.* 2.2.9.

91. Plut. *Mor.* 369e; Parker, 2004, 137 n.17.
92. Hdt. 4.70.
93. Hdt. 1.74.6. On the Scythian drinking of blood, see Hobden, 2013, 86–87.
94. Plat. *Crit.* 119d.
95. Hartog, 1988, 113–19.
96. Hom. *Il.* 3.103–10, 245–52.
97. The libations of wine made to the gods (normally as the plural *spondai*) provided the word used to denote a truce; on *spondai*, see Karavites, 1984.
98. Hom. *Il.* 3.298–301.
99. Hom. *Il.* 4.66–67, 71–72.
100. Hom. *Il.* 4.66–67, also 70–72.
101. Hom. *Il.* 4.155–62.
102. Hom. *Il.* 4. 161–62.
103. Hom. *Il.* 4.163–68. Eustathius *Il.* 1.727.23 notes that this passage shows that Agamemnon expects Troy to be destroyed because of the Trojans' *epiorkia* (perjury).
104. Thuc. 1.78.4.
105. Thuc. 1.87.2: 'Spartans, all of you who think that the treaty has been broken and the Athenians are in the wrong.' For discussion of Thucydides' account of this decision, cf. Badian, 1993, 145–52.
106. Thuc. 1.87.4–6.
107. Thuc. 7.18.2–3: for this reason, they believed that their misfortune was well deserved.
108. Thuc. 7.18.3: at that time, the Spartans believed that the same unlawful behaviour which had previously harmed them, had now turned right around to fall on the Athenians.
109. Xen. *Anab.* 2.5.7.
110. Xen. *Anab.* 2.6.1–15; see Roisman, 1985–1988.
111. Xen. *Anab.* 2.5.20–21.
112. Xen. *Anab.* 2.5.31–32, 2.6.1, see also 2.4–6, 2.10, 3.1.19–23, 5.5. Xenophon's depiction of Tissaphernes as treacherous towards Cyrus is clear: *Anab.* 1.1.2, 1.3. On Xenophon's account of this episode, see Bassett, 2002; on Xenophon's attitude to such treachery, see Danzig, 2007.
113. On Xenophon's focus on the deceit of Tissaphernes, see Hirsch, 1985, 25–32. Xenophon knew of Tissaphernes' fate and may be foreshadowing it here (Xen. *Hell.* 3.4.25): Tissaphernes was accused of treachery and executed by the Persian king after a military failure.
114. Xen. *Hell.* 2.4.42.
115. Thuc. 1.103, about 455 BC; see Hornblower, 1991, 160.
116. 409 BC; Xen. *Hell.* 1.2.18.
117. Thuc. 4.16, 4.23.1.
118. See Krentz 2002.
119. Plut. *Sayings of Spartans* 45.2–3 (*Mor.* 223b); Herodotus has a quite different account: Hdt. 6.77–78. Scott, 2005, 294, rightly rejects Plutarch's version of events as an 'urban myth'.
120. Paus. 6.18.2–4. A similar apocryphal story is told about Hagnon: Polyaen. *Strat.* 6.53.
121. For this narrative device in Herodotus, see for example, Hdt. 4.154.3, 9.109.2–3.
122. At Notium in 427 BC: Thuc. 3.34. Gomme, 1956, 297 treats this example as historical, the kind of strategy necessary in war to save lives; for the setting of the

episode in Thucydides' narrative for thematic development of the idea of *logos* in war, see Connor, 1984, 80–81.

123. Set in the 390s BC, Thibron's story is vague ('when he was attacking a fort in Asia'): Polyaen. *Strat.* 2.17.

124. Polyaen. *Strat.* 2.6 (cf. Xen. *Hell.* 3.1.20); Jul. Afric. *Kest.* 7.1.11 (cf. Polyaen. *Strat.* 2.2.9); Wheeler, 1988, 34–35; Bayliss, 2014, 262–65.

125. See for example, Thuc. 5.18.9. On 'anti-deceit clauses', see Bolmarcich, 2007, 31–38.

126. For military thank offerings, see Pritchett, 1979, 240–95, and Michael Schmitz in this volume; on the terminology for Greek religious offerings, see Jim, 2012, 310–37.

127. For further examples of the hero making a vow before his military action, see Hom. *Il.* 7.76–86, 10.283–94.

128. Hom. *Il.* 4.119–21.

129. Hom. *Il.* 4.101–03.

130. Hom. *Il.* 4.104.

131. For example, Theseus' fulfilment of his vow provided a charter for the Attic festival *Pyanopsia* (Plut. *Thes.* 22.1, 4); the prayers and libations before the sailing of the Athenian fleet (Thuc. 6.32.1).

132. Hom. *Il.* 6.269–80, 6.297–311. For the request of another to make a vow, see also *Od.* 17.49–51.

133. For Zeus granting only part of a request, see *Il.* 16.249–52.

134. For discussion of examples of such vows, see Pritchett, 1979, 230–39.

135. Xen. *Anab.* 3.2.12. See also Plut. *On the Malignity of Herodotus* 2 (*Mor.* 862); cf. Ael. *Var. Hist.* 2.25; schol. Ar. *Knights* 660.

136. Hdt. 6.117.

137. The phrase 'it was resolved by them' in Xen. *Anab.* 3.2.12 suggests an official resolution of the *dêmos*.

138. Xen. *Anab.* 3.2.9.

139. Xen. *Anab.* 3.2.9: 'And they all raised their hands in agreement. Afterwards they made the vow.'

140. Xen. *Anab.* 4.8.25–28.

141. Dem. *Ep.* 1.16: after making a vow to all the gods over the victory-offerings. On the authenticity of this letter, see Goldstein, 1968.

142. Dem. 24.120, 129.

143. Pritchett, 1971, 100; for the evidence for the tithe from booty, see 93–100; for booty in general, 53–84.

144. Hdt. 7.132, Diod. 11.3.3, Polyb. 9.39.5, Lycurg. *Leocr.* 81; Xen. *Hell.* 6.3.20.

145. Diod. 11.29; cf. Plut. *Arist.* 21.1–2; Thuc. 2.71.2, 3.58.4; Strabo 9.2.31; Paus. 9.2.5–6; Plut. *On the Malignity of Herodotus* 42 (*Mor.* 872f).

146. Justin *Epit.* 20.3.1.

147. *IG* ii² 112 (*GHI* ii, no. 144). The alliance proposed is with Arkadia, Achaia, Elis and Phleious.

148. On the importance of shame in Greek culture, see Dodds, 1951, 28–63; Cairns, 1993; Konstan, 2003.

149. Aesch. F394.

150. Plut. *Alex.* 59.4.

151. Plat. *Laws* 10.886d–e, 12.948b–e.

152. Paus. 3.20.9; Eur. *Iph. Aul.* 58–65.

153. As Hornblower, 1991, 31.
154. Thuc. 1.9.1.
155. As Thuc. 5.105; on the nature of power in Thucydides, see Romilly, 1963; Woodhead, 1970; Immerwahr, 1973; Hunter, 1982, 33–45.
156. For a full treatment of this issue, see Rubel, 2014.
157. Dion. Hal. *On. Thuc.* 40; cf. Thuc. 5.103.2. For discussion, see Hornblower, 2008, 242.

Bibliography

Andrewes, A., and Lewis, D.M., 1957, 'Note on the Peace of Nikias', *JHS* 77.2, 177–180.

Badian, E., 1993, *From Plataea to Potidaea: Studies in the History and Historiography of the Pentecontaetia*, Baltimore.

Baltrusch, E., 1994, *Symmachie und Spondai: Untersuchungen zum griechischen Völkerrecht der archaischen und klassischen Zeit (8.-5. Jahrhundert v. Chr.)*, Berlin.

Bassett, S., 2002, 'Innocent Victims or Perjurers Betrayed? The Arrest of the Generals in Xenophon's Anabasis', *CQ* 52.2, 447–61.

Bayliss, A.J., 2013, 'Oaths and Citizenship', in Sommerstein, A.H., *Oath and State*, 9–32.

—— 2013a, 'The Formulation and Procedure of Interstate Oaths', in Sommerstein, A.H., *Oath and State*, 151–84.

—— 2014, '"Artful Dodging", or the Sidestepping of Oaths', in Sommerstein, A.H., *Oaths and Swearing*, 240–80.

Boedeker, D., 1984, *Descent from Heaven: Images of Dew in Greek Poetry and Religion*, Atlanta.

Bolmarcich, S., 2007, 'Oaths in Greek International Relations', in Sommerstein, A.H., and Fletcher, J., *Horkos*, Exeter, 26–38.

—— 2007a, 'The Afterlife of a Treaty', *CQ* 57, 477–89.

—— 2008, 'The Date of the "Oath of the Peloponnesian League"', *Historia* 57.1, 65–79.

Bremmer, J.M., 1998, 'Reciprocity of Giving and Thanksgiving in Greek Worship', in Gill, C., Postlethwaite, N., and Seaford, R. (eds), *Reciprocity in Greek Religion*, Oxford, 127–37.

Buck, R.J., 1994, *Boiotia and the Boiotian League, 432–371 B.C.*, Edmonton.

Burkert, W., 1985, *Greek Religion*, Cambridge MA.

Cairns, D.L., 1993, *Aidôs: The Psychology and Ethics of Honour and Shame in Ancient Greek Literature*, Oxford.

Cartledge, P., 2013, *After Thermopylae: The Oath of Plataea and the End of the Graeco-Persian Wars*, Oxford.

Cawkwell, G., 2005, *The Greek Wars: The Failure of Persia*, Oxford.

Connor, W.R., 1984, *Thucydides*, Princeton.

Danzig, G. 2007, 'Xenophon's Wicked Persian or, What's Wrong with Tissaphernes? Xenophon's Views on Lying and Breaking Oaths', in Tuplin, C. (ed.), *Persian Responses: Political and Cultural Interaction With(in) the Achaemenid Empire*, Swansea, 27–50.

Daux, G., 1965, 'Deux stèles d'Acharnes', in Zakythenos, D. *et al.* (ed.), Χαριστήριον εἰς Ἀναστάσιον Κ. Ὀρλάνδον 1, Athens, 78–90.

Davies, J.K., 1996, 'Documents and "Documents" in Fourth-Century Historiography', in Carlier, P. (ed.), *Le IVe siècle av. J.-C.: Approches historiographiques*, Nancy, 29–39.

Dodds, E.R., 1951, *The Greeks and the Irrational*, Berkeley.

Faraone, C.A., 1993, 'Molten Wax, Spilt Wine and Mutilated Animals: Sympathetic Magic in Near Eastern and Early Greek Oath Ceremonies', *JHS* 113, 60–80.

Fletcher, J., 2012, *Performing Oaths in Classical Greek Drama*, Cambridge.

Fornara, C.W., 1983, *Archaic Times to the End of the Peloponnesian War*, Cambridge.

Giangiulio, M., 1992, 'La φιλότης tra Sibariti e Serdaioi (Meiggs – Lewis, 10)', *ZPE* 93, 31–44.

Goldstein, J.A., 1968, *The Letters of Demosthenes*, New York.

Gomme, A.W., 1956, *A Historical Commentary on Thucydides*, vol. ii, Oxford.

Gomme, A.W., Andrewes, A., and Dover, K.J., 1970, *A Historical Commentary on Thucydides,* vol. iv, Oxford.

—— 1981, *A Historical Commentary on Thucydides*, vol. v, Oxford.

Goodman, M.D., and Holladay, A.J., 1986, 'Religious Scruples in Ancient Warfare', *CQ* 36.1, 151–71.

Hartog, F., 1988, *The Mirror of Herodotus: The Representation of the Other in the Writing of History*, Berkeley.

Henry, A.S., 2002, 'The Athenian State Secretariat and Provisions for Publishing and Erecting Decrees', *Hesperia* 71, 91–118.

Hirsch, S.W., 1985, *The Friendship of the Barbarians: Xenophon and the Persian Empire*, Hanover.

Hobden, F., 2013, *The Symposion in Ancient Greek Society and Thought*, Cambridge.

Hornblower, S., 1991, *A Commentary on Thucydides. Volume i: Books i–iii*, Oxford.

—— 1996, *A Commentary on Thucydides. Volume ii: Books iv–v.24*, Oxford.

—— 2008, *A Commentary on Thucydides. Volume iii: Books v.25–viii*, Oxford.

How, W.W., and Wells, J., 1912, *A Commentary on Herodotus*, vol. ii, Oxford.

Hunter, V., 1982, *Past and Process in Herodotus and Thucydides*, Princeton.

Immerwahr, H., 1973, 'Pathology of Power and the Speeches of Thucydides', in Stadter, P. (ed.), *The Speeches of Thucydides*, Chapel Hill NC, 15–31.

Jim, T.S.F., 2012, 'Naming a Gift: the Vocabulary and Purposes of Greek Religious Offerings', *GRBS* 52, 310–37.

Joyce, C., 2015, 'Oaths (ὅρκοι), Covenants (συνθῆκαι) and Laws (νόμοι) in the Athenian Reconciliation Agreement of 403 BC with an Appendix by Edward Harris', *Antichthon* 49, 24–49.

Kagan, D., 1981, *The Peace of Nicias and the Sicilian Expedition*, Ithaca.

Karavites, P., 1984, '*Spondai-Spendein* in the Fifth Century B.C.', *AC* 53, 63–70.

Karavites, P., 1992, *Promise-Giving and Treaty-Making. Homer and the Near East, Mnemosyne,* Supplement 119, Leiden.

Kearns, E., 1989, *The Heroes of Attica*, London.

Kellogg, D.L., 2008, 'Οὐκ ἐλάττω παραδώσω τὴν πατρίδα: The Ephebic Oath and the Oath of Plataia in Fourth-Century Athens', *Mouseion* series 3.8, 1–22.

—— 2013, 'The Place of Publication of the Ephebic Oath and the "Oath of Plataia"', *Hesperia* 82, 263–76.

Konstan, D., 2003, 'Shame in Ancient Greece', *Social Research* 70.4, 1031–60.

Kostuch, L., 2011, 'Pantes theoi, Polemos and Ares on the Battlefield. The Greek Concept of the War Deity', *Symbolae Philologorum Posnaniensium Graecae et Latinae* 21.1, 41–48.

Krentz, P., 2002, 'Fighting by the Rules: the Invention of the Hoplite Agôn', *Hesperia* 71.1, 23–39.

—— 2007, 'The Oath of Marathon, Not Plataia?', *Hesperia* 76.4, 731–42.

Lazenby, J.F., 1985, *The Spartan Army*, Warminster.

Liddel, P., 2003, 'The Places of Publication of Athenian State Decrees from the 5th Century BC to the 3rd Century AD', *ZPE* 143, 79–93.

Lombardo, M., 2008, 'Il trattato tra i Sibariti e i Serdaioi: problemi di cronologia e inquadramento storico', *Studi di Antichità* 12, 49–60.

Mactoux, M.-M., 1993, 'Phobos à Sparte', *RHR* 210, 259–304.

Mattingly, H.B., 1976, 'Three Attic Decrees', *Historia* 25, 38–44.

—— 1992, 'Epigraphy and the Athenian Empire', *Historia* 41, 129–138.

—— 1996, *The Athenian Empire Restored: Epigraphic and Historical Studies*, Ann Arbor.

Mikalson, J.D., 2003, *Herodotus and Religion in the Persian Wars*, Chapel Hill NC.

—— 2010, Greek Popular Religion in Greek Philosophy, Oxford.

Mosley, D.J., 1961, 'Who Signed Treaties in Ancient Greece?', *PCPhS* 187, 59–63.

—— 1972, 'Theban Diplomacy in 371 B.C.', *REG* 85.406–08, 312–18.

Ostwald, M,. 2002, 'Athens and Chalkis: A Study in Imperial Control', *JHS* 122, 134–43.

Parker, R., 1998, 'Pleasing Thighs: Reciprocity in Greek Religion', in Gill, C., Postlethwaite, N., and Seaford, R. (eds), *Reciprocity in Greek Religion*, Oxford, 105–25.

—— 2004, 'One Man's Piety: The Religious Dimension of the *Anabasis*', in Lane Fox, R. (ed.), *The Long March: Xenophon and the Ten Thousand*, New Haven, 131–53.

Pritchett, W.K., 1971, *The Greek State at War. Part I*, Berkeley.

—— 1979, *The Greek State at War. Part III: Religion*, Berkeley.

Raubitschek, A.E., 1960, 'The Covenant of Plataea', *TAPhA* 91, 178–83.

—— 1964, 'The Treaties Between Persia and Athens', *GRBS* 5, 151–59.

Rhodes, P.J., 1993, *A Commentary on the Aristotelian* Athenaion Politeia, revised edn, Oxford.

Rhodes, P.J., and Osborne, R. (eds), 2003, *Greek Historical Inscriptions: 404–323 B.C.*, Oxford.

Robert, L., 1938, *Études Épigraphiques et Philologiques*, Paris.

Roisman, J., 1985–1988, 'Klearchos in Xenophon's *Anabasis*', *SCI* 8–9, 30–52.

Romilly, J. De, 1963, *Thucydides and Athenian Imperialism*, trans. Thody, P., Oxford.

Rubel, A., 2014, *Fear and Loathing in Ancient Athens: Religion and Politics During the Peloponnesian War*, London.

Scott, L., 2005, *Historical Commentary on Herodotus Book 6*, Leiden.

Siewert, P., 1972, *Der Eid von Plataiai*, Munich.

—— 1977, 'The Ephebic Oath in Fifth-Century Athens', *JHS* 97, 102–11.

Sommerstein, A.H., 2013, 'Introduction', in Sommerstein, *Oath and State*, 1–8.

—— 2014, 'What is an Oath?', in Sommerstein, *Oaths and Swearing*, 1–5.

—— 2014a, 'How Oaths are Expressed', in Sommerstein, *Oaths and Swearing*, 76–85.

Sommerstein, A.H., and Fletcher, J. (eds), 2007, *Horkos: The Oath in Greek Society*, Exeter.

—— and Bayliss, A.J. (eds), 2013, *Oath and State in Ancient Greece*, Berlin.

—— and Torrance, I.C. (eds), 2014, *Oaths and Swearing in Ancient Greece*, Berlin.

Ste Croix, G.E.M. de, 1972, *The Origins of the Peloponnesian War*, London.

Steinbock, B., 2011, 'A Lesson in Patriotism: Lycurgus Against Leocrates, the Ideology of the Ephebeia, and Athenian Social Memory', *ClAnt* 30.2, 279–317.

Wees, H. Van, 2006, '"The Oath of the Sworn Bands": The Acharnae Stela, the Oath of Plataea and Archaic Spartan Warfare', in Luther, A., Meier, M., and Thommen, L. (eds), *Das frühe Sparta*, Stuttgart, 125–64.

Wheeler, E.L., 1988, *Stratagem and the Vocabulary of Military Trickery*, Leiden.

Woodhead, A.G., 1967 'Olympia. Foedus inter Sybaritas et Serdaeos, s. VIa p. post', *SEG* 22.36, Leiden.

—— 1970, *Thucydides on the Nature of Power*, Cambridge MA.

Chapter 5

Sacred Truces and Festivals Interrupting War: Piety or Manipulation?[1]

Ian Rutherford

One of the few occurrences which could interrupt war in ancient Greece was a sacred truce accompanying a religious festival which took place at a specific point in the calendar. Such sacred truces were of two types. Some were confined to a single city or territory, corresponding to a local festival: these are best attested at Sparta and Argos in the Peloponnese. Some festivals, however, had as their catchment area a region or even the whole Greek world (and as such were Panhellenic, applying to 'all the Greeks'), and in these cases the sacred truce applied more broadly. The best attested cases of the latter truces were those accompanying the Panhellenic festivals of Olympia, Delphi, Nemea, the Isthmus and Eleusis. At an intermediate level between these seem to be the regional sacred truces, an example of which is the mysterious 'Samian Truce' in Triphylia in the western Peloponnese; it was apparently announced by the city of Makistos, of which little is known.[2] The usual terms for a sacred truce were the same as for ordinary truces, i.e. *ekekheiria* (literally 'restraining hands') and *spondai* ('libations'). A related term is *hieromenia* ('sacred month'), which may be broader in scope. Sacred truces covered the time of the festival and sometimes the period around it, which may indeed be a month. In the case of the Panhellenic festivals, the time covered could be longer, including the whole period taken to spread word of the imminent festival, which could be several months (see below).

Two general patterns seem to emerge. Firstly, local sacred truces sometimes prevented cities in the region from participating in military campaigns, though this was far from being a general rule. This may have been in part because there was a specific incompatibility between war and religion, but it is also because worshipping the gods was an activity which precluded all other activities for that period, including warfare. Secondly, Panhellenic sacred truces did not prevent general combat, and were designed mainly to protect people travelling to and from festivals. There was, however, a tendency to treat the Panhellenic sanctuaries themselves and the cities who administered them as sacrosanct, especially during the periods of the festivals. Even here, there was considerable discretion allowed.

Sacred truces of this sort have probably existed in many cultures. Tacitus, the Roman historian, describes a type of truce in his account of the Germanic Suebi; in this case the truce was observed when the chariot of the goddess Nerthus (mother Earth) was led around by a priest from one territory to another.[3] In Islam, the Hajj-pilgrimage is supposed to be a time of sacred truce, apparently based on pre-Islamic tradition; indeed, the Quran lays down a period of four 'sacred months' (months one and seven, and eleven and twelve, the last being the month of the Hajj).[4] The 'Truce of God' in Medieval Europe has some similarities, being a period of peace correlated with festivals. Strikingly, however, no such sacred truces are known from the Ancient Near East; the closest approximation to these, perhaps, is the information that the Hittite King Mursili II (around 1300 BC) interrupted a campaign against the polity of Kalasma (probably in north-west Turkey) early in the twentieth year of his reign so that he could return to the Hittite capital and celebrate the *purulli* festival of the goddess Lelwani there (cf. the behaviour of the Amyclaeans mentioned below). Whether this festival was fixed in the Hittite calendar, however, is not certain.[5] Analogous practices have been documented in tribal cultures elsewhere in the world: in his study of the Maring tribe of New Guinea, the anthropologist Roy Rappaport observed alternation between periods of warfare and sacred truces, during which the tribesmen were expected to pay their obligations to gods and ancestors,[6] and Fortes describes an obligatory truce imposed during the festival cycle among the Tallensi of Ghana.[7]

Truces and War

In Greece, a religious festival was often conceived of as a time of celebration and worship, during which conflict ceased and the community came together in harmony. In the preface to his account of the death of Socrates in the *Phaedo*, Plato reports that at Athens during the *hieromenia*, relating to the regular sacred embassy (*theoria*) to the island of Delos for Apollo, executions were suspended.[8] In epigraphic sources relating to festivals in some sources from the Hellenistic period, the word *ekekheiria* seems to refer specifically to the suspension of judicial activity.[9] In religious terms, one might say that violence is impure and offensive to the gods (thus, executions during the Delian festival might offend Apolline purity). Just as all forms of conflict between different groups within the community were banned, so by extension there may have been a sense that festivals precluded hostilities between the community and external enemies. Yet this last factor is not an absolute: festivals could celebrate military victories as well, and serve as a focus for pride in glorious martial victories.[10] A second reason that festivals precluded warfare is that they obliged people to devote themselves to religious activities for their duration. There may be a sense that if the gods were not sufficiently cultivated, military endeavours would fail anyway. These two factors (harmony-over-conflict, and religious-obligation-trumps-military-obligation) may of course overlap, and it is not always easy to distinguish one from the other (see below on the Hyakinthia).

Observance of religious festivals affected warfare because in Greece, as in many cultures, these celebrations were embedded in the calendar, usually identified with a specific month (which would often take its name from the festival), and thus be associated with a particular time of year. All Greek states had calendars which were in principle 'lunar-solar', i.e. based on the cycle of twelve lunar months, which was periodically adjusted to match the solar year, usually by adding an 'intercalary' month every few years. Considerable variation, however, is apparent in the calendars of individual Greek states, both in the terms of the names of months and in so far as they were never synchronized throughout the Greek world: different states inserted intercalary months at different times of the year, and the day when the month began varied as well. This underlying flexibility in the calendar meant there was some flexibility in the timing of festivals. Thus, in 419 BC, the Argives seem to have postponed their month of Karneios by inserting days into the previous month. And in 417 BC, the Spartans are said to have postponed the Gymnopaidiai festival (see below), which almost certainly also involved postponing the month in which it was celebrated.[11]

In Xenophon's account of the events of 387 BC, Agesipolis criticized the Argives because they 'pleaded the sacred months' whenever the Spartans invaded, which might mean bringing forward a sacred month. There is a strong probability that both postponements and advancements of festivals and months were not uncommon. Alexander the Great did something similar just before the Battle of the Granicus, when he inserted a second month of Artemisios to avoid conflict taking place during the ill-omened month of Daisios.[12] A willingness to move a month should not be assumed to imply a degree of cynicism towards religion and its observances: the important issue was that the festival happen in the month of the right name; exactly when in the seasons the festival happened was unimportant.[13]

Military conflict was mainly affected by festival truces in that observation of a local sacred truce was a reason for the citizens of that place not to engage in military engagements. There was no expectation that such a local truce would protect the inhabitants against external attack, although it was normal to protest about such attacks if they occurred. Thus, the Plataeans protested that they had been attacked by the Thebans during a *hieromenia* in the spring of 431 BC. Another accusation of truce-breaking occurred around 229–224 BC: Lyciscus, an Acarnanian envoy, accused the Aetolians of various acts of sacrilege, among them that Lattabos and Nicostratus violated the truce (*paraspondeô*) during the time of the peace of the Pamboiotia festival.[14] A few years later, in the summer of 428 BC, the Athenians planned to attack Mytilene while the Mytilenaeans were celebrating their local festival for Apollo Maloeis outside the walls of their city, but the Athenians' plan was frustrated when the Mytileneans learned of it and did not go outside their city to celebrate it.[15] Polyaenus' *Strategemata* (second century AD) mentions several examples of military actions which succeeded because the soldiers on the opposing side were preoccupied with a festival; for example, Aristomenes of Messenia and a friend, impersonating the Dioskouroi, attacked the Spartans at a drunken festival for the Dioskouroi,[16] and in 212 BC, the Roman general Marcellus captured Syracuse during a three-day festival of Artemis.[17] The only recorded case where the observance of a local festival may have given pause to a potential attacker is Agesipolis' attack on Argos in 387 BC;[18] the anomaly surely suggests, however, that this was not a local festival, but the Nemean Games (see below).

Surviving Evidence

As far as can be ascertained, the tendency for local truces to be observed was at its strongest in the Peloponnese. Most of the evidence relates to Sparta; isolated cases in Phlius and Mantineia are also known. In 394 BC at the Battle of Coronea, the Phliasians declined to fight alongside the Spartans because of an *ekekheiria* (sacred truce); similarly, the Spartans accused the Mantineians of not having fought alongside them because of an *ekekheiria*.[19] For Sparta, there is evidence for truces relating to three major festivals – the Hyakinthia, Gymnopaidiai and Karneia – all celebrated in honour of Apollo. The Hyakinthia in the month of Hyakinthios (early summer) coincided with the Isthmian festival in 390 BC, but general coincidence cannot be inferred in this or analogous cases, because different city-states might have inserted intercalary months at different times. The Gymnopaidiai was held in late summer, probably in the month before the month of Karneios. Most importantly, the Karneia festival was held from the seventh to the fifteenth days of Karneios, which was probably the month in which the

autumn equinox occurred.[20] This festival is described by Thucydides as
hieromenia Dorieusi ('the sacred month for the Dorians'),[21] and was of central
importance to Sparta.[22] Apparently it coincided, quite unusually, with the
Olympic Games in 480 BC.

Several incidents are recorded involving the Karneia, with the first case
involving the Battle of Marathon in 490 BC. According to Herodotus, the
Spartans, having been warned by Pheidippides of the imminent arrival of
the Persians, refused to go to war, declaring that it was against their *nomos*
(custom) to begin a campaign on the ninth of the month if the moon was not
full.[23] Herodotus does not mention the Karneia or any other festival here,
but it seems likely that this was the context, since the Spartans respected the
Karneian truce more than any other. A general principle about not going to
war on the ninth or if the moon was not full is otherwise not known.[24]

Secondly, in the build-up to the Battle of Thermopylae, the Spartans
refused to leave their country during the Karneia, and the rest of the allies
also declined because they were celebrating the Olympic Games,[25] which
in this case seems to have coincided with the Karneia. (Possibly some of
the other Dorians were celebrating the Karneia as well, but Herodotus does
not say that.) Leonidas and 300 Spartiatai were allowed by the Spartans to
march to Thermopylae, in order to discourage other Greeks from taking
the Persian side. Later, Herodotus comments that even after the Battle of
Thermopylae, at a time when the Greeks were seeking to make a stand at the
Isthmus, a number of Peloponnesian peoples failed to show up, even though
the Olympic and Karneian festivals were over.[26]

The next recorded incident was during the Peloponnesian War in 419 BC,
when, according to Thucydides, King Agis of Sparta initially planned an
expedition in the month before Karneios,[27] but when he reached the border,
the offerings for crossing (*diabateria*) proved unfavourable, so he decided to
spend the month of Karneios in Sparta, and told the allies that their campaign
would start in the month after Karneios. This is the passage where Thucydides
describes Karneios as the '*hieromenia* for the Dorians'. Meanwhile, the Argives
invaded Epidaurus just before the start of Karneios on the 27th of the preceding
month (in Greek terms the 'fourth of the waning third of the month': *tetras
phthinontos*), claiming that every day of their subsequent campaign was the
27th, in order to postpone the month of Karneios.[28] Epidaurus called on its
allies for military assistance, but some of them excused themselves precisely
on the grounds that the month was Karneios. Epidaurus also had a month
Karneios, but that was apparently not an issue.[29]

There is another Karneia-related issue in 418 BC, according to
Thucydides.[30] After the Battle of Mantineia, where Sparta and its allies had

defeated the Argives, Athenians and their allies, the Spartans went home at once to celebrate the Karneia. Meanwhile, Epidaurus was attacked by the Argives, Eleans and Athenians, who had arrived too late for the battle. The Karneia at Argos has sometimes been thought to be the festival implied in Xenophon's account of Agesipolis' invasion of Argos via Nemea in 387 BC,[31] when the Argives demanded that the Spartans not invade because of a truce (*spondai*): the view that this festival was the Nemean Games is to be preferred.[32]

In three cases, the celebration of the Hyakinthia earlier in the year is said to have interrupted warfare. According to Pausanias,[33] a truce of forty days was declared during the Second Messenian War (seventh century BC) so that the Spartans could return to their homeland to celebrate the Hyakinthia. Given that there was probably no written account of this before the third century BC, this information cannot be regarded as an historical record, but it tells us the sort of thing that was believed to have happened.

Herodotus reports that in the summer of 479 BC, the Athenians on Salamis sent messengers to Sparta urging them to support them.[34] The Spartans were at that time celebrating the Hyakinthia and finishing the fortification of the Isthmus, and put off answering the Athenians for ten days. Eventually, the Athenian messengers lost patience and criticized the Spartans because 'you celebrate the Hyakinthia and play', whereupon they were told that the Spartans had that very morning sent off a large army. Thus in the end, the festival functioned as a sort of decoy, concealing the Spartans' true actions from the visitors. In any case, it is clear that in this instance celebration of the festival was not a bar to action.

In 390 BC, according to Xenophon,[35] King Agesilaus led an army to the Isthmus during the month when the Isthmian festival took place, driving off the Argives and allowing some Corinthian exiles to sacrifice there. At some point during this, the Amyclaeans (those of the Spartan village of Amyclae) decided to return to Sparta to celebrate the Hyakinthia and sing the paean (hymn); Xenophon writes that this was their usual practice, as might be expected, since the cult of Hyakinthos was in Amyclae.[36] A group of horsemen escorted them some of the way, but on the way back to the Isthmus they suffered heavy casualties. Xenophon says that Agesilaus himself went home to sing the paean as an ordinary member of the chorus, something which is not mentioned in the *Hellenica*, though not incompatible with it.[37] Celebrating the Hyakinthia was thus a religious obligation for the Spartans, especially for the Amyclaeans, but none of these sources mention a sacred truce.

Only one incident related to the Gymnopaidiai festival is recorded: according to Thucydides,[38] in 417 BC, the Argive *dêmos* attacked the oligarchs, having waited for the time of the Gymnopaidiai, during which celebration they anticipated that the Spartans would not want to intervene. Eventually, the Spartans decided to 'postpone' (*anaballô*) the Gymnopaidiai (and presumably the month it was in as well), and they marched out to assist; learning of the defeat of the oligarchs, however, they returned. Again, no sacred truce is mentioned, and this may have been simply a matter of religious obligation. On the basis of this, it seems that the Karneia was taken more seriously, at least by the Spartans, than the Hyakinthia (which was strictly observed only by the men of Amyclae in Sparta) or the Gymnopaidiai (which could be postponed).[39]

The Interstate Dimension: Major Festivals and their Proclamation

Panhellenic sanctuaries proclaimed truces that were intended to cover the whole of the Greek world, and sent out delegates with the double function of proclaiming the truce and inviting worshippers to the imminent festival. Such truces are attested for all four Panhellenic festivals, as well as the Great Mysteries at Eleusis. Other major sanctuaries probably proclaimed Panhellenic or regional truces as well, though little evidence has survived for it, and it was probably not recorded at all in many cases.[40] In the Hellenistic period, truces were proclaimed by a number of cities aiming to establish new festivals, often in the context of a campaign to have themselves recognized as deserving the privilege of 'inviolability' (*asylia*) on the basis of their religious and cultural status in the wider Greek world;[41] some of these festivals, and their associated truces, were probably short lived, but the principle of civic 'inviolability' itself can be thought of as amounting to a sort of truce between the individual city and all other states that would seek to attack it.[42]

At some major sanctuaries, the time of the festival together with the periods immediately before and afterwards was known as the *hieromenia*, which seems despite the name (sacred month) to have often been longer than a single month. Where it existed, the *hieromenia* was probably longer than the *ekekheiria*, which came into operation only at the point when the truce-bearers reached each individual city, as suggested by Thucydides' account of the Lepreon incident.[43]

Scholars generally agree that, in practical terms, these truces were not intended to generate a period of interstate peace, since nothing like that actually happened. Their main effect was to facilitate the safe passage of pilgrims and athletes, as well as that of delegates announcing the truce. Similar protection is found in non-sacred treaties, such as the Peace of Nicias between Athens and Sparta and their allies in 421 BC, which, as reported by Thucydides, guaranteed access of various groups to sanctuaries.[44] The hypothesis that sacred truces applied mainly to those in transit is confirmed by the fact that states made formal complaints when their citizens were attacked or otherwise obstructed when in transit during a sacred truce. In any case, the truce was a bilateral agreement between the city organizing the festival and each individual participating state, not between all the participating states.

It is possible that truces were more generally effective in the territory immediately adjacent to the sanctuary itself, rather like local festival truces. During the period of the festival, even groups that were at war might engage in cultic activity together. This happened at the Isthmian Games of 412 BC, for example, when Corinth insisted on carrying out its responsibilities *à propos* of the festival, and even sacred delegates from Athens, with which it was at war, took part. In the same way, literary texts suggest a sense that the Panhellenic festivals were occasions of peace and fellow feeling between participants. Thus, Aristophanes' character Lysistrata complains that Athens and Sparta fight each other even though, 'You two sprinkle altars from the same cup like kinsmen, at Olympia, at Thermopylae, at Pytho – how many other places could I mention if I had to extend the list.'[45] This idea of the territory of the sanctuary as peaceful was taken one step further in the case of Elis, which was often said to be permanently inviolable and to enjoy a perpetual peace, a claim that may go back to the local intellectual Hippias (late fifth century BC).[46]

Since these festivals were notionally 'Panhellenic', it would be expected that the truce would be extended to all Greek cities, at least in principle. Military conflict, however, may have made that impracticable or undesirable. Information about what actually happened is in short supply, but it may be noted that Thucydides, describing the Isthmia of 412 BC, specifies that the Athenians attended 'because they had been invited', a detail which suggests that the invitation (which usually accompanied the announcement truce) was not a given.[47] Related to this is the possibility that the state controlling a sanctuary would reject delegates from another state, whether they had been included in the official truce and formally invited or not. The only case known from the Classical period is the Spartans' exclusion from the Olympics of 420 BC because they had failed to pay the fine imposed in the case of Lepreon. Something similar, however, is suggested by Aelius Aristides,[48] when he mentions an unknown occasion when the Athenians had not been invited to the Isthmian Games, and their delegation was refused admission; in response, the Athenians sent both soldiers and *theoroi* to the Corinthian border in order to guarantee that they would be admitted, and the Corinthians came to Eleusis to offer a truce, at which point the Athenians sent their troops home.[49]

Although in practice these truces did not prevent general conflict, in theory the *hieromenia* may have been meant to apply generally. Thus, at Delphi, the *hieromenia* was said to be 'equal for all', which may mean all Greeks (see below). According to Pindar, the *hieromenia* of Nemea (i.e. the Nemean Games) was also celebrated in Aegina, which suggests that it was imagined as extending broadly, perhaps over the whole of Greece. Worth bearing in mind also, as noted above, is that Thucydides described the Karneia as a '*hieromenia* for the Dorians', as if its effect transcended any one Dorian state.

Evidence of Different Sanctuaries

Practice and terminology predictably varied from sanctuary to sanctuary and from period to period. For the fifth and fourth centuries BC, the surviving evidence relates to Olympia, Delphi, Eleusis and Nemea. At Olympia, the truce, according to tradition, was supposed to go back to an early king of Elis, Iphitus, who inscribed it on a disc which was still on display at Olympia.[50] Thucydides refers to the truce *à propos* of the Lepreon episode,[51] and other early sources for its announcement include a recently discovered bronze disc with a regulation concerning the announcement of the festival and the Sacred Law from Selinous in Sicily, which correlates the truce with the local Kotytia festival.[52] There is no direct evidence for the length. A *hieromenia* of at least four months is referred to by the imperial writer Lucian of Samosata, although the context is humorous (Zeus explains that executing the philosophers was illegitimate during that period).[53] One early document from Olympia refers to an 'Olympic Month',[54] which seems to be a reference to a *hieromenia*. The minimum length of the truce itself must have been the two lunar months immediately before and after the full moon when the festival took place, and probably at least three months, since the athletes seem to have been required to have been present at Olympia for a period of training before the contests.[55]

At Delphi, an inscription from the fourth century BC refers to a Delphic *hieromenia*, apparently a year in length, 'equal for all', and also a truce.[56] This *hieromenia* at least partly coincided with the mission of the festival announcers, who left six months before the festival, but it carried on longer, extending six months afterwards. (Sixth months may seem a long time for the festival's announcers to undertake their role, but cases are known from the Hellenistic period when announcers must have started out the year before the festival took place.)[57] The qualification 'equal for all' is ambiguous in this context: it could refer to members of the Delphic Amphiktiony, but it could also mean 'all Greeks'.[58]

For Eleusis, the Eleusinian truce was proclaimed by messengers called *spondophoroi* ('libation carriers'), who are first attested in a mid-fourth-century BC law.[59] The journey of the Eleusinian *spondophoroi* may have been symbolized iconographically by the Eleusinian hero and prince Triptolemos, who is often depicted in Athenian vase scenes making libations. For example, an Athenian red-figure calyx-krater dating to about 475–425 BC is typical of many such vase scenes. Triptolemos is depicted enthroned on a bewingéd chariot: for he must travel throughout the Greek world. He holds a libation bowl (*phialê*) into which Demeter, goddess of the Mysteries, pours a libation. This symbolizes the libation which would have been poured by the *spondophoroi* and the state officials of a city accepting the announcement of the Eleusinian sacred truce (Figure 5.1).[60]

Figure 5.1: Triptomemos, prince of Eleusis, wearing a wreath and holding a sceptre of authority in his left hand, sits on a throne mounted on a chariot with bewingéd serpents on its wheels, holding in his right hand a wide libation bowl (*phialê*) into which the goddess Demeter pours wine; Athenian red-figure calyx-krater by the Niobid Painter, dating to about 475–425 BC; Ferrara, Museo Nazionale di Spina: T313. (*Courtesy of Alamy*)

An Athenian honorary decree from the later third century BC reveals that at that time the *spondophoroi* proclaimed truces for three major Athenian festivals, the Eleusinia, the Panathenaia and the Mysteries,[61] and perhaps this was the practice earlier as well. An Athenian sacred law from around 470–460 BC indicates that the truces (*spondai*) of the Greater and Lesser Mysteries were about fifty-five days long each: that for the Greater Mysteries, held in the month Boedromion, extended from the middle of Metageitnion, the previous month, until the 10th of Pyanopsion, the following month; that for the Lesser Mysteries, held in the month of Anthesterion, extended from the middle of the preceding month of Gamelion until the 10th of the following month of Elaphebolion. It identifies their scope as 'the cities that use the sanctuary',[62] which strongly suggests that these truces were widely proclaimed. It may well be that the Eleusinian truce goes back to the time of the tyrant Pisistratus in the sixth century BC.[63]

Nemea, too, had a sacred month: in his victory ode for Aristocleidas of Aegina, apparently performed on the island in 475 BC, Pindar invited the Muse to come to Aegina during the *hieromenia* of Nemea.[64] This may imply that Aegina was within the penumbra of the *hieromenia* associated with the Nemean festival in honour of Poseidon, and also that the performance took place during the period, though perhaps not in the same year.[65]

Infringements of Truces

Despite the existence of truces, several cases are known where people were attacked, robbed or kidnapped either announcing truces or on their way to the festivals. *Spondophoroi* announcing the Eleusinian Mysteries in Aetolia were arrested by the people of Trichoneia in 367/366 BC, after the Aetolians as a whole had accepted the truce.[66] The Athenians subsequently appealed to the *Koinon* ('League') of the Aetolians to secure their release.[67] In 348 BC, Phrynon, an Athenian citizen from Rhamnous, was attacked by the soldiers of Philip of Macedon on his way to Olympia (either to watch the contests or to take part);[68] he had to ransom himself, and later demanded that Philip compensate him for the ransom, which makes some sense since, as Dillon points out, Philip must have accepted the Olympic Truce, though it is still not clear why Philip specifically was involved.[69] Competitors bound for the Nemean Games at Argos in 235 BC were captured and enslaved by Aratus of Sicyon, commander of the Achaean League. Aratus was at this time holding his own Nemean Games at Kleonai.[70] Finally, a Delphic decree of 192 BC reveals that two Delphians announcing the Pythia in the Black Sea area had to be ransomed by the city of Tauric Chersonesos, presumably after they had been captured by pirates.[71]

General Peace

For a general peace during the Panhellenic truces, there is, as noted above, little evidence. Perhaps the only case is Herodotus' account of the events of 480 BC,[72] where the (non-Dorian?) Greek allies are said to have delayed going to fight at Thermopylae because of the Olympic contests, just as the Spartans (and other Dorians?) delayed because of the Karneia. On the face of it, this means that the reason or pretext of the allies for refusing to fight was that participating in the Olympic festival came first, and that this ruled out fighting the Persians. That might be either because the truce forbad any fighting or that one cannot do two things at once. Elsewhere, the Panhellenic sanctuaries tend to be a focus for resistance to Persia, so it seems odd that the duty of participating in the greatest Panhellenic festival could be a deterrent to fighting a foreign enemy that threatened the existence of Greece.

Usually, however, undertaking military activity during the period of the Olympic and other common festivals seems to have had no consequences.[73] A well-known example is Thucydides' account of the Olympics of 428 BC,[74] when the Mytileneans, present at Olympia to plot future strategy while the Athenians were besieging their city, did not complain that their city was besieged during the truce. Another is the Isthmian festival of 412 BC, when the Spartans were perfectly happy to initiate a revolt in Chios, an action hostile to Athens (see below).[75]

Attacks on sacred sanctuaries during festivals were not unknown. According to Xenophon,[76] in 390 BC, the Spartan King Agesilaus invaded the Isthmus during the Isthmian games; finding the Argives sacrificing to Poseidon, 'as if Corinth were Argos' (i.e. without using local *proxenoi* [representatives for foreigners] to carry out the sacrifice for them?), the Spartans drove them off and performed the sacrifice themselves, which resulted in a double Isthmian Games. Similarly, around 225 BC, Cleomenes III of Sparta seized Argos during the Nemean Games.[77] But above all there was the famous 'Anolympiad' ('no-Olympic festival') of 364 BC, when the contests coincided with war between Elis and Arcadia and their respective allies. Xenophon describes how the Arcadians occupied Olympia and commenced celebrating the festival with the assistance of the men of the town of Pisa (which was said to have been responsible for organizing the games in the distant past before Elis took over).[78] In Xenophon's narrative, the Eleans themselves, together with their Achaean allies, attacked the Arcadians and Pisatans, supported by Argive and Athenian allies, in the middle of the first day of competitions.[79] A ferocious battle took place in which the Eleans gained the upper hand, but were put under pressure by the Arcadians who were raining down projectiles from the roofs of buildings. After the Eleans withdrew, the Arcadians converted their festival-pavilions into a stockade, which was enough to deter the Eleans from a second day of fighting. The festival and its contests were abandoned.

It was not, however, always as chaotic as this. In two cases, there may be evidence that sanctuary authorities attempted to police infringements of the truce. One case here is Thucydides' account of the dispute between Elis and Sparta over Phyrkos and Lepreon in Triphylia in 420 BC.[80] An Olympic court fined Sparta because these attacks were alleged to have taken place during the truce for the Olympic contests, and when the Spartans refused to pay the fine, they were banned from future celebrations of the festival. When Lichas of Sparta tried to compete in the Olympic contests as a Theban, he was whipped on the order of the Elean authorities. The Spartans claimed the truce had not yet been announced in Sparta when the attack took place. Everything here is uncertain. Possibly, as Paradiso and Roy have argued,[81] the issue was not the truce at all but the Olympic *hieromenia*, which started earlier. At any rate, it is clear that this may have been a special case because Spartan aggression threatened Elis itself, and Elis may have thought of itself as being specially protected by the truce.

Another possible case of truce-enforcement was provided by a relatively recently discovered document from Olympia in which some magistrates of Olympia acted as arbitrators between other states, lifting a previous judgment that had been made against Boeotia and Thessaly.[82] This was interpreted by Siewert as referring to the Medising (pro-Persian) activities of these states, and he took it as evidence that the Olympic Truce had a wider force.[83] This text, however, can be explained in other ways; Minon herself, the editor of the inscription, suggests that the magistrates of Olympia may have functioned as international arbiters, rather like the Delphic Amphictyony.[84]

Two other cases may illustrate the complexity of attitudes towards Panhellenic truces. In 387 BC, Agesipolis decided to invade the territory of Argos, which in response claimed that there was a truce, though for which festival is not stated in Xenophon's account.[85] Agesipolis then consulted the oracular centres of Delphi and Olympia whether his invasion was legitimate, claiming that 'it was not when the appointed time came, but when the Lacedaemonians were about to invade their territory, that they pleaded the sacred months (*hypepheron tous menas*)'. Presumably he wanted to show the Greek world that the Spartans had divine authority on their side. Zeus at Olympia agreed, and then Agesipolis asked Delphic Apollo whether he agreed with his father, and Apollo naturally did so.[86] Despite the Argives then sending out heralds, the Spartans invaded anyway. Then while the latter were having dinner, there was an earthquake, and they sang the paean to Poseidon (apparently a paean regularly sung when there was a earthquake); such seismic activity was probably interpreted as a signal of divine displeasure with the invasion. Xenophon notes that on an earlier occasion when there was an earthquake on a campaign, the Spartans had withdrawn.[87] Subsequent omens were also bad.

What was the identity of the festival which the Argives claimed a truce for? Some have suggested the Argive Karneia,[88] but Parker favoured the view that it was the Nemean Games.[89] The problem with it being the Argive Karneia is that it is difficult to understand why Agesipolis needed to justify his behaviour in the way he did if this was a local festival, unless, perhaps, the Spartans felt a special respect for the Karneia because it was common to all Dorians. (There is also the problem that one might have thought that if this was the time of the Karneia in Argos, it would be the Karneia in Sparta as well, in which case the Spartans would themselves be reluctant to fight; but perhaps there was a discrepancy between the Argive and Spartan calendars.) If it was the Nemean Games, then, following the principle set out earlier above, the territory of Argos would be specially protected by the truce, and Xenophon's narrative indicates the complex attitude that the Spartans had towards it: they would break the truce, but only after securing the consent of the gods.

A similarly complex picture emerges from Thucydides' narrative of the events at the Isthmian Games of 412 BC.[90] Agis decided to set sail to support the imminent revolt of Chios and wanted the Corinthians to take part, but the Corinthians insisted on celebrating the Isthmia; the Spartans consented so as 'not to break the truce' (*me luein tas spondas*), and were willing to sail off on their own, but the Corinthians insisted that they stay until after the festival. This created a delay, allowing the Athenians to find out more information; the Athenians in fact sent a delegation to the festival ('since they had been invited'), where they heard rumours about the Chian revolt. Here, then, the Corinthians, who had a special responsibility for the festival, insisted on observing the truce, while the Spartans themselves were willing to ignore it, though there was no fighting in the territory of the sanctuary itself.

Conclusion

Sacred truces announced by *spondophoroi* aimed to allow the safe passage of those attending religious festivals. These were generally observed, but occasionally there were transgressions. Sacred truces in no way meant that warfare ceased throughout the Greek world; rather, conflicts went on unaffected. For the purpose of a truce was to protect worshippers travelling to and from sacred sites. Sparta's annoyance and exasperation at the Argive 'manipulation' of their calendar months, and hence sacred truces, led them to seek the intervention of oracular centres to provide divine support for their contention that the Argives were organizing their calendar and sacred truces in order to keep Spartan invasions at bay. Nevertheless, the concept of the sacred truce was intrinsic to the celebration of festivals, and in a sense, as revealed in the Peace of Nikias, held that all Greeks had the right to travel to sanctuaries for purposes of worship, a right that all the states which accepted sacred truces announced by *spondophoroi* were expected to adhere to. The relatively few incidents in which *spondophoroi* and worshippers were attacked indicate that the concept was an accepted one, and adhered to. Attacks on festival sites as festivals were being celebrated at them were few, and reflect the fact that control of sanctuaries was considered so important by those contesting their jurisdiction. Truces aimed to guarantee that Greeks could worship the gods at festivals and sacred places, and in this they generally succeeded, so that the gods received their due worship, honours and gifts.

Notes

1. I would like to thank J.D. Morgan for assistance and advice in writing this piece.
2. Strabo 8.3.13; Tausend, 1992, 19–21; Mylonopoulos, 2006, 137–40.
3. Tac. *Germ.* 40, cf. 44.3.
4. Quran 9.36.
5. *Annals of Mursili* 2 (KBo2.5iii 13–26); Goetze, 1933, 188–90, Del Monte, 1993, 129; this was pointed out in Goodman and Holladay, 1986, 151 n.2.
6. Rappaport, 1968, 151–52.
7. Fortes, 1987, 48, 99–100.
8. Plat. *Phaedo* 58b.
9. Robert, 1937, 177–79: *Ekekheiria* in inscriptions often refers to a judicial truce; Roman period: Ziegler, 1985; Chaniotis in *ThesCRA* vii.17–18, 35 n.334. The practice is also referred to in the Greek novel: see Achilles Tatius 7.12.13; Chariton 5.3.11 and 6.1.4 (referring to Babylon), and made into a joke by Luc. *Icar.* 33 (see n.53 below).
10. Pritchett, 1979, 154–209.
11. See Pritchett, 1999, 1.
12. Plut. *Alex.* 16.2; Edmunds, 1979.
13. Contrast, however, Ar. *Clouds* 615–26: it was important that a festival for a god be held on the right day of a lunar month.
14. Plataea: Thuc. 3.56.2; Lyciscus: Polyb. 9.34.11.
15. Thuc. 3.3.
16. Polyaen. *Strat.* 2.31.3. Cf. Paus. 4.27.1–3, where the same tale is told of two other Messenians named Gonippus and Panormus.
17. Polyaen. *Strat.* 8.11. Cf. Polyb. 8.37; Livy 25.23.13; Front. *Strat.* 3.3.2; Plut. *Marc.* 18.3.
18. Xen. *Hell.* 4.7.2.

19. Phlius: Xen. *Hell.* 4.2.16; Mantineia: Xen. *Hell.* 5.2.2.
20. See Morgan and Iverson, forthcoming.
21. Thuc. 5.54.2.
22. Richer, 2012, 455.
23. Hdt. 6.106. See Popp, 1957, 75–87. The idea that the full moon could be on the 9th in a lunar-solar calendar seems counter-intuitive, but this shows how little is known about ancient calendars: see Dunn, 1998.
24. An Athenian principle that an army is not led out before the 7th is known from Hesychius and the Suda: see Pritchett, 1971, 117. The source seems to be Callimachus *SH* 277: Robertson, 2002, 36, or possibly Istros the Callimachean (see *SH* 277).
25. Hdt. 7.206, 8.72.
26. Hdt. 8.72.
27. Thuc. 5.54.1–2.
28. For another case of calendar manipulation in Argos from around the same time, see Kritzas, 2006, 433–34 (celebrating two months simultaneously).
29. As the Epidaurian Karneios, see Trümpy, 1997, 141.
30. Thuc. 5.75.4–6.
31. Xen. *Hell.* 4.7.2, 5.
32. The festival of Heracles in Syracuse which prevented the Syracusans pressing their advantage against the Athenians, mentioned in Thuc. 7.73.2, was also in the month of Karneios, to judge from Plut. *Nic.* 28.
33. Paus. 4.19.4.
34. Hdt. 9.7–11.
35. Xen. *Hell.* 4.5.1–2.
36. Xen. *Hell.* 4.5.11. On the Hyakinthia, see Richer, 2004. The importance of the Hyakinthia is shown also by the stipulation in the Peace of Nikias that the renewal of the treaty in Sparta shall take place at the Hyakinthia, witnessed by the Athenians, just as in Athens it shall take place at the Dionysia, witnessed by the Spartans (Thuc. 5.23.4–5).
37. Xen. *Ages.* 2.17. As a child, Agesilaus sang in a chorus at the Gymnopaidiai, according to Plut. *Mor.* 208d–e.
38. Thuc. 5.82.2.
39. See Goodman and Holladay, 1986, 159.
40. See Rutherford, 2013, 72–76.
41. See Rutherford, 2013, 76–81. An *ekekheiria* is mentioned in acceptance decrees for Cos, Magnesia on the Maeander, Cyzicus and the Ptoion: Cos: e.g. Rigsby, 1996, no.16.6; Magnesia: e.g. Rigsby, no.73.13; Cyzicus: e.g. Rigsby, no.168.6; Ptoion: e.g. Rigsby, no.3.10.
42. For asylia, see Rigsby, 1996, 1–29.
43. Thuc. 5.49.
44. Thuc. 5.18.1; Hornblower and Morgan, 2007, 30–35; Lämmer, 1982–1983.
45. Ar. *Lys.* 1129–35; see Rutherford, 2013, 266.
46. See Rigsby, 1996, 41–44; Strabo 8.3.33.
47. Parker, 1983, 156 n.61.
48. Arist. *Panath.* 372 (cf. schol. Dem. 3.100c in Dilts, 1983).
49. For Hellenistic parallels, see Rutherford, 2013, 252–53.
50. See for example, Bollansee, 1999.
51. Thuc. 5.49.

52. See Rutherford, 2013, 88–90. For the disc, see Siewert, 2002; for the sacred law from Selinous, see Jameson, Jordan and Kotansky, 1993, column A, 7–8; Robertson, 2010, 69–82 views the Kotytia as a local version of the Kronia festival, a characteristic of which was the suspension of social norms; Roberston, 2010, 81 sees the Olympic Truce as embodying the spirit of the Kronia: 'It is a means of showing how the new dispensation succeeds the old.'

53. Luc. *Icar.* 33: 'It is the *hieromenia*, as you know, over the next four months, and I have already sent round an announcement of the truce.'

54. Minon, 2007, n.7, 2.

55. See Robertson, 2010, 65–66.

56. *CID* 4.1, 44; see Rutherford, 2013, 91.

57. See Rutherford, 2013, 78.

58. Rougemont, 1973, 99, preferred to see the *hieromenia* as longer than the truce, but also relatively local, so that he preferred the amphictyonic interpretation.

59. *Agora* 16.56 (Clinton, 1994, 138, n.26); see Rutherford, 2013, 92.

60. *ARV²* 602.24 (Ferrara, Museo Nazionale di Spina, T313). See Hayashi, 1992, and for this vase: 144 no. 67.

61. *I.Gonnoi* 2.109 (*IG* ii³ 1145).

62. *IG* i³ 6B.6–47.

63. Clinton, 1994, 172–73.

64. Pin. *Nem.* 3.2.

65. See Pfeijffer, 1999, 245.

66. See Rhodes and Osborne, 2003, n.35.

67. 'Since the Aetolians of the *koinon* have accepted the truce of the Mysteries of Eleusinian Demeter and Kore, but those of the Eumolpidae and Kerykes announcing the truce, Promakhos and Epigenes, have been imprisoned by the Trichonians contrary to the common laws of the Greeks, the council shall forthwith choose heralds from all the Athenians who upon arrival at the *Koinon* of the Aetolians, shall demand the release of the men.'

68. Aeschin. 2.12; hypoth. 2, 3 to Dem. 19 (Dilts, 1986); Dillon, 1995; Rougemont, 1973, 83.

69. Dillon, 1995.

70. Plut. *Arat.* 28.4.

71. Frei-Stolba and Bielman, 1994, 162–65, n.45. For the safety of *spondophoroi*, and of pilgrims travelling to sacred sites, see Dillon, 1997, 27–59.

72. Hdt. 7.206.

73. Hornblower and Morgan, 2007, 31–33; Lämmer, 1982–1983, 44.

74. Thuc. 3.8–14.

75. A more problematic example is Thucydides' account of the expulsion of the Delians in 422 BC (Lämmer, 1982–1983, 45). Thucydides says this happened ἐν τῇ ἐκεχειρίᾳ. The transmitted text of the preceding sentence is τοῦ δ' ἐπιγιγνομένου θέρους αἱ μὲν ἐνιαύσιοι σπονδαὶ διελέλυντο μέχρι Πυθίων (literally: 'During the next summer the year-long truce came to an end until the Pythia'). The drawing up of the year-long truce was previously described in Thuc. 4.117–18. Something may well be missed out before μέχρι Πυθίων, giving a sense like 'and a new one was made to last until the Pythia' (see Gomme 1970 and Hornblower's 1996 commentaries on this passage). It is not clear what the relation is between the year truce, the Pythia and the Pythian truce (see Gomme), nor when in this sequence the expulsion of the Delians happened. But it is at least possible that the Athenian action coincided with

the Pythian truce. It is a pity that the text of the opening of Thuc. 5.1 is so uncertain, because there is a unique suggestion here that the sacred truce accompanying one of the Panhellenic festivals might have been regarded as on a level with the general year-long truce.

76. Xen. *Hell.* 4.5.1–2: see above.
77. Plut. *Cleom.* 17; Walbank, 1933, 96–98.
78. Xen. *Hell.* 7.4.28–32.
79. According to Chaniotis, 2005, 179, the Romans alleged in 171 BC that Perseus had come with his army to Delphi during the sacred truce: *SIG*³ 643; Austin, 1981, n.76.
80. Thuc. 5.49–50; Dillon, 1997, 46–47.
81. Paradiso and Roy, 2008.
82. Minon, 2007, n.15: 'Offering to Zeus. Charixenos and the *mastroi* have decided in revision that the condemnations that Menandros and Aristolokhos have pronounced against the Boeotians in favour of the Athenians, have not been pronounced justly in favour also of the Thespians and their allies, and they have removed (the condemnation) of the Thessalians.'
83. Siewert, 1981; followed in Mackil, 2013, 414–15.
84. Minon, 2007, 112; for other possibilities, see Schachter, 2016, 59–60.
85. Xen. *Hell.* 4.7.2, 5. See the discussion of Bruce LaForse in this volume.
86. On the passage, see Parker, 2016, 123.
87. On Xenophon and religion, see Bowden, 2004.
88. Dillon, 1997, 49–50.
89. Parker, 1983, 155. The Nemean Games are also favoured by Stengel, 1920, 217 n.14, and Hanell, 1935, 2,325; Popp, 1957, 144 is undecided. If it was the Nemea, the date of the invasion must have been 387 BC (unless the truce was over a year long; in the Hellenistic period, festival announcers sometimes left the previous year, as in the case of the Nikephoria at Pergamum: Robert, 1930, 182; cf. Rigsby, 1996, 365; Rutherford, 2013, 78). In favour of Agesipolis' invasion in 387 BC, see Pascual, 2009.
90. Thuc. 8.9–10.

Bibliography

Austin, M.M., 1981, *The Hellenistic World from Alexander to the Roman Conquest*, Cambridge.

Bollansee, B., 1999, 'Aristotle and Hermippos of Smyrna on the Foundation of the Olympic Games and the Institution of the Sacred Truce', *Mnemosyne* 52, 562–67.

Bowden, H., 2004, 'Xenophon and the Scientific Study of Religion', in Tuplin, C. (ed.) *Xenophon and His World*, Stuttgart, 229–46.

Chaniotis, A., 2005, *War in the Hellenistic World: A Social and Cultural History*, Oxford.

Clinton, K., 1994, 'Eleusinian Mysteries and Panhellenism in Democratic Athens', in Palagia, O., and Coulson, W.D.E. (eds), *The Archaeology of Athens and Attica under the Democracy: Proceedings of an International Conference Celebrating 2500 Years Since the Birth of Democracy in Greece*, Oxford, 161–72.

Connor, W.R., 1988, 'Early Greek Land Warfare as Symbolic Expression', *P&P* 119, 3–29.

Del Monte, G.F., 1993, *L'annalistica ittita*, Brescia.

Dillon, M.P.J., 1995, 'Phrynon of Rhamnous and the Macedonian Pirates: The Political Significance of Sacred Truces', *Historia* 44, 250–54.

—— 1997, *Pilgrims and Pilgrimage in Ancient Greece,* London.

Dilts, M.R., 1983–1986, *Scholia Demosthenica,* 2 vols, Leipzig.

Dunn, F.M., 1998, 'Tampering with the Calendar', *ZPE* 123, 213–31.

Edmunds, L., 1979, 'Alexander and the Calendar (Plut., *Alex.* 16.2)', *Historia* 28, 112–17.

Fernández Nieto, F.J., 1975, *Los acuerdos bélicos en la antigua Grecia: época arcaica y clásica,* 2 vols, Santiago de Compostela.

Fortes, M., 1987, *Religion, Morality and the Person: Essays on Tallensi Religion,* Cambridge.

Frei-Stolba, R., and Bielman, A. (eds), 1994, *Epigraphie grecque et latine,* Lausanne.

Goetze, A., 1933, *Die Annalen des Mursilis,* Leipzig.

Gomme, A.W., Andrewes, A., and Dover, K.J., 1970, *A Historical Commentary on Thucydides,* vol. iv, Oxford.

Goodman, M.G., and Holladay, A.J., 1986, 'Religious Scruples in Ancient Warfare', *CQ* 36, 151–71.

Hanell, K., 1935, 'Nemea (Spiele)', *RE* 16.2, 2,325.

Hayashi, T., 1992, *Bedeutung und Wandel des Triptolemosbildes vom 6.–4. Jh. v. Chr.: religionshistorische und typologische Untersuchungen,* Würzburg.

Hornblower, S., 1996, *A Commentary on Thucydides. Volume ii: Books iv–v.24,* Oxford.

Hornblower, S., and Morgan, C., 2007, 'Introduction', in Hornblower, S., and Morgan, C. (eds), *Pindar's Poetry, Patrons and Festivals. From Archaic Greece to the Roman Empire,* 1–43.

Jameson, M.H., Jordan, D.R., and Kotansky, R.D., 1993, *A 'Lex Sacra' from Selinous,* Durham NC.

Kritzas, C., 2006, 'Nouvelles inscriptions d'Argos: les archives des comptes du Trésor sacré (IVe s. av. J.-C.)', *CRAI* 150, 397–434.

Lämmer, M., 2010, 'The So-Called Olympic Truce in Ancient Greece', in König, J. (ed.), *Greek Athletics,* Edinburgh, 36–60 (English translation of 'Der sogenannte Olympische Friede in der griechischen Antike', in Lämmer, M. (ed.), *Stadion* 8/9 1982/1983, 47–83).

Legun, R.P., 1967, 'Phliasian Politics and Policy in the Early Fourth Century B.C.', *Historia* 16, 324–37.

Mackil, E., 2013, *Creating a Common Polity,* Berkeley.

Minon, S., 2007, *Les inscriptions Éléennes dialectales. VIe–IIe si.cle avant J.-C.,* 2 vols, Geneva.

Morgan, J.D., and Iverson, P., forthcoming.

Mylonopoulos, J., 2006, 'Von Helike nach Tainar und von Kalaureia nach Samikon: Amphiktyonische Heiligtümer des Poseidon auf der Peloponnes', in Freitag, K., Funke, P., and Haake, M. (eds), *Kult, Politik, Ethnos: überregionale Heiligtümer im Spannungsfeld von Kult und Politik,* Stuttgart, 121–55.

Paradiso, A., 2013, 'Usi politici della tregua sacra in Tucidide', in Birgalias, N., Buraselis, K., Cartledge, P., Gartziou-Tatti, A., and Dimopoulou, M. (eds), *War, Peace and Panhellenic Games: In Memory of Pierre Carlier / Πόλεμος-ειρήνη και πανελλήνιοι αγώνες,* Athens, 583–603.

Paradiso, A., and Roy, J., 2008, 'Lepreon and Phyrkos in 421–420', *Klio* 90, 27–35.

Parker, R., 1983, *Miasma: Pollution and Purification in Early Greek Religion,* Oxford.

—— 2016, 'War and Religion in Ancient Greece', in Ulanowski, K. (ed.), *The Religious Aspects of War in the Ancient Near East, Greece and Rome*, Leiden, 123–32.

Pascual, J., 2009, 'Xenophon and the Chronology of the War on Land from 393 to 386 B.C.', *CQ* 59, 75–90.

Pettersson, M., 1992, *Cults of Apollo at Sparta. The Hyakinthia, the Gymnopaidiai and the Karneia*, Stockholm.

Pfeijffer, I.L., 1999, *Three Aeginetan Odes of Pindar: A Commentary on Nemean v, Nemean iii, and Pythian vii*, Leiden.

Popp, H., 1957, *Die Einwirkung von Vorzeichen, Opfern, und Festen auf die Kriegführung der Griechen im 5. und 4. Jahrhundert v. Chr.*, Erlangen.

Pritchett, W.K., 1971, *The Greek State at War, Part i*, Berkeley.

——1979, *The Greek State at War. Part iii. Religion*, Berkeley.

—— 1999, 'Postscript: the Athenian Calendars', *ZPE* 128, 79–93.

Rappaport, R.R., 1968, *Pigs for the Ancestors. Ritual in the Ecology of a New Guinea People*, New Haven.

Rhodes, P.J., and Osborne, R. (eds), 2003, *Greek Historical Inscriptions: 404–323 B.C.*, Oxford.

Richer, N., 2004, 'The Hyakinthia of Sparta', in Figueira, T.J. (ed.), *Spartan Society*, Swansea, 77–102.

—— 2012, *La religion des Spartiate: croyances et cultes dans l'Antiquité*, Paris.

Rigsby, K., 1996, *Asylia: Territorial Inviolability in the Hellenistic World*, Berkeley.

Robert, L., 1930, 'Sur les Nikephoria de Pergame. Notes d'epigraphie hellénistique XXXVII', *BCH* 54, 332–46 (Robert, 1969, i.151–65).

—— 1937, *Études Anatoliennes. Recherches sur les inscriptions grecques de l'Asie Mineure*, Paris.

—— 1969, *Opera minora selecta: Epigraphie et antiquités grecques*, vols i–vii, Amsterdam.

Robertson, N., 2002, 'The Religious Criterion in Greek Ethnicity: The Dorians and the Festival Carneia', *AJAH* 1.2, 5–74.

—— 2010, *Ritual and Reconciliation in Greek Cities. The Sacred Laws of Selinus and Cyrene*, Oxford.

Rougemont, G., 1973, 'La hiéroménie des Pythia et les "trèves sacrées" d'Éleusis, de Delphes et d'Olympie', *BCH* 97, 89–106.

Rutherford, I., 2013, State Pilgrims and Sacred Observers in Ancient Greece: A Study of Theôriâ and Theôroi, Cambridge.

Schachter, A., 2016, *Boiotia in Antiquity: Selected Papers*, Cambridge.

Siewert, P., 1981, 'Eine Bronze-Urkunde mit elischen Urteilen über Böoter, Thessaler, Athen und Thespiai', *OlBer* 10, 228–48.

—— 2002, 'Die wissenschaftgeschichtliche Bedeutung der Bronze-Urkunden aus Olympia mit der Erstedition einer frühen Theorodokie-Verleihung als Beispiel', in Kyrieleis, H. (ed.), *Olympia 1875–2000. 125 Jahre Deutsche Ausgrabungen*, Mainz, 359–70.

Stengel, P., 1920, *Die griechischen Kultusaltertümer*, Munich.

Tausend, K., 1992, *Amphiktyonie und Symmachie. Formen zwischenstaatlicher Beziehungen im archaischen Griechenland*, Stuttgart.

Trümpy, C., 1997, *Untersuchungen zu den altgriechischen Monatsnamen und Monatsfolgen*, Heidelberg.

Walbank, F.W,. 1933, *Aratos of Sicyon*, Cambridge.

Ziegler, R., 1985, *Städtisches Prestige und kaiserliche Politik. Studien zum Festwesen in Ostkilikien im 2. und 3. Jahrhundert n. Chr.*, Düsseldorf.

Chapter 6

Militarizing the Divine:
The Bellicosity of the Greek Gods

Matthew Dillon

Greek gods and goddesses were, in Greek belief, as reflected in literature and religious practices, no strangers to warfare: they had been involved in a major struggle for dominance and survival against the Giants (the Gigantomachia), in which all of the Olympian gods had participated, a theme depicted on the sixth-century BC Treasury of the Siphnians at Delphi, and later on the Hellenistic great altar of Pergamon. In the struggle of the Trojan War, too, individual gods took sides with either the Greek or Trojan forces, and participated actively on the battlefield. In the *Iliad*, for example, Athena emerges as the pre-eminent warrior god, while Zeus sits aloof and watches the conflict from afar, although in the end he will determine that Troy must be sacked. Whilst the gods do fight for either the Greeks or the Trojans, individual gods are especially concerned in coming to the aid of their favourite heroes. In historical times, the Greek gods were also considered to be active in human affairs, and to have taken an interest in military conflict, both against foreign outsiders and between Greek city-states. Yet the major deities themselves are missing as such on the battlefields of Salamis and Plataea, although there are numerous epiphanies of divine beings recorded by Herodotus. Thucydides' account of the Peloponnesian War has no gods personally present at all on his canvas, but he considers the religious practices of states to be important, and festivals, temples, access to sanctuaries, and above all oracles, are presented in his narrative as significant aspects of the conflict. Xenophon's account of the Ten Thousand Greek mercenaries who had fought at Cunaxa in Persia in 401 BC and made their way home through foreign, hostile territory reflects the religious beliefs of this general and his comrades – that the gods deliberately gave directions through signs to indicate courses of action to be undertaken by the mortal protagonists, and showed their support in battle through omens and other portents. Throughout the Greek world in the Classical period, deities of war such as Aphrodite, Athena, Ares and Enyalios received cult offerings in order

✂ DISCOVER MORE ABOUT PEN & SWORD BOOKS

Pen & Sword Books have over 4000 books currently available, our imprints include: Aviation, Naval, Military, Archaeology, Transport, Frontline, Seaforth and the Battleground series, and we cover all periods of history on land, sea and air.

Can we stay in touch? From time to time we'd like to send you our latest catalogues, promotions and special offers by post. If you would prefer not to receive these, please tick this box. ☐

We also think you'd enjoy some of the latest products and offers by post from our trusted partners: companies operating in the clothing, collectables, food & wine, gardening, gadgets & entertainment, health & beauty, household goods, and home interiors categories. If you would like to receive these by post, please tick this box. ☐

Mr/Mrs/Ms ....

Address..

Postcode................................ Email address...

Website: www.pen-and-sword.co.uk Email: enquiries@pen-and-sword.co.uk
Telephone: 01226 734555   Fax: 01226 734438
Stay in touch: facebook.com/penandswordbooks or follow us on Twitter @penswordbooks

Freepost Plus RTKE-RGRJ-KTTX
Pen & Sword Books Ltd
47 Church Street
BARNSLEY
S70 2AS

to win their military support. Wars could not be fought without the support of the divine, which had to be sought actively; it could not be taken for granted.

Athena: *the* God of War

In the Trojan War, the gods' involvement is best illustrated in *Iliad* Book 20, when destruction is fast approaching for the Trojans and their city. At this point in the conflict, Zeus has summoned the gods to Mount Olympus, to send them to enter the fray, and he rouses, 'war unabating'. He states that he himself, however, will not participate in the fighting but sit back on Olympus and enjoy the battle. In Book 21, he is shown as laughing aloud when he sees the gods fighting with each other.[1] Hera, Athena, Poseidon, Hermes and Hephaestus join the Greeks, while Ares, Apollo, Artemis, Leto, the river Xanthus and 'lover of laughter' Aphrodite fight for the Trojans. Zeus has noted that the contest is already uneven, with Achilles on the rampage, and the gods will tilt the battle even more in favour of the Greeks, for the gods assisting them do so more effectively than the gods supporting the Trojans. Troy's destruction approaches, and in Book 22, Hector will be slain by Achilles: but it is not a fair fight, for Athena will be assisting him. In Book 20, Athena had already turned aside Hector's spear from Achilles, and while Apollo then protects Hector, it is but a delay of the Trojan's doom.[2]

In Book 21, Hephaestus boils off the waters of the river Skamandros who has attacked Achilles when the latter has come into his waters, which Achilles has clogged with the bodies of Trojans he has slain, while Ares fights Athena, who knocks him senseless with a rock and laughs at him, and boasts that he ought to know that she is mightier than he. When Aphrodite comes to Ares' rescue, Hera reacts by setting Athena upon her, striking her on the breast so that Aphrodite falls, at which Hera smiles.[3] Various verbal arguments break out amongst the gods, until they all finally retire to Olympus. As will be seen further below, the gods are portrayed by Homer as intervening directly in battle. While this is not articulated as such in later accounts of specific, historical battles, the Homeric background indicates that combatants and non-combatants alike in the Archaic and Classical period considered that the gods did fight with them in the sense of providing divine support and guidance, even if they were not physically present.

Athena the War-Goddess

'Mourning Athena', the modern name given to a marble sculpture relief some 48cm high, is arguably one of the finest pieces of Classical Athenian sculpture (Figure 6.1). Athena, wearing a crested Corinthian-style helmet, is shown with a spear in her left hand and is clearly placing her weight on the spear, leaning against it. That her spear is in her left and not her right hand signifies that she is not at war, but at peace, as is also indicated by her not wearing sandals. Her head inclines towards a carved stele in front of her, which she is contemplating. There are differing modern interpretations of this scene, but the most accepted is that the stele, which is side-on for the viewer, would be engraved as a funerary monument. Her expression is decidedly melancholic and thoughtful, and also sad: she is clearly contemplative, perhaps even pensive. This may indicate that she is looking at an Athenian casualty list of those killed in battle, which saddens her as the goddess who protects Athens.[4] Such lists are known to have existed, with the most famous example being the inscribed casualty list of the Athenian Erechtheis tribe, dating to 460 or 459 BC, which lists the names of all those from this tribe killed in battle: 'Of the tribe Erechtheis these died in the war: in Cyprus, Egypt, Phoenicia, Halieis, on Aegina, at Megara in the same year.'[5]

Athena as noted is armed in this relief, which is common in her iconography, and this theme first emerges in the narrative of her birth. Hesiod recorded the genealogy of the gods in his *Theogony* (*The Race of Gods*), and includes the account of Zeus marrying Metis, the goddess of wisdom, who became pregnant: but there was a prophecy that Metis would have a second child, a son, who would overthrow Zeus, and he therefore put Metis into his stomach. But one day Zeus had a mighty headache: to cure him, Hephaestus split his head in half, and out leapt the goddess Athena, fully armed, waving a sharp spear, a scene so frightening that the sun god Helios stopped his chariot in the sky.[6] At some stage she came into possession of Zeus' aegis (see below), which she used to frighten enemies. Of the two myths of Athena represented in stone sculptures on the pediments of her temple, the Parthenon on the Athenian acropolis, constructed 447–432 BC and showing the very real importance placed on the armed goddess by the Classical Athenians, the east pediment represented the birth of Athena from Zeus' head, and the western her contest with Poseidon for control of the city.[7] Vase-painters frequently employed the theme, and there are dozens of representations of Hephaestus with his axe and Athena springing from Zeus' head.[8] An Athenian black-figure vase dating to *c.* 550 BC shows Athena emerging from Zeus' head (Figure 6.2). Hephaestus is not present, but this vase is significant because Athena is born in the presence of gods: on the left, immediately behind Zeus (shown holding his thunderbolts), is Poseidon with his trident (due to his role in the contest for Athens with Athena), while

Figure 6.1: The 'Mourning Athena', a marble relief showing Athena contemplating a stele, almost certainly an engraved casualty list: height, 48cm, dating to about 460 BC. Athens Acropolis Museum 695. (*Courtesy of Art Resource (392399)*)

behind Poseidon stands a goddess of unknown identity; in front of Zeus, a goddess, perhaps Eileithyia (a birth goddess), greets Athena, and behind her the god Ares, fully armed. His presence is important, for while they would be enemies in the Trojan War, they have similar characteristics and roles in battle.[9]

The two *Homeric Hymns to Athena* (11 and 28), while short, encapsulate what was seen as her essence. Written in the seventh century BC at Athens, they embody the Athenian attitude to the goddess, and in both she is celebrated as 'guardian of the city':[10]

> I begin to sing of Pallas Athena, the city's guardian. Terrible is she, and with Ares she delights in the works of war, the sacking of cities, and battles. She is the one who saves the armed host as it goes off to war and returns.

Moreover, the *Homeric Hymn to Aphrodite* (5) draws a specific contrast between Aphrodite and Athena: Aphrodite has no sway over three goddesses: Athena, Artemis or Hestia, the ever-virgin goddesses. While nothing warlike is said of Artemis, who is described here and in her own two hymns as a huntress delighting in the wilderness,[11] the hymn provides a contrast between passive Aphrodite and bellicose Athena. The latter 'finds pleasure in wars and in Ares' deeds, in strife and battle ... She it was who first taught craftsmen to devise war-chariots.'[12] Sixth-century BC sources describe her as 'Pallas [Athena] who stirs up battles', and she who 'finds joy in tumults, wars and battles'.[13]

Constant Homeric references drawing readers' attention to the differences between Athena and Aphrodite have almost a programmatic nature. Why did the composers of the *Iliad* and the *Homeric Hymns* feel it so important to draw this distinction, to the extent, in a sense, of hijacking the actual *Hymn to Aphrodite* to praise Athena's bellicosity and denigrate Aphrodite's martial prowess? This continual emphasis on Athena as a war-goddess is understandable, as in the eighth century BC she was the Greek war deity par excellence, who could drive Ares the war-god himself from the battlefield. Yet the constant allusion to Aphrodite's non-military side and her uselessness in battle needs a further, albeit brief, comment. Athena was worshipped widely throughout the Greek world, but, of course, especially by the Athenians and the Ionians in general. The Homeric epics and *Homeric Hymns* derive from the Ionian world, to which Aphrodite as a war goddess was unknown. But this was not the case at Corinth, a Dorian city, with the Dorians being rivals of the Ionians (see further below on Aphrodite at Corinth). Perhaps this

Figure 6.2: Athena, fully armed, emerging from Zeus' head in the presence of gods and goddesses. Athenian black-figure vase, dating to *c*. 550 BC. Louvre F32. (*Courtesy of Art Resource (149979)*)

might help explain the Ionian determination to deny Aphrodite a role as a martial deity, for the Homeric poems hailed from the Ionian world. Perhaps, more particularly, it was thought that as Aphrodite was on the Trojan side in the Trojan War, her assistance could not then be effective.

This, however, is very much a case of Homeric revisionism, for Aphrodite appears elsewhere, in actual Greek cult as opposed to the Homeric epic narrative and hymnography, as very much a warlike goddess. The cause of the emphasis on Athena's hatred of Aphrodite is never revealed (much of the relevant battle action relating to Aphrodite is in *Iliad* Book 5, for which see the discussion below on Aphrodite). But it probably reflects earlier and/or different versions of the Trojan War saga, in which Aphrodite may have been a warlike and bellicose goddess who encountered Athena in battle on the Trojan plain. Yet the war goddess of the Greeks was victorious, and the written epic itself refashioned the story to such an extent as to denigrate the war goddess of the Trojans. While Zeus also aids the Trojans as and when it suits his purposes (especially to draw attention to Achilles' absence from the battle, so as to increase his fame), he is also cognisant that the Trojans will be defeated, and there comes a point when he must withdraw his support, even to the extent of allowing his son Sarpedon to be killed in battle (see below). Ares, also on the Trojan side, is a very ineffective war god in Homer: he is, on the one hand, belittled by his own father for being a gore-loving reprobate, but on the other he in fact fights diligently for the Trojans. Yet even the blood insatiate war-god is tricked by Athena into leaving the battlefield, abandoning the Trojans, and Athena will defeat him in battle in *Iliad* Book 21 (see below).

Athena had numerous cult titles, the vast majority of which related to war. Indeed, she had more war epithets than any other god or goddess, even Zeus or Ares. She was, in fact, the most important military deity of the ancient Greeks, and in these epithets are encapsulated many aspects of both her bellicosity and protective nature. A listing of these epithets, as well as adjectives, demonstrates how multi-faceted she was as a war divinity, with her roles as such encapsulating everything from being a guardian and defender, fighter in the front ranks, preserver and 'driver of the spoils' of war. It is not simply the sheer number of these epithets which delineate her as the supreme war deity, but the numerousness of these occurrences as compared to the war-epithets of any other divinity. Moreover, her martial cult titles occur in numerous contexts: in the history of war as in the *Iliad*, in references relating to the Persian Wars and in information concerning temples and statues as recorded by the Greek travel writer Pausanias in the second century AD. Moreover, they cover a wide geographical and historical range, from all over mainland Greece from the Homeric poems on, and were known to the tenth-century AD Byzantine lexicographer whose work is known as the Suda.

The epithets for Athena, as well as some adjectives, include the following: Athena *Agelaie* ('Driver/herder of the Spoils');[14] Athena *Agestrate* ('Leader of the Army');[15] Athena *Alea* ('escape to place of safety or refuge');[16] Athena *Alalkomenêis* ('Protector');[17] Athena *Alkimache* ('Strong in War');[18] Athena *Areia* ('Ares-like Athena'), who was worshipped in a temple at Plataea which the inhabitants constructed from the proceeds of their share of the spoils from the defeat of the Persians at Marathon in 490 BC: clearly the temple was a gift to her for services rendered in the campaign,[19] and the cult statue there was sculptured by Pheidias; the Persians destroyed her shrine in 479 BC,[20] but the victorious Greeks gave the Plataeans eighty talents from the war-booty to rebuild it.[21] Athena is one of the deities in the ephebic oath from Acharnai (see below), and she had an altar on the Areios Pagos hill in Athens;[22] there is also Athena *Atrytone* ('Unwearied'), which Hera calls Athena several times when she wants Athena to get stuck into the battle;[23] Athena *Eryma* ('Defender');[24] Athena *Glaukopis* ('Flashing-eyed'), indicating her zeal for battle;[25] Athena *Gorgopis* ('Fierce-Eyed');[26] Athena *Itonia* (Iton was the name of a hero and also a place named after him), under which epithet she had a well-attested cult of Athena as a war-goddess in Koroneia in Boeotia, and coins from there show her in the 'Promachos' stance;[27] shields captured from the Gauls were dedicated in her temple in Thessaly;[28] Athena *Laossoos* ('Preserver of the People');[29] Eris is also so titled;[30] Athena *Leitis*, as Athena of war-booty, with a sacrifice made to her at Elis;[31] Athena *Niké*, Athena of Victory, with her temple on the Athenian acropolis; there was also a temple to her in the city of Megara;[32] Athena *Persepolis* ('Sacker of Cities');[33] Athena *Phobesistrate* ('Striker of Fear into an Army') could be a comic invention of Aristophanes, as the word only occurs once in Greek literature;[34] Athena *Polemedokos* ('War Sustaining');[35] *Athena Polias* or *Poliatis* ('Keeper of the City');[36] Athena *Polioukhos* ('Protector of the City');[37] Athena *Polyleidis* ('Giver of Bounteous Booty');[38] Athena *Promachos* ('Athena Fighter in the Front Line'), which was the most bellicose of all her cult epithets, and it was as Athena Promachos that she stood as a statue outside the Parthenon (see below), and most of the images of Athena are in fact in this style;[39] Athena *Promachorma* ('Fighting before the Battle Ranks' or 'Champion of the Anchorage'), and she had a shrine as such on the island of Troezen;[40] Athena *Rhysiptolis* ('Saviour of the City'): this epithet occurs when the Trojan priestess Theano, in company with the Trojan women, presents Athena with a magnificent *peplos* to propitiate her to 'break the spear' of Diomedes, who was running amok, causing devastation in the Trojan lines: he was, however, Athena's favourite, whom she was helping, and she refused to hear their prayer;[41] Athena *Salpinx* ('Athena of the War-trumpet'), with a temple on the Athenian acropolis;[42] Athena *Soteira* ('Saviour'), as in of the city or an individual, with a shrine in Arkadia said to have been built by Odysseus;[43] Athena *Sthenias* ('Athena the Strong');[44] and Athena *Stratia* ('Athena of the Army').[45]

There are numerous armed Athena (Athena Promachos) iconographic representations, consisting of statuettes, marble reliefs, vases and coinage. An Athenian bronze statuette of the sixth century BC, for example, shows Athena with an enormous crest on her helmet, while her hands originally held a spear (now missing).[46] The most famous armed statue of Athena is of course that of Athena Polias (Athena [defender of] the City) in the Parthenon, sculpted by Pheidias in 438 BC. The statue, long destroyed, is described by various ancient sources, but particularly Pausanias,[47] and was copied in antiquity, with the most famous copy being the Varvakeion marble statuette, one metre high, of the first half of the third century AD, which shows her with her shield resting against one leg, high crested winged horses on her helmet (in the original these were actually griffins), and in her right hand, outstretched, a statuette of a wingéd victory, Athena Nikê, about to take off to award victory to someone. The original statue in the Parthenon held a spear, but the Varvakeion marble copy in its present state does not (it presumably was a metal one, resting perhaps in the crook of her left arm).[48] Outside the Parthenon itself was a colossal bronze statue of Athena Promachos (Athena the Warrior), also the work of Pheidias.[49] The prize vases presented to the winners in the Panathenaic contests all depicted the goddess on the obverse, fully armed.[50] Armed Athena is by far the most common way in which the goddess is depicted – a war deity, armed to the teeth, ready to defend Athens and other states that worshipped her in this capacity.

Athena's abandonment of Troy is signalled by her collusion with the Greek heroes when Diomedes – her definite favourite amongst the Greeks at Troy – and Odysseus sneak into Troy and steal the Palladion, a small ancient statue of Athena said to have fallen from heaven when the city was founded by Ilias. *The Little Iliad* epic provides the narrative, while the scene is represented on vases which depict Diomedes running or walking stealthily with a statuette of an armed Athena; on one such vase, Athena with spear, and holding her helmet, looks on approvingly.[51]

Even when goddesses felt affection for individual Trojan heroes, this did not save them: Skamandrios is slain, even though he was a mighty hunter whom Artemis herself had instructed in the slaying of all the wild beasts of the mountains: 'In no way did the archer Artemis aid him now.' Artemis, in fact, is conspicuously absent from the *Iliad*, except (ineffectually) towards its end. Phereklos the Trojan warrior is slain, even though 'Pallas Athena loved him more than any other man'.[52] The goddess Athena was hell-bent on the destruction of Troy, and had laid aside her feelings for this Trojan mortal. Athena's attitude is made clear by two separate prayers offered to her: one by the Greek warrior Diomedes in *Iliad* Book 5, and one by the women of Troy to her in Book 6. Diomedes calls upon Athena to hear and assist him, just as she had stood beside his father in battle. Athena does hear and act, and makes him stronger, like his father, and speaks to him by his side, removing the mist from his eyes so that he could distinguish mortal from god, advising him thus not to attack any gods who might be in the battle, except for Aphrodite: if she entered the battle, he was to strike her with his sharp bronze spear. This relationship between Diomedes and Athena stems from her previous relationship with his father, and Diomedes can call upon this. In assisting him, Athena guides his spear through the nose of the Trojan Pandaros and into his teeth, 'and his spirit and his strength were loosed'. [53] Athena does not listen to the prayer of the Trojan women in Book 6, to break the spear of Diomedes, and simply ignores it.

Yet this personal involvement belongs to the heroic world, and in the Archaic and Classical ages, gods and heroes are not described as intervening directly to assist individual mortals, but rather support mortals as a group fighting as an army. Gods and heroes assisting the Greeks at Salamis, for example, aid the Greek forces as a whole, or the body of Athenians. This represents the end of the heroic warrior age and the emergence of the communal military group, whether the hoplite phalanx or the rowers in the navy as a collective whole. With the age of the individual fighter over, it was the community of warriors who as a whole fought the enemy which received divine assistance.

Related to this is the Spartan general Brasidas' attitude to an incident he was involved in during the Peloponnesian War (431–404 BC). Thucydides has Brasidas promising to award a prize of thirty minas to the man who was the first to scale the walls of the fort at Lekythos, held by the Athenians. Yet when he did in fact capture it, he felt rather that it had been captured 'in some other way rather than the human', and so dedicated the thirty minas to the temple of Athena at Lekythos, and then in fact demolished the fort and consecrated the land as a sacred place (*temenos*), presumably to Athena. (In contrast, the Athenians attacked the sanctuary of Apollo at Delion in 424/423 BC and profaned it through human activities, at which the Thebans unsuccessfully complained.) Thucydides focuses on Brasidas' virtue, and the incident at Lekythos is important for this. It is not to say that other commanders did not think in a similar way about the gods, but that Brasidas' attitude to Athena here is part of Thucydides' presentation of Brasidas as a pious and virtuous commander.[54]

Ares the Man-Slaughterer

As seen above, Athena could be worshipped in martial guise as Athena Areia ('Athena as Ares'). Ares and the goddess fight on opposite sides in the Trojan War. But elsewhere they are paired: the scene of an army besieging a city as crafted on Achilles' shield by Hephaestus showed Athena and Ares together as leading the defendants of a city under attack.[55] He certainly also had his own identity as a war god. In two epigrams in the *Palantine Anthology*, Ares speaks, objecting that helmets and spears not used in war have been dedicated in his temple: the shields are not stained with blood, the spears are not broken, the helmets not crushed: for he is 'Ares, Man-Slaughterer, delighting in smashed weapons of war dedicated to me, and the gore of dying men'.[56] Captured weapons were dedicated to Ares, even in the temple of another god in one case – hence the famous lines of Alcaeus: 'Alcaeus has escaped, but his armour has been nailed up as a dedication to Ares in the temple of Athena Glaukopis by the Athenian army.'[57] Pindar writes of him that Ares prospers in the presence of young men's 'destructive spears'.[58]

Ares is probably the first of many Greek personifications, in which abstract concepts were transformed into objects of worship. After Ares, others were to come, such as Nemesis ('Retribution'); in the Roman world too, Virtus and Pietas emerge as separate deities. Ares is found in the Linear B tablets in religious contexts, indicating that he was the recipient of some form of cult worship then, as in the Classical period. His name also appears as a personal name in the tablets – but no mortal in the Classical period bore his name.

Ares was the child of Zeus and Hera, but his father in anger tells Ares that he hates him most of all the gods, even though he is his son, for Ares loves 'strife (*eris*), battles and fighting'; Zeus, however, blames Hera for these aspects of Ares' character, for she is nearly uncontrollable and has passed her traits onto their son. For Zeus, war is not a way of life, particularly as he is a god of justice and of the civilized order of the city-state (*polis*), and Ares' attachment to blood and gore and the enjoyment of battle and death purely for its own sake, with no moral interest in who won or lost the battle, is seen by Zeus as despicable, while in the *Iliad* Ares is described as the bane of men in battle (see next quotation). Ares had a sister, Eris, a personified deity who was the daughter of Zeus and Hera: she was Strife, a key component of battlefield slaughter (see below).[59] Alcaeus of Mytilene in the sixth century BC urges his countrymen to peace after civil war: he advises them to be at ease until Ares once more delights to stir them to war:[60]

> Even as Ares, the slaughterer of men, marches forth to battle, and with him goes his beloved son Phobos, strong, unfearing, inducing fear (*phobos*) in a warrior, no matter how stalwart.[61]

What is also interesting here is that Ares and his son are referred to as coming from Thrace, considered by the Greeks to be backward, being a non-Greek area, an area known for its lack of urbanization, in contrast to the *polis* life of the Greeks: it is a case of they versus the other, *polis* versus non-*polis*, Greek versus non-Greek, and this picture of these deities must be a deliberate reflection of their liminality. So it could be said that Ares does not belong in the Greek civilized world with its ordered *polis* and sophisticated rules of combat.[62] Moreover, because he prefers neither side, according to Zeus, he is an outside, liminal, indiscriminate force of battle gore. Ares stands for indiscriminate slaughter: 'hateful Ares', 'insatiate of war Ares', the 'slaughterer of men'.[63]

Yet this is not completely the case for Ares in the Trojan War, and his father Zeus has been unfair towards and overall critical of him. Ares, as a participant on the Trojan side, does not slaughter indiscriminately, but harries the Greek forces consistently. He is such a menace that Athena (despite her belittling of his prowess) has to lure him from the battle by a ruse, to give the Greeks a respite from his attentions. And despite Zeus' description of his son, the mighty warrior Menelaos is frequently described by Homer in terms of a relationship with Ares: Menelaos is described by both Agamemnon and by Zeus, and throughout the *Iliad's* narrative, as 'beloved of Ares'. No other hero receives this epithet in the *Iliad*, indicating Menelaos' pre-eminent zeal and valour as a warrior amongst the Greeks (even more so than Achilles, who only defeats Hector with divine assistance, which Hector does not receive). Another warrior, the Greek Pylaimenes, is 'Ares' peer', and Agamemnon describes the Greek soldiers as 'attendants of Ares'.[64] Looking much further forward in time, Gaius Caesar was referred to in an Athenian inscription of 2 BC as the 'New Ares' on the strengths of his conquests.[65]

Ares did possess cult centres throughout Greece, with worship specifically addressed to him, as Pausanias' description of various statues of Ares and sanctuaries to the god attests, and numerically he has his fair share of Greek cult places in Pausanias' account. He was worshipped in all areas of mainland Greece: at Athens, on the road from Argos to Mantineia (with an image of Ares and one of Athena), Hermione (on the site where Theseus was said to have defeated the Amazons), Troizen, Sparta, Geronthrai (women were forbidden to enter his sanctuary at his annual festival), Elis (where there was an altar of Ares Hippias [Horse-Ares] and one of Athena Hippia [Horse-Athena]), Triteia in Achaea, Megalopolis, Tegea and Boeotia. His cult as Ares Gynaikothoinas (*Ares, Feasted by the Women*) at Tegea, in which only women could make sacrifices, might not necessarily, however, be a warlike manifestation. Pausanias also notes several statues of the god, some at the above cult places.[66] Priestly personnel dedicated to this god would have staffed these temples and shrines, and such are specifically known at Hermione and Orchomenos, where each place had a priest of Ares-Enyalios.[67] At Sparta, a bull was sacrificed to Ares (probably by the kings) when the army won a battle through superior generalship.[68] Cults with priests of Ares are known from Asia Minor in the Roman period, such as at Metropolis, but are outside the chronological scope of the discussion here, and may at any rate be the result of syncretism with a local, pre-Greek Anatolian war god.[69] At Ephesos, an inscription of the Roman period refers to cult members of the combined deity Ares-Enyalios as Areistai.[70] That Ares did not receive cult and worship is therefore a misnomer: as a war-god it was considered important to have him 'on side' and actively to seek his support.

Enyalios

Another attested Greek war god is Enyalios, and the name *E-nu-wa-ri-jo*, equating to the later Enyalios, appears in a Mycenaean Linear B tablet from Knossos.[71] He was one of the gods to whom the Athenian ephebes swore taking their oath to defend Attica. From the city of Lindos on Rhodes comes the most detailed evidence for his worship, where an inscription of the late fifth century BC records that both citizen soldiers and mercenaries fighting for the city were to pay a tax of one-sixtieth of their remuneration to the god's cult.[72] The money was to be collected by the *strategos* (general), who was to be held guilty of impiety if he did not collect the money, as too would be the soldiers who did not present their tithe of one-sixtieth. Enyalios' cult at Lindos had a priest, who at the end of every year was to provide a written account for the town council of how much money had been collected for the god, and the money was to go towards building a shrine for Enyalios (presumably he did not have one at the time the decree was passed, and the tithe is clearly being instituted to pay for this). There was to be an annual sacrifice to the god and procession in his honour in the month of Artemision (Artemis' month – presumably chosen because of her martial aspect as Artemis Agrotera: see below) in which as many soldiers as the city council decided could participate, accompanying the sacrificial offerings of a boar, dog and goat. Of course, here the accidents of survival need to be considered, and it is possible that there were other cult regulations like this which have not survived. The practice at Lindos, which was a legal requirement, was possibly an informal practice not codified into law in other cities, and prior to the regulation, soldiers may have informally donated a fraction of their pay to Enyalios.

Enyalios was in particular associated with the war-cry voiced as soldiers charged into battle. Thrasyboulos, for example, leader of the Athenian democratic forces in 404 BC, tells his troops as they go into battle to take Athens from the pro-Spartan oligarchs that he will strike up the paean (hymn), and then all together will call upon Enyalios.[73] In Philostratos, the sounding of the war-trumpet gives the signal of Enyalios, ordering the young men to arm themselves.[74] Enyalios was the god believed to be present when men were being killed and killing in battle, who supervised and presided over their arms, their besieging of towns and the driving off of war-booty; he was god of war, battle and heroic struggle.[75] Archilochos of Paros in his poetry referred to himself as the 'servant' of Enyalios, because he played a leading military role in the civil war on his island, and another poet, Ibycus, wrote that discord and strife were the offshoot of Enyalios.

According to Pindar, the warrior Chromios of Etna in Sicily warded off the onslaught of Enyalios in many battles in the 490s BC with the aid of the goddess Aidos (Shame), while he describes Ajax, the mighty Greek hero at Troy, as 'awesome amongst the armed host in the labours of Enyalios'.[76] When the Spartan King Cleomenes I (reigned *c.* 519–490 BC) destroyed the Argive army in battle, the poet Telesilla and the other Argive women defended the walls of the city, but Kleomenes did not attack. Afterwards, the women dedicated a statue of Enyalios, and Telesilla was depicted in a stone relief with her books and portrayed as putting on her armour. There is no particular reason to doubt this story.[77] There was a Delphic oracle relating to Argos that women would be victorious over men: but this, like many oracles, might have been invented after the event.[78]

While Ares and Enyalios could be thought of by the ancient Greeks as the same deity, Ares-Enyalios,[79] evidence indicates, however, that generally they were viewed as separate and distinct gods,[80] and their separate cults support this. Yet there was a clear link between the two deities, and when in Aristophanes' *Peace* the characters drink a toast to gods connected with the goddess Peace (Eirene), Hermes, who is present, emphatically declares that they will drink neither to Ares nor to Enyalios.[81] Enyalios was particularly associated with the spear (Pindar refers to 'Enyalios' spear'), the principal weapon of the hoplites: the connection was so strong that Plutarch in his *Roman Questions* noted that the Romans called Enyalios 'Quirinus', which related to the Roman *Juno Quiritis* (*Juno of the Spear*), as most of her statues represented her with a spear.[82]

Aeneas Tacticus' *On the Defence of Fortified Positions* specifically gives some examples of passwords for armies, including 'Dioskouroi', 'Ares', 'Enyalios', 'Athena' and 'Pallas', as being words suitable for armed forces; when the the enemy was approaching, 'Enyalios' could be the password.[83] Pausanias describes the customary fighting which took place (he does not specify a date or month) between companies of ephebes at Sparta: each company (*moira*) of the Spartan ephebes, by tradition, sacrificed a puppy at night to Enyalios on the day before the fighting, the puppy representing the most valiant of all animals. Clearly, each *moira* was attempting to gain Enyalios' assistance. In the city of Sparta itself, there was a temple to Ares but not apparently to Enyalios: his ancient, fettered statue stood outside a temple of the athletic hero Hipposthenes, and was kept in chains in a ritual attempt to ensure that Enyalios would always abide with the Spartans.[84] Clearly both deities were worshipped as gods at Sparta, which need not occasion surprise, and Enyalios received specific worship from the ephebes.[85]

At Athens, each year's War-Archon (Polemarchos-Archon) made annual sacrifices to Artemis Agrotera and Enyalios, as well as organizing funerary contests for those who had been killed in war. Artemis Agrotera had received the vow of goats before the Battle of Marathon in 490 BC, and it was probably this sacrifice which the Polemarchos-Archon presided over. The linking of the two gods in their military capacities – and the funerary contests – was deliberate. There was an ancient temple to Enyalios at Athens, said to have been erected by Solon in the 590s BC after he had defeated Athens' neighbouring city of Megara.[86]

Enyalios' worship might have been one of the men-only cults in the Greek world. Teles, in the third century BC, stated that women were forbidden at all his shrines. Such exclusion of women was not unusual in some 'masculine' cults, such as those of Heracles, and can be explained by the desire not to have the potency of the war-god 'diluted' by the presence of 'unwarlike' women.[87] Enyalios was, in many ways, much more of a war god than Ares: he possessed more cults and received regular sacrifices, as a war god who was trusted to assist his worshippers; like all the gods, it was believed that it was best to worship him formally, as in the cult at Lindos.

Deimos, Phobos and Other Lesser Deities of War

A range of minor deities was also concerned with Greek warfare: Terror, Fear, Death and the evil Keres. These deities lacked the personal characterization of the Greek gods; rather, they were personifications of brutal forces operating without mercy on the battlefield. Incapable of being placated, they pursued their roles without pity or mercy, their role being one of blood-lust, carnage and the removal of the souls of the battle-dead. Ares and Aphrodite were believed to have had several children: two reflected Aphrodite's love, Eros and Anteros ('Anti-Love'), as well as her role in civic concord: Harmonia. Those who more clearly took after their father (but also the mother, if due recognition is given to her warlike nature) were Deimos (Fear) and Phobos (meaning both Terror and Panic). Panic or Fear could be concepts,[88] or they could be deities, forces so important, and overwhelming in battle, that they were deified by the Greeks. For the panic in battle, the panic of the rout, was a real, significant force: Pindar writes that panics – *phoboi* – in war were sent by the gods, and in battle even the sons of gods trembled before these.[89] Their particular association with war is indicated by their appearance on shields: a Gorgon monster of 'terrifying gaze' decorated the shield of Agamemnon as described by Homer, with Deimos and Phobos shown next to her as her companions, while in Hesiod's lengthy description of the shield of Heracles, Phobos was depicted: he was intrinsic to battle as a terrifying force that could afflict any army. In Book 5 of the *Iliad*, the aegis of Athena is described as a tasselled, shawl-like garment worn around her shoulders when she is engaged in battle, which struck sheer terror into her enemies: 'all about which Phobos [panic] is set as a garland, and there is Eris [Strife], Battle-strength [Alke], and Ioke [Onset] who chills the blood, and thereon is set the head of the Gorgon, dread and awful monster, a portent of Zeus.'[90]

Enyo

When Diomedes in *Iliad* Book 5 at the behest of Athena pursues Aphrodite to attack her, he pursues her in her capacity as Cyprian Aphrodite (a title redolent of love), 'a weakling goddess', unfavourably compared with Athena and Enyo the city-sacker: Aphrodite is, unlike Athena and Ares, not one who masters men in battle. When Diomedes wounds Aphrodite in the wrist and she drops her son Aeneas whom she was protecting, he warns her to stay away from war and battle; her role is to ensnare helpless women, and she should learn to fear the very name of war.[91] Later in the same book, Ares, with his huge spear, is said to be leading the Trojans along with Enyo, who carries with her the tumult of battle.[92] They were linked in worship, for Pausanias comments on the temple of Ares in Athens in which there were two statues of Aphrodite, one of Ares, one of Athena and one of Enyo.[93] Soldiers could be described as Enyo's belted-warriors,[94] and in legend the Seven against Thebes swore an oath by Ares, Enyo and Phobos to capture Thebes.

The ephebes at Athens in the fourth century BC swore an oath to defend Attica, and a number of gods are listed on the inscription which records this, including Enyo and other martial deities. She was clearly a war goddess of some significance, and with the other military gods would punish any ephebes who broke their oaths. Given her terrifying nature in battle, her inclusion in the oath was meant as a serious deterrent to cowardice.[95] The context of the inscription is important, as it was set up in the shrine of Ares and Athena Areia ('Ares-like Athena') in the deme of Acharnai, Attica. She was, interestingly, not included in a list of gods in a similar oath of the ephebes of the city of Dreros on Crete, from *c.* 220 BC, despite Ares' presence.[96] Perhaps it was thought that Ares covered the role of war deity sufficiently, without her. Around 600 BC, an individual named Lyraqos dedicated a small marble cylinder pillar to Enyo.[97] Why did he do so? Perhaps he was a warrior returned safely home from battle who had sworn a vow to her for his return, or possibly on his arrival home decided to thank Enyo in this way.[98] In the third century AD, the poet Oppian described Ares' gifts as swords, helmets, spears and bronze tunics, and 'whatever things with which the goddess Enyo is delighted'.[99] Etymologically, Enyo is clearly a female version of Enyalios, but is not particularly associated with him.

Aphrodite: Goddess of Love or War?

Aphrodite's portrayal as a goddess in the *Iliad* is not a flattering one. In addition to the material in the *Homeric Hymns* (discussed above), there is the decided emphasis in the *Iliad* on her role as a goddess of love. Most famously, this is revealed in *Iliad* Book 5.[100] When Diomedes and Aeneas came to blows, Diomedes struck him on the hip with a massive stone: 'And now would Aeneas, a king amongst mortals, have met his end had not Aphrodite, Zeus' daughter, been quick to perceive his peril', and started to bear him from the battle. When Aphrodite flees from Diomedes, she goes to her father Zeus, who advises her that 'the works of war have not been given' to her, but to Ares and Athena, and she is to stay with 'her province of marriage', while Hera and Athena laugh at her.

Yet it is a very simplistic version of Aphrodite which is presented in the *Iliad*, and the goddess was much more multi-faceted than the Homeric epics and hymns present. Perhaps her portrait is affected by the fact that she was a goddess who in the *Iliad* fought for the Trojans, for the situation was different historically. At Corinth, she was the protector and tutelary deity of the city, with a large and impressive temple complex on the Acrocorinth. When the Persians were invading Greece in 480 BC, the Corinthians, including Aphrodite's sacred prostitutes there, turned to their city's deity and sought her help, and according to them, received it. This was quite regular as an expectation, for Chamaileon of Herakleia (writing in the late fourth and early third century BC) noted that it was an 'ancient custom' that when the Corinthians prayed communally as a city for the assistance of their goddess, they invited the prostitutes to attend as well – for as many, in fact, as possible to come.[101] In 480 BC, both the good citizen women and Aphrodite's prostitutes prayed to the goddess to save them from the barbarian, and the latter joined in the sacrifices to ensure Aphrodite's assistance. And when she did save them, the Corinthians in gratitude dedicated a plaque (*pinax*) to her, on which was a painting of the prostitutes supplicating the goddess, along with their names. Simonides, the author of several poems about the Persian War of 480–479 BC, composed an epigram for the plaque:[102]

> These women on behalf of the Greeks and their fair fighting fellow citizens were set up to pray with heaven-sent power to Kypris [Aphrodite] for the goddess Aphrodite did not choose to hand over the acropolis of the Greeks [Corinth] to the bow-carrying Persians.

Herodotus does not mention this incident, and Plutarch took him to task for this (as part of his attack on Herodotus for alleged bias against the Corinthians, for they in fact played a very important role at the Battle of Salamis which Herodotus devalues). Plutarch considered that the divine attention and assistance which the Corinthians had received from Aphrodite should have been acknowledged by Herodotus.[103]

Given this, it seems that Aphrodite might once in fact have played a much more vigorous and effective role in the Trojan War saga, and that Homer has redacted this myth and not only omitted her role but edited it – Aphrodite's part is reduced to that of the deity who organized Helen's seduction for Paris, and this is the only role present in the *Iliad*. Moreover, it suited Homer's purpose to have two powerful goddesses, martial and bellicose, on the Greek side, but to deprive the Trojans of any substantial assistance: Ares being easy to trick and Aphrodite ineffectual.

Scholarship frequently draws a connection between the armed warrior goddess Ishtar and Aphrodite, assuming that Aphrodite has a connection of some kind with this eastern goddess.[104] This is interesting speculation, but not relevant to the discussion here. Aphrodite is presented as the wife of Ares in Hesiod and iconography, and this could be significant, especially as in Homer she is Hephaestus' wife (but he also includes the episode of her adultery with Ares, pointing to the other tradition). As the wife of Ares, she gave birth to Panic and Phobos ('terrifying creatures herding in disorder the men close-ranked in war chilling to the bone, aided by Ares the city-destroyer'), as well as, by contrast, the goddess Harmonia.[105] There are also various representations of Aphrodite with spear, shield and the like, as Aphrodite Hoplismene – the 'Armed Aphrodite' (also Aphrodite Enoplion, also meaning 'Armed Aphrodite'). While it is possible to argue that these represent Aphrodite using the tools of war in her capacity as the conquering power of love,[106] it is more likely that these relate to her role as a goddess of war. Pausanias reports three statues of Aphrodite Hoplismene: at Corinth, Sparta (where he also mentions a temple of Aphrodite Areia, 'Ares like Aphrodite') and Cyprus.[107] The statue of 'Armed Aphrodite' at Sparta is the subject of some epigrams in the *Palatine Anthology*, owing to their authors' curiosity about the contrast between this aspect and her role as the goddess of love.[108] Plutarch notes of the Spartans in the second century AD:

> The Spartans worship Aphrodite arrayed in her full armour. All the statues of the gods, both the female and the male, they present with a spear in their hands, demonstrating that all their gods have the courage demanded by battle.[109]

In Sparta, all the gods had to 'pull their weight' in war and military enterprise, and Plutarch also notes the Spartans' account that, when Aphrodite crossed the River Eurotas into Spartan territory, she abandoned her mirrors and ornaments, and instead took up a spear and shield.[110] It was probably the case that Aphrodite was always a war-goddess at Sparta. Elsewhere, a life-size statue of Aphrodite, from Asklepios' sanctuary at Epidaurus in the Peloponnese and dating to about 400 BC, indicates that her left hand originally held a spear, while a strap indicates she carried a sword.[111] Similarly, an exquisite ring-gem dating to about 250–200 BC with a garnet centre, circled by gold and signed by the engraver, one Gelon, depicts Aphrodite (the only goddess ever shown nude or semi-nude) arming herself with a shield, with a spear shown resting against her; it was found in a tomb at Eretria on the island of Euboea.[112] If the evidence for a non-warlike goddess in Homer is set aside, the evidence for Aphrodite as a goddess of battle and defender of the city at Sparta and Corinth is quite compelling.

Zeus, Poseidon and Other Gods at War

Zeus, despite his love of Priam and Troy, is determined that Troy will fall; whether this was his own will or whether he is impelled by Fate to do so is impossible to ascertain.[113] He was in a very real sense 'in charge' of the divine conduct of the war: in Book 8, he tells all the gods to withdraw from the battle, and they obey, only returning later; he looses the gods upon the battlefield in Book 20. His involvement is, however, from a distance, and he does not enter the actual fray: to do so would presumably be beneath his dignity.

Zeus makes Agamemnon appear more powerful in Book 2 to stress his authority over the Greeks: 'his eyes and head like that of Zeus who hurls his thunderbolt, his midriff as of Ares, and his chest unto Poseidon'. On this occasion, Zeus makes Agamemnon reflect the appearance of the three most powerful gods. Similarly, Hector must go to his doom, with Athena assisting in his death, but Zeus gives him honour and glory on the battlefield first. While Athena was hastening on the day when Hector would be killed by Achilles, in the meantime Zeus himself was his defender, for out of all the warriors on the battlefield, Zeus granted to Hector alone honour and glory in the absence of Achilles.[114]

Even though Zeus does not engage in the fighting himself – it amused him to remain aloof and watch the other gods in the battle – he was nevertheless a god of war. This is not often clearly articulated in the ancient sources, but it is important to note that the Spartans always sacrificed to him before setting out on campaign. Xenophon in a section of his *Lacedaemonian Politeia* (*Spartan Constitution*) dealt with Spartan army sacrifices, in which the king (only one of the two kings went on campaign from the late sixth century BC on) as war-leader (Polemarchos) sacrificed to 'Zeus and to the Twin Gods' (Kastor and Polydeukes: Castor and Pollux) when setting out for war.[115] If this sacrifice was well-omened, that is, if the entrails were propitious, the army set forth for the border, where the king sacrificed again, this time to Zeus and Athena. Only when the sacrifice to both gods was propitious (implying a separate sacrificial victim for each) was the border crossed.

Such an association of Zeus with Athena was deliberate: he was the supreme deity, and Athena was *the* deity of war. Zeus was also Agetor ('Leader') in that he was conceived of as 'leading' the army, and this epithet was employed for no other Greek god.[116] Fire from his altar at Sparta was taken with the Spartan army and used whenever the king sacrificed to the gods at the daily sacrifices before dawn, sacrifices which it was compulsory for all the army officers to attend, for the purposes of which 'animals of all kinds follow the army'. Herodotus, in discussing the roles and privileges of the Spartan kings, notes that the kings when on campaign can sacrifice to the gods 'as many animals as they wish'.[117] After the sacrifices, the king then gave his orders for the day. Nothing on campaign was ventured without the approval of the gods, and Spartan law required that all the Spartan warriors on campaign had to take daily exercise in the evening, after which the army sacrificed to the gods 'to whom they have sacrificed with propitious omens'.[118] Simonides, in his elegy on Plataea, has the Spartans leaving for the Battle of Plataea (479 BC) 'accompanied by the horse-taming sons of Zeus, the Tyndarid heroes [Kastor and Polydeukes]'.[119] Spartan kings had a very regular sacrificial role, not just when at war.[120]

Poseidon was a very important deity for the Spartans, primarily because their own territory was particularly prone to earthquakes. When on campaign and an earthquake struck, Spartan hoplites would spontaneously strike up the 'paean' (see further below) – a hymn in honour of Poseidon, which hopefully would end the earthquake.[121] Such earthquakes could end military campaigns, being seen as divine warnings. Yet while Poseidon has a role in the fighting of the *Iliad*, it is more as one of the gods in general, rather than because he possessed specific bellicose attributes; even navies did not particularly venerate him. In the *Iliad*, being on the Greek side, he was bitterly angry with Zeus in Book 13 for allowing the Trojans the upper hand in the battle, and after Hera has seduced Zeus and he lies sleeping, Sleep then urges Poseidon to go and rally the Greeks, as Hera desired. In Books 20–21, he, with all the other gods, joined the mêlée, and he stood paired against Apollo, but was not portrayed as a war deity *per se*.[122] Similarly, other gods appear on the battlefield in the *Iliad*, but this is because they are gods generally, rather than military deities. Many of the gods and goddesses participated in the episode in Book 20 in which they are ranged on different sides: Poseidon against Apollo, Enyalios against Athena, Hera against Artemis, Leto against Hermes and Hephaestus against the river-god Skamandros: 'so gods went out against gods.'[123]

Apart from her support of the Greeks in the *Iliad*, Hera's most significant involvement in war was at the Battle of Plataea (479 BC). Pausanias, the Spartan regent and commander, in desperation because his men were being attacked by the Persians, wished to respond but he could not as the sacrifices he kept making were not propitious. He therefore turned towards the temple of Hera on the plain and prayed to her that the Greek hope of victory not prove false. She answered his prayers, the omens became propitious and the Greeks went on to defeat the Persians. Pausanias here called upon Hera for assistance in a moment of dire military necessity.[124] This, however, is very much the result of the coincidence of the battle being fought near her temple: she was not a deity upon whom Pausanias would normally have called, although his trust in the goddess is implicit and unqualified, and she immediately answers his prayer for propitious omens and Herodotus presents Pausanias' action as natural and expected for a Greek commander.

Artemis has a small role in the *Iliad*, where she is rather Artemis the archer and huntress.[125] In Book 20, as seen, she is named as one of the gods who descend from Mount Olympus to aid the Trojans, but is unable to save her favourite Skamandrios (not to be confused with the river god Skamandros) from death in battle. Notably, in the battle in Book 21, she is attacked by Hera, after Athena has just bested Ares and mocked him, after which Hera, angered by Artemis' presence in the battle, abuses her:

> Of a certainty it would be far preferable for you to be on the mountain-sides, slaughtering the beasts and wild deer rather than undertaking a contest of strength with those far stronger than you are.

Having said this, Hera beat Artemis about the ears with Artemis' own bow, laughing while she did so: Artemis fled.[126] In the *Iliad,* therefore, Artemis is ineffectual as a warrior, but elsewhere in Greek myth and cult there are, as with Aphrodite, indications that Artemis was inextricably connected with warfare in her manifestation as Artemis Agrotera, 'Artemis of the Wilderness'. The Athenians, according to Xenophon, swore before the Battle of Marathon (490 BC) that if they defeated the Persians they would sacrifice to Artemis as many she-goats as the number of Persians they killed. After the battle there were not enough she-goats, so they commuted the sacrifice to an annual one of 500 goats to her, on the sixth day of the month Boedromion (the anniversary date of the battle), and were still doing this in Xenophon's time, even though the number of dead must have been equalled by the number of sacrificed goats over a century earlier,[127] for Herodotus reports that the Athenians claimed that they had lost 192 citizens for about 6,000 Persians slain. There are many questions unanswered here. Why, for example, did Herodotus not mention the vow? Why was Artemis not involved when the Persians invaded again in 480–479 BC, or rather, not mentioned in the Herodotean narrative? Why was she so important at the battle of Marathon?

Although Xenophon does not give Artemis an epithet, he must mean her to be Artemis Agrotera, for it is in this role that she was sacrificed to before battle, with a goat being the animal of sacrifice. Xenophon notes with respect to the Spartans that when they were about to go into battle in 394 BC, they sacrificed a goat to Artemis Agrotera, 'as was their custom',[128] and it was Artemis Agrotera who was invoked by the Greeks whenever they made the sacrifice of the *sphagia* immediately prior to battle. She was a liminal goddess, a goddess of mountains, hills and wild places, and a deity present on the liminal place of the battlefield, where the civilized values of the *polis* were lacking. Marathon was decidedly an Athenian battle (with aid from the nearby city of Plataea), and fought against overwhelming odds.

Apollo is the first deity met in the *Iliad*, a deity of vengeance against the Greeks, who have captured the daughter of his priest Chrysis. The priest, an old man, goes to the Greek camp and beseeches Agamemnon to return his daughter. Agamemnon refuses. Chrysis, bitterly downcast and shedding tears as he makes his way along the seashore, called upon his god, Apollo, reminding him of all the acts of piety he has rendered to him. Apollo stormed down from Mount Olympus, and with his arrows killed dogs, horses and then men. Funeral pyres smoked constantly: a plague had struck the camp. Calchas, the Greek mantis (seer), is frightened to address the Greek assembly but Achilles encourages him to do so: so he reports that Apollo has sent the sickness and must be placated by the daughter being returned. In a sense, this has nothing to do with the actual war and its progress, but Agamemnon's insistence that he be compensated for the loss of the daughter, by taking in turn Achilles' sex-slave Briseis, leads Achilles to go to his tent and sulk, forbidding his men to fight and allowing the Trojans to take the lead in the battle, a process Zeus encourages in order to bring eventual honour to Achilles. In the war, Apollo fights alongside his sister Artemis, but not particularly effectively, and she upbraids him for not doing his share.[129]

Numerous festivals for Apollo were celebrated at Sparta, but these were not connected with warfare. Noteworthy, however, is that the Spartans did not undertake military activity while they were celebrating his festival of the Karneia, and, because of the celebration of the Karneia in 480 BC, the Spartans sent only 300 Spartiates (and helots) to Thermopylae. If the army was on campaign when the Karneia was due to be celebrated, the Spartan king in the field would add extra days to the month so that the day of the Karneia did not technically occur. The Spartans were prevented from arriving for the Battle of Marathon until the Athenians and Plataeans had won, as they had to wait until the full moon; this might well have been a reference to the celebration of the Karneia.[130]

Interestingly, Herodotus' account of the divine intervention at Delphi when the Persians attacked it in 479 BC includes sacred weapons moving outside of their own accord from within the temple, thunderbolts, rocks falling from Mount Parnassus and the intervention of two local heroes (Phylasus and Autonous) whose shrines were near Apollo's temple – but he records no specific role for Apollo himself.[131] When the Gauls invaded Greece in 279 BC and battle ensued at Thermopylae, Pausanias records that the Athenians surpassed all the other Greeks in the battle, and that the bravest of them was Kydias, who died in this, his first battle: his family dedicated his shield to Zeus Sôtêr ('Zeus the Saviour'). A further battle took place at Delphi: Pausanias writes that ill omens more direct than ever before were recorded, sent 'by the god' (Apollo), instancing thunder, lightning, earthquakes and the appearance of local heroes, including again Phylakos, while rocks fell from Parnassus (but Pausanias attributed these to a severe frost). Pausanias records that the god Apollo himself announced to the Delphians who had fled in terror to his temple that he would defend his shrine, but this perhaps refers to the priestess herself declaring this as an oracle. At night, Pan himself sent fear (*phobos*) amongst the Gauls, who attacked each other in their confusion, after which they were completely routed and their forces destroyed. A festival, the Sôtêria ('Deliverance'), was instituted at Delphi in thanks to Apollo for saving the sanctuary.[132] Much closer in time than Pausanias, an inscription of the very year of the battle records that Apollo himself appeared at Delphi and assisted the Greek soldiers to repel and defeat the Gauls; the same inscription indicates that shields captured from the Gauls were dedicated in Apollo's temple.[133]

So in the post-Homeric world, gods are recorded to have aided the Greeks but without actually fighting or appearing in battle: the divine presence, when seen, is that of local heroes. Of demi-gods, the Dioskouroi are the most prevalent in the recorded epiphanies – and not only for the Spartans.[134] What is to be made of this Homeric-style direct interference of a god in battle, something Herodotus and the later historians Thucydides and Xenophon did not countenance? In 279 BC, the actual presence of Apollo was claimed, and not merely the intervention of heroes via epiphanies. The threat to Delphi from the Gauls was of such a scale that the god himself could be envisaged as having a personal interest, along with the local heroes. Why did these stories of epiphanies and Apollo's direct appearance exist? It is probably that word had spread amongst the Greek hoplites that the god had been sighted, and that the heroes of the land had come to their aid – as they had in the past, in the case of Phylakos – doubly assuring their success based on his previous involvement. These tales had much the same purpose as the omens of armour and weapons miraculously appearing outside temples before battles, of propitious omens from the gods or of supportive oracles: all demonstrated to the soldiers entering and engaging in battle that the gods took an interest in them and ensured their victory. This was more than a mere psychological boost for the combatants but a very real encouragement for them. Onasander comments that a belief that the gods supported the reason for their war caused combatants to fight more effectively and enthusiastically (see below).

On the eve (432 BC) of the Peloponnesian War, the Spartans enquired at Delphi about whether they should go to war against the Athenians. Through the medium of the Pythian priestess, they received the reply: 'Apollo would be on their side if they fought with all their might, whether they called upon him for help or not.' Thucydides' narrative certainly does not include any reference to any Spartan calling upon Apollo for military assistance, and it is clear that he himself was not inclined to believe this oracle, for he prefaces Apollo's answer with a very telling 'so it is said', despite the fact that he himself believed in oracular responses and on a few occasions actually explained how prophecies came to be fulfilled.

But the intention of the 'story' is that it was credible that the Spartans received this oracle. And an important if little-mentioned point is the identity of the god who replied, for just as the Pythia was the mouthpiece of Apollo, so Apollo in fact forwarded the will of Zeus: while Apollo inspired the Pythia, he himself did not make the decisions – it was believed that Zeus communicated his will to Apollo. In this case, the oracle probably meant that Zeus would aid the Spartans if they did go to war (if they fought with all their might), and this support is logical given that the Spartan kings claimed descent from him.[135]

Famously, the Athenians sent an embassy to consult the Delphic oracle prior to the Persian invasion of 480 BC, and were told, basically, that the Athenians should flee their city. Yet, unhappy with this response, the ambassadors asked for a second oracle, and were told that Athena had entreated Zeus on their behalf, and, although she could not fully persuade him, he granted that, while their city would be burned, their wooden walls (that is, their triremes) would be safe.[136] This emphasizes the Greek notion of prayer and worship – that the will and decisions of the gods, even of Zeus, could be changed with appropriate entreaties, prayer and sacrifices. Hence it was that a commander such as Pausanias in 479 BC could keep making sacrifices at Plataea until the gods had changed their minds and allowed him to attack the enemy.

Thanatos: The Deity of Death on the Battlefield

A particularly magnificent Athenian red-figure calyx-krater of *c.* 510 BC by the potter Euxitheos and the painter Euphronios (both have their names on the vase) depicts on its obverse the dead Sarpedon, son of Zeus. Here, the gods Thanatos (Death) and Hypnos (Sleep), both bewingéd and armed as warriors, lift the prostrate body of Sarpedon, who fought for the Trojans, while the god Hermes with his herald's staff, in his guise as *psychopompos*, guider of the souls of the dead, looks on, making a male gesture of mourning, raising his right hand over the body (Figure 6.3). Sarpedon is shown with several wounds literally gushing blood: he has fought the good fight and died heroically, and deserves this honourable treatment. Two mortal Trojan warriors, Laodamas and Hippolytos, stand either side of the corpse, in respectful silence; even Zeus wept tears of blood at the death of his own son.[137] A small Athenian black-figure amphora also shows Thanatos and Hypnos carring off Sarpedon, but in this case there hovers a small 'stick-figure', an armed eidolon, that is, an image of Sarpedon, representing his psyche (soul) which will now speed to Hades.[138] Mere mortal warriors cannot expect such treatment: in Homer, their souls (*psychai*) are carried off by Keres (see below).

This is an interesting episode. For as Patroclus and Sarpedon approach each other to do battle, Zeus, Sarpedon's father, looks on from Mount Olympus: pity stirs him, and in speaking to his wife Hera, he laments that

Figure 6.3: Thanatos (Death) and Hypnos (Sleep), both bewingéd, and dressed and armed as warriors, lift the prostrate body of Sarpedon, who fought for the Trojans, while the Trojan warriors Laodamos and Hippolytus look on. Athenian red-figure calyx-krater, by the potter Euxitheos and the painter Euphronios; dating to about 510 BC. Museo Nazionale di Villa Giulia, Rome 1972.11.10. (*Courtesy of Art Resource (407274)*)

Sarpedon must die, and wonders aloud to her whether he ought not in fact to snatch him from the battle and set him down in his native land, Lycia, rather than acquiesce in his being slain. Hera, pitiless, abuses her husband: if Sarpedon is saved from the battle, she argues, why should not the other gods save their own offspring from death as well, for many of the warriors battling around Troy are sons of the immortals (*athanatoi*: the deathless gods) Zeus must suffer Sarpedon's death, for he is after all mortal, and must die anyway. But she softens the blow for Zeus, suggesting that Thanatos and Hypnos take his body to Lycia, where his kin can bury it, placing over him a burial mound and stone marker. Zeus harkened to her words, but wept tears of blood upon the earth. [139] Even the gods suffer personal loss from war.

The Keres

Sarpedon, as a son of Zeus, is carried off by Thanatos; mere mortals, however, in the world of the *Iliad*, were dealt with by the *Keres*, female *daimones* (very loosely, 'spirits'), who carried off those who died violent deaths in combat. *Ker* itself as a singular noun in the Homeric poems does not reflect a deification of death but is a concrete noun, simply referring to the state of death. But Keres (the plural of *ker*) appears three times, personified directly, in the *Iliad*, especially in the well-known description of the scene which Hephaestus crafted on the shield he made for Achilles at Thetis' request, to replace that which Patroclus wore in battle and which was taken by Hector when he slew him. The portrayal is a grisly one:

> Then the soldiers set their ranks in order and fought astride the banks of the river, ever striking at one another with bronze-tipped spears. And in the fray amongst them Strife (Eris) and Tumult (Kydoimos) and murderous Death (Ker) joined in, grasping one man, fresh-wounded, still living, another yet without a wound, and another dead she dragged by the feet through the bloodbath; reddened with the blood of men was the raiment on her shoulders. As if they were living mortals they entered into the fray and fought; each was carrying off the slaughtered corpses of those fallen. [140]

Hesiod too described a shield, this time of Heracles, with a battle scene depicting Pursuit, Flight, Fear (Phobos), Slaughter, Eris, Tumult (Kydoimos) and murderous Ker (as in the *Iliad* passage just cited) amidst the fray. Moreover, in his *Theogony*, Hesiod provides a revealing family history: Ker (singular) is the daughter of the goddess Night, and her siblings included Fate, Death, Sleep and the race of Dreams. [141]

Were these descriptions of Homer and Hesiod poetic licence? Did hoplites think that their bodies were borne away by Keres? Homer and Hesiod were both read, and in the case of Homer recited publicly: hence it is possible that hoplites marching into battle considered that this might be their fate – for their *psychai* to be borne away to Hades by the Keres. Hence in Simonides' epitaph, the Spartan seer (*mantis*) serving at Thermopylai in 480 BC who predicted his own death at the hands of the Persians knew that 'the Keres' were approaching him, placing him in an heroic context.[142] They remained associated with violent death throughout the centuries:[143] Quintus Smyrnaeus in his fourth-century AD account of the fall of Troy refers repeatedly to them in company with Eris (Strife), Phobos (Panic), Deimos (Terror), Enyo, Kydoimos and Thanatos; the Keres laugh at the warrior who attempts to escape them.[144] Kydoimos accompanies Enyo in battle, and a scholiast on Homer explains Kydoimos as, in fact, an object which Enyo swings, as if it were a weapon.[145]

The Dioskouroi March into Battle

Kastor and Polydeukes (Castor and Pollux) did not fight at Troy for they had died earlier in their native Sparta.[146] At some stage, the two brothers were heroised and worshipped as gods at Sparta, and a statue of each of them was carried into war with the Spartan army, clearly so that they would participate actively in the campaign. Both Spartan kings went to war with the Spartan army, until about 506/505 BC, when the Spartan kings Kleomenes and Demaratos disagreed publicly in front of the army and the allied contingents, when they had arrived in Attica, as to whether or not to invade Attica. This was much to the embarrassment of the Spartan state, and caused the aborting of the campaign. Consequently, it was decided that in future only one king would go on campaign, and the other would remain in Sparta: similarly, only one statue would be taken to war.[147] This seems to be the only case in which what could be termed 'religious icons' were carried with a Greek army into battle. They made an appearance at the Battle of Plataea.[148]

The Iconography of Divine Intervention

Vase paintings, in an iconographic reflection of the literary discourse, depict individual hero-combatants with gods present who were particularly involved in duels between opposing Greek and Trojan warrior pairs. A particularly fine example is a sixth-century BC red-figure Athenian vase by the Andokides

Painter which shows two unnamed warriors with shields raised and spears aimed for each others' loins (Figure 6.4). Athena stands on the left, also with a spear and wearing her aegis, from which a snake seems to prepare to strike. Her lack of pity for the other warrior is indicated by the motif of her casually holding a lotus flower; Hermes as the messenger god has probably arrived to indicate Zeus' will as to who will win and hence survive the duel, or it could be that he is there as the psychopompos, ready to lead the right-hand warrior, who will be slain by his opponent, who has Athena's support, into Hades.[149]

On one side of the exterior of an Athenian red-figure cup, by the Douris Painter and dated to about 490–480 BC, Ajax and Hector are shown duelling while Athena and Apollo look on. Athena stands behind the Greek hero Ajax, while Apollo is behind Hector. All four are named. The artists depict the partisanship of the gods, with Athena supporting the Greeks, Apollo the Trojans. In this case, however, Hector will live to fight another day, despite the presence of Athena, for it is Zeus' will that Hector be slain by Achilles;

Figure 6.4: Athena standing behind the left-hand warrior indicates her support for him, which dooms the right-hand warrior, behind whom Hermes as leader of the souls of the dead awaits, to escort him to Hades. Red-figure Athenian hydria by the Andokides Painter, dating to the late sixth-century BC. Louvre G1. (*Courtesy of Art Resource (149986)*)

Ajax also survives. The other side of the cup shows Menelaos and Paris (both named: Paris as Alexander), with Menelaos dashing after a fleeing Paris. Behind Menelaos stands Artemis, and behind Paris, Aphrodite, who holds his bow for him (for the Greeks, a weapon not used by warriors), while the spear he holds is ineffectual, as he is holding it with its point to the ground as he runs away from Menelaos' furious onslaught. Interestingly, the vase painter has closely followed Homer's narrative – other deities stand behind fighting warriors, while Aphrodite is present as Paris flees, and Artemis, also on the Trojan side, watches helplessly as Menelaos sprints towards the fleeing Paris. On the interior of the same cup is a different but related theme, with Eos carrying off the body of her son Memnon (both are named), after he has been killed in battle (Figure 6.5).[150] In these scenes, the head-scarves of Eos

Figure 6.5: Eos carries off the body of her son Memnon. The interior of an Athenian red-figure cup by the Douris Painter, dating to about 490–480 BC: height 12cm. Louvre G115. (*Courtesy of Art Resource (150247)*)

and Aphrodite (and the hair ribbon of Artemis), as opposed to the helmet of Athena, symbolize their non-martial nature. Here, the vase painter accepts the portrait in the *Iliad* of the unwarlike Aphrodite.

Eos is depicted on another vase, an Athenian sixth-century BC black-figure amphora, mourning for her son who lies prostrate on the ground: she cuts off a lock of her hair over him; behind her are Memnon's armour and weapon, piled up as a monument to his death.[151] Another vase, an Athenian red-figure volute krater by the Berlin Painter, dating to about 500–480 BC, pictorially narrates the duel between Achilles and Memnon which both their mothers watch anxiously. Thetis stands behind her son Achilles, Eos behind Memnon, who is shown staggering before Achilles, about to meet his doom. Thetis stretches out her right hand in worry for her son, but Eos has her left hand in her hair, which she will soon rip and tear out as a sign of mourning for her son, who will soon be dead. The divine mothers' pain, suffering and worry reflect the universal grief of mothers whose sons go to war and die in battle. This pain is one which mortals also feel, for Priam and Hecabe are described by Homer as watching, from the walls of Troy, the slaughter of their son Hector by Achilles.[152]

Interestingly, the other side of this vase continues the theme: the final confrontation between Achilles, with Athena behind him, and Hector, with Apollo behind him; all four are named on the vase. Before Achilles' dynamic onslaught, Hector is staggering back, with blood spurting from wounds in his chest and left thigh. Athena, to emphasize her martial character, is shown wearing the dreadful aegis, which strikes terror into foes, together with a helmet and spear; Apollo, grim-faced, is leaving the scene, casting a backward glance at the hero who has met his bane, and whom the god cannot assist.[153]

Heroes and their Bones Winning Battles

Gods were part and parcel of Greek warfare. In addition, mere mortals could be raised posthumously and even, from the fifth century BC on, in their own lifetime to heroic status. Several heroes of myth were accorded this treatment, such as Orestes, the son of Agamemnon. After the Spartans in the sixth century BC had lost their war against the city of Tegea, they consulted the oracle at Delphi, and were instructed to discover the bones of Orestes, which they did: in Tegea in fact. Having brought his bones back to Sparta, the Spartans then had major military successes with his support. Although not specifically stated by the source of this information (Herodotus), Orestes' bones would have been reburied at Sparta and venerated with a hero cult.

Another case is that of Theseus, in mythology the first king of Athens: his bones were brought from the Aegean island of Skyros to Athens in 476 BC, and thereafter venerated, clearly in the expectation that their first king would assist the Athenians in battle. In Sophocles' play, *Oedipus at Colonus*, written shortly before Sophocles' death in 406 BC, Oedipus, after blinding himself, left Thebes for Athens, and promised the Athenians to aid them in war against the Thebans. At this point Athens and Thebes were deadly enemies, and Oedipus' assistance in war will be 'better than many shields and the imported spear of neighbours'.[154]

Historical examples are also evident. Founders of colonies (*oikistai*) were routinely honoured after death with religious rites and worshipped as a divine hero. Amphipolis had been founded in Thrace by the Athenian general Hagnon in 437/436 BC, and he was venerated there with a cult. But the city was captured by the Spartans in 425 BC, and when the Athenians tried to reclaim it in 421 BC, the Spartan general Brasidas was killed in battle but the city remained in Spartan hands. The inhabitants buried Brasidas with great ceremony and 'sacrificed to him as a hero and gave him the honour of contests, and annual sacrifices'. They stopped honouring Hagnon as a hero on the grounds that 'because they were at war with the Athenians, Hagnon could no longer be honoured with similar benefit or contentment'. Clearly, Hagnon's support in war would no longer be forthcoming, while that of Brasidas, as a great military leader, would be far more effective.[155]

Invoking the Gods with Song: the Paean

The Greeks sang hymns (*hymnoi*) to the gods in a variety of contexts. A particular genre of hymn was the paean, especially associated with supplication. Such paeans were mainly addressed to Apollo, but they could more generally invoke the gods as helpers and thank them for their assistance, and paeans were especially associated with battle.[156] Ancient Greeks expressed this as 'to strike up the paean' (start singing it). When Xenophon addressed the Ten Thousand in Persia as they made the decision to march back to Greece, they voted to make sacrifices if the gods returned them home safely: the soldiers made their vows and spontaneously struck up the paean.[157] When the Sicilian naval expedition was setting sail, all the Athenians, those who had come to watch the fleet depart and those on it, said the prayers together to the gods, and sang the paean; it was also struck up by rowers in fleets about to engage the enemy.[158]

Thucydides, with his attention to religious matters, and Xenophon in particular, repeatedly mention this battle-paean. Soldiers would pray and then sing the paean enthusiastically and eagerly, as Xenophon notes on several occasions, as they went into battle. Clearly, though the ancient sources might not note it on every occasion, the paean to the gods would be struck up spontaneously by soldiers as they went into battle, seeking the assistance of the gods.[159] On one occasion, Xenophon notes, the Ten Thousand were lined up for battle: 'Then the paean was struck up, and at the same moment as the trumpet sounded, they raised up a war-cry to Enyalios, and the hoplites charged, running, at the enemy.'[160] The singular importance of the paean is indicated by Aeschylus' inclusion of it in his play *Persians*, of 472 BC, dealing with the defeat of the Persians at Salamis (480 BC). As the Greek ships moved out to engage the Persians at Salamis, the entire Greek fleet took up the 'sacred paean', followed by a trumpet call, striking terror into the Persians. Hekabe also describes how when the Greeks arrived by ship at Troy, they sang the 'hateful paean'.[161]

Victorious armies would sing it to thank and praise the gods who had granted them victory, and when the victory monument itself was erected.[162] Aristocratic Samians sang a paean in honour of the victorious Spartan naval commander Lysander when he ended the Athenian-supported democracy on the island.[163] Interestingly, Thucydides notes that when the Athenians and Syracusans met in a night-battle at Epipolai (in which the Athenians were defeated) in 413 BC, the Syracusans had the upper hand, partly because they overheard the Athenian password. But what also caused a great deal of confusion was the paean, for the Dorian paean sung by the Dorians in the Athenian force was similar to that of the enemy Syracusans, who were also Dorians:

> But what placed the Athenians to greatest disadvantage, causing them the most harm, was actually the singing of the paean. For the paean of both armies was quite similar, and this caused perplexity amongst the Athenians. Whenever the Argives or the Corcyraeans or any other Dorian contingent of the Athenian army raised the paean, the Athenians were as much struck with terror as when the enemy sang theirs.[164]

Both sides (if Greek) would of course sing the paean, hoping to win the favour of the gods, as this case demonstrates.[165] Paeans were a prelude to battle, involving heartfelt singing as men walked or rushed into battle; they invoked the gods as a general body and called upon their aid, and could in turn be sung in thanks to the gods after a victory. A subsidiary purpose, as with all battle cries, would have been an attempt to strike fear into the enemy (as it did with the Athenians as just discussed). As the army sang, it would have served the time-honoured role of the battle-cry, raising the soldiers' spirits, thus enthusing them for the coming contest. Paean singing was also a recognition that the gods were interested in battle and could affect its outcome, if combatants were pious and sought their assistance.

Declaring War: The 'Just War'

Related to this is the historical concept of the 'just war'. Combatants throughout history have often taken pains to indicate that their cause was just and that the gods – or God – were on their side. The Romans declared war with an elaborate ceremony involving specially designated priests, the *fetiales*, which ensured that the gods approved of a particular military undertaking: it was a 'just war'. This concept, however, seems to have been largely missing from Greek warfare.[166] While the Greeks clearly believed that they received the assistance of the gods as a group in warfare, particularly against the barbarians, and while there was a concept that individual gods would assist a particular army in battle (the Dioskouroi in the case of the Spartans, or Athena for the Athenians), they did not wage war in the name of the gods.

But there was a feeling that war could be justified, particularly if oaths had been broken, which would mean that sacred vows to the gods had been dishonoured.[167] This was the case when the Spartans commenced the siege of the Boeotian city of Plataea in 430 BC, the site of the defeat of the Persians in 479 BC. Thucydides, with his usual attention to religious matters when these impinge on his narrative, writes that Archidamos, the Spartan king leading the campaign, when he heard that the Plataeans would not surrender, called upon the 'gods and heroes that protect' the land of Plataea to witness that it was only after the Plataeans had broken their oaths and the Spartans' 'reasonable' demands had been rejected that Archidamos decided to punish their city. He asked the gods and heroes to give their consent to punish the wrongdoers, and after he made his appeal to the gods (an *epitheiasmos*), he began the successful siege of Plataea.[168] In 432/431 BC, the ephor Sthenelaidas, in urging the Spartan assembly to declare war on the Athenians, had finished his speech thus: 'With the gods let us punish the unjust deeds of the Athenians.'[169]

Much later, Onasander, in his first-century AD *Strategikos* (*Advice for a General*), must have been echoing the philosophy of Classical warfare when he wrote that soldiers fight better and more courageously for a 'just cause'. He further commented that the gods also looked favourably upon these and will assist soldiers by becoming 'comrade soldiers' fighting with them side-by-side, while those soldiers who participate in an unjust war which is displeasing to heaven enter such a war with trepidity.[170] As with Archidamos, the emphasis is on fighting a 'just war' (*to dikaion polemon*), which the gods will support, and this was a vital facet of the campaign. Onasander also advises that a general must purify his army before leading it out, by rites dictated by the law or by the advice of his diviners (*manteis*), and should carry out expiatory sacrifices for any wrong the state or any citizen has committed before commencing the campaign.[171] This will ensure the gods' support, for, in the final analysis, no matter how many gods fought for Troy and how enthusiastically, the 'crime' of Paris' abduction of Helen and his adultery spelt Troy's doom. In Onasander's section on undertaking divination before battle, if the omens are good, the general should tell his troops that the gods in fact are ordering them to fight: soldiers are more courageous if they fight believing they have divine good will on their side.[172] Onasander also believed that those who have suffered wrongs could not simply expect that the gods would exact vengeance for them: 'Whoever trusts to the gods for revenge for what they have suffered are indeed thinking piously, but on the other hand they are not acting for their own safety.'[173] Clearly he was intending that one had to march to war, invoking the gods, to exact retribution for wrongs done to one.

In contrast to Onasander, however, Aelian the Tactician in his fourth-century BC work *Concerning the Defence of Fortified Positions* has absolutely no mention of the gods or of divination, but deals with purely practical means for defending a city; similarly, Asklepiodotos' first-century BC *Taktika* has no reference to the gods. In the case of these two authors, there is a completely secular, human-orientated focus. Presumably they did not regard the gods as irrelevant, but rather were focussing purely on the profane military aspects of campaigning and warfare. Polyainos' second-century AD *Strategika*, however, does record several 'ruses' involving religion, which were obviously considered legitimate, but this was not the intervention of the gods as such.

Conclusion

In Homer, the gods were present at the battles around Troy; in accounts of historical battles, individual local heroes could appear, but the gods' assistance occurred without their direct military intervention, as in the case of Brasidas' campaign at Lekythos. Only a dire case, such as the threat of Gauls to Delphi in 279 BC, compelled a god – Apollo himself, not a military deity in his own right – to appear. For direct divine aid, it was the 'local hero' who could be relied upon. Whatever the level of their manifestation, hoplites, naval rowers and their generals in the Archaic and Classical periods firmly believed that the gods could and would assist them. Prayer, sacrifice and paeans would invoke the gods and bring them to the army's assistance. Without question, the ancient Greeks embraced an ideology of divine assistance in which the gods were not disinterested viewers in the military conflicts of their worshippers, but were willing to render assistance.

Notes

1. Hom. *Il.* 20.31–40, quotation: 31; laughs aloud: 21.388–90.
2. Hom. *Il.* 20.428–54.
3. Hom. *Il.* 21.391–414, 420–35.
4. See, for various interpretations of the 'Mourning Athena': Bloedow, 1999 (extensive bibliography at 27–28 n.3); *LIMC* ii Athena no. 625. Copenhagen Ny Carlsberg Glyptotek 231a (*LIMC* ii Athena no. 198) is a similar relief in which Athena holds and contemplates her helmet before a stele seen from the side. For casualty lists at Athens, see now esp. Arrington, 2015, 91–123.
5. *IG* I³ 1147.
6. Hes. *Theog.* 886–900, 924–29, with F343. The story was a popular one, found next in the *Hom. Hymn* 28 *Athena* 4–15, then in numerous writers; more sources are cited at *LIMC* ii.1 p. 985. Cf. Deacy, 2000, 289.
7. Paus. 1.24.5.
8. *LIMC* ii Athena nos 334–80.
9. Louvre F32; *ABV* 135.43 (not in *LIMC* ii Athena, but *LIMC* ii no. 352 is very similiar).
10. *Hom. Hymns* 11, 28 *Athena*.
11. *Hom. Hymn* 5 *Aphrodite* 16–17; *Homeric Hymns* 9, 27 *Artemis*.
12. *Hom. Hymn* 5 *Aphrodite* 10–13.
13. *Hom. Hymn* 3 *Demeter* 424; Hes. *Theog.* 924–26.
14. *Agelaie*: Hom. *Il.* 4.128, 5.765, 6.270, 6.279, 15.213; Hes. *Theog.* 318, *Shield Her.* 197; Hesych. and Suda *sv* Agelaie.
15. Agestrate: Hes. *Theog.* 925.
16. Hdt. 1.66.1–4; Paus. 8.23.1, 8.45.4–46.1, 8.47.1. Athena *Alea* had a temple in Tegea, now badly ruined, where the Tegeans dedicated the chains which the Spartans had brought with them when they invaded Tegea, with the intention of enchaining their Tegean prisoners: the Tegeans, however, defeated the Spartans, and used these chains on them instead.
17. *Alalkomenêis*: Hom. *Il.* 4.8, 5.908; Bacchyl. F15; Paus. 9.33.5–7; Ael. *Var. Hist.* 12.57; Steph. Byz. *sv* Alalkomenion; Schachter, 1981, 1.112–14. Athena *Alalkomenêis* was worshipped at a sanctuary (the Alalkomeneion) in the city of Alalkomenai in Boeotia, and the goddess as its protector was said to have kept the city independent.
18. *Alkimache*: *Pal. Anth.* 6.124.2; Suda *sv* Alkimache.
19. Paus. 9.4.1–2.
20. Paus. 7.27.2; Davison, 2009, 1.39–43.
21. Plut. *Arist.* 20.3.
22. Paus. 1.28.5.

23. *Atrytone*: Hom. *Il*. 2.157, 5.115, 5.714, 10.284, 21.420, *Od*. 4.762, 6.323; Hes. *Theog*. 925; Suda *sv* Atrytone.
24. *Eryma*: Paus. 8.47.5.
25. *Glaukopis*: Hom. *Il*. 1.206, 2.166, 2.172, 5.29, 5.133, 5.405, 8.30, 9.390, 10.483, 10.553, 22.177, 22.446.
26. *Gorgopis*: Soph. *Ajax* 450–52; Suda *svv* Adamastos, Gorgopis.
27. *Itonia*: Luyster, 1965, 157; esp. Lagos, 2001.
28. Bacchyl. F15; Paus 1.13.3 (shields' dedication), 9.34.1–5; Hesych. and Suda *sv* Itone.
29. *Laossoos*: Hom. *Il*. 13.128, *Od*. 22.210; Suda *sv* Laossoos.
30. Eris *Laossoos*: Hom. *Il*. 20.48.
31. *Leitis:* Hom. *Il*. 10.460; Paus. 5.14.5; Suda *sv* Leitis, cf. Suda *sv* Leias.
32. *Nikê*: acropolis; Paus. 1.22.4; Suda *sv* Nikê Athena; Megara: Paus. 1.42.4.
33. *Persepolis*: Suda *sv* Teleporon.
34. *Phobesistrate*: Ar. *Knights* 1177, with schol.
35. *Polemedokos*: Strabo 9.2.29.
36. *Poliatis*: Paus. 8.47.5.
37. *Polioukhos*: Ar. *Knights* 581; Paus 3.17.2.
38. *Polyleidis*: Alcaeus F298.9.
39. *Promachos*: Paus 2.34.8.
40. *Promachorma*: Paus. 2.34.8.
41. *Rhysiptolis*: Hom. *Il*. 6.305, cf. *Hom. Hymn* 9 *Athena* 3, *Hom. Hymn* 29 *Athena* 3.
42. *Salpinx:* temple: Paus. 2.21.2; trumpet: Thuc. 6.69; see also Aesop *Fables* 289; cf. Achilles' voice like a trumpet at Hom. *Il*. 18.219.
43. *Soteira*: Paus. 8.44.4.
44. *Sthenias*: Paus. 2.30.6, 2.32.5.
45. *Stratia*: Plut. *Mor*. 801e (and Ares Enyalios).
46. Athens National Museum 6447 (*LIMC* ii Athena no. 146; Dillon, 2002, 16 fig. 1.2).
47. Paus. 1.24.5–7.
48. Athens National Archaeological Museum 129 (*LIMC* ii Athena no. 220, vi Nikê no. 196).
49. Paus. 1.28.2: the spear and crest of her helmet were visible out at sea as soon as ships sailing to Athens passed the promontory at Sounion; Davison, 2009, 277–96.
50. *LIMC* ii Athena nos 151–52.
51. *The Little Iliad* 1; vases and coins: *LIMC* ii Athena nos 103–10; Athena looks on: no. 105.
52. Skamandrios: Hom. *Il*. 5.49–57; Phereklos: *Il*. 5.59–68.
53. Hom. *Il*. 5.95–132, cf. 260. Quotation: *Il*. 5.290–96.
54. Brasidas at Lekythos: Thuc. 4.116.1–3. For Brasidas and Athena, see Burns, 2011, 510, and 508–23 on Thucydides' portrayal of Brasidas' virtue; Pausanias sacrifices to Zeus Eleutherios: Thuc. 2.71.2; Delion: Thuc. 4.76–98. See also Lara O'Sullivan in this volume for the possibility that Brasidas had an epiphany at Lekythos.
55. Hom. *Il*. 18.516–19. The apposition when Ares and Athena work together, and the opposition of Ares and Athena in conflict with each other, is examined in detail by Deacy, 2008, with particular reference to Homer's *Iliad*.
56. *Pal. Anth.* 9.322–23.
57. Strabo 13.38 (Alcaeus F32).
58. Pin. *Olym*. 13.23.

59. Ares as child of Zeus and Hera: Hes. *Theog.* 921–23, hated by Zeus: Hom. *Il.* 5.889–95; bane of men: Hom. *Il.* 5.31; Strife: Hom. *Il.* 4.440 (see also below); for Ares' son Phobos, see below. Scholars over-emphasize Zeus' complaint about Ares (Dewald, 2013, 31), but it is not the case that Ares received little or no cult.
60. Alcaeus F70.
61. Hom. *Il.* 13.298–300; Phobos at Sparta: Plut. *Cleom.* 9.
62. For the 'rules' of hoplite battle, see esp. Krentz, 2002; Lanni, 2008.
63. Hom. *Il.* 2.385, 5.388, 5.455.
64. Menelaos as 'beloved of Ares': Hom. *Il.* 3.21, 3.52, 3.69, 3.90, 3.136, 3.206, 3.253, 3.307, 3.323, 3.430, 3.432, 3.452, 3.457, 4.13, 4.150, 5.561; Menelaos as 'Ares-like': Hom. *Il.* 4.98, 4.195, 4.205; Pylaimenes as 'beloved of Ares': Hom. *Il.* 5.576; 'attendants of Ares' (Hom. *Il.* 19.78).
65. *IG* ii² 3250 (*SEG* 35.147).
66. Paus. 1.8.4, 2.25.1, 2.32.9, 2.35.10, 3.19.7, 3.22.6–7, 5.15.6, 7.22.9, 8.32.3, 8.37.12, 8.44.7, 9.10.5; Ares Gynaikothoinas: Paus. 8.48.4–6. Statues (some at the above cult places): 1.8.4, 2.25.1, 2.35.10, 3.19.7, 5.18.5, 5.20.3, 6.19.12, 7.21.10, 8.48.4.
67. *IG* iv 717, *IG* v.2 343.
68. Plut. *Mor.* 238f.
69. *SEG* 32.1167, 43.844, 58.1341. There was a priest*ess* of Ares at Selge in Asia Minor in the Roman period: *SEG* 53.2245.
70. *SEG* 33.945.
71. See Gonzales, 2008, 132 n.68 for references.
72. *SEG* 4.171, 58.812; *LSCG Suppl.* 85. See esp. the most recent and detailed discussion of this decree in Gonzales, 2008 (esp. 121–31), who also collates and discusses the evidence for the cult of Enyalios throughout Greece (131–34). See also Guarducci, 1985, 11.
73. Xen. *Cyr.* 7.1.26, *Anab.* 1.8.18, 5.2.14, (cf. 6.5.27), *Hell.* 2.4.17 (Thrasyboulos).
74. Philost. *Gymnast.* 7.
75. Plut. *Mor.* 757d.
76. Archilochos F1; Ibycus F319; Chromios: Pin. *Nem.* 9.36–37; Ajax: Pin. *Isthm.* 6.53–54.
77. Telesilla: Paus. 2.10.8–10; *Plut.* Mor. 42c; Polyaen. *Strat.* 8.33; Socrates of Argos *FGrH* 310 F6; cf. Luc. *Love* 30; Graf 1984: 247–48 unnecessarily rejects the historical authenticity of the story.
78. Parke and Wormell, 1956, no. 84; Fontenrose, 1978, Q134.
79. Plut. *Mor.* 801e; Apoll. Rhod. *Argon.* 3.1365.
80. For example, Alcman F344.
81. Ar. *Peace* 457, with schol.
82. Pin. *Dithyramb* 2, 70b, lines 15–16; Plut. *Mor.* 285c–d.
83. Ael. Tac. 24; Luc. *The Wishers* 36.
84. Paus. 13.15.7.
85. Spartan ephebes: Paus. 3.14.9–10, 3.20.2; Ares' temple: statue of Enyalios: Paus. 3.15.7.
86. Artemis Agrotera and Enyalios: [Arist.] *Ath. Pol.* 58.1 (see Rhodes, 1993, 650); Solon: Plut. *Sol.* 9.4.
87. Paus. 3.22.6; Teles of Megara 24.11; Graf, 1984, 252; Cole, 1995, has examined male-only cults.
88. See Lara O'Sullivan in this volume.
89. Pin. *Nem.* 9.27.

90. Agamemnon: Hom. *Il.* 11.31–37; Heracles: Hes. *Shield Her.* 155; aegis: Hom. *Il.* 5.738–42.

91. Hom. *Il.* 5.330–33, 348–51.

92. Hom. *Il.* 5.592–93.

93. Paus. 1.8.4, cf. Philost. *Imag.* 2.29.

94. Callim. *Hymn to Apollo* (2) 85–86.

95. Seven: Aeschylus *Seven Against Thebes* 41; ephebic oath: *GHI* ii: no. 204 (*SEG* 16.140; also see Lycurg. *Leocr.* 76–79; Plut. *Alc.* 15.4; Stob. *Flor.* 43.48; Poll. 8.105–06; *SEG* 57.117; Dillon, 2008, 237 n.15 with bibliography). For these oaths which included Enyo, see Ian Plant in this volume.

96. *SIG*³ 527 (*ICret.* I 9,1; *SEG* 46.1210; Rhodes and Osborne, 2003, no. 88). See Krentz, 2007.

97. Dreros: *LSAG* 311 no. 1; *SEG* 27.620, 46.1210.

98. Naxos: *SEG* 35.1014, 42.872, 44.774, 46.1267; Guarducci, 1985, 8 (fig. 1), 11–12 for Enyo.

99. Oppian *Halieutica* 2.23–25.

100. Cf. Plut. *Mor.* 472 b: Zeus sends Aphrodite to the marriage chamber as she has no part in war.

101. Chamaileon of Herakleia F34 (from Athen. *Deip.* 573c; see Dillon, 2002, 200; Budin, 2008, 140–41).

102. Simonides F104a–c; Athen. *Deip.* 573d–e; Plut. *Mor.* 871b; schol. Pin. *Olym.* 13.32b.

103. Plut. *Mor.* 871a–b.

104. Marcovich, 1996, esp. 48 on Aphrodite as a war-goddess.

105. Hes. *Theog.* 933–37.

106. Flemberg, 1995.

107. Corinth: Paus. 2.5.1 (cf. Strabo 8.6.21); Sparta: 3.15.10 (Hoplismene: Armed), 3.17.5 (temple of Aphrodite Areia), cf. 3.18.8; Cyprus: 3.23.1. See Budin, 2010, 85–89; Cyrino, 2010, 51–52.

108. *Pal. Anth.* 9.320, 16.171, 173 (Aphrodite Enoplios, 'Armed Aphrodite'), 175, 176; Nonnus *Dion.* 35.175–76. Note Hesych. *sv* Encheios: (a statue) Aphrodite ('[Spear] in the hand'). For armed Aphrodite at Sparta, see Budin, 2010, 85–89.

109. Plut. *Mor.* 239a (Aphrodite Enoplios: 'Armed Aphrodite').

110. Plut. *Mor.* 317f.

111. Athens National Archaeological Musuem no. 262; Flemberg, 1995, 184; Budin, 2010, 91 fig. 5.3; Stewart, 2005, 235–36, fig. 4. See also the statue of Aphrodite arming herself with a sword in Florence at the *Accademia di Belle Arti* (Roman marble copy of a Greek original which dated to *c.* 300 BC).

112. Boston MFA 21.1213 (3.2cm high); Flemberg, 1995, 117 fig. 6; Budin, 2010, 92–93, fig. 5.4; Stewart, 2010, 235, 237 fig. 5, 238.

113. For these issues of Zeus' motive, see Clay, 1999.

114. Agamemnon: *Il.* 2. 477–83; Hector: *Il.* 15.610–12.

115. Xen. *Lac. Pol.* 13.2. I adopt here the *Oxford Classical Text Thucydides* (1900) reading of E.C. Marchant at 13.2: *toin sioin* ('the twin [gods]') rather than *tois syn autoi* ('the gods associated with him [Zeus]'). The latter is vague, and reading the twins makes better sense. Despite the fact that only one of the twin gods travelled with the king in the Classical period, it would make sense that the kings would continue what would have been the traditional sacrifice (to both twins) before the

change around 506 BC to only one king going on campaign. See also Plut. *Mor.* 478a for the Dioskouroi accompanying the Spartan army.

116. For these border crossings, the *diabateria*, consult Sonya Nevin in this volume.
117. Xen. *Lac. Pol.* 13.3; Hdt. 6.56.
118. Xen. *Lac. Pol.* 12.7, 13.2–5; Dillon, 2008, 237–38.
119. Hdt. 6.57.1–2; Xen. *Lac. Pol.* 15.2–5. See below on the Dioskouroi.
120. Simonides *Elegy* 11.30–31; translation: Dillon and Garland, 2010, 385–86, doc. 11.48.
121. Xen. *Hell.* 4.7.4.
122. Poseidon's bitter anger: *Il.* 13.16, 13.37–38, 13.351–60, 13.551–63; Poseidon into the fray for the Greeks: *Il.* 14.352–90; Book 20: esp. 20.57–75; involvement generally, for example, 15.8, 15.41–43, 15.51–54, 15.158–219, 20.132–52, 20.318–39, 21.286–97.
123. Hom. *Il.* 20.67–75 (quotation: line 75).
124. Hdt. 9.61–62 (cf. 9.52, 9.69); Plut. *Arist.* 17.6–18.2; Mikalson, 2003, 94–96.
125. For example, Hom. *Il.* 24.606.
126. Hom. *Il.* 21.478–513, quotation: 485–88.
127. Xen. *Anab.* 3.2.11–12.
128. Xen. *Hell.* 4.2.20. For a discussion of Artemis and war, see Budin, 2016, 59–67.
129. Hom. *Il.* 21.471–77.
130. Limited Spartan force sent to Thermopylai due to Karneia: Hdt. 7.206.1; Marathon: Hdt. 6.106.3, 6.120. Cf. Pettersson, 1992, 62–66, who argues that the Karneia itself was a military festival for Apollo, but the evidence does not strongly support this. For the insertion of extra days into months, see Ian Rutherford in this volume.
131. Hdt. 8.37–39; Pritchett, 1979, 25.
132. Paus. 10.21–23; festival: *IG* ii³ 11005 (*SIG*³ 408); other inscriptions: Champion 1995. Kydias: Paus. 10.21.5.
133. *SIG*³ 398; other ancient sources: see Pritchett, 1979, 31–32; Champion, 1995.
134. Pritchett, 1979, 19–46.
135. Thuc. 1.118.3. See Marinatos, 1981, 138; Dillon, 2017b.
136. 'Wooden Walls': Hdt. 7.139–41. There is an immense bibliography on these oracles; see recently Barker, 2006, 19–23, with some bibliography. The oracles: Parke and Wormell, 1956, nos 94–95; Fontenrose, 1978, Q146–47.
137. Museo Nazionale di Villa Giulia, Rome Inv. 1972.11.10 (no *ARV²*). All five figures are named. The theme is also shown on vases: The Metropolitan Museum of Art 56.171.25 (*ARV²* 509137) and British Museum E12 (*ARV²* 126.24). See Chris Matthew in this volume for the gendered nature of Greek mourning.
138. Louvre F388 (no *ABV* no.). The Diosphos Painter was fond of painting warrior duels.
139. Hom. *Il.* 16.419–58; described also by Philostr. *Imag.* 10. In *Il.*12.310–29, Sarpedon has told Glaukos, also fighting for the Trojans, that they go into battle to win glory, even if this might mean their death.
140. Hom. *Il.* 18.533–40. See also Suda *svv* Anamplaketoi, Ker: the Keres are inescapable and death-bringing. Homer also has them as black (*Il.* 3.454); 'murderous Ker' occurs at *Il.* 13.665. See Harrison, 1908, 183–87; Garland, 1981, 44–45; *LIMC* vi Keres. The Keres were 'dog-faced: Eur. *El.* 1252–53.
141. Hes. *Theog.* 211–17, *Shield Her.* 154–56.

142. Simonides 6 (Hdt. 7.228, with 219, 221); Dillon and Garland, 2010, doc. 11.28, p.374; Dillon and Garland, 2013, 233–34.
143. Mimnermus F2; Aeschyl. F44 (schol. Soph. *Ajax* 833); Paus. 5.19.4.
144. Quint. Smyrn. 1.307–13, 2.81–84, 5.34–40, 8.11–12, 9.146–47, 11.7–15, 14.563–64; see esp. the description at 11.151–63.
145. Hom. *Il.* 5.591–93, 18.535; schol. Hom. *Il.* 5.593.
146. Hom. *Il.* 3.236.
147. Hdt. 5.75 ('one of the sons of Tyndaros [i.e. Kastor and Polydeukes] was also to be left behind'). See also Plut. *Mor.* 1140c (they invented the Spartan war-dance).
148. See Lara O'Sullivan in this volume.
149. Louvre G1 (*ARV²* 3.2; *LIMC* v Hermes no. 859).
150. Louvre G115 (*ARV²* 434.74).
151. Museo Gregoriano Etrusco, Vatican 16589 (*ABV* 140.1).
152. Hom. *Il.* 22.410–515.
153. British Museum E468 (*ARV²* 206.122). This theme of the two divine mothers watching appears on other vases, and must have been a popular, poignant scene: see for example British Museum E77 (*ARV²* 837.1).
154. Orestes: Hdt. 1.67–68 (Huxley, 1979; Barker, 2006, 15–19; Arrington, 2015, 31–35); Theseus: Plut. *Kim.* 8.5–7 (Arrington, 2015, 198–99); Oedipus: Soph. *Oed. Col.* 1518–34 (quotation at line 1525).
155. Thuc. 5.11.1; Jones, 2010, 24–26; Dillon, 2017b.
156. For the paean, see esp. Bremmer, 1981; Furley, 1995.
157. Xen. *Anab.* 3.2.9.
158. Sicilian expedition: Thuc. 6.32.2. 7.75.7; rowers: Thuc. 1.50.5, 2.91.2; see also Diod. 13.15.3.
159. Hdt. 5.1.1; Thuc. 4.43.4, 4.96.1, 7.44.6–7, 7.83.5; Xen. *Anab.* 1.10.10, 1.8.18, 4.3.19, 4.3.29, 4.3.31, 4.8.16, 6.5.25 (cf. 6.1.5), *Hell.* 4.2.19; Diod. 4.23.1; note Timotheus F800. A fragment of Bacchylides *Dithyramb* 2.1–3 mentions a 'god-sent army' and the paean. Note how when the Spartans were on campaign, and the time came for the paean to Apollo to be sung at their festival of the Hyakinthia, those of the Spartans who were from the village of Amyklai would leave the campaign and return home: Xen. *Hell.* 4.5.11.
160. Xen. *Anab.* 5.2.14: other occurrences of the paean and Enyalios: *Anab.* 4.3.19, *Hell.* 2.4.17.
161. Aesch. *Pers.* 384–95; Eur. *Troj.* 126.
162. Hom. *Il.* 22.391 (which indicates the long history of the paean); Xen. *Hell.* 7.2.23, 7.4.36; Diod. 5.29.4, 33.14.5; Aesch. *Seven* 735; victory monument: Xen. *Hell.* 7.2.15.
163. Plut. *Lys.* 15.3
164. Thuc. 7.44.6–7.
165. As does Eur. *Phoen.* 1100–02.
166. For the justifications for war in ancient Greece, see Dewald, 2013, 38–42.
167. For the examples from Thucydides and Onasander discussed here, see Pritchett, 1979, 322–33.
168. Thuc. 2.74–75; cf. 7.18.2.
169. Thuc. 1.86.5. Gomme and Hornblower do not mention this important religious point in their commentaries.
170. Onas. *Strat.* 4.1–3, 10.26; cf. Xen. *Cyr.* 3.3.21. See the detailed discussion of Chlup 2014; cf. Smith, 1998.

171. Onas. *Strat.* 5.
172. Onas. *Strat.* 10.25–26.
173. Onas. *Strat.* 37.4.

Bibliography

Arrington, N.T., 2015, *Ashes, Images, and Memories: the Presence of the War Dead in Fifth-Century Athens*, Oxford.

Barker, E., 2006, 'Paging the Oracle: Interpretation, Identity and Performance in Herodotus' History', *G&R* 53, 1–28.

Bloedow, E.F., 1999, 'The "Mourning"/"Sinnende" Athena. The Story Behind the Relief', *Athenaeum* 87, 27–50.

Bremmer, J.M., 1981, 'Greek Hymns', in Versnel, H.S. (ed.), *Faith, Hope and Worship: Aspects of Religious Mentality in the Ancient World*, Leiden, 193–215.

Budin, S.L., 2008, *The Myth of Sacred Prostitution in Antiquity*, New York.

—— 2010, 'Enoplion Aphrodite', in Smith, A.C., and Pickup, S. (eds), *Brill's Companion to Aphrodite*, Leiden, 79–112.

—— 2016, *Artemis*, Oxford.

Burns, T., 2011, 'The Virtue of Thucydides' Brasidas' *The Journal of Politics* 73.2, 508–23.

Champion, C., 1995, 'The Soteria at Delphi: Aetolian Propaganda in the Epigraphical Record', *AJPh* 116, 213–20.

Chlup, J.T., 2014, 'Just War in Onasander's ΣΤΡΑΤΗΓΙΚΟΣ', *JAH* 2, 37–63.

Clay, J.S., 1999, 'The Whip and Will of Zeus', *Literary Imagination* 1, 40–60.

Cole, S.G., 1995, 'Women, Dogs, and Flies', *AncW* 26, 182–91.

Cyrino, M.S., 2010, *Aphrodite*, London.

Davison, C.C., 2009, *Pheidias: the Sculptures and Ancient Sources*, 3 vols, London.

Deacy, S., 2000, 'Athena and Ares: War, Violence and Warlike Deities', in Wees, H. van (ed.), *War and Violence in Ancient Greece*, London, 285–95.

—— 2008, *Athena*, London.

Dewald, C., 2013, 'Justice and Justifications: War Theory Amongst the Ancient Greeks', in Neusner, J., Chilton, B.D., and Tully, R.E. (eds), *Just War in Religion and Politics*, Lanham, 27–46.

Dillon, M.P.J., 1997, *Pilgrims and Pilgrimage in Ancient Greece*, London.

—— 1999, 'Post-Nuptial Sacrifices on Kos (Segre, *ED* 178) and Ancient Greek Marriage Rites', *ZPE* 124, 63–80.

—— 2002, *Girls and Women in Classical Greek Religion*, London.

—— 2008, '"Xenophon Sacrificed on Account of an Expedition" (Xenophon *Anabasis* 6.5.2): Divination and the Sphagia Before Ancient Greek Battles', in Brulè, P., and Mehl, V. (eds), *Le sacrifice antique. Vestiges, procédures et stratégies*, Rennes, 235–51.

—— 2017a, *Omens and Oracles in Classical Greece*, Oxford.

—— 2017b, '"Festive Crowds Welcome the God with the Piping of the Flute, Competing with the Courageous Strength of Their Limbs." Pindar *Nemean Ode* 5.37–39', in Scanlon, T., and Futrell, A. (eds), *The Oxford Handbook of Sport in the Ancient World*, Oxford.

Dillon, M.P.J., and Garland, L., 2010, *Ancient Greece*, third edition, Oxford.

—— 2013, *The Ancient Greeks*, Oxford.

Flemberg, J., 1995, 'The Transformations of the Armed Aphrodite', *The Norwegian Institute at Athens*, no vol., 109–22.

Flower, M.A., 1988, 'Agesilaus of Sparta and the Origins of the Ruler Cult', *CQ* 38, 123–34.

Fontenrose, J., 1978, *The Delphic Oracle, Its Responses and Operations, With a Catalogue of Responses*, Berkeley.

Furley, W.D., 1995, 'Praise and Persuasion in Greek Hymns', *JHS* 115, 29–46.

Garland, R., 1981, 'The Causation of Death in the *Iliad*: A Theological and Biological Investigation', *BICS* 28, 43–60.

Gonzales, M., 2008, 'New Observations on the Lindian Cult-Tax for Enyalios ("SEG" 4.171)', *ZPE* 166, 121–34.

Graf, F., 1984, 'Women, War, and Warlike Divinities', *ZPE* 55, 245–54.

Guarducci, M., 1985, 'Una nuova dea a Naxos in Sicilia e gli antichi legami fra la Naxos siceliota e l'omonima isola delle Cicladi', *Mélanges de l'Ecole française de Rome. Antiquité* 97, 7–34.

Harrison, J., 1908, *Prolegomena to the Study of Greek Religion*, second edition, Oxford.

Hornblower, S., 1992, 'The Religious Dimension to the Peloponnesian War, or, What Thucydides Does Not Tell Us', *HSPh* 94, 169–97.

Huxley, G., 1979, 'Bones for Orestes', *GRBS* 20, 145–48.

Jones, C.P., 2010, *New Heroes in Antiquity: From Achilles to Antinoos*, Cambridge MA.

Jordan, B., 1986, 'Religion in Thucydides', *TAPhA* 116, 119–47.

Krentz, P., 2002, 'Fighting by the Rules: the Invention of the Hoplite Agon', *Hesperia* 71, 23–39.

—— 2007, 'The Oath of Marathon, Not Plataia?', *Hesperia* 76, 731–42.

Lagos, C., 2001, 'Athena Itonia at Koroneia (Boiotia) and in Cilicia', *NC* 161, 1–10.

Lanni, A., 2008, 'The Laws of War in Ancient Greece', *LHR* 26.3, 469–89.

Luyster, R., 1965, 'Symbolic Elements in the Cult of Athena', *HR* 5, 133–63.

Marcovich, M., 1996, 'From Ishar to Aphrodite', *The Journal of Aesthetic Education* 30.2, 43–59.

Marinatos, N., 1981, 'Thucydides and Oracles', *JHS* 101, 138–40.

Matthaiou, A.P., 2003, 'Athenaioisi Tetagmenoisi en Temenei Herakleos (Hdt. 6.108.1)', in Derow, P., and Parker, R. (eds), *Herodotus and His World*, Oxford, 190–202.

Mikalson, J., 2003, *Herodotus and Religion in the Persian Wars*, Chapel Hill.

Parke, H.W., and Wormell, D.E.W., 1956, *The Delphic Oracle*, vols i–ii, Oxford.

Pettersson, M., 1992, *Cults of Apollo at Sparta. The Hyakinthia, the Gymnopaidiai and the Karneia*, Stockholm.

Pritchett, W.K., 1979, *The Greek State at War. Part iii: Religion*, Berkeley.

Rhodes, P.J., 1993, *A Commentary on the Aristotelian* Athenaion Politeia, revised edn, Oxford.

Rhodes, P.J., and Osborne, R. (eds), 2003, *Greek Historical Inscriptions: 404–323 B.C.*, Oxford.

Sanders, L.J., 1991, 'Dionysius I of Syracuse and the Origins of the Ruler Cult in the Greek World', *Historia* 41, 275–87.

Schachter, A., 1981, *Cults of Boiotia*, vol. 1, London.

Smith, C.J., 1998, 'Onasander on How to be a General', *BICS* 42, 151–66.

Stewart, F., 2010, 'Two Notes on Greeks Bearing Arms: The Hoplites of the Chigi Jug and Gelon's Armed Aphrodite', in Dally, O. *et al.* (eds), *Medien der Geschichte – antikes Griechenland und Rom*, Berlin, 227–43.

Winiarczyk, M., 2013, *The 'Sacred History' of Euhemerus of Messene*, Berlin.

Chapter 7

Epiphanies in Classical and Hellenistic Warfare

Lara O'Sullivan

Now, assuming the war tunic of Zeus who gathers
the clouds, she armed in her gear for the dismal fighting.
And across her shoulders she threw the betasselled, terrible
aegis, all about which Terror hangs like a garland,
and Hatred is there, and Battle Strength, and heart-freezing Onslaught,
and thereon is set the head of the grim gigantic Gorgon,
a thing of fear and horror, portent of Zeus of the aegis.
Upon her head she set the golden helm with its four sheets
and two horns, wrought with the fighting men of a hundred cities.
She set her feet in the blazing chariot and took up a spear
heavy, huge, thick, wherewith she beats down the battalions of fighting
men, against whom she of mighty father is angered.[1]

Thus that most warlike of goddesses, Athena, readies herself to enter the fray on Homer's fields of Troy to rally the spirits of Diomedes, son of Tydeus. She encourages him to return to a battle which the presence of Ares has caused him to quit, and to manifest further her interest in Diomedes' success against the god of war she assumes the place of his charioteer; standing at the mortal's side, the goddess deflects the spear that Ares launches at the hero, and instead guides Diomedes' own spear into Ares' stomach, causing the god to retreat in pain from the battlefield. Such divine presence is scarcely unusual in the world constructed by the epic poet, whose Trojan plains bear frequent witness to the interventions of powerful beings into the realm of mortal battle.

Such intermingling of gods and men retained a place in the imagination of Greek poets beyond Homer, but the phenomenon was not confined to the world of poetry. A number of historical clashes bore witness to the claimed presence of non-mortals, whether gods or, more frequently, heroes – that is, of those chthonic 'powerful dead' who received cult worship and who were felt to exert an influence in the world of the living. It is to epiphanies on the historical battlefields of Greece in the Classical and Hellenistic periods that the following chapter is devoted.[2] The phenomenon is necessarily a complex one, a product of the psychological stress of combat on the one hand and of the cultural and literary constructs that shaped ancient historical narratives on the other. Considered here will be the function of epiphany narratives, ranging from their articulation of the experience of violence in battle to their deployment as claims to kudos in the wake of fighting. Before an examination of the contexts and impacts of extraordinary battlefield appearances, however, some consideration needs to be given to the typology of epiphanies in the ancient records.

Heroes and Gods Manifest: What did an Encounter Entail?

Both gods and heroes assumed active roles in the warfare of the Classical and Hellenistic periods, but broad differences may be discerned in the manner and treatment of their interventions. In the case of claimed interventions by heroes, battlefield appearances are commonly conceived as a manifestation of the hero in anthropomorphic form within the fighting ranks. Illustrative of this is the reported experience of the Athenians at Marathon in 490 BC, of whom some 'thought they saw an apparition of Theseus in arms rushing on in front of them against the Barbarians'.[3]

Plutarch's account here is typical of many literary reports of epiphanies in distinguishing the anthropomorphic apparition from his more corporeal fellow-fighters by employing the term 'apparition' (*phasma*).[4] For those fighting alongside the hero, however, the recognition of the non-mortal presence in their midst was often ascribed to a number of visual indicators.[5] Unusual size was sometimes a factor. The inhabitants of Delphi identified as their local heroes Phylacus and Autonous, the 'two gigantic soldiers – taller than ever a man was' of whom the Persian survivors from the assault on Delphi in 480 BC spoke, while a heroic presence encountered at Marathon by an Athenian, Epizelus, was 'a man of great stature in heavy armour, whose beard overshadowed his shield'.[6] Peculiarities of dress might also distinguish the hero; so too, at times, might his miraculous disappearance once the battle was done. The presence of the Dioskouroi among the Locrians at the Battle of the River Sagra was marked out by such devices:

> On the wings also were seen two young men fighting in armour different from the rest, of an extraordinary stature, on white horses and scarlet cloaks; nor were they visible longer than the battle lasted.[7]

Marked out by similar means was the appearance of the rather obscure hero Echetlaus at Marathon, described by witnesses as 'a man of rustic appearance and dress' who, having dispatched many of the enemy with a plough, disappeared after the engagement.[8] Such visual clues were not confined to heroic epiphanies. It was the stature, beauty and dress of a captive maiden (so Plutarch) or of a priestess (so Polyaenus) at Pellene that led to the apprehension of her as a goddess (Artemis or Athena) by the Aetolian forces besieging Pellene in 241 BC.[9]

Some heroes opted for a less anthropomorphic form on the field.[10] In ancient iconography, heroes are frequently represented as (or associated with) snakes, and when the hero Cynchreus intervened at Salamis in 480 BC, he reportedly took the form of a serpent. Indeed, it is as a serpent that a hero manifests himself in what is perhaps the earliest claimed context for a divine or heroic epiphany, at the establishment of the Olympic Games. According to an Olympic tradition, an invading army of Arcadians was thrown into disarray when an infant, set naked before the Eleans' defensive line, miraculously transformed into a snake; the creature was subsequently identified as Sosipolis.[11] In a number of epiphany anecdotes the heroic presence that has been suggested by outstanding size or serpentine form was later confirmed and clarified by oracles, with oracular statements providing the Athenians with the identities both of the curious plough-wielding apparition at Marathon and of the serpent at Salamis.[12]

In some cases of epiphany, it is possible that the presence of heroes in war may have been affected through their cult statues or through an assemblage of cultic objects and weapons, material items through which the person of the hero could be invoked or invited.[13] Just such a mechanism may underlie the story of the assistance rendered by the Dioskouroi at the Battle of the River Sagra. The sources report that the Locrians had applied to the Spartans for help, and that the aid proffered by the Spartans was an alliance with the sons of Tyndareus (that is, the Dioskouroi); the Locrians thus took the Dioskouroi with them back to Locri, and the twin heroes duly made an appearance in the ensuing battle. The claim that the Dioskouroi came from Sparta on a couch especially prepared for them on the Locrians' vessel might indicate that the conveyance of a material talisman such as statues was involved.[14] Similarly present via their statues may have been the 'sons of Aeacus', the Aeacidae, witnessed by some as the 'phantoms of armed men from Aegina' who manifested in front of the Greek ships at the Battle of Salamis in 480 BC.[15] Herodotus records that a ship had been sent to Aegina to bring these heroes,[16] and once more perhaps a ritualistic fetching of cult images or objects is to be imagined.

While identification of statues or cult objects within the epiphany narratives outlined above is largely conjectural,[17] other episodes are more directly suggestive of such a mechanism. The traditions concerning the appearance of the Messenian hero Aristomenes against the Spartans at Leuktra in 371 BC are interesting in this regard, for the Messenian claims that their hero fought for the Thebans at this battle stand alongside claims that the Theban commander, Epaminondas, was advised by an oracle to take the shield of Aristomenes into battle, and that the shield was used to adorn the *tropaion* ('trophy') set up in the Theban lines.[18] The dual presences of Aristomenes – as active hero and as talismanic shield – may in fact be inter-related, with the Theban possession of the shield serving to evoke its heroic owner. A possible nexus between statues and epiphanies is more firmly posited again in one of the variant explanations of an episode of divine manifestation that occurred during an Aetolian siege of Pellene.[19] According to Plutarch, the Pellenians' own explanation of the divine presence that threw the invaders into disarray was that a statue of their goddess – a statue too terrible for men to gaze upon, and taken out into the fray by the priestess for that very reason – had driven off the enemy.[20] For the Pellenians, the presence of the statue did not diminish the sense of divine agency; that is, the statue is not to be understood as the explanation by which the story of epiphany was rationalized away. Rather, the goddess was felt to be present in her statue, and the power of the divinity was made manifest through it.

It is important to recognize this potential for epiphanies to entail something other than an anthropomorphic appearance in battle. The manifestations of gods in particular were often more indirect and less anthropomorphic than those of their heroic counterparts.[21] The events at Delphi in 480 BC neatly illustrate the difference. The advance of the Persians was met by the miraculous appearance of Apollo's sacred weapons outside his temple and, when the Persians themselves reached the sanctuary of Athena Pronaia, they were thrown into disarray by lightning bolts and landslides; a din emanating from Athena's sanctuary further panicked the invaders. The Persians were then slaughtered in flight by the Delphians, with some dispatched by the heroes Phylacus and Autonous.[22] Aptly described by Mikalson as the 'most remarkable series of miracles' in the Persian Wars,[23] the defence of Delphi clearly betrays for Herodotus the signs of divine intervention by Zeus and Apollo, but unlike the two heroes (Phylacus and Autonous), neither god makes himself visible on the battlefield;[24] rather, the power and presence of the gods are manifest through tangible demonstrations of their power, whether through lightning bolts or miraculously moved sacred weapons.

Many divine manifestations take place prior to an armed engagement rather than in its midst, and in a number of such pre-battle episodes it is via dreams that the gods make their presence felt. The Greeks were guided to the site of Plataea for their clash with the Persians in 479 BC by Zeus Soter; Athena gave crucial advice to the Rhodians (to solicit aid from Ptolemy I) when they were besieged by Demetrius Poliorcetes in 305 BC; Heracles, Apollo and Hermes all appeared in a dream to guide to safety the population of Themisonium in 287/286 BC when they were under threat from the Gauls.[25] Similarly, it was through the medium of dream that goddesses manifested themselves to the people of Cyzicus and Ilium during the Mithridatic Wars; in the case of Cyzicus, Demeter's dream-appearance was followed by the destruction of the enemy's siege towers by devastating winds.[26]

It would be misleading to deny the more indirect manifestations of gods the status of epiphanies. Comparison between the miraculous events at Delphi in 480 BC and a later, very similar set of prodigies at that very shrine is particularly instructive in this regard. When a contingent of Gauls approached Delphi in 279 BC, they were met with thunderbolts, earthquakes and rock-falls from Parnassus, and then, in flight, found themselves faced with apparitions of local heroes.[27] As detailed by Pausanias and Diodorus, this divine intervention appears construed consciously to recall the Persian episode of almost exactly two centuries earlier; in both episodes, the local population consults Apollo about the protection of the treasures in his sanctuary and is advised that the god will safeguard his own affairs; in both, the attackers are driven back by the weather and by rock-falls, and are then confronted with epiphanies of heroes – even, in the case of one Phylacus, by the very same hero on both occasions.[28] In contrast to the Herodotean version of the Persian assault, however, the preservation of Apollo's sanctuary in 279 BC is explicitly and immediately couched in the language of epiphany.[29] From the year following the repulse of the attack (278 BC), we have an inscription from Cos detailing the despatch of sacred ambassadors from Cos to Delphi to offer sacrifices of thanksgiving to Pythian Apollo as well as to Zeus Soter and Nikê, and the motivational clauses of the decree speak directly of the god's epiphany: the *polis* of Cos pays thanks-offerings 'to the god for manifesting himself during the perils which confronted the sanctuary'.[30]

Unambiguously epiphanic language recurs in subsequent epigraphical allusions to the event, and also in the literary accounts. Cicero, in the *De Divinatione*, has the Pythia address an oracle to the Gallic leader, Brennus, in which he is warned that Apollo and 'the white virgins' will see to his impious attack on Delphi, with the result that 'the virgins were seen fighting against the Gauls, and [the Celtic army] was overwhelmed with snow'; Justin knows not only of epiphanies by Athena and Artemis (thus Cicero's 'white goddesses', as Diodorus confirms), but also, very explicitly, of Apollo, who is witnessed 'jumping down' from the roof of the temple at the barbarian foe.[31] The language of 'epiphany' is further applied to dream-appearances and meteorological phenomena in the treatment of the manifestation of Athena at the Rhodian *polis* of Lindus during the Persian Wars. The goddess' appearance is listed on a column headed 'Epiphanies' (*Epiphaneiai*) in a lengthy inscription from the local temple of Athena Lindia of 99 BC (the so-called *Chronicle of Lindus*). The inscription describes Athena's miraculous intervention in detail. Lindus was besieged by the Persian general, Datis, and the *polis* was on the verge of surrender because of the lack of water; Athena then appeared in a dream to one of the leaders, encouraging the Lindians not to capitulate since she was going to ask her father for water on their behalf. In response, the Lindians negotiated a five-day truce with the Persians (a period for which their existing water supplies would suffice); the condition of the truce was that they would surrender after this if their situation was unchanged. A day later, a great storm cloud delivered the much-needed rain to the citadel, and it was the besieging Persian force that found itself waterless. Datis, who had met the Lindian proposal with laughter, was now 'astounded at the manifestation (*epiphaneia*) of the goddess' and made dedications of his own to her temple.[32] The interweaving in the Delphic and Rhodian traditions of meteorological and geological phenomena with statements of divine epiphany confirm that, in the formulation of Versnel, epiphanies at the divine level encompass both the appearance of the god and also the manifestations of his power through his miraculous deeds.[33]

The Narratives: Classical Origins and Hellenistic Elaborations?

From a temporal perspective, the phenomenon of divine or heroic encounters in battle seems to have been an enduring one, as the catalogue of epiphanies compiled by Pritchett in his multi-volume *The Greek State at War* attests.[34] Pritchett's survey spans from the Archaic period to the time of Roman domination. Of examples to which a date may be nominally assigned, one of the earliest must be the appearance of the Dioskouroi to assist the Locrians in their mid sixth-century BC clash with Croton at the River Sagra; at the other end of the chronological spectrum stand cases such as those of Athena, who appeared at Ilium after she had aided the people of Cyzicus against Mithridates in 73 BC.[35]

A note of caution, however, is warranted. The traditions concerning many of the earlier battlefield epiphanies are clustered in late sources, notably in Plutarch, Pausanias and (to a lesser extent) Diodorus and Justin. This is not to suggest that epiphany as a notion is a late one. Its existence in the Classical age is established by Herodotus' inclusion not only of the Delphians' report concerning the manifestation of their heroes, Phylacus and Autonous, at Delphi, but also of the tale told by an Athenian, Epizelus, of his narrow encounter at Marathon with a fighter whose immense stature betrayed his non-mortal status; Herodotus refers also to the Greek summoning of the heroic Aeacidae to fight with them at Salamis, and of the appearance of a phantom woman at that battle.[36] Reflective too of early traditions around epiphanies at Marathon is a cup by the Brygos Painter, a cup produced not long after the battle itself and associated with that conflict through its depiction of warring Greeks and Persians on its exterior. The tondo of the cup (Figure 7.1) shows two armed figures, whose emergence from an altar-like structure strongly suggests that these are heroes rising from their *heroon* (hero–shrine) to stand by the Greeks on the Marathonian plain.[37]

Figure 7.1: Two armed figures rising from their *heroon*; detail of tondo (interior) of an Athenian red-figure cup (kylix) by the Brygos Painter, dating to shortly after the Battle of Marathon. Ashmolean Museum, AN1911.615. (*Image © Ashmolean Museum, University of Oxford*)

It is nonetheless striking that the traditions concerning epiphanies become more explicit in later sources.[38] While Herodotus himself maintains a pious reticence in his stories of miraculous intervention, all of which are carefully attributed to his sources, later testimonies are less circumspect. This is evident even in the most overt divine epiphany narrative in Herodotus, namely that of Pan prior to the Battle of Marathon.[39] The Athenian runner Philippides (or Pheidippides) claimed to have encountered the god in the mountains near Tegea, and to have been quizzed on the lack of worship accorded him at Athens – a city to which, Pan asserted, he had been useful in the past and to which he would be useful in the future. In the words uttered by Pan there is an insinuation that the god will aid the Athenian defence at Marathon, but Herodotus does not go on to report any claims for Pan's presence in his narrative of the actual clash at Marathon.[40] Herodotus tells the story, moreover, at some remove: it is what the Athenians say that Philippides said.[41] In Pausanias, by contrast, the encounter with Philippides prompts a more explicit undertaking from the god that he would come to Marathon and fight for the Athenians; the Suda even seeks to find Pan on the field at Marathon by identifying him, in garbled fashion, with the strange apparition that blinded Epizelus.[42] Epiphanies are not only more overtly but also more frequently claimed in later authorities than in earlier ones. Plutarch and Pausanias put heroes undocumented in Herodotus' account on the field at Marathon (Theseus and Echetlaus) and at Salamis (Cynchreus).[43]

While some of these later accounts of epiphanies may be preserving traditions that stretch back to the battles in question, some of the proliferation of epiphany episodes that is found in Hellenistic sources may be the result of later accretions. The kudos attached to epiphanies in battle (discussed in detail below) will generally have acted as an incentive to introduce such episodes into historical narratives. That tendency became particularly pronounced after the preservation of Delphi in 279 BC, for this famous instance served as a model for emulation, triggering a raft of divine interventions against the invading Gauls in various locales.[44] The influence of Apollo's defence of his sanctuary is suggested also by the surge of divine appearances in battle after this date, for epiphanies prior to 279 BC are predominantly enacted by heroes.

There is a distinct possibility, too, that some of the epiphany traditions may have been shaped by the placement of victory thanks-offerings in sanctuaries, a placement that had the potential to be understood by later viewers as indicating the active contribution – sometimes in the form of epiphany – of the resident god or hero to the victory itself. The erection of a *tropaion* near the sanctuary of Poseidon is thought, for example, to underpin the tradition of that god's epiphany in a battle at Mantineia in the mid-third century.[45] Monuments commemorating victories had the potential to influence epiphany stories also through the depiction of some gods and heroes alongside mortal combatants. Such visual representations – whether statue groups or paintings – effectively made tangibly present these divine helpers in a way that conceivably encouraged, among later viewers, the extrapolation of stories of epiphanies during the course of the battle itself.[46] The Athenian commemorations of the victory at Marathon are a case in point.[47] That success saw the dedication at Delphi of a statue group in which were represented the gods Athena and Apollo, the victorious general Miltiades and ten heroes (among whom was Theseus); it was commemorated also in a famous painting put on display in the Stoa Poikile ('Painted Stoa') in Athens, in which were depicted portraits:

> of the hero Marathon, after whom the plain is named, of Theseus represented as coming up from the under-world, of Athena and of Heracles. ... Of the fighters the most conspicuous figures in the painting are Callimachus, who had been elected commander-in-chief by the Athenians, Miltiades, one of the generals, and a hero called Echetlaus.[48]

These displays present an amalgam of figures, some of whom figure in literary epiphany narratives (thus notably Echetlaus and Theseus; so too Pan, whose presence in the Stoa Poikile painting is indicated in other accounts)[49] while others do not; the inclusion among the ten heroes in the Delphi group of a number of the Athenian tribal *eponymoi* (the legendary heroes after whom the Athenian tribes were named) might be taken, for instance, as a visual short-hand for the Athenian tribal contingents rather than as indicative of epiphanies of the heroes themselves. The statue group and painting do not, however, distinguish semantically between these various modes of heroic presence, and such ambiguity will have invited a variety of interpretation. It is striking, in this context, that only late literary accounts ascribe to Theseus an active role at Marathon. The Delphi group and the Stoa painting may attest to an early belief in Theseus' presence that is lacking in Herodotus (with the painting in particular showing him emerging from the ground), but equally they may have provided the impetus for the elaboration of stories of his participation as a fighter in later traditions.[50]

The narratives of battlefield epiphanies in the ancient sources are, therefore, potentially the products of diverse cultural, political, literary and historical factors. Some will reflect the claimed experiences of combatants on the field; others may be the fruit of later elaborations. This complexity of formulation suggests that such narratives performed a multiplicity of functions, and these issues can now be considered, commencing with consideration of the dynamics of the encounters of gods, heroes and men on the battlefield.

Heroes, Gods and Mortals Engaged: the Impact of Epiphanies

What was the impact of seeing a hero or god in action? Our sources betray a range of effects and reflect on the experience from a diversity of perspectives. Heroes have a tendency to appear alongside the ranks of citizen fighters in open battle; given this, the prevalence of young warrior-types (such as the Dioskouroi and Aeacidae) among the heroes who manifest themselves is entirely apposite.[51] There is often emphasis on communal solidarity; the hero is a fellow-fighter, an ally who shares in the toil of battle. This emerges consistently from the language for the summoning of heroes before battle, and from the descriptions (both literary and visual) of the heroes in action in battle. It is, for example, for an alliance (*symmachia*) and assistance (*boetheia*) in their looming clash with Croton that the Locrians appeal to Sparta and receive from it the Dioskouroi, and when Herodotus' Greeks send out a summons to the Aeacidae before the Battle of Salamis, it is as fellow-fighters (*symmachoi*) that the heroes are invoked.[52] Heroes appear in the thick of battle, with the painting of the Battle of Marathon in the Stoa Poikile depicting the hero Echetlaus 'among those fighting'; at times a close identification of the hero with the troops on the field is patent, as it is in the description of the epiphany of Hermes who, 'armed with a scraper like an *ephebos*', fought alongside the ephebes at Tanagra. Much later in date is an inscription recording a sacrifice and statue offered to Heracles by three Epirote warriors; these soldiers, thankful for their safe return home from campaign, acknowledge the assistance given them by a saviour Heracles who 'stood beside them in all battles'.[53]

The hero's identification with his mortal fellow-combatants is often heightened by the existence of a close association of the hero with a particular territory and its people.[54] Indeed, many of the epiphany narratives state the close proximity of the hero's shrine to the field of battle.[55] The heroes who come to the defence of Delphi, for example, are local heroes and are specified as such by Herodotus, while it is the quintessentially Athenian Theseus who assumes an important place in the narratives about Marathon.[56] Heroes act as champions of their particular *polis*, particularly in battles between cities with a long history of tension. Messenia and Sparta enjoyed just such a turbulent relationship, and heroic epiphanies occur on both sides in the narratives concerning hostilities between the two. As general of the Messenians during his lifetime (seventh century BC), Aristomenes was diverted from his pursuit of a retreating Spartan army (and thus prevented from inflicting full-scale destruction) by the intervention of the Spartan Dioskouroi; much later, when Aristomenes himself had been heroised, he appeared among the ranks of Sparta's foe, the Thebans, at Leuktra in 371 BC.[57] Heroes could, admittedly, be 'borrowed' from other people, as attested for example in the Thebans' request for the aid of the Aeginetan Aeacidae after a defeat inflicted by Athens in 506 BC. Even here, however, there were links, with the Thebans affiliated to the Aeginetans through mythological genealogies upon which the request for aid was based. As it turned out, the Thebans' borrowing proved unfruitful and they were forced to apply to Aegina a second time for aid: this time in the form of real men.[58] Heroes respond, then, to the special ties – be they of cult or kinship – that bind them to the mortal combatants, and share with them a sense of defending their own land and championing their own *polis* and its interests.

In taking his place alongside the hoplite line of his allies or fellow citizens, the hero serves as a model for the mortal combatants themselves. He acts to strengthen the steadfastness of the citizen in the terrors of battle – a tangible counterpart to the kind of exhortations to courage composed so famously by the poet Tyrtaeus in the seventh century:

> Fear not the throng of men, turn not to flight
> but straight toward the front line bear your shields ...
> Those who bravely remain beside each other
> and press toward engagement at the front
> die in less numbers and save the ranks
> behind; of those who run all virtue is perished.[59]

The hero's galvanizing function at times sees him portrayed as leading the onslaught. This *topos* is apparent in the epiphany of Hermes mentioned above, in which Hermes 'led the ephebes into battle'; his epithet *Promachos* ('fighter in the front line') reinforces the point. It is present also in the behaviour of Theseus, who was reported to have been seen at Marathon 'clad in full armour and charging ahead of [the Athenians] against the barbarians'.[60] Theseus' action is of particular significance given the highly unusual circumstances of the Athenian assault at Marathon. Sources for the battle, both literary and visual, make much of the fact of the Greeks attacking the Persian lines 'at a run' (*dromoi*). Thus Herodotus writes:

[The Athenians] were the first Greeks, as far as I know, who charged their enemies at a run, and the first who endured the sight of Persian garments and men dressed in them; till then, the Greeks were frightened by the very name of the Persians.[61]

While the import (and indeed feasibility) of Herodotus' description has been endlessly debated in modern scholarship,[62] of concern here is not the *realia* of the fighting as much as the emphasis in the traditions on the unusual Greek charge.[63] In the light of the very audacity of the Greek assault and its perceived unconventional nature, the sighting of Theseus in front of the advance functions as implicit guarantor of the Greeks' success and thus as encouragement in the face of overwhelming danger.

The potency of heroes seems to have been especially valued in conflicts in which the opposing forces were mismatched. There was a clear perception, for instance, that the Greeks were outnumbered in the Persian invasions of 490 BC and 480–479 BC; the presence of a Theseus and an Echetlaus at Marathon, or a Cynchreus and the Aeacidae at Salamis, helped to redress this imbalance. Aiding in a similar way was the alleged presence of the Messenian hero, Aristomenes, among the ranks of the Thebans at Leuktra in 371 BC, although the imbalance at issue between the Thebans and Spartans at this clash stems not so much from a numerical mismatch but a perceived inequality in the prestige of the opponents, with the Spartans seemingly invincible before their unexpected humbling at the Thebans' hands.[64] A nexus between non-mortal combatants and a superior opponent is present too in the traditions concerning the battle between Croton and Locri at the Sagra River in the sixth century. The victory of the 15,000 Locrians over a 130,000-strong army from Croton (according to Justin) was so unexpected as to become proverbial (thus Strabo, explaining that the saying 'it is more true than the victory of the Sagras' was directed at the incredulous). Justin's account of the clash is replete with an epiphany by the Dioskouroi and the implicit support of Zeus (via his bird, the eagle), while the mythographer Conon puts Ajax also in the ranks of the Locrians, who had left a space clear for the manifestation of the hero.[65]

Perhaps the clearest indication of the galvanizing effect of the presence of heroes on mortal troops comes not from the claimed actual epiphanies themselves, but from the staging of epiphanies as a stratagem of warfare. In a number of accounts, our sources admit the possibility of human contrivance. Xenophon, for example, describes the manner in which the Thebans were induced by their own generals to engage with the Spartans at Leuktra in 371 BC. In addition to oracles and the opening of doors of temples, there were reports 'that the arms in the temple of Heracles had disappeared, showing that Heracles himself had set out for the battle'. Xenophon adds:

> Some people, to be sure, say that all these reports were invented by the Theban leaders. But at any rate in the battle itself, everything certainly turned out badly for the Spartans.[66]

The device employed here – the movement of the hero's weapons – echoes the traditions attested at Delphi during the Persian Wars, where Apollo's intention of defending his sanctuary against the Persians was vouchsafed by his oracular pronouncement and by the reported appearance of his weapons in front of the temple. (The possibility of human staging at Delphi is implicitly acknowledged and countered by the assurance that these weapons were 'sacred weapons, which no human hand may touch'.[67]) Polyaenus goes so far as to include entries on epiphanies in his treatise on military stratagems.[68] He reports, for example, that the Spartan King Archidamus secretly arranged two panoplies of armour on an altar, and led horses around it so that the ensuing tableau of armour and hoof-prints might convince his troops that the Dioskouroi had come to aid them in their fight against the Arcadians; the result was that the soldiers, 'because they were thus filled with courage and inspired by their belief in assistance from the gods, fought bravely and defeated the Arcadians'.[69]

On rare occasions, the experience of epiphany is presented from the perspective of the heroes' opponents rather than his comrades. Central here is the experience at Marathon of the Athenian hoplite Epizelus, whose close encounter with a towering heroic presence left him alive; it was the man at Epizelus' side who was cut down by the phantom, while Epizelus himself was struck blind, his sight never to return.[70] Modern scholarship has seen in this anecdote a reflection of the psychological strain of battle. Tritle adduces the case of Epizelus in a discussion of the 'terror and anger' attendant upon hoplite warfare; he reads Epizelus' blindness as the body's response to the acute distress of battle, noting the fear attendant upon fighting a foreign enemy and Epizelus' likely horror at witnessing the man at his side cut down. On this understanding, the epiphany of a hero serves to sublimate something of the psychological trauma of warfare experienced by the mortal combatant. Viewed from the perspective of historical probabilities, such interpretation is entirely plausible and it is widely reflected in modern scholarship.[71] The concern of the ancient traditions in Epizelus is, however, rather different, and will be considered below.

In accounts of epiphanies by the gods rather than by heroes, an interest in the response of the enemy is much more typical. While the (benevolent) impact of the deity on the local population is sometimes addressed,[72] the focus is frequently on the fear among the enemy and the resultant disorder on the battlefield that the divine manifestation elicits.[73] When Herodotus' Persians approached the shrine of Athena Pronaia at Delphi, for example, the manifestations of divine wrath caused the attackers to flee in fear, and the mortal defenders of Delphi were thus able to cut them down in their disarray. So Herodotus writes, having described the lightning and rockfalls:

> All these things together caused a panic (*phobos*) amongst the Persian troops. They fled; and the Delphians, seeing them on the run, came down upon them and attacked them with great slaughter.[74]

Comparison may be sought in the tradition concerning the impact of the epiphany at the siege of Pellene, where the appearance outside the sanctuary of Artemis of a statuesque and helmet-clad woman who was mistaken for the goddess (according to Plutarch) – or of the goddess' priestess at the head of a procession (says Polyaenus) – induced such terror in the invading Aetolians that they were rendered incapable of fighting:

> The enemy thought they saw an apparition from heaven and were struck with amazement and terror, so that not a man of them thought of defending himself.[75]

The terror inspired by the divine apparition is central also to the Pellenians' own version (known to Plutarch), in which the epiphany was effected through the parading by the priestess of the cult image of the goddess:

> But the Pellenians themselves tell us that the image of the goddess usually stands untouched, and that when it is removed by the priestess and carried forth from the temple, no man looks upon it, but all turn their gaze away; for not only to mankind is it a grievous and terrible sight, but trees also, past which it may be carried, become barren and cast their fruit. This image, then, they say, the priestess carried forth from the temple at this time, and by ever turning it in the faces of the Aetolians robbed them of their senses and took away their reason.[76]

The interventions of Zeus and Hecate at Panamara in 42 BC similarly induced terror in the invading forces, throwing them into disorder and causing them to slaughter each other in the mayhem.[77] Manifestations of gods seem, then, to articulate a quite specific phenomenon of warfare: the sudden apprehending of an army by fear in the throes of battle, a fear that descends without readily identifiable human causation, that renders the army incapable of fighting and thereby irrevocably swings the tide of the fighting.

One minor god claimed an especially close identification with a fighting force's fear. Pan gave his very name to the phenomenon of panic.[78] His was a very particular fear, for his presence is often offered as an explanation of the mass terror that can strike an army from within its own ranks, often while it is encamped or still awaiting engagement with the enemy.[79] The idea is encapsulated in the Suda's definition of a 'panic terror', which 'happens in army camps, when all of a sudden the horses and men are startled, for no apparent reason'; the same passage considers also attributable to the presence of Pan a phenomenon that strikes an army for no reason:

> For example, the enemy seems to attack, and [the soldiers] pick up their weapons in the commotion, form ranks, and attack one another.[80]

It is in exactly this guise that Pan has a place in the traditions around the Gallic attack on Delphi in 279 BC. Having described the divine manifestations, the epiphanies of local heroes and the staunch defence by the Greeks themselves that beset the Gauls during their attack on the shrine, Pausanias claims that, after the Gauls had withdrawn to camp for the night:

> There fell on them a 'panic'. For causeless terrors are said to come from the god Pan. It was when evening was turning to night that the confusion fell on the army, and at first only a few became mad, and these imagined that they heard the trampling of horses at a gallop, and the attack of advancing enemies; but after a little time the delusion spread to all.[81]

The effect of the panic, described in the ensuing passage by Pausanias, was a wholescale self-slaughter of the Gauls, who had been rendered insensible to all the signs that they were in fact slaying each other:

> So rushing to arms they divided into two parties, killing and being killed, neither understanding their mother tongue nor recognizing one another's forms or the shape of their shields. Both parties alike under the present delusion thought that their opponents were Greek, men and armour, and that the language they spoke was Greek, so that a great

mutual slaughter was wrought among the Gauls by the madness sent by the god.[82]

Prominent in these narratives concerning Pan is the notion of emotional or psychological disturbance. Such disturbance is certainly a component in the epiphanies of other gods, and indeed Cicero in his *On Divination* precedes his discussion of the epiphanies of the two 'white virgins' who fought at Delphi in 279 BC with comments about the gods seizing the minds of poets and about the psychological disturbances that make men see as substantial beings things that are merely apparitions.[83] These latent psychological dimensions of divine epiphanies are brought to the fore with Pan. The god is not anthropomorphically visible on the field, nor is he experienced as an external force (such as snow or thunder), but he is present rather as a madness that seizes the minds of warriors. On this basis, it has been suggested that Pan's supposed involvement in the Battle of Marathon is to be associated with a panic experienced in the Persian ranks; given, however, that no such Persian panic is claimed in the battle narratives, and moreover that 'panic' is more often associated (at least in our later sources) with armies at rest, not in the heat of battle, the suggestion cannot be pressed.[84]

The Honour(s) of Battle

If battlefield epiphanies articulate something of the experiences and emotions of battle, they also serve an important function in the subsequent memorialization of the conflict. The cultural primacy of warfare – the correlation of battlefield success with the kudos and standing of both the *polis* and the individual – is amply attested through the prominent display of trophies and dedications in the wake of conflicts and through the focus on warfare in Greek historical narratives. In the following will be examined the ways in which epiphanies of gods and heroes have a part to play in the construction of the kudos derived from military conflict. The mechanisms involved are diverse. Epiphanies serve, for example, to witness the close relationship between a city or individual and the gods and heroes, a relationship that confers prestige. In narrative terms, moreover, by introducing traits evocative of Homeric epic they serve also to elevate the conflicts in which they occur.[85] The magnitude of the Persian Wars is conveyed by the multiplicity of divine and heroic interventions associated with its battles, both in the 'historical' accounts and the poetic celebrations of them; the Persian Wars themselves become in turn a template for the narratives of later conflicts, with the inclusion of epiphanies again being key to this historical echoing.[86]

Indications of the prestige value of epiphanies may be identified in the competing traditions concerning the death at Argos of the Macedonian King Pyrrhus, who was felled by a tile cast down by a woman during his invasion of the city. Pausanias, Plutarch and Strabo all describe Pyrrhus' assailant as simply a woman; Plutarch goes so far as to specify that she was an old woman of lowly birth.[87] For the Argives themselves, however, this was no mere woman, but the goddess Demeter. The Argive tradition acts as a corrective to the more profane alternative and is cited as such by Pausanias. It bestows more kudos on the *polis* by advertising the goddess' personal interest in their fate. It serves also to promote the prestige of the local sanctuary of the goddess, a fact hinted at by Pausanias' citation for the Argive material of a poem by one Lyceas, whom Pausanias specifies to be the local guide for the neighbourhood in which Pyrrhus' death occurred. Pausanias observes further that Pyrrhus' death occurred near Demeter's sanctuary and that Pyrrhus' remains were allegedly interred within it.[88] The vested interest of a guide in publicizing to visitors (presumably a Roman tourist audience) the divine favours shown his native *polis* is clear.

The kudos attendant upon divine intervention in a battle is evident also in the concern of *poleis* and individuals to document and broadcast the epiphany.[89] By the Hellenistic period, inscriptions became a favoured mode for display of such episodes.[90] Notable here is the inclusion, on the monumental *Chronicle of Lindos*, of a catalogue of divine epiphanies (of which two-thirds belong to military contexts); the assistance rendered to the Cyzicenes in the Mithridatic Wars by Athena of Ilium was, according to Plutarch, similarly documented on a stele, on which were published 'certain decrees and inscriptions relating to this matter'.[91] The most thorough form of 'publication', however, involved manifold avenues of dissemination. The preservation of Delphi from Gallic attack in 279 BC prompted the institution of a festival, the Soteria, and the invitation to this festival of *theoroi* (sacred envoys) from other states provided an occasion for the promulgation of the stories of the epiphanies at Delphi. Inscriptions preserve both the fact of the institution of the festival and the epiphanies that motivated it. Likewise, at Cnidus, the epiphanies of Artemis Hyacinthophorus (during what is assumed to be Philip V's unsuccessful siege in 201 BC) were commemorated through the institution of a festival; additionally, an inscription documents the response from Cos to the announcement of the festival, and in doing so records the epiphanies of the goddess.[92] The pattern of responses to epiphanies at Delphi and Cnidus reveals not only the commemorative activities within the *polis* that experienced the epiphany, but also the active promulgation to other *poleis* of news of the epiphanies and their commemoration.

Epiphanies may further have played a role in advancing individual claims in cases where battle prestige was later contested among combatants. Athens and Aegina were rival claimants to honours from the naval clash at Salamis in 480 BC (with Aegina the winner),[93] and this rivalry is mirrored in Herodotus' narrative of the battle itself by competing claims of divine and heroic assistance. According to the Athenians, the Greek fleet had been giving way to the Persians until a decisive move was made by an Athenian vessel; the Aeginetans by contrast held that the first to go into action was an Aeginetan vessel, and moreover that it was the very vessel that had carried the Aeacidae from Aegina.[94] Prior connections between the Aeacidae and Aeginetan thalassocracy had been drawn in poetry,[95] and the historical tradition recounted to Herodotus seems to draw on this *topos*, with the detail that battle was initiated by the Aeacidae's ship bolstering Aegina's entitlement to glory over the rival Athenian claim.[96] Athens had, however, also contributed to the divine assistance bestowed on the Greeks at Salamis, with the quintessentially Athenian gods of Eleusis signalling their intent prior to the engagement;[97] Plutarch, by directly juxtaposing the miraculous signs from Eleusis with the epiphany of the Aeginetan Aeacidae in his account of Salamis, contributes to this impression of competing narratives of prestige from Aegina and Athens.[98]

The augmentation of military prestige through the involvement of heroes and gods functioned at the level of the individual as well as the *polis*. Commemorations of the Battle of Marathon offer a case study in this regard. The Athenians' victory dedication at Delphi and the painting of the battle in the Stoa Poikile have been associated with Miltiades' son, Cimon, who rose to great prominence in the 470s and 460s BC.[99] These commemorations place great emphasis on the collaboration of the heroes and gods, and do so in a fashion that reflects not only on the *polis* of Athens but on Miltiades himself: thus the inclusion of figures of Echetlaus and Epizelus alongside Miltiades in the Stoa painting of Marathon, and of Theseus, the heroes and gods with Miltiades at Delphi. Cimon may also have been instrumental in the introduction of a cult of Pan in the wake of Marathon and the dedication, in Miltiades' name, of a statue of the goat-footed god in his new Acropolis sanctuary.[100] Such monuments insinuated a close personal connection between Miltiades and the heroes and gods, a connection to which their epiphanies bore witness, and a political agenda is discernible. Cimon had good cause to want to redeem the posthumous memory of his father, whose reputation after Marathon had been tarnished by subsequent military failures at Paros.[101] Representation of Miltiades fighting alongside heroes and gods of the Attic state will have functioned as an implicit bid for the restoration of the prestige of the general, and indeed served by extension to elevate Cimon's own status.

Strikingly, the presence of heroes and gods on the battlefield could lend prestige not only to the victor but also to the vanquished. This potential is illustrated by an epigram which, it is argued, belonged to the state grave, or *polyandrion*, in which were buried the Athenian dead from the Battle of Coronea in 447 BC. This was an engagement in which the Athenians suffered defeat by the Thebans,[102] but the epigram for the Athenians casts their opponent as a 'demi-god':

> Enduring ones, how you lasted to the end your struggle in the hopeless fight, and lost your lives by divine power in war – not by the strength of men who opposed you, but one of the half-gods came into the goddess' road against you and wrought your undoing.[103]

In an article on this inscription, Bowra observed the rarity for such epigrams to acknowledge explicitly the fact of a defeat, much less for a cause to be offered.[104] The effect of the Coronea epigram is reminiscent of the earlier (*c.* 540 BC) inscription from the funerary *kouros* (portrait statue) of the Athenian Croesus, who is described as having been destroyed by 'violent Ares' in the front rank of battle.[105] By ascribing defeat to heroic or divine agency, such epigrams bestowed honour in the face of defeat; those who perish do so only in the face of forces much superior to themselves, in a conflict itself elevated above the realm of the merely mortal.

This 'elevating' function of epiphanies is, in fact, fundamental to the response in ancient testimonia to the claimed encounter of the Athenian hoplite Epizelus with an unnamed hero at Marathon. While the modern tendency is to read Epizelus' blinding as reflective of stress-induced trauma, Herodotus' narrative conveys instead the prestige bound up in the events.[106] Epizelus' personal bravery is explicitly asserted (when struck blind, he was 'in the thick of the fighting, and fighting bravely himself') and his wounding is less a marker of individual fallibility than an affirmation of the wisdom of Homer's Hera, who warns in the *Iliad* that the gods when manifest pose dangers to men.[107] Against this backdrop, the encounter with the daunting *phasma* augments Epizelus' individual valour and prestige; his *logos* is thereby thematically aligned to the programme of Herodotus' entire work, namely the display of astonishing acts and achievements. Confirmation of Epizelus' enhanced status can be found from the visual realm, for he was individually portrayed in the famed painting of the Battle of Marathon displayed in the Stoa Poikile at Athens; thanks to this painting, Epizelus subsequently featured alongside the polemarch Callimachus (who died in battle) and Cynegirus (who lost a hand while holding onto a Persian ship, preventing its flight) in what became the canonical list of the bravest Greeks at Marathon.[108]

Apportioning Credit

The presence of gods and heroes on the battlefield thus elevates the stature of the combatants. But what of the kudos of victory itself, and its apportionment to the heroes or gods who contributed to victory by manifesting themselves (or their power) in battle? The evidence here reveals a range of responses. Victory dedications from the Persian Wars indicate that, while gratitude to the gods would be acknowledged (through the dedication of spoils to them and occasionally by explicit statements of thanks), military successes of this period tended ultimately to remain those of the mortal combatants on the field.[109] Illustrative here is the epigram from the *tropaion* erected near the sanctuary of Athena Pronoia by the victorious Delphians in the wake of their defence of Delphi in 480 BC – a victory which, as detailed above, was encouraged by the presence of local heroes and the intervention of the gods. Known from its quotation by Diodorus and from the transcription of a (now lost) inscribed version, the epigram reads thus:

> The Delphians who drove back the city-sacking ranks of the Medes
> and protected the bronze-crowned sanctuary
> erected me as a memorial of man-warding-off war
> and as a witness of the victory,
> showing gratitude (*charizomenoi*) to Zeus and Phoebus.[110]

A debt to the gods is latent in the gratitude expressed in the final line and in the fact of the dedication of the *tropaion* itself, a *tropaion* which Diodorus describes in his preamble to the epigram as an 'undying memorial to the epiphany of the gods'.[111] The active agency of the victory is, however, reserved for the Delphians themselves; it is they rather than the gods who have driven back the marauding Persian foe.[112] By 279 BC, by contrast, when the same sanctuary again faced a barbarian foe, the approach to the apportionment of kudos had shifted, with punishment of the sanctuary's aggressors inflicted by 'the god and by the men who came to defend it'.[113] This division of credit did not, however, go unchallenged. The Aetolians, to whom much of the human credit for the defence of Delphi was due, were subsequently keen to gloss over the epiphany narratives in order to emphasize their own agency; this, at least, is the impression conveyed by a dossier of inscriptions relating to the Aetolian reorganization of the Soteria festival at Delphi in 246/245 BC.[114]

Credit for victory might thus be contested between mortal and divine agents, and it is not only in the episode at Delphi that such contestation is revealed. In his discussion of the deliverance of Pellene from its Aetolian attackers in 241 BC, Plutarch isolates a source discrepancy over the reason for the Aetolians' sudden flight. Having recounted the Pellenians' story of the parading of the statue of Artemis and the resulting terror among the invaders, Plutarch observes that:

> Aratus, however, in his *Commentaries*, makes no mention of such a thing, but says that after routing the Aetolians and bursting into the city with them as they fled, he drove them out by main force, and slew seven hundred of them.[115]

Plutarch appears to isolate here a divergence between a population keen to promote its close identification with its *polis* deity on the one hand, and mortal combatants keen to promote their own valour on the other.[116]

On rare occasions, a god might receive sole credit. Just such a case is documented in the most unlikely of authors, Thucydides, whose silence concerning the religious dimension of warfare is notorious. In his narrative of Brasidas' action against an Athenian-held Lekythos in 424/423 BC, however, a perceived divine epiphany has been discerned.[117] Preparing to meet an assault by the Peloponnesian attackers, so Thucydides reports, the defenders of Lekythos overburdened a parapet with weapons and men, causing it to collapse. While the cause of the din was clear to those close to the scene, those at further remove mistakenly concluded that the invaders had breached the defences; they thus fled their posts and yielded the city to the Spartans. Thucydides himself gives no divine colouring to the events, but not so Brasidas: on the grounds that 'the capture was scarcely due to human means', the Spartan general gave to the goddess Athena the thirty *minae* that he had promised to the first man to breach the walls of Lekythos, and indeed consecrated to her the entire territory of the razed *polis*.[118] Brasidas' gesture may have been shaped by considerations beyond any simple belief in divine intervention: the destruction of Lekythos reduced by one the number of Chalcidian *poleis* that Peloponnesian resources (already suffering strain) would be required to protect from Athenian recapture, while the cultivation of Athena (a goddess so closely aligned with Athens) would have been an adroit stroke of religious brinkmanship. Brasidas' gesture nonetheless establishes the conceptual possibility of a god receiving prime credit for a victory through an act of epiphany.

Some Concluding Remarks

The diversity of episodes canvassed above suggests that the phenomenon of epiphanies in battle is a complex one, one resistant to generalization. Like the phenomenon of epiphanies more broadly, the experience of gods and heroes within battle is to be situated within a culturally specific construct of beliefs about the involvement and immediacy of supra-mortal beings within the mortal realm, and about ways of seeing gods and validating their manifestations. Thus, while it has proved tempting to rationalize some epiphanies through the lens of modern medical understandings of trauma – the encounter between an exhausted Philippides and Pan, or Epizelus' blinding by his encounter with an unnamed presence at Marathon feature prominently in this regard – such rationalizations run the risk of 'reading' these episodes within a culturally unhistorical framework; moreover, the assumption of the diachronic universality of disorders such as post-traumatic stress disorder (of which Epizelus is now commonly diagnosed) underlying these rationalizing tendencies has been problematized in some modern scholarship.[119] This is not to deny that epiphany is a phenomenon often localized in moments of crisis such as war, but rather to emphasize that the ancient experience was mediated largely by its own set of culturally framed narratives.

Intrinsic to epiphany, whether in battle or elsewhere, is the Greeks' belief not only in the reality of their gods, but in the anthropomorphic form of those gods and in their ready involvement in human affairs.[120] Such beliefs lie at the heart of the Greeks' fundamental willingness to identify divine manifestation in a variety of phenomena – whether the encounter of unusually potent combatants on the field or the fortuitous occurrence of weather and meteorological events. They are at the heart too of the Greeks' willingness to transform their experience of these phenomena, where necessary, into a more overtly anthropomorphic discourse. Graf's survey of the testimonia to the gods' interventions against the Gauls at Delphi in 279 BC neatly illustrates one such transformation across time.[121] As noted above, the signs at Delphi that were understood as manifestations of divine power were essentially meteorological and physical (earthquake, snowstorm, lightning and the like); while these interventions did not consist therefore of anthropomorphic appearances by individual gods, it is clear from the decree moved by Cos only a year later that the phenomena were immediately conceptualized, by a people culturally conditioned to recognize the presence of the divine in their realm, as manifestations of divine presence. In some later traditions, written at great temporal remove from any personal experience of the events, the articulation of the divine intervention has been enhanced by transformation into a narrative of anthropomorphic epiphany. Pompeius Trogus, for example, records priestly sightings of Apollo, bodily present as a beautiful youth, leaping into his temple, and of the emergence of two armour-clad virgins from the temples of Artemis and Athena; in Trogus' account, the concomitant earthquake and storm are included as affirmations of the presence of the sighted deities.[122] The translation of physical phenomena into the presence of the gods, and the further recasting of that presence as an anthropomorphic manifestation, are products of the receptiveness to and expectation of divine involvement on the part of the witnesses and of later generations.

Warfare arguably afforded one of the prime sites at which beliefs in divine presence and involvement were most effectively reinforced, because conflict provided a means of verifying as divine (or heroic) a presence that had been subjectively identified as such by witnesses. The fact of victory encouraged acceptance that the witnessed epiphany was legitimately that of a god or hero, just as oracular pronouncements confirm and identify heroes in a number of our epiphany traditions. This mechanism is deployed, for example, in Isyllus' account of his encounter with Asklepios, in which the god announced his intention of aiding the Spartans against King Philip of Macedon; Isyllus reports that he himself then went to the Peloponnese to inform the Spartans of the god's intentions, and that the Spartans subsequently instituted a festival for Asklepios Soter after they were saved.[123] The validity of Isyllus' encounter with the god was thus substantiated for the Spartans by their preservation. A similar pattern may be implicit in Herodotus' account of Pan's epiphany before Marathon. The sole witness to that epiphany was the runner Philippides, who duly recounted his experience to the Athenian assembly. Herodotus says that the Athenians believed him, but it is notable that the introduction of a cult for Pan happened somewhat later; while Herodotus ascribes the delay to the disorder of the state in 490 BC, the victory at Marathon in the interim may well also have been a factor in the public acceptance of the legitimacy of the epiphany.[124] This affirmation of a suspected epiphany through an ensuing victory is particularly pronounced for those epiphanies located in conflicts in which the odds were felt to be skewed heavily in favour of one side over another, and in which the victory of the underdog was thus particularly remarkable; as noted above, a number of epiphanies belong to this category.

On this basis, epiphany and victory are mutually reinforcing phenomena. Their symbiotic relationship extended well beyond the immediate temporal context of the victory itself, for recognition of the epiphany of the god or hero often led, in the aftermath of victory, to a public affirmation through the institution of cult. The institution of a Soteria at Delphi as a result of the Gallic victory in 279 BC is one of the most explicitly attested instances, but a great many battle epiphanies are associated with subsequent cult observance;[125] so entrenched was the nexus of epiphany, victory and cult that such a pattern is woven into the fabric of the ancient novel, with Achilles Tatius alluding to a wartime epiphany of Artemis after which the Byzantines, 'since they won, thought it necessary to send a sacrifice to her as a victory offering for her support'.[126] Religious commemoration of epiphanic gods and heroes allowed the *polis* to recall, on an ongoing basis, simultaneously the epiphany itself (a token of divine support that bestowed kudos on the city) and the *polis'* resultant victory in war. These proffered a powerful combination in the articulation of a *polis'* prestige, one that had diplomatic potential for the polis' future military engagements; a *polis* that had enjoyed divine protection in the past, and had duly fostered its relationship with the god or hero concerned, could well hope to benefit from such support in the future.[127] These diverse traditions on battlefield epiphanies thus illuminate not only something of the dynamics and strains of hoplite warfare, but shed light also on the strategies through which the prestige of conflict could be contested and articulated. It is little wonder, then, that the epiphany in battle proved so attractive a *topos* within ancient discourses.

Notes

1. Hom. *Il.* 5.736–47; trans. Lattimore 1951.
2. Historical instances have been catalogued by Pritchett, 1979, 11–46. For an overview of battlefield epiphany, see also Speyer, 1980; Petridou, 2015, 107–41.
3. Plut. *Thes.* 35.5. The Battle of Marathon is the locus of a number of epiphanies, on which see in general, Kearns, 1989, 44–46; Kron, 1999, 62–65; Petridou, 2015, 114–15. Theseus' presence there constitutes one element of a pattern of interest in that hero for fifth-century BC Athenians, by whom he was regarded as a virtual founder and protector of the democratic state; see Lavelle, 1993, 44–47.
4. Compare Hdt. 6.117.3 (unnamed hero at Marathon), cf. 8.84 for the *phasma* of a woman at Salamis; Plut. *Them.* 15.1 (Aeacidae at Salamis); Paus. 4.16.9 (of Helen and the Dioskouroi). For this terminology, see Marinatos and Kyrtatas, 2004, 230.
5. Recognition of the deity (or hero) as something different from a mortal presence is an important component of what Cioffi, 2014, 3–4 terms the 'protocols' of epiphany: the divine revelation is followed by mortal perception and finally – and crucially – recognition.

6. Delphi: Hdt. 8.38. Epizelus at Marathon: Hdt 6.117; Plut. *Mor.* 347d, 305b; Polemon *Call.* 44, *Cyn.* 56; Ael. *Nat. An.* 7.38; Diog. Laert. 1.56; and Suda *svv* Hippias, Polyzelus have a version of same story, although giving the name as Polyzelus. See further Scott, 2005, 395–96.
7. Justin *Epit.* 20.3; trans. Watson, 1853. The episode is attested also by Diod. 8.32; Strabo 6.1.10. For discussion, see Pritchett, 1979, 21–22.
8. Paus. 1.32.5 (cf. 1.15.3). See also Pritchett, 1979, 24; see also below, n.56.
9. Plut. *Arat.* 32; Polyaen. *Strat.* 8.59.
10. See further Platt, 2015, 495–96 on the multiplicity of forms of epiphany in general.
11. Snakes: Bravo, 2004, 71–72; Cynchreus: Paus. 1.36.1; Sosipolis: Paus. 6.20.3–5.
12. Paus. 1.32.5, 1.36.
13. Pritchett, 1979, 14–16.
14. Diod. 8.32; Justin *Epit.* 20.2. Hornblower, 2011, 46–47, sees in the Sagra episode a reflection of an 'exchange of cult' more broadly between Sparta and its colonies in Southern Italy, an exchange further attested in the reciprocal presence of a (South Italian) 'Zeus Messapeus' in Sparta (*SEG* 39.376).
15. Plut. *Them.* 15.1. For other epiphanies and divine signs at Salamis, see further Pritchett, 1979, 25–26; Mikalson, 2003, 75–80; Bowie, 2007, 150–53.
16. Hdt. 8.64, with Bowie, 2007, 151; Nagy, 2011a, 50. Compare Hdt. 5.79 for a similar invitation to the Aeacidae, this time by the Thebans.
17. Figuiera (online) canvasses, but rejects, the possibility that statues, or even the supposed bones of the heroes, were at issue in such instances.
18. Paus. 4.32.5–6. The advice alludes to another tradition, that Aristomenes (when mortal) lost his shield to the Dioskouroi: Paus. 4.16.4–6. For analysis of the story, see Ogden, 2004, 59–74.
19. For other explanations of the goddess' epiphany at Pellene, see Plut. *Arat.* 32.1; Polyaen. *Strat.* 8.59.
20. Plut. *Arat.* 32.2–3.
21. For forms of divine epiphany in general, see Petridou, 2015, 29–106. Epiphanies could be experienced also as auditory phenomena: consider, for example, the triumphal cry emanating from Athena's sanctuary at Delphi (Hdt. 8.37). Platt, 2015, 495, notes that Philippides' experience of Pan also seems to have been largely auditory.
22. Hdt. 8.35–39.
23. Mikalson, 2003, 69. On this episode, see also Harrison, 2000, 94–95.
24. Even in Homer's imagined world, the presences of gods in battle are often unseen. When Athena enters the fray, she in fact makes herself invisible by donning the 'helmet of Hades' (*Il.* 5. 844–45); the same goddess will later take to the field in the guise not of her own person, but of the mortal combatant, Deiphobos (*Il.* 22.225–27).
25. Zeus Soter: Plut. *Arist.* 11.5–8; Athena at Rhodes: *I.Lindos* II.2 D.95–115, with Higbie, 2003, 48–49, for text and translation; gods at Themisonium: Paus. 10.32.4–5. Given that epiphany via dreams was the *modus operandi* in Asklepios' sanctuary at Epidaurus, it is tempting to posit that the alleged epiphany of that god to Isyllus near Epidaurus (*IG* iv² 1.128.62–64, of *c.* 280 BC, on which see Kolde, 2003 may also have its basis in a dream encounter, although it is not overtly cast as such. Asklepios' epiphany is not a battlefield epiphany (Isyllus had come to seek healing from the god), but a wider military context is suggested: the god appears in shining

armour, and claims to be on his way to Sparta where there was a threat from a King Philip (so *IG* iv² 1.128.57–59, 63–64).

26. Plut. *Luc.* 10.2–3. Habicht, 2005, 98, notes the similarity of this episode to the epiphany of Athena at Rhodes.

27. Paus. 1.4.4, 10.23.2.

28. For the consultation of the god in 480 BC, see Hdt. 8.36; in 279 BC, Cic. *Div.* 1.81; Diod. 22.9.5; Suda *sv emoi melesei*. For Phylacus, Hdt. 8.39; Paus. 10.23.2. In addition to these similarities, Scott, 2014, 170–71, notes the display of Gallic shields on the Temple of Apollo, matching the Persian shields that had been hung by the Athenians.

29. See Platt, 2011, 149–150, on the emergence of the noun *epiphaneia* for the phenomenon of divine appearances in the Hellenistic age.

30. *SIG*³ 398.16–19 (trans. Austin, 2006, no. 60, pp.129–30).

31. For inscriptions, consider *FD* iii.1.483.6, of 245 BC (referring to 'the epiphany of the gods'). Literary accounts: Cic. *Div.* 1.81; Justin *Epit.* 24.8; Diod. 22.9. On the identification of the various divine and heroic participants and the elaboration of the tradition, see Champion, 1995, 215–17; Graf, 2004, 120–21.

32. *I.Lindos* II.2 column D.1–59. For text and translation, see Higbie, 2003, 43–47. This epiphany story may have been formulated well after the Persian Wars: see below, n.44.

33. Versnel, 1987, 52. On this basis the assistance rendered to the Athenians by Boreas at Artemisium (Hdt. 7.189) might be deemed an epiphany, and it is counted as such by Pritchett, 1979, 24, in his catalogue of battle epiphanies.

34. Pritchett, 1979, 11–46.

35. Sagra River: above n.7. Cyzicus: Plut. *Luc.* 10.2–3.

36. At Delphi: Hdt. 8.39; Marathon: Hdt. 6.11; Salamis: Hdt. 8.64, 83–84. The prodigies reported near Eleusis prior to the battle at Salamis also contain epiphanic elements: see Hdt. 8.65. On these, see Graf, 2004, 115–18; Bowie, 2007, 129–30, 151–53, 172–74, and, for Epizelus, see below. For other Classical attestations of epiphanies, cf. also *IG* i³ 1163.

37. On this cup, see Morris, 1992, 327; Kron, 1999, 65–68; also Barrett and Vickers, 1978 (associating the cup, however, with Plataea rather than Marathon).

38. Compare the observations of Graf, 2004, 122, on the treatment of epiphanies in inscriptions.

39. Hdt. 6.105. On the epiphany of Pan, see Garland, 1992, 47–63; Harrison, 2000, 82–92; Hornblower, 2001, 143–45; Scott, 2005, 369–70.

40. In modern scholarship, a more explicit claim for Pan's active presence on the field at Marathon is sometimes implied by translations of the epigram (*Pal. Anth.* 16.232, attributed to Simonides) which supposedly graced the statue of Pan dedicated at Athens by Miltiades. Some of these translations supply a verb of fighting where the Greek original lacks any such form. Thus Garland, 1992, 50, has, 'Miltiades erected me, goat-footed Pan of Arcadia, the one who fought against the Medes and with the Athenians'; in the Greek, Pan is in fact described simply as being 'with the Athenians, and against the Medes'.

41. This is not to argue that Herodotus is implicitly denying credence to the story; the observation is simply that the presentation of similar stories by later sources is more direct. For discussion of Herodotus' attitude to epiphanies, see Harrison, 2000, 89–92 (with particular emphasis on the Pan episode); Mikalson, 2003, 145–46.

42. Pan present at Marathon: Paus. 1.28.4; Suda *sv* Hippias; see also Lucian *Philopseud.* 3, *Deor. Dial.* 22.3.

43. Marathon: Plut. *Thes.* 35.5; Paus. 1.32; Salamis: Plut. *Thes.* 10.3; Paus. 1.36.1.

44. Chaniotis, 2005, 160. For epiphanies in the context of Gallic threat post-279 BC, see Paus. 10.32.4–5 (Themisonium) and 10.30.9 (Celaenae). Pritchett, 1979, 32, includes in his list of epiphanies a possible appearance by Heracles at Cyzicus, c. 278/277 BC, the evidence for which is discussed below, n. 53. In a similar vein, the formulation of the story of the epiphany of Athena at Rhodes (see above) may also be later than its narrative context (the fifth century). The historicity of a Persian attack on Rhodes is debatable, and the historical authorities cited for the episode on the *Chronicle of Lindos* all post-date the fifth century BC: Higbie, 2003, 232–35.

45. Paus. 8.10.8, with Pritchett, 1979, 34–35 (citing earlier scholarship). Pritchett, 1979, 20, deduces an epiphany from a statue group described at Paus. 10.13.10.

46. On further complexities around the interface of epiphanies and of representations of deities in art, see Bravo, 2004; Platt, 2011, 253–87; Platt, 2015, 491–92.

47. Another epiphany possibly influenced by a victory monument is that of the Dioskouroi at Aegispotami in 405 BC. For the epiphany, see Plut. *Lys.* 12.1, and for the monument, Paus. 10.9.7, with Pritchett, 1979, 27.

48. Monument at Delphi: Paus. 10.10.1–2; Stoa Poikile (Athens): Paus. 1.15.3; trans. Jones, 1918.

49. For Pan in the Stoa painting, see Polemon *Call.* 35, *Cyn.* 41, 62; Aristid. *Panath.* 88.

50. Cimon, whose interest in the Marathon epiphanies is discussed above, may well have encouraged speculation about Theseus. Cimon cultivated a close personal association with that hero, whose bones he reclaimed from Scyros (Plut. *Cim.* 8); the insinuation of a place for that mythical Athenian king at Marathon will have served Cimon's own agenda.

51. Similarly, heroes are sometimes represented as warriors in hoplite attire in the visual arts: see Salapata, 1997, 247–49; Bravo, 2004, 70–71.

52. Locrian appeal: Diod. 8.32.1–2. Aeacidae at Salamis: Hdt. 8.64.1. Cf. Polemon *Cyn.* 62 of the gods and heroes as *symmakhoi* in the Stoa Poikile painting of Marathon. For aid as a dominant *topos* of heroic epiphany, see Bravo, 2004, 65.

53. Stoa painting: Paus. 1.15.3. Hermes at Tanagra: Paus. 9.22.2. Epirote soldiers: *SEG* 36.555, *c.* 129 BC. The examples could be multiplied: consider, for instance, the manifestation of the Dioskouroi 'in the battleline (*in nostra acie*)' of the Romans at Lake Regillus *c.* 495 BC: Cic. *Nat. Deor.* 2.6. Possibly indicative of an active battlefield intervention too is the representation of Heracles overcoming a Gaul depicted on a relief dedicated by the generals and phylarchs of Cyzicus in 278/277 BC (*BCH* 56 [1932] pl. 25), although the reading of this image is far from certain. The brief text accompanying the relief (*IMT Kyz Kapu Dağ* 1547) does not establish beyond doubt that an epiphany as such motivated the dedication, which may rather have been an offering to entreat Heracles' protection. See Launey, 1944, 217–36; Robert and Robert, 1946, 347 no. 177.

54. Mikalson, 2003, 129–31.

55. For Cynchreus at Salamis, see Paus. 1.36; for the presence of an altar to the Dioskouroi at the Sagra River, see Strabo 6.1.10 (an altar mentioned in the context of Strabo's report on the battle between Locri and Croton at this site).

56. Delphi heroes: Hdt. 8.39.1. At Marathon, heroes too may have had local significance: see Jameson, 1951. Propinquity is a factor in the influence of Heracles

at Marathon (an influence suggested by the inclusion of him in the picture of the battle displayed at the Stoa Poikile: Paus. 1.15.3; Stafford, 2012, 169, but questioned by Kearns, 1989, 46); it was at Heracles' sanctuary that the Athenians set up camp prior to battle (Hdt. 6.108), while Pausanias (1.15.3, 1.32.4) attests to the close ties with Heracles claimed by the Marathonian demesmen, who asserted that they had been the first to worship Heracles as a god.

57. Paus. 4.16.4–6 (Messenia), 4.32.4 (Leuktra). For other encounters between Aristomenes and the Dioskouroi, cf. Paus. 4.16.9.

58. Hdt. 5.79–81. On the genealogical links, see Nagy, 2011a, 75–78. The Spartan provision of the Dioskouroi to the Locrians affords a parallel, with Sparta being the mother-city of Locri.

59. Tyrtaeus F11 (West, 1989–1992).

60. Plut. *Thes.* 35.5.

61. Hdt 6.112; modified trans. of Godley, 1922.

62. Scott, 2005, 618–25, gives a summary of issues raised by Herodotus' narrative of the whole engagement. Krentz, 2010a, 143–52, suggests that the point of the rapid deployment was to cross the plain of Marathon and close on the Persian infantry at first light, before the Persians could equip and deploy their cavalry; the speedy charge was essential to neutralize the element that otherwise gave the Persians an immense advantage – their cavalry.

63. Compare also Ar. *Wasps* 1081–83, of Marathon: 'At once *we ran up* and … gave them battle.' In iconography, a running hoplite became emblematic of conflict with the Persians: see Morris, 1992, 303, and for a particular example, see the cup by Douris (Johns Hopkins University Museum B8), with discussion by Krentz, 2010b. The Athenian claim to have been the first to engage at a run, however, is dismissed as spurious by Wees, 2004, 180.

64. On Leuktra, see Cawkwell, 1983; Roche, 2013, 96–98, with valuable discussion of the unexpectedness of Sparta's defeat in 371 BC. The ending of the myth of Spartan invincibility at Leuktra made possible subsequent helot rebellions and the creation of the state of Messenia; hence the attribution in Messenian tradition to the Messenian hero Aristomenes of a pivotal role in the battle (Paus. 4.32.4) is entirely apposite.

65. Justin *Epit.* 20.3; Strabo 6.1.10; Conon *FGrH* 26 F1.18.

66. Xen. *Hell.* 6.4.7; adapted trans. of Brownson, 1921; compare Diod. 15.53.4; Polyaen. *Strat.* 2.3.8; Callisthenes *FGrH* 124 F22a. For Xenophon's careful treatment of the issue of divine influence at Leuktra, see Tuplin, 1993, 136–37.

67. Hdt. 8.37.

68. The examples above concern the staging of epiphanies in order to encourage bravery; for an epiphany staged for financial motives, see Polyaen. *Strat.* 6.1.3, and for one staged to dupe the enemy, Paus. 4.27.2–3, Polyaen. *Strat.* 2.31.4. On epiphanies as strategies generally, see Petridou, 2015, 142–67.

69. Polyaen. *Strat.* 1.41.1 cf. Front. *Strat.* 1.11. At Polyaen. *Strat.* 8.59 the epiphany of Athena at Pellene is described as a ruse by her priestess; for discussion, see Platt, 2011, 12–14.

70. Hdt. 6.117 for Epizelus.

71. Tritle, 2000, 159–60; compare also Sekunda, 2002, 69; Wees, 2004, 151. Scott, 2005, 369, 396, explains both Philippides' encounter with Pan (see above) and Epizelus' blindness as responses to physical strain and trauma. Wheeler, 2004, identifies stress as a driving factor in epiphanies generally; compare further Hermann, 2011.

72. Plut. *Arat.* 32 (Pellene), *Luc.* 10.2 (Cyzicus).
73. Divine epiphanies are similarly treated in poetry, with fear and terror dominant in the description of Athena's preparations for battle in Hom. *Il.* 5.736–47.
74. Hdt. 8.38.1; trans. Selincourt and Marincola, 1996.
75. Plut. *Arat.* 32.1; trans. Perrin, 1926; Polyaen. *Strat.* 8.59. For a 'phantom procession' presaging divine intervention in warfare, compare the epiphany on the plain of Eleusis prior to the Battle of Salamis, with the presence of the gods indicated to the observers by visual and auditory means (a great dust cloud, and the singing of the Iacchus song): Hdt. 8.65.
76. Plut. *Arat.* 32.2–3; trans. Perrin, 1926.
77. *I.Stratonikeia* 10, with Petridou, 2015, 138–41 for Panamara. Compare also the panic induced in the invading Arcadians by the epiphany of Sosipolis at Elis: Paus. 6.20.3–5.
78. For Pan as metaphor for fear, Eur. *Rhes.* 36–37.
79. Occasionally it is Dionysus rather than Pan who operates thus, as for example in Eur. *Bacch.* 300–05. The overlap between Pan and Dionysus is reflected in their association in literature and art: see *LIMC* viii Pan 219, with Polyaen. *Strat.* 1.2 (Pan as general of Dionysus).
80. Suda *sv Panikoi deimati*.
81. Paus. 10.23.7; trans. Jones, 1935.
82. Paus. 10.23.8.
83. Cic. *Div.* 1.80–81, with Schulz, 2014, 159.
84. For Pan as inducing Panic at Marathon, see Garland, 1992, 51–54. For doubts, see Hornblower, 2001, 143–45; Parker, 2005, 401.
85. Feeney, 1991, 216, isolates as a distinguishing differentiator between epic and historical narrative the 'characterful narration of divine action'. The intrusion of divine agents into historical battle thus tends to lend a Homeric colouring, and in consequence it is unsurprising that descriptions of epiphanies sometimes borrow from Homeric language. See for example the commentary of Kolde, 2003, 185, 198–99, on Isyllus' narrative of his claimed encounter with Asklepios.
86. The multitude of epiphanies in the Persian Wars is treated by Petridou, 2015, 113–22. For poetic epiphanies in the Persian Wars, note Simonides' Plataean elegy: FF11–17 (West, 1989–1992) in which the Spartans are depicted as marching out in the company of the Dioskouroi and Menelaus (see esp. F11.29–31); the elegy serves more generally to assimilate the Battle of Plataea with the Trojan War.
87. Paus. 1.13.8; Plut. *Pyrr.* 34; Strabo 8.6.18.
88. Paus. 1.13.8. It is tempting to see the presence of the sanctuary of Demeter, and the burial of Pyrrhus within its confines, as central to the construction of the Argive version of events. Demeter's willingness to manifest herself as an old crone in myth (*Hom. Hymn 2: To Demeter* 101–04) will have further facilitated the Argive interpretation.
89. Pertinent here also are the victory dedications in which epiphanic heroes and gods are depicted; these serve both to demonstrate gratitude to the benefactions of the deities concerned and to publicize the fact of the benefactions to viewers of the dedication.
90. Platt, 2011, 147–63, discusses epigraphic responses to epiphanies in general, with keen observations on the ways in which the display of the epiphany narrative mirrors the materiality of the epiphany itself.
91. Plut. *Luc.* 10.3. Pritchett, 1979, 29, 35–39, catalogues additional inscriptional instances as following: the epiphanies of Asklepios at Sparta; of the Parthenos in

a time of great danger at Chersonesus in the mid-third century BC, and again in 108 BC; of Athena at Pergamum in 167 BC against the Galatians; of Artemis Cindyas at Bargylia in the second century BC; of Hecate at Lagina in the first century BC; of Zeus and Hecate at Stratonicea in 40 BC (on which episode, see Graf, 2004, 118–20). See also Hermes at Tanagra: Paus. 9.22.2.

92. Delphi Soteria and epiphanies: *SIG*³ 398; Artemis at Cnidus: *SEG* 38.812, *I.Knidos* 220. On both, see further Platt, 2011, 154–57.

93. Hdt. 8.93.1.

94. Hdt. 8.84. Compare Pind. *Isth*. 5.48 for the prowess of Aegina at the Battle of Salamis.

95. Hesiod F205; Pind. *Pyth*. 9.98–100, with Nagy, 2011a, 45–48; Irwin, 2011, 383–84, on Aeacidae and Aegina's thalassocracy.

96. The contestation between Athens and Aegina over 'ownership' of the Aeacidae themselves will have heightened these tensions. Two locales for the Aeacidae – Aegina and Salamis – are attested when the Greeks invoke these heroes before the naval battle (Hdt. 8.64.1–2), and those on Salamis had come largely under the aegis of Athens. On the rival sets of Aeacidae, see Nagy, 2011b, 201–04. Athens had even tried to appropriate Aeacus himself, with the construction of an Aeaceum undertaken in the context of hostilities with Aegina (Hdt. 5.89.2; cf. Hdt. 5.80.3; for Aegina's claimed retention of the remains of Aeacus, see Paus. 2.29.6–8). At the Battle of Salamis, then, there were present as 'fellow fighters' both the Aeacidae whom the Athenians had claimed as their own, and the Aeacidae of Aegina, and it is tempting to see in the post-battle rivalry between the two poleis a concern also for the perceived effectiveness of their heroic connections.

97. Hdt. 8.65. Note also Paus. 1.36 for the contribution of the Athenian/Salaminian hero Cynchreus to this battle.

98. Plut. *Them*. 15.

99. On the commemoration at Delphi (the influence on which of Cimon's family is suggested by the inclusion among the heroes depicted on it of Philaios, the progenitor of Cimon's own Philaid clan: so Pherecydes *FGrH* 3 F2), see Neer, 2004, 82–83. The Stoa was funded by Cimon's brother-in-law, Peisianax: Diog. Laert. 7.1.5; on the 'Cimonian' flavour of the paintings displayed in it, Massaro, 1978, 458–59, 462–65.

100. On the cult of Pan, see below, n.124. For Cimon's possible influence in its introduction, see Podlecki, 1984, 187–88. Cimon may not have been the only individual interested in promoting Pan. Garland, 1992, 51, seeks to identify Pan with a reference to the 'messenger of the immortals' on *IG* i³ 784, the dedication on the Acropolis offered in the name of the *polemarch* Callimachus; given that the column on which the dedication is inscribed supported a statue of Nikê, however (Keesling, 2010, 119–26), the allusion may instead be to that goddess.

101. Hdt. 6.136; Plut. *Cim*. 4.

102. Thuc. 1.113; Diod. 12.6.

103. *IG* i³ 1163. The translation is that of Bowra, 1938, 80, with his restorations.

104. Bowra, 1938, 85–86. For a rare comparison, see Plut. *Nic*. 17, where the acknowledgement of defeat is, however, much less explicit.

105. *IG* i³ 1240.

106. Christ, 2006, 115, thus includes Epizelus in his examples of individual hoplites' strategies for laying claim to personal glory after battles. For another wounding of a hoplite by a hero, with subsequent indications of the hoplite's prestige, see Conon

FGrH 26 F1.18, cf. Paus. 3.19.12–13 with Brown, 2002, 144–47, on Autoleon of Croton, wounded by Ajax at the Battle of the Sagra River.

107. Hom. *Il.* 20.131. Platt, 2015, 493, notes other injurious (or fatal) epiphanic experiences from myth.

108. For Epizelus in the Stoa painting, Polemon *Call.* 44, *Cyn.* 56; with Harrison, 1972, 367–69. For lists of the outstanding warriors at Marathon, see Ael. *Nat. An.* 7.38; Diog. Laert. 1.56; Plut. *Mor.* 305b–c, 347d. A counter-case against Epizelus' prestige is mounted by Keaveney and Bartley, 2014.

109. Mikalson, 2003, 70–71. Contrast (albeit at the level of an entire war rather than an individual battle) Themistocles' speech at Hdt. 8.109.2: 'Not we but the gods and heroes have accomplished these things.' Themistocles puts forward this view, however, in the context of the abandonment of the Greek pursuit of the Persians, a decision which such pious thoughts could be usefully deployed to legitimize.

110. Diod. 11.14.4 (trans. Page, 1981, no. 106). The date of the epigram is disputed. Compare Meritt, 1947 (*c.* 400 BC, based on the description of the inscribed version); Page, 1981, 411 BC (contemporary with the war). Dawe and Diggle, by whom Page, 1981, was prepared for publication, ventured a reconciliation between these two positions by venturing that the inscription was a re-publication of an earlier text.

111. The contribution of heroes might similarly be acknowledged; see Hdt. 8.121 for the dedication to Ajax of a trireme from the Battle of Salamis.

112. Mikalson, 2003, 70–71, notes the tendency of some scholars to emend the text in order to transfer credit to the gods, and argues against this by comparing this text to other dedicatory texts of the period, for which see Hdt 5.77; Plut. *Them.* 8.2–3; and other comparanda gathered at Mikalson, 2003, 213 n.221.

113. *SIG³* 398.5–8.

114. Champion, 1995, cf. 1996, 317–18.

115. Plut. *Arat.* 32.3; trans. Perrin, 1926.

116. Marasco, 2011, 112, suggests that the version of this episode in which an epiphany was indeed responsible for the rout (albeit an epiphany based on the mistaken identification of a statuesque, helmeted woman: Plut. *Arat.* 32.1) was designed to detract from Aratus' glory.

117. Hornblower, 1996, 355–56.

118. Thuc. 4.116.

119. See esp. Crowley, 2014 (from whom I have borrowed the term 'diachronic universality'). Crowley subtly teases out the shift in the religious and moral frameworks of war, noting the potential difference between fighters in antiquity and those whose outlook has been heavily informed by a Judaeo-Christian perspective.

120. Graf, 2004, 113–15.

121. Graf, 2004, 120–21.

122. Trogus' account is preserved in Justin *Epit.* 24.8.

123. *IG* iv² 1.128.72–77; for the context of this supposed intervention, see Kolde, 2003, 257–64.

124. See Hdt. 6.105 and Paus. 1.28.4, with Garland, 1992, 58–62, for the introduction of Pan's cult after Marathon, although it should be acknowledged that neither Herodotus nor Pausanias explicitly links the cult to the victory.

125. The Marathon victory may also have had an effect on Heracles' cult (on which see Stafford, 2012, 179–80): Garland, 1992, 57. Compare also Paus. 1.32.5 for the worship of Echetlaus; Plut. *Thes.* 35.5 for recognition of Theseus as a 'demigod' after Marathon; Hdt. 7.189 for Boreas (after Artemisium). Ajax's help at Salamis was recognized by the Athenians through the Aianteia that they established at

Salamis: see Parker, 1996, 153–54. Garbrah, 1986, argues that the Theophaneia festival celebrated in Chios in Hellenistic and Roman times may have been prompted by a wartime epiphany.

126. Ach. Tat. 7.12.4. At Cic. *Nat. Deor.* 2.6 comes an explicit articulation of the relationship of cult to epiphany.

127. See for example the repeated protection afforded by Zeus to Panamara: *I.Stratonikeia* 10. On the political currency of epiphanies generally, see Platt, 2015, 496–500. Kolde, 2002, 161, suggests that the publication of Asklepios' epiphany to Isyllus (*IG* iv² 1.128.57–77, with n.25 above) may have been in part a strategy to encourage military support for the rebellion of the Spartan Areus against Antigonus Gonatas through the implicit promise of another epiphany by Asklepios in aid of the Spartan cause.

Bibliography

Austin, M.M., 2006, *The Hellenistic World from Alexander to the Roman Conquest*, 2nd edn, Cambridge.

Barrett, A.A., and Vickers, M., 1978, 'The Brygos Cup Reconsidered', *JHS* 98, 17–24.

Bowie, A.M., 2007, *Herodotus*: Histories, *Book 8*, Cambridge.

Bowra, C.M., 1938, 'The Epigram on the Fallen of Coronea', *CQ* 32, 80–88.

Bravo, J., 2004, 'Heroic Epiphanies: Narrative, Visual and Cultic Contexts', *ICS* 29, 63–84.

Brown, M.K., 2002, *The Narratives of Konon*, Beiträge zur Altertumskunde 163, Munich.

Brownson, C.L., 1921, *Xenophon* vol. 2, Cambridge MA and London.

Cawkwell, G., 1983, 'The Decline of Sparta', *CQ* 33, 385–400.

Champion, C., 1995, 'The Soteria at Delphi: Aetolian Propaganda in the Epigraphical Record', *AJPh* 116, 213–30.

—— 1996, 'Polybius, Aetolia and the Gallic Attack on Delphi (279 B.C.)', *Historia* 45, 315–28.

Chaniotis, A., 2005, *War in the Hellenistic World: A Social and Cultural History*, Oxford.

Christ, M.R., 2006, *The Bad Citizen in Classical Athens*, Cambridge.

Cioffi, R., 2014, 'Seeing Gods: Epiphany and Narrative in the Greek Novels', *AN* 11, 1–42.

Crowley, J., 2014, 'Beyond the Universal Soldier: Combat Trauma in Classical Antiquity', in Meineck, P., and Konstan, D. (eds), *Combat Trauma and the Ancient Greeks*, New York, 105–30.

Feeney, D., 1991, *The Gods in Epic*, Oxford.

Figueira, T., 'The Aiakidai, the Herald-less War, and Salamis', in *Donum Natalicium Digitaliter Confectum Gregorio Nagy Septuagenario a Discipulis Collegis Familiaribus Oblatum* (http://chs.harvard.edu/CHS/article/display/4610).

Garbrah, K., 1986, 'On the Θεοφάνεια in Chios and the Epiphany of Gods in War', *ZPE* 65, 207–10.

Garland, R., 1992, *Introducing New Gods: The Politics of Athenian Religion*, Ithaca.

Godley, A.D., 1922, *Herodotus: The Persian Wars. Books V–VII*, vol. iii, London.

Graf, F., 2004, 'Trick or Treat? On Collective Epiphanies in Antiquity', *ICS* 29, 111–30.

Habicht, C., 2005, 'Notes on Inscriptions from Cyzicus', *EA* 38, 93–100.

Harrison, E., 1972, 'The South Frieze of the Nike Temple and the Marathon Painting in the Painted Stoa', *AJA* 76, 353–78.

Harrison, T., 2000, *Divinity and History. The Religion of Herodotus*, Oxford.

Hermann, G., 2011, 'Greek Epiphanies and the Sensed Presence', *Historia* 60, 127–57.

Higbie, C., 2003, *The Lindian Chronicle and the Greek Creation of their Past*, Oxford.

Hornblower, S., 1996, *A Commentary on Thucydides. Volume ii: Books iv–v.24*, Oxford.

—— 2001, 'Epic and Epiphanies. Herodotus and the "New Simonides"', in Sider, D., and Boedeker, D. (eds), *The New Simonides: Contexts of Praise and Desire*, Oxford, 135–47.

—— 2011, *The Greek World 479–323 BC*, 4th edn, London and New York.

Irwin, E., 2011, 'Herodotus on Aeginetan Identity', in Fearn, D. (ed.), *Aegina: Contexts for Choral Lyric Poetry. Myth, History and Identity in the Fifth Century* BC, Oxford, 373–425.

Jameson, M.H., 1951, 'The Hero Echetlaeus', *TAPhA* 82, 49–61.

Jones, W.H.S., 1918, *Pausanias: Description of Greece, Books i and ii*, vol. i, London.

—— 1935, *Pausanias: Description of Greece, Books viii.22–x*, vol. iv, London.

Kearns, E., 1989, *The Heroes of Attica, BICS* Supplement 57, London.

Keaveney, A., and Bartley, A., 2014, 'The Case of Epizelus (Herodotus 6.117) Revisited', *GIF* 66, 9–26.

Keesling, C.M., 2010, 'The Callimachus Monument on the Athenian Acropolis (*CEG* 256) and the Athenian Commemoration of the Persian Wars', in Baumbach, M., Petrovic, A., and Petrovic, I. (eds), *Archaic and Classical Greek Epigram*, Cambridge, 100–30.

Kolde, A., 2002, 'Is Isyllos of Epidauros' Poetry Typically Hellenistic?', *Hermathena* 173/174, 155–64.

—— 2003, *Politique et religion chez Isyllos d'Épidaure*, Basel.

Krentz, P., 2010a, *The Battle of Marathon*, New Haven and London.

——2010b, 'A Cup by Douris and the Battle of Marathon', in Trundle, M., and Fagan, G. (eds), *New Perspectives on Ancient Warfare*, Leiden, 183–204.

Kron, U., 1999, 'Patriotic Heroes', in Hägg, R. (ed.), *Ancient Greek Hero Cult. Proceedings of the Fifth International Seminar on Ancient Greek Cult, Organized by the Department of Classical Archaeology and Ancient History, Göteborg University, 21–23 April 1995*, Stockholm, 61–83.

Lattimore, R., 1951, *The Iliad of Homer*, Chicago.

Launey, M., 1944, 'Un épisode oublié de l'invasion galate en Asie Mineure (278/7 av. J.-C.)', *REA* 46, 217–36.

Lavelle, B.M., 1993, *The Sorrow and the Pity. A Prolegomenon to a History of Athens under the Peisistratids, c. 560–510 B.C.*, Historia Einzelschriften 80, Stuttgart.

Marasco, G., 2011, 'The Hellenistic Age: Autobiography and Political Struggles', in Marasco, G. (ed.), *Political Autobiographies and Memoirs in Antiquity. A Brill Companion*, Leiden, 87–120.

Marinatos, N., and Kyrtatas, D., 2004, 'Conclusions Epiphany: Concept Ambiguous, Experience Elusive', *ICS* 29, 227–34.

Massaro, V., 1978, 'Herodotus' Account of the Battle of Marathon and the Picture in the Stoa Poikile', *AC* 47, 458–75.

Meritt, B.D., 1947, 'The Persians at Delphi', *Hesperia* 16, 58–61.

Mikalson, J., 2003, *Herodotus and Religion in the Persian Wars*, Chapel Hill and London.

Morris, S.P., 1992, *Daidalos and the Origins of Greek Art*, Princeton.

Nagy, G., 2011a, 'Asopos and His Multiple Daughters: Traces of Preclassical Epic in the Aeginetan Odes of Pindar', in Fearn, D. (ed.), *Aegina. Contexts for Choral Lyric Poetry. Myth, History and Identity in the Fifth Century* BC, Oxford, 41–78.

Nagy, G., 2011b, 'A Second Look at the Poetics of Re-enactment in Ode 13 of Bacchylides', in Athanassaki, L., and Bowie, E. (eds), *Archaic and Classical Choral Song: Performance, Politics and Dissemination*, Berlin and Boston, 173–206.

Neer, R., 2004, 'The Athenian Treasury at Delphi and the Material of Politics', *ClAnt* 23, 63–93.

Odgen, D., 2004, *Aristomenes of Messene. Legends of Sparta's Nemesis*, Swansea.

Page, D., 1981, *Further Greek Epigrams*, revised and prepared for publication by R.D. Dawe and J. Diggle, Cambridge.

Parker, R., 1996, *Athenian Religion: A History*, Oxford.

—— 2005, *Polytheism and Society at Athens*, Oxford.

Perrin, B., 1926. *Plutarch's Lives, with an English Translation*, vol. 11, Cambridge MA and London.

Petridou, G., 2015, *Divine Epiphany in Greek Literature and Culture*, Oxford.

Platt, V., 2011, *Facing the Gods. Epiphany and Representation in Graeco-Roman Art, Literature and Religion*, Cambridge.

—— 2015, 'Epiphany', in Eidinow, E., and Kindt, J. (eds), *The Oxford Handbook of Greek Religion*, Oxford, 491–504.

Podlecki, A., 1984, *The Early Greek Poets and their Times*, Vancouver.

Pritchett, W.K., 1979, *The Greek State at War. Part III: Religion*, Berkeley.

Robert, J., and Robert, L., 1946, 'Bulletin épigraphique', *REG* 59/60, 298–372.

Roche, H. 2013, 'Spartan Supremacy: a "Possession Forever"? Early-Fourth Century Expectations of Enduring Ascendancy', in Powell, A. (ed.), *Hindsight in Greek and Roman History*, Swansea, 91–112.

Salapata, G., 1997, 'Hero Warriors from Corinth and Laconia', *Hesperia* 66, 245–60.

Schulz, C.E., 2014, *Commentary on Cicero* De Divinatione 1, Ann Arbor.

Scott, L., 2005, *Historical Commentary on Herodotus Book 6*, Mnemosyne Supplementum 268, Leiden.

Scott, M., 2014, *Delphi. A History of the Center of the Ancient World*, Princeton.

Sekunda, N., 2002, *Marathon 490 BC: The First Persian Invasion of Greece*, Oxford.

Selincourt, A. De, and Marincola, J., 1996, *Herodotus*, Harmondsworth.

Speyer, W., 1980, 'Die Hilfe und Epiphanie einer Gottheit, eines Heroen und eines Heiligen in der Schlacht', in Dassman, E., and Frank, K.S. (eds), *Pietas. Festschrift für Bernard Kötting*, Munster, 55–77.

Stafford, E., 2012, *Heracles. Gods and Heroes of the Ancient World*, London and New York.

Tritle, L.A., 2000, *From Melos to My Lai: War and Survival*, London.

Tuplin, C., 1993, *The Failings of Empire. A Reading of Xenophon* Hellenica *2.3.11–7.5.27*, Stuttgart.

Versnel, H., 1987, 'What Did Ancient Man See When He Saw a God? Some Reflections on Greco-Roman Epiphany', in Plas, D. van der (ed.), *Effigies Dei*, Leiden, 42–55.

Watson, J.S., 1853, *Marcus Junianus Justinus. Eptiome of the Philippic History of Pompeus Trogus*, London.

Wees, H. Van, 2004, *Greek Warfare: Myth and Realities*, London.

West, M.L., 1989–1992, *Iambi et Elegi*, 2nd edn, vols 1–2, Oxford.

Wheeler, G., 2004, 'Battlefield Epiphanies in Ancient Greece: a Survey', *Digressus* 4, 1–14.

Chapter 8

Fate, Predestination and the Mindset of the Greek Hoplite in Battle

Christopher Matthew

One of the factors which has greatly contributed to the success or failure of any military operation, in the ancient world or the modern, has been the morale of the individual combatant. Without the willingness of soldiers to engage in the fighting, any military action simply cannot take place. Furthermore, history has shown that, when the occasion has called for it, the willingness of a soldier to stand his ground amidst the carnage of combat is one of the things that has dictated the outcome of an engagement. Such willingness to maintain their position was essential to the warfare of the ancient Greeks, whose primary mode of offensive action was the employment of groups of men arranged in the ranks and files of the phalanx. Many different socio-political aspects of the ancient Greek hoplite's home city-state combined to influence his morale in battle. Some of these were specific to that city-state, while others had a broader sphere of influence. Despite the numerous influences placed on the ancient Greek hoplite in battle, the one socio-political aspect that almost all hoplites would have been influenced by would have been religion.

War is a variable entity – full of vagaries and seemingly random acts and outcomes – where death on both sides is an all too common occurrence.[1] Why does a person's weapon fail at a particularly critical point in a battle when his opponent's does not? Why does one warrior only receive a minor injury when another is killed instantly? Why does one warrior get hit by a volley of projectiles while the man standing beside him does not? These are the sorts of questions that warriors have been asking for millennia. Conditioning and/or inspiring men to participate in this apparently indiscriminate environment of violence, at least for the ancient Greeks, was part of the socio-political mechanisms of the city-state. Any number of reasons could inspire the men of a city-state to go off to war: a sense of duty to the state, the defence of one's homeland against an invader, religious or political fervour, the inspiration of strong leadership, a quest for revenge, blatant aggression, the level of professionalism of the warrior, and the list goes on. Once deployed on the field of battle, however, forces were called into play (and occasionally questioned) which were arguably far stronger than those which had initially led the men to march out to battle – and it is these forces which dictated how the soldier would perform on the battlefield.

For the hoplites of ancient Greece, combat was a very up-close and personal experience. Even before any fighting commenced, hoplites would be formed up in the densely packed formation of the phalanx where those around them could be, almost literally, shoulder to shoulder, or spaced in a slightly more open, yet still closely packed, order.[2] Hoplites could be deployed, as in the case of the Athenians, in clan or regional groups – meaning that those within the sub-units of the phalanx would be familiar with, and possibly related to, each other.[3] In the case of the Spartans, children were assigned to mess groups as part of the rigorous *agogé* education system and, as these boys grew to adulthood, would fight in their mess groups as part of the Spartan phalanx – again meaning that those in the phalanx would be familiar with, and have close bonds with, those around them.[4]

Hoplites would be equipped with a large heavy shield (*aspis*) and a long thrusting spear (*doru*) as the minimum requirements for fighting in the phalanx.[5] They may additionally, depending upon the social structure of their *polis* and personal wealth if applicable, have been further encumbered with heavy body armour, greaves, padding and a helmet which, depending upon its style, could inhibit such things as hearing and ventilation – making hoplite combat also somewhat burdensome and claustrophobic.[6] The nature of the battlefield could additionally be inhibiting by way of heat, dust, sun glare, precipitation and other environmental factors, and by such things as hunger, thirst and/or disease.

The fighting between two hoplite phalanxes (or one hoplite phalanx against a contingent of other troops, such as those from Persia) was undertaken at very close quarters. Due to the length of the hoplite spear, its configuration and the manner in which it was wielded, an enemy was, at best, fought at a 'spear length' of around 2 metres.[7] At this distance, and using a hand-held weapon, a hoplite would be able to see everything about his opponent. He would be able to see (depending upon the style of headwear the opponent had) the fear on his face and if he had lost control of his bowels in the terrifying moments before the clash of forces.[8] He would be able to see if his opponent was hesitant, if his hands were trembling with fear or if his eyes were burning with rage. As weapons clashed, the hoplite would be able to feel every impact that he delivered with his spear as it reverberated down the shaft, and feel every hit delivered against his shield and armour.

The hoplite would feel his weapon penetrate the armour and flesh of his opponent as he delivered a killing blow, and would see the life drain out of the man in front of him. Yet behind this falling enemy would be standing rank upon rank of the opposing phalanx, all driving forward to try and push his own formation back, and the man who had occupied the second rank of the opposing phalanx would step forward to take the place of his fallen comrade and continue the fight.

Under certain circumstances, formations would literally press each other 'shield against shield'. In such a scenario, the lengthy spear was practically redundant as a weapon, swords could be drawn if possible and the battle would develop into a physical shoving match as each side strove to break the opposing formation apart through the sheer application of force.[9]

Amid such carnage, the ground would become littered with the detritus of battle – the torn and bloodied bodies of the fallen, broken and discarded weapons and shields, urine, excrement and vomit from those overcome by fear.[10] The anguished cries of the wounded and dying, and the enraged screams of those still fighting, would fill the air amongst the clash of arms, instructions and exhortations yelled by officers and commanders, trumpet blasts to relay orders and music that may have been played to help keep the formation in step and together.[11] If one side's morale failed, and the men in the formation broke and attempted to flee, the carnage would not stop. Encumbered by their heavy equipment, the hoplite was not agile enough to operate in long-distance pursuits. Lightly armed skirmishers or cavalry, however, could chase the routed side at will, cutting down all whom they caught.[12]

Such a method of combat could result in casualty rates, even for the winning side, that would be considered military disasters in modern terms.[13] What was it that motivated hoplites to stand and fight in this manner and amid such terrors? To suggest that this was the case because it was a violent time in human history seems overly simplistic and naive. Standing one's ground would have partly come down to training, tradition and convention. Herodotus, for example, relates that Spartan law prohibited retreating from battle and gave the hoplite only two choices: victory or death.[14] Similarly, the Athenian Ephebic Oath outlined the necessity for hoplites to remain in position and maintain their formation.[15] These social aspects of warfare in ancient Greece, however, while still essential to understanding the combat of the time, are more about the culture of the *polis* that the hoplite belonged to, and about the actual style of warfare itself, rather than being an indication of what drove the individual hoplite to maintain his position and fight. For the individual, there must have been an additional psychological element which prompted him to stand amongst, and contribute to, such ferocious carnage where the chance of survival was seemingly random. Religion, as a general concept across the Hellenic world, would have had a large part to play in this. One factor that was both religious and psychological in nature that would have had a direct impact on the hoplite's bearing and mindset on the field of battle would have been a belief in the Fates.

The influence and/or role of the Fates and the accompanying concept of predestination is an area of study that has not permeated much of the scholarship on warfare in ancient Greece. Indeed, many of the major works on this subject, which include discussions of the place of morale and religion on the battlefield, contain little or no reference to the Fates (let alone any analysis of their importance to the conduct of ancient warfare).[16] Similarly, works on Greek religion and mythology, while outlining the stories involving the Fates, contain no discussion of their place on the battlefield or within the mindset of the inhabitants of Greece.[17] Despite this, however, there is a vast array of evidence which shows that these divinities held a dominant position in Greek religion and, as a result, would have had a direct impact on the psyche of the Greek hoplite in battle.

Although not major deities in the Greek pantheon of gods, the Fates (*Moirai/Moῖραι*) still held an eminent place within Greek religion – and had a particular impact on the nature of war in ancient Greece. Their collective name translates as 'parts' or 'allocated portions', and it was the Fates who personified the predetermined destiny of mankind. There were three Fates: Klotho 'the Spinner', who wove the thread of each person's life at the moment of their birth; Lakhesis 'the Divider', who measured each person's thread of life; and Atropos 'the Inescapable', who cut the thread of a person's life at the time of their death.[18] Thus the three Fates determined the course of everyone's life from the moment they came into the world to the moment they left it.[19] What the Fates dictated was considered, for the most part, unknowable to mortals and inescapable, and even the other gods had to bow to what had been predetermined.[20] Herodotus goes so far as to openly declare that 'no one can escape his lot, not even a god!'[21] Such a statement clearly illustrates the power that the Greeks felt the Fates had over the course of events in everyone's life.

The *Moirai* were the daughters of Zeus – although their maternal parent seems to have been uncertain. The poet Hesiod claimed that the Fates were the daughters of Nyx (Night),[22] and also that their mother was the goddess Themis – the personification of divine order.[23] Plato claimed that they were the offspring of Zeus and Anagnke (Destiny).[24] Regardless of their parentage, it is clear that the ancient Greeks associated the Fates with something inevitable and all of their potential mothers bear connotations relating ultimately to death. As such, the Fates are regularly associated with both the Death-Spirits (Keres) and/or with the Furies (*Erinyes*).[25]

The concept that the time and means of a person's death had been predetermined by the gods was, for the Greeks, as old as the works of Homer (if not older), and the gods played their own part in ensuring that what had been predetermined for heroes and warriors on the battlefield came to pass. Hesiod paints the most vivid portrayal of the active role that the divine played on the field of battle through a description of the actions of the Keres:

> [Men were engaged in battle] and behind them the dark Keres, gnashing their white teeth, depressing, grim, and unfriendly, sought those who were dying, for they desired to drink dark blood. As soon as they caught a man slain, or falling just injured, one of them would wrap her great claws about him, and his spirit would descend to Hades and bitter Tartarus. And when they had satiated their souls with human blood, they would discard that one behind them, and again rush back into the confusion and conflict.[26]

In a common literary motif, Homer regularly states that Death (*Thanatos*) and Fate (*Moira*) stood beside or behind individual warriors on the battlefield, and similarly took them when they fell in the fighting – suggesting that the warrior had only died because his allotted time had come.[27]

The Keres, Fates and Death were not the only divinities to roam the battlefield either to save warriors or drag them to their doom. In the *Iliad*, the goddess Hera, speaking on behalf of other gods, states:

> We have all descended from Olympus to join in this battle, so that Achilles may suffer no harm amidst the Trojans today; but later he will suffer whatever Fate has spun for him with her thread at his birth.[28]

Even Patroclus, whose death is the cause of so much calamity throughout the remainder of the *Iliad*, is killed through the actions of Fate and the god Apollo, and because the gods will it to happen at a certain time. At one stage in the epic, the Greeks had pushed forward and were scaling the very walls of Troy, and Patroclus was almost the man who captured the city. As this was not his predetermined fate, however, the god Apollo kept pushing him back. Eventually Apollo declared:

Back! Patroclus! It is not the fate of the Trojans that their proud city be sacked by your spear, or even by that of Achilles, a man far greater than you![29]

Hector also knew that the outcome of his eventual fight with Achilles would be decided by the gods.[30] Agamemnon even blamed Zeus, Fate and the Furies for his quarrel with Achilles – suggesting that all of the events that resulted from this, the attacks and counter-attacks, the deaths of so many on both sides and the eventual meeting between Achilles and Priam were part of a divine grand plan.[31] As such, all of the seemingly random events of the battlefield, such as when a warrior might die, were in some way seen by the Greeks as the result of divine intervention.

The survival of a warrior on the battlefield was also seen as part of a divine plan. In his poem the *Thebiad,* Statius outlines how a single survivor of a campaign believed that 'the commands of the gods snatched destruction away from me, and Atropos, whose pleasure knows no denial, and the Fate that long since shut against me this door of death'.[32] Homer outlines how the failure of a piece of equipment like a sword, or the failure to land a killing blow on an enemy, which could then lead to an opposing warrior living to fight another day, was also seen to have been caused by divine intervention.[33] Such passages clearly demonstrate how it was believed that whether a warrior was victorious, wounded, slain or saved in battle had been determined years earlier at the time of their birth, and that the gods would see to it that circumstances aligned, to the point of divine intervention, so that harm would only befall the warrior when the predetermined time was reached.[34]

What happened to a hero or warrior, even after he was slain, was also predetermined. The savage mutilation of the corpse of the Trojan prince Hector by Achilles, by dragging it behind his chariot and then leaving it for dogs to eat, had been dictated by the Fates at the moment Hector was born:

[Queen Hecuba said] let us now lament far from him we mourn [i.e. Hector] … In this way did restless Fate (*Moira*) spin with her thread at his birth … that he should feed fleet-footed dogs far from his parents.[35]

Yet even though a warrior was destined to die in a certain conflict, the exact time of his demise was far from certain. Zeus, the main deity of the Greek pantheon and guarantor of cosmic order (which included ensuring that what the Fates had determined came to pass in his guise as *Zeus Moiragetes*), contemplated what time he was going to allow Hector to kill Achilles' comrade Patroclus.[36] Similarly, when Hector and Achilles finally clashed, the gods debated whether they should let Achilles kill Hector then or at a later time. Athena, favouring the Greek cause, argued that Hector had been fated to be killed by Achilles for a long time and that it should therefore happen immediately. Zeus, in his role as cosmic-guarantor, agreed.[37] Yet even as the fight continued, Zeus pulled out a set of scales, with Hector on one side and Achilles on the other, to see who would kill whom.[38] Even though Homer states that the scales immediately tipped in favour of Achilles, the symbolism of the scales suggests that the outcome of the fight between Achilles and Hector, despite Zeus' agreement with Athena, was still literally in the balance.

Thus Fate seems to have been a somewhat transient concept for the Greeks, with the exact time of the fulfilment of what had been predestined by the Fates determined by the gods – Zeus in particular. Yet it is important to note that the time of a warrior's demise was still out of his hands and was determined by divine will – either by the Fates themselves or by the actions and interventions of the other gods. Apollo's turning back of Patroclus from the walls of Troy on a number of occasions additionally shows that, in the Greek mindset, mortals still possessed a certain level of free agency in their daily lives to do what they wanted, so long as their actions did not jeopardize the predestined course of events that had been set out for them. It was at these moments that the gods intervened to make sure that each person's correct path was followed. This seems to have been how the ancient Greeks explained and accepted the seeming randomness of the battlefield, and how they explained why some ventures (military, domestic, commercial or otherwise) succeeded while others, despite their best efforts, resulted in failure.

Achilles is also one of the few characters in the *Iliad* who seems to be able to dictate his own fate to some extent. He is fully aware that the course of his life holds two options: a long life without glory, in which his name will be forgotten within a few generations, or a short, glorious life, tempered in the fires of conflict, which will ensure that his name and exploits will live on forever.[39] Achilles, however, other than actually knowing what the choices before him are, and knowing the consequences of taking either path, is not aware of the exact time or means of his death, regardless of which course he chooses for his life to take. This is because the final outcome of his life is still part of a divine plan, the details of which Achilles himself is not privileged to know. It is only following the death of Patroclus and Achilles' decision to exact revenge on Hector, as part of his right of free agency, that the course of Achilles' fate seems to have been irreversibly set upon. Once Achilles has chosen his path, his mother, divine Thetis, cries, 'then, child, I must lose you to a swift death … for immediately after Hector dies is your own doom certain.'[40] Later, Hera tells Achilles that the time of his destruction is drawing near, but that many of the gods will not be to blame for this; rather it will be the result of the actions of 'a great god [i.e. Zeus] and strong Fate'.[41]

In a military context, the predestination of a time of death was not confined to warriors on the field of battle in the ancient Greek mindset. The fall of besieged cities was also said to have been predetermined by the Fates. Troy itself, for example, is said to have had the time of its destruction dictated at the time of its 'birth' (i.e. founding).[42] Statius also outlines how the city of Thebes had the thread of its 'life' cut by Death at the moment of its destruction.[43] This severing of the thread of life for a city is the same as when the predetermined course of a person's life reached its end.

The Archaic Greek belief that the Fates and the other gods played a dominant role in the course of a person's life did not end with the advent of the Classical Age, and many writers of the time detail the intervention of the divine in human affairs. Xenophon outlines how it was believed that almost everything was part of the machinations of the gods, and that these interventions could in part be discerned via oracles and divinations.[44] Within the literature of the Classical Age are found passages relating to the Fates and the destinies of individuals and cities which bear close parallels to those written by Homer centuries beforehand – demonstrating a continuance in the belief of the role that the Fates played in the outcome of events such as wars and campaigns.

Herodotus, for example, outlines how the fall of the city of Sardis had been predetermined by the Fates.[45] This bears many similarities to accounts of how the city of Troy had been fated to be destroyed by the Greeks.[46] Similarly, Herodotus states that Fate had decreed that the offspring of Eetion would bring troubles to the city of Corinth.[47] In contrast to these passages, which detail the predetermined ills of a city, Herodotus also outlines how the people of the island of Naxos were not fated to be destroyed by the force led by Aristagoras of Miletus, and how, because of this predetermined course of events, an entirely different train of incidents takes place to influence the course of Greek history.[48]

Nor does Herodotus confine the influence of fate only to cities. Kings and other individuals, for example, are said to have been fated to die at certain times.[49] Indeed, Herodotus' regular reference to, and use of, oracles throughout his narrative, while possibly just a literary motif to highlight the importance of what is to follow in the text, also highlights a strong belief that almost every major event of the conflicts between Greece and Persia had been divinely inspired, either by the Fates or some other deity, long before they came to pass.[50] Thucydides additionally outlines how 'there is much that is unpredictable in war' – particularly volleys of missile fire – the randomness of which could slay brave or cowardly men alike without distinction.[51] This sentiment bears many similarities to descriptions of how the ancient Greeks saw the workings of Fate as predominantly unknown.

The works of Xenophon also contain passages which directly refer to the influence of fate, the divine or the Fates, on the field of battle and how what came to pass had been predetermined, but was sometimes unknown to the individual, or that what would happen to a person was out of their hands and was to be decided by the gods.[52] During his command of the Ten Thousand in Persia, Xenophon himself describes how:

> [He] arose, arrayed for war in his finest attire. For he thought that if the gods (*theoi*) should grant victory, then the finest dress was suited to victory; and if it should be his fate to die, it was proper, he thought … [that] in this attire he should meet his death.[53]

Oracles and prophets seem to have been able somehow to know what the result of a particular course of action would be – even if involving themselves. In the struggle against the Thirty Tyrants in Athens in 404 BC, an anonymous seer (*mantis*) believed that the gods had determined that he was to die in an impending battle but that, if the forces he was with waited until one of their number was killed before advancing, the gods had additionally decreed that they would then be able to move against the enemy and secure a victory.[54] Xenophon then states of the seer:

> His prophecy came true. When they had taken up their shields, he, inspired by some kind of fate … sprang forward in front of them, fell upon the enemy and was killed.[55]

Even the decision to go to war (or not), it seems, was directed by the gods. Xenophon outlines how a divine power (δαιμόνιον) directed the Lacedaemonian assembly along a certain path towards conflict with Thebes – a course of action which led ultimately to their defeat at Leuktra in 371 BC.[56]

A sense of fate, predestination and/or divine influence over events (not just on the battlefield but everywhere else as well) is also found in many of the plays, both tragic and comic, of the Classical Period.[57] Aristophanes, for example, states that all that Zeus and fortune favour goes forward according to a plan.[58] In Aristophanes' *Peace,* Hermes announces that the character

Trygaeus has been sentenced to death for attempting to rescue Peace from the Heavens. Trygaeus counters this, however, with a declaration that Hermes normally selects victims by lot and that even Hermes cannot be sure that Trygaeus' number will come up.[59] When Hermes continues to announce 'you will die', Trygaeus enquires if Hermes knows the exact date when his death with occur.[60] This shows that the gods knew the time of a person's impending demise, even if the person themselves did not and thought that the whole process was somehow random. The unknowable nature of this divine plan is also outlined by Euripides at the end of his play *Medea*, when he has the chorus leader state how many things that mortals expect do not come to pass, but a god finds some way to accomplish the unexpected.[61] In the *Persae*, Aeschylus uses the concept of a divine plan to account for the Persian defeat at the Battle of Salamis in 480 BC when he has a Persian messenger declare:

> I hardly imagine you will consider we were inferior in that regard [i.e. numbers] in battle! It was some deity (*daimôn*) that destroyed our fleet like this, weighting the scales so that fortune did not fall out even: the gods have saved the city of the goddess Pallas [Athena].[62]

Aeschylus also states, using a prophecy as a literary trope, that the Persian army that had been left behind in Greece following the defeat at Salamis was destined to be destroyed at the Battle of Plataea the following year.[63] His references to both a divine plan and the use of scales by the gods to decide the outcome of events like the Battle of Salamis bear close similarity to Homer's account of Zeus using scales to decide the outcome of the fight between Hector and Achilles in the *Iliad* – it is only the scale of the confrontation which is different. This again shows a continuance from the Archaic Age to the Classical Period of the notion that death and destruction in battle was part of a divine plan, yet still somehow seemingly random to mortals.

Further evidence for a strong belief in the role of the Fates comes from the references to the cults of these divinities. Pausanias details the presence of at least seven different shrines or temples dedicated to the *Moirai* on mainland Greece – including at major cult centres like Delphi and Olympia, and in major military *poleis* such as Sparta, Thebes and Corinth.[64] Apollonius also relates the existence of a cult to the Fates on the island of Corcyra, which at one time possessed the second largest naval fleet in Greece.[65] The widespread nature of these religious sites honouring the Fates, and the references to them found in the literature of the Classical Age, demonstrates that the belief in the power of these deities was both Panhellenic and seen to have been an integral part of how events were seen to have played out – from the conduct of military campaigns by various city-states to the actions of individual warriors on the battlefield.

A strong belief in the workings of Fate, divine sanction of one's actions and/or divine protection would have had a powerful impact on the mindset of those on the ancient Greek battlefield. Religion, as a holistic concept, would have been a prime motivator not only for campaigns themselves, but for people to take part in them. As Holmes states: '[F]or centuries men have been spurred on into battle and consoled in defeat by religion.'[66] For the ancient Greeks, a belief that the divine was in favour of their venture, or was intending to grant them victory on the battlefield, would have been intensified by the receipt of oracles by the *polis* prior to the campaign, by means of divination such as the pre-battle sacrifice (*sphagia*), and by the witnessing of other heavenly portents before fighting actually began.

Belief in the workings of the Fates, in particular the idea that a warrior would only die when their allotted time had come, would have also removed much of the fear associated with operating in a frantic combat environment. While not detailed to a great extent in the ancient literature due to the focus of many of the works on recounting, or explaining, the great events of the time, the analysis of the impact of religion and fatalism in alleviating fear on the battlefield is found in many modern studies of the psychology of combat and has worked its way into how combat operations in the modern age are conducted and understood. Much of this literature suggests that those who view the chaotic nature of the battlefield with a sense of a divine plan are able to perform, at least for a limited time, more actively (and potentially more effectively). As Regan states: 'Fear … must be channelled so that its control becomes the first step in becoming an efficient soldier.'[67]

The nineteenth-century French military soldier-theorist Ardant du Picq outlined the origins of such action on the battlefield by commenting: 'Absolute bravery, which does not refuse battle even on unequal terms, trusting only to God or destiny, is not natural in man; it is the result of moral culture.'[68] For both the ancient Greek hoplite and the modern soldier, the greatest purveyor of this 'moral culture' would have been the religious principles of the individual and the state. For the ancient Greeks, this would have included a strong belief in the concept of Fate. In the Judeo-Christian tradition, the literature also outlines how the divine similarly knew when events involving mortals would come to pass.[69] Such sentiments bear many similarities to the workings of the divine in Greek mythology.

The US Army Field Manual on combat stress outlines how faith and/or a sense of fatalism can impact the mindset of a combatant:

> Many soldiers and civilians do find that danger, and especially the
> unpredictable danger of modern war, stimulates a new or stronger
> need for faith in God ... In some cultures and religions, acceptance of
> God's will, fatalism, faith in the afterlife, or the reward for dying in a
> holy cause may also contribute to exceptional bravery and disregard for
> death.[70]

Not only would a sense of fatalism remove much of the fear of death, but the
main advantage in such a system of belief is that it allows a soldier to find
relief, distractions and/or consolation in relation to the horrors of war which
may be unfolding around him.[71] In studies conducted by the US Army at the
end of the Second World War, when combat veterans were asked 'while you
were in combat, did you have the feeling that it was just a matter of time until
you would get hit?', more than 60 per cent answered in the affirmative.[72]
These responses demonstrate that many combat veterans believed that,
regardless of what they did, circumstances would eventually align in such
a way that they would be wounded or killed. While potentially without the
religious connotations, this finds close parallels to ancient Greek references
to the nature of combat where the decision about whether a soldier lived or
died was solely in the hands of an outside power.

Religious belief ('there are no atheists in foxholes'), superstition (carrying
a lucky charm like a rabbit's foot or other talisman) and/or a sense of
fatalism (the military maxim that 'somewhere out there is a bullet with
my name on it') played a strong part in helping US combat troops cope
with Second World War battlefields. When enlisted men were asked what
motivated them to continue to fight when the going got tough, prayer was
the largest response (70 per cent in the research conducted in the Pacific
theatre of operations and 83 per cent in the Mediterranean theatre) – well
above the idea of not wanting to let one's comrades down (61 per cent for the
Pacific and 56 per cent for the Mediterranean).[73] The extent to which prayer
was said to have helped, and in what form (for example, a plea for divine
protection or a fatalistic acknowledgement that what was to come was part of
a divine plan), was not examined. Such a high response rate amongst combat
troops, however, shows that the notion of divine support or intervention in
some guise helped make the experience of combat more bearable for many
soldiers, as these provided modes of adjustment to situations of high stress
and unpredictability.[74] Shalit states that faith or fatalism 'does not only
mean that we delegate responsibility to another agent; it also means that
we restructure our perception of the environment', and this, in turn, allows
things like the random and chaotic nature of war to, from the soldier's

perspective, somehow make sense.[75] This would be as true for the ancient Greek warrior as it would be for the modern soldier.

Of these modes of adjustment to a stressful environment such as combat, faith and superstition employ what are termed 'suprarational techniques' to create confidence in the believer and possibly alter the course of events (or at least a belief that the divine is changing events in one's favour).[76] Fatalism, conversely, accepts that what is to come has all been predetermined by a higher authority, in a course that cannot be altered and, consequently, worrying about potential outcomes like injury or death is pointless.[77] Thus any perceived threat from the unpredictable nature of the combat environment is removed as the outcome is seen as inevitable rather than mostly random.[78] The ancient Greek belief in the workings of the Fates would have had a similar result. If the Greek warrior believed that he would die only when the thread of his life reached its end, as determined by the gods, that this end was inescapable regardless of what he did, his belief would have alleviated much of the concern he may have had about what was going on around him on the battlefield as he would have seen no randomness in the chaos of war, but rather a fulfilment of a divine construction.

It was also found amongst US combat troops that those who relied on faith as a comfort on the battlefield were those who needed it the most. Amongst the respondents who stated that prayer helped them endure combat 'a lot', it was found that the vast majority of them were those who were less likely to become accustomed to the traumas of war, who demonstrated more of the physical symptoms of fear in combat, were more prone to fear, were less willing to engage in combat, were new to the battlefield or lacked confidence in themselves.[79] Belief in a higher power, and the intervention thereof in the events of one's life, thus went a long way to removing fear in what would otherwise be a traumatic and troubling environment. Again, this would have been similar, if not more entrenched, in the pious hoplites of ancient Greece.

For the polytheistic Greeks, the loss of divine favour by one god did not mean that all of the gods had abandoned them. On the contrary, different gods could be seen as fighting on both sides of a conflict (as occurs in the *Iliad*). In the more monotheistic modern world, on the other hand, belief in the sanction of one's actions by a higher power (especially one that is attributed to benevolence, love, peace, righteousness, forgiveness and salvation) can result in the feeling that this divine spirit had abandoned one's cause in the event of defeat.[80] Furthermore, in the monotheistic modern world, many soldiers have had trouble reconciling which side God was on as, in the case of American troops fighting the Germans in the Second World War, both sides held to Judeo-Christian values and both believed that God was on their side.[81] The Biblical book of Romans adds to this contention by stating, 'If God is for us, who can be against us?'[82] This then raises the question in the minds of many modern soldiers that, if both sides believe the same God is favouring them, and God cannot support both sides in a conflict, which side is God actually on? This can result, depending upon how the answer to this question is perceived, in a sense of divine abandonment for one's cause.[83] The ancient Greeks, however, would not have experienced such a sense of divine abandonment as there were always seen to be different gods favouring both sides of any encounter or action. Thus the very structure of the polytheistic ancient Greek religious system meant that the gods and Fate were ever-present on both sides of the battlefield – with the divine intervening to ensure compliance with predetermined destinies for all of the combatants involved. This sense of overall divine protection and interference would have gone a long way to alleviating much of the stress associated with worrying about death or injury in ancient Greek combat.

This is not to say that fear was removed totally from the battlefields of ancient Greece by a belief in the Fates. On the contrary, the literature from ancient Greece contains some of the first recorded references to the manifestation of psychological responses to heightened states of fear. The sophist Gorgias, for example, states that:

> Some who have seen terrible things have lost their presence of mind in the present time; as such, fear extinguishes and drives out understanding. And many fall into useless labours and terrible diseases and incurable insanities; thus sight engraves in the mind images of things seen. And the frightening ones, many of them, remain.[84]

Tritle sees this as an ancient reference to some of the symptoms of Post-Traumatic Stress Disorder (PTSD) and post-combative depression.[85] In a similar statement about how fear can reduce combat effectiveness, the Athenian commander Phormio is said to have remarked that 'fear drives out all memory of previous training, and without the will-power to resist, skill [in battle] is useless.'[86] Euripides' Heracles is also maddened following war in another possible ancient reference to PTSD – although the attribution of his madness to the actions of the gods also bears similarities to the actions of the gods affecting other 'unknown' aspects of conflict.[87]

The ancient literature of the Greeks also contains some of the first recorded references to physiological responses to fear in combat. Herodotus describes how Epizelus became suddenly blinded at the Battle of Marathon after seeing a large, well-armed opponent.[88] It has been suggested that this may be the first recorded case of 'shell shock'.[89] However, it is more probably the first reference to the acute narrowing of the vision known as 'hysterical blindness', where a person experiences such an extreme state of fear that the brain actually impedes their visual input.[90] In another reference to a physiological consequence of extreme fear, in his play *Peace*, Aristophanes twice refers to warriors defecating themselves on the battlefield.[91] This description is likely a reference to the common battlefield condition where the body's Sympathetic Nervous System takes over during a 'fight or flight' situation such as combat, usually resulting in a loss of bowel control.[92]

Such references to the psychological and physiological effects of fear on the ancient Greek battlefield demonstrate that a belief in the Fates and divine intervention was not absolute, or that some hoplites' beliefs were stronger or weaker than others, as they were still prone to fearing the environment in which they found themselves. However, the fact that ancient writers like Herodotus seem to place an emphasis on detailing accounts such as that of Epizelus suggests that similar extreme reactions to fear on the battlefield were somewhat rare in ancient Greece. It must also be considered that both fear and a belief in the concept of Fate are not mutually exclusive of each other. A warrior may accept the notion that they will die only when their allotted time is reached, but may still fear this eventuality and the process (i.e. combat) that may bring it about. It is thus little wonder that militaristic city-states like Sparta contained a cult centre to Fear (*Phobos*).[93] The presence of a cult of Fear in places like Sparta additionally shows that other means to alleviate stress and cope with the traumas of the battlefield were sought beyond just a blind belief in the Fates.[94] This also finds parallels in modern times. Combat soldiers have often employed their religious principles in conjunction with the use of talismans and a fatalistic approach to endure the environment of combat in the belief that no possibility of safeguarding oneself should be overlooked.[95]

Furthermore, in both ancient and modern times, if the belief was universally held that death on the battlefield only occurred at a time predetermined by a higher power, the question must be asked: what is the point of training? If the divine would only take a warrior when his appointed time had arrived, then that warrior should, by default, be able to perform well enough on the battlefield to survive without any training at all. The fact that the hoplites of ancient Greece underwent some level of training depending upon the principles of their city-state demonstrates how it was thought that human free agency could have some influence on the battlefield – although most likely over issues of victory and defeat rather than matters of life and death – and that experience still played a large part in the outcome of an engagement. Daddis outlines how realistic and rigorous training provides the soldier with advantages in dealing with real combat situations by allowing them to recognize how their bodies will react to such an environment and to develop a 'combative mindset that mitigates the psychological and physiological effects of fear'.[96] The training of hoplite forces in ancient Greece, especially for the militaristic Spartans, who began their harsh acclimatization to the turmoils of war at an early age, can be seen as yet another way that they employed means other than religious devotion to ensure combat effectiveness. The lack of a dogged belief in Fate alone by the Greek hoplite also explains why in many encounters the morale of one side failed, leading to a rout. Had Greek warriors simply accepted that their time would come only when the gods willed it, it is unlikely that their morale would have failed. Panic within an army, however, and defeat in battle was also seen, in many cases, to have been the result of divine intervention (see Chapter 7 'Epiphanies in Classical and Hellenistic Warfare' in this volume). This further demonstrates that belief in the concept of Fate was not absolute, that it was acknowledged that human free-agency within the construct of a divine plan could still result in a person's death or the defeat of a whole army, and that hoplites could still fear the combative environment regardless of their religious ideals.

For the ancient Greeks, a sense that one would only die at the time allotted by the gods would have not only removed much of the fear associated with the conditions of close-quarter combat, but would have also alleviated much of the sense of loss over fallen comrades. Homer describes how grief for a fallen comrade was short-lived because it was seen as part of the workings of Fate and/or a divine plan:

> A man may have lost one dearer even than this man [Patroclus] was – a brother, whom the same mother bore, or perhaps a son; yet surely when he has wept and lamented for him he is then done; for an enduring heart have the Fates given to men.[97]

In the ancient Greek world, the only people who regularly and openly displayed prolonged periods of grief over loss were women.[98] Greek vase paintings from as early as the Archaic Age regularly feature processions of women in mourning funerary scenes. In such scenes, the women are depicted with their hands raised (or grasping their hair) in an overt public display of grief. In comparison, men in similar scenes are depicted in a much less animated way – suggesting a less open display of grief – and in some scenes the men seem to be stoically waving farewell to, or saluting, the deceased (Figures 8.1–2).[99]

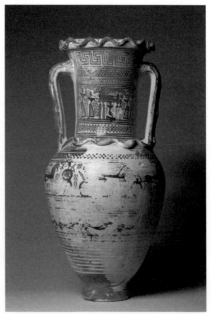

Figure 8.1 a–b: An early Attic amphora depicting animated women in a funerary procession on the neck. The *Dipylon Amphora*, dating to the eighth century BC, attributed to 'Workshop of Athens 894': height 60cm. The Cleveland Museum of Art, purchase from the J.H. Wade Fund 1927.6. (*Courtesy of The Cleveland Museum of Art*)

In the account of Pericles' famous funeral oration, Thucydides similarly states that the women witnessing the funerary procession were to make their public lamentations at the tomb of the fallen while the men, in contrast, were meant to find inspiration in the actions and sacrifices of those who had died.[100] Ancient Greek funerary monuments also reflect this ideal of commemorating war dead, rather than mourning them. Epitaphs ascribed to Anacreon, Simonides and others, for example, detail the valour and noble sacrifice of the deceased rather than lament their loss.[101] As Wolfe states, Greek epitaphs of the Classical Age were vivid in their comments, not morbid, and in Classical Athens, one's duty to the state often overshadowed any display of personal emotion.[102] This clearly accounts for the subdued nature of ancient, male, Greek funerary practices relating to war dead.

A concept of restrained grief amongst warriors in the ancient Greek world places the actions of one of the characters central to the concept of Fate into an interesting perspective – those of Homer's Achilles. In the *Iliad*, Achilles does experience a brief moment of extreme grief for the death of his friend Patroclus, a point in time where he wails uncontrollably, rubs dirt into his hair and his friends fear that he may kill himself (all womanly traits to the

 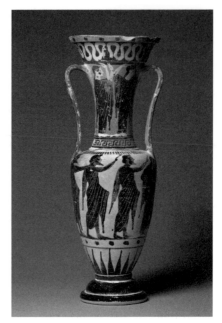

Figure 8.2 a–b: An Athenian black-figure funerary vase *(loutrophoros)* depicting stoic men and animated women in a funerary procession, dating to about 500 BC: height 43.5cm. The Cleveland Museum of Art, Charles W. Harkness Endowment Fund 1927.145. (*Courtesy of The Cleveland Museum of Art*)

Greeks). His grief, however, is soon eclipsed by a new emotional state and the focus of Homer's story: rage.[103] 'Rage' (*mênis* in Greek) is the very first word of Homer's *Iliad* and may have even been its original title. The opening lines also detail how everything that is to follow in the poem is the result of the will of Zeus. This clearly illustrates the underlying themes of the epic.

Achilles' anger manifests itself almost immediately following Patroclus' death and Achilles vows to slay Hector before his own death overtakes him.[104] When Patroclus' body was brought back to the Greek camp, Achilles led 'all of the Greeks' in mourning because a 'bitter fury' gripped him.[105] Achilles declares that he will cut the throats of twelve Trojan children over the grave of Patroclus because of 'my anger for your [plural] killing'.[106] The important part of this passage is that Achilles is declaring that he is extracting revenge for the death of his 'companions' and not just for the death of Patroclus. Thus Achilles' rage has almost immediately moved beyond that for loss of a single comrade, and Hector is killed on behalf of all of the Greeks who had previously fallen in battle.

At Patroclus' funeral, the Myrmidons are roused to tears by Thetis, and Achilles promises the body of Patroclus that he will drag Hector's body close to the pyre to let dogs eat it raw, and again to sacrifice twelve Trojan children 'in my *anger* for your killing'.[107] Achilles also declares that he will not wash until Patroclus is buried, 'since no second *pain* like this will come to touch my heart so long as I am in the land of the living'.[108] Following the funeral of Patroclus, when Achilles is given a new set of armour, '*the anger* reached deeper into his heart and his *eyes glared* out from his lids as if they were flames'.[109] Achilles is so enraged that he even challenges the god Apollo to try and stop him from killing Hector.[110] When they finally fight, Achilles declares to Hector, 'now you will make a lump payment for the pain of my companions' deaths – all those you killed when your spear was raging' (again, note the use of the plural 'companions').[111]

As Hector dies, Achilles says to him, 'Doubtless as you killed Patroclus you thought you would be safe, and you had no fear of me as I was far away. You fool! Behind him there was I, left to avenge him … now the dogs and birds will maul you hideously, while the Achaeans will give Patroclus full burial.'[112] Again, the themes of anger and revenge permeate the tale. This is no more clearly displayed than when the dying Hector asks Achilles to return his body to his father and Achilles responds, 'The fury in my heart would drive me to cut you to pieces and eat your flesh raw for all that you have done to me. So no man is going to keep the dogs away from your head … not even … if Priam offers to pay your own weight in gold.'[113] These passages highlight that it is anger, not grief, that is the driving force behind Achilles' actions.[114]

The concept of Fate then paints the anger that drives Achilles in an interesting light. Achilles is not just angry at Hector for killing Patroclus, he is also angry at himself for not being able to save his companion. Achilles feels guilty over the loss of Patroclus for several reasons. Firstly, Achilles had actually asked the gods to let the Trojans push the Greeks back to their ships in the hope that this would show to Agamemnon, with whom Achilles was in disagreement over a matter of pride and honour, that he was indispensible to the Greek army.[115] However, unknowingly, it is this Trojan attack that leads to the death of Patroclus, and so Achilles feels directly responsible. Additionally, Achilles' plan does not work. He does not immediately become reconciled with Agamemnon, and so lends his armour to Patroclus and tells him to go out and save the Greeks if he wants to – an act which directly leads to his death.[116] This merely compounds the guilt that Achilles feels and the anger that he has with both himself and Hector.

Thus in the *Iliad*, Achilles is suffering from the first recorded example of what modern military psychiatrists call 'survivor guilt'.[117] Yet is such guilt, and its subsequent anger, in Achilles warranted? Even the shade of

Patroclus itself informed Achilles that 'hateful Death' had grasped him from the moment of his birth – in reference to Patroclus' fate having been decided long before the actual time of his demise.[118] If the time of the death for all Greek warriors was part of the machinations of Fate and the gods, can Achilles really become that upset about the loss of Patroclus? Why does the loss of Patroclus become such a burden on Achilles' psyche and what is Achilles trying to 'say' through his anger? Is Achilles suggesting that he is not beholden to the gods and that he thinks he somehow has either the right or the ability to go against them (he is part divine himself after all)? His challenge to Apollo to try and prevent him from killing Hector would certainly suggest so. Thus the negative consequences of hubris can potentially be added to the list of morals and ideals that the *Iliad* is commenting on.

Grief, as a feminine characteristic, and Fate place certain elements of the character of Achilles in the *Iliad* into context. The brief episodes of grief experienced by Achilles portray him, at least for these short moments in time, as acting in a decidedly un-Greek manner (at least from a masculine perspective). This explains why grief is so quickly replaced by anger, rage and/or a desire for revenge (all masculine characteristics) each time Achilles is momentarily overcome. Yet Achilles' rage is the product of his sense of guilt over his failure to save Patroclus in arrogant defiance of what the gods had predetermined his fate should be. As such, the *Iliad*, as well as being a morality tale about the negative consequences of pride, anger and revenge, and being a commentary on the Greek belief of pre-destination and Fate, also has a deeper, underlying message about the futility of trying to act contrary to divine will.

The belief that the time of a warrior's demise was solely in the hands of the Fates and the gods would have affected almost every facet of ancient Greek warfare. Soldiers would have found comfort in the idea that they would only die on the battlefield as part of a larger divine plan that had mapped out the course of their life from the moment of their birth. This would, in many cases, have removed much of the fear and stress of combat. The acceptance that a comrade had only been killed as part of this same predestined course would have also alleviated much of the grief and guilt that survivors of conflict felt in relation to their lost brothers in arms. The idea that an outside power determines the course of events is known as extrinsic religiousness.[119] It is only when someone questions or loses faith in the concept of Fate that many of the physiological and psychological side-effects of combat, such as guilt and fear, manifest themselves in the combatant. The strong belief in the Fates across the panhellenic world, combined with other religious principles of the individual and the state, partially explains why the warriors of ancient Greece were both physically and mentally capable of standing their ground and engaging in some of the fiercest forms of close combat known to any age.

Notes

1. Clausewitz (*On War*, 1.3) describes war as being, 'the province of Chance. In no sphere of human activity is such a margin to be left for this intruder, because none is so much in constant contact with him on all sides. He increases the uncertainty of every circumstance, and deranges the course of events.' For a list of many of the major variables in modern warfare – including such things as terrain, climate, weather, supply, replacements, leadership, training, level of opposition, level of support, communication, objectives, chance of success, duration of fighting and number of casualties – see Stouffer *et al.* 1949, 66.
2. For the different intervals of the phalanx, see: Asclep. *Strat.* 4.1; Ael. *Tact.* 11, 14; Arr. *Tact.* 11, 12; for a discussion of the different formations of the phalanx, see Matthew, 2012, 168–204.
3. For the methods of Athenian recruitment and mobilization, see: [Arist.] *Ath. Pol.* 21.1–22.2, 61.1–3; Ar. *Peace* 1181–84; Diod. 11.81.4, 11.84.4–5, 18.10.2.
4. For the Spartan *agogē*, mess and military systems, see: Xen. *Lac. Pol.* 2.1–5.4, 9.1– 12.7; Plut. *Lyc.* 10–12, 16–19, 24; Hdt. 1.65.
5. When Athens began issuing arms and armour to its citizens at state expense following their defeat at Chaeronea in 338 BC, only a shield and spear were provided ([Arist.] *Ath. Pol.* 42.4; Lycurg. *Leocr.* 76–78, 80–82; Isoc. 8.82; Aeschin. 3.154). This suggests that these two items were considered the minimum requirements for fighting in the Athenian phalanx. Conversely, Bertosa (2003, 361–79) suggests that the spear and shield may have been the minimum requirements for garrison duties but the remainder of the panoply would have been required for battle.
6. For the available range of vision, hearing and ventilation of Greek helmets, see Matthew, 2012, 96–101, 109.
7. For the distance of engagement in hoplite battles, see Matthew, 2012, 71–92, 205– 37.
8. Aristophanes *Peace* 237 refers to War as 'the emptier of bowels', while at line 1173 Aristophanes describes how a soldier in combat could 'dye' his cloak with excrement due to his fear. Stouffer *et al.*, 1949, 201–02, state that during the Second World War, approximately 18 per cent of the troops interviewed from four combat divisions in the Pacific vomited as a result of fear-induced stress. There are no references to similar reactions found in the extant ancient Greek literature, and Crowley, 2012, 92, suggests that this was the case because the Greeks did not have a revulsion to killing – a cause which may contribute to levels of stress in modern combatants. However, even if the Greeks did have less of a reluctance to kill, vomiting, as a physiological response to fear, cannot be discounted on the ancient battlefield – unless it is assumed that fear, in general, was not common on the ancient battlefield.
9. For the different ways in which a hoplite battle could be fought, see Matthew, 2012, 205–37.

10. For examples of the carnage on the hoplite battlefield, including broken and discarded weapons and piles of dead and dying, see Xen. *Ages.* 2.14; Diod. 15.55.5; Plut. *Pel.* 4, 32; for a Homeric example of similar carnage, see Hom. *Il.* 16.661.

11. For the use of music, see: Thuc. 5.70, also Plut. *Mor.* 210f; Athen. *Deip.* 14.627d; Polyaen. *Strat.* 1.10.1; Paus. 3.17.5.

12. In some encounters, hoplites maintained or reformed their positions, rather than attempting to pursue routed enemies, in order to preserve unit cohesion in the face of new threats or to comply with other battlefield strategies – for example, see Hdt. 6.113; Thuc. 6.70; Xen. *Hell.* 7.4.30; Xen. *Anab.* 1.8.19; Paus. 4.8.11; for a discussion of the casualty rates in victorious and vanquished hoplite armies, see Krentz, 1985, 13–20.

13. Gabriel, 2013, 33, outlines how in Homer's *Iliad*, 93 per cent of all injuries delivered at close range resulted in a fatality. This is contrasted to modern engagements, such as the Normandy landings in 1944, where, despite the more mechanized and distant nature of the fighting, allied forces suffered an average of 39 per cent casualties, or the war in Korea, where US troops suffered 22 per cent casualties. In comparison, Krentz, 1985, 13–20, calculated that the victorious side of a single hoplite vs hoplite engagement in the fifth century BC could expect to suffer 2–10 per cent casualties (average 5 per cent), while the vanquished side could lose 5–25 per cent (average 14 per cent) of their forces. See also Ray, 2009, 301–05.

14. Hdt. 7.104. Marshall, 2000, 78, states that an American soldier is 'what his home, his religion, his schooling and the moral code of his society have made him'. This would have also been true for the ancient Greeks.

15. *GHI* ii: no. 204; see also Plat. *Apol.* 28d; Soph. *Ant.* 670; Plut. *Alc.* 15; Lycurg. *Leocr.* 76–77; for modern discussion of the oath, see Rhodes and Osborne, 2003, 440–49; Siewert, 1977, 102–03.

16. For example, see the indices in: Hanson, 1989; Wees, 2004; Hanson, 2004; Wees, 2009; Crowley, 2012; Kagan and Viggiano, 2013.

17. For example, see: Graves, 1992, 4.a.1, 13.a.3, 17.h, 18.l, 35.e, 35.g, 36.c.3, 52.a.2, 60.2, 69.c, 73.9, 80.a, 81.l, 90.6, 101.k, 105.b, 115.f; Harris and Platzner, 2008, 63, 183, 186, 352, 650–51; Powell, 2010, 142–43, 303, 495, 499.

18. For a person's fate being 'spun' at their birth, see: Hom. *Il.* 20.127, 24.209, 24.525; Hom. *Od.* 7.193; Bacchyl. F24; Callimachus *Bath of Pallas* 103; Pin. *Olym.* 2.21, 2.35; Ibycus F282a; Aesch. *Eum.* 964–65, *Prom. Bound* 511; for the cutting of a person's 'thread' at the time of their death, see: Hom. *Od.* 2.100, 3.238, 24.29; Stat. *Theb.* 1.632; Plato *Rep.* 617c describes the roles of the Fates through a comparison to singing. Of their songs, he states that Klotho sung of the things that are (i.e. the arrival of a person at the moment of birth), Lakhesis sung of things that were (i.e. the events of a person's life up to the present) and Atropos sung of the things that were to be (i.e. the events of a person's life from the present until the time of their death).

19. Homer refers to the Fates many times in the *Iliad*. However, Homer only once refers to the Fates in the plural (*Il.* 24.29) and, as such, Homer's *Moira* (singular) can be seen as a collective reference to all three of the Fates, who are also treated as a synonym for Destiny (Aisa) (*Il.* 20.127, 24.209). Similarly, Pin. *Pyth.* 1.40 (see also Pin. *Nem.* 5.40) uses Klotho as a collective reference to all three Fates. See also, *Orphic Hymn to the Fates* 59.

20. For the inescapable nature of what had been determined, see Eur. *Alc.* 781–83, 1070; Aesch. *Prom.* 511, 515; for the gods being beholden to what had been determined,

see Hdt. 1.91; Aesch. *Prom.* 515; Paus. 5.15.5, 8.42.3; other deities had their divine roles dictated by the Fates: see Callimachus, *Hymn 3. To Artemis* 22; Aesch. *Eum.* 334; Clausewitz followed a similar concept when he wrote (*On War*, 2.5) that, 'no human eye can trace the thread of the necessary connexion of events'. It is interesting that Clausewitz uses the term thread – possibly an indirect reference to the spinning of the thread of a person's life at the time of their birth by the Fates in Greek myth. Du Picq (1921, 117) similarly said that on the modern battlefields of the industrial age, 'many more chances are left to fate'.

21. Hdt. 1.91.
22. Hes. *Theog.* 211.
23. Hes. *Theog.* 901.
24. Plat. *Rep.* 617c.
25. For example, see Hes. *Shield Her.* 258; Aesch. *Eum.* 961; for other associations of the Fates with the Underworld, see Hom. *Il.* 3.101, 5.83, 16.434, 16.853, 20.477, 21.101, 24.132; Ar. *Frogs* 453. For the Keres, see Matthew Dillon in this volume.
26. Hes. *Shield Her.* 248–57. For a similar literary correlation between the Fates and the Furies, see Aesch. *Eum.* 310–11.
27. For example, see Hom. *Il.* 3.101, 16.853, 24.477, 21.100, 24.132; Hom. *Od.* 3.238.
28. Hom. *Il.* 20.125–28; in the so-called *Prayer to the Fates*, Aisa is listed as one of the three Fates along with Klotho and Lakhesis – all of whom are regarded as daughters of Night. For a discussion of this fragmented text, see Bowra, 1958, 231–40; Hansen, 1990, 190–92.
29. Hom. *Il.* 16.698–708.
30. Hom. *Il.* 22.130.
31. Hom. *Il.* 19.86–89.
32. Stat. *Theb.* 3.67–68; Statius' poem comes from a much later time (the first century ad), but recounts the story of the Seven Against Thebes of Aeschylus' play from the fifth century BC. While containing many elements of the Roman period in its descriptions, the *Thebaid* also contains elements more relevant to the earlier Greeks, and ones that seem to have continued across the centuries.
33. Hom. *Il.* 3.355–68, 12.400–04, 15.458–73.
34. There are a number of instances in the *Iliad* of 'lucky escapes', where a weapon is aimed at one individual but somehow hits someone or something else (for example, see 4.592, 8.134, 8.344, 13.209, 13.466, 13.588, 14.519, 15.600, 16.593, 16.844, 17.339, 17.689). This seemingly random avoidance of death or injury is regularly attributed to the predetermined fate of both the slain and the survivor and/or the intervention of the gods.
35. Hom. *Il.* 24.208–10.
36. Hom. *Il.* 16.643–49.
37. Hom. *Il.* 22.166–85.
38. Hom. *Il.* 22.208–13.
39. Hom. *Il.* 9.408–14.
40. Hom. *Il.* 18.94–96.
41. Hom. *Il.* 19.410; in a later passage (*Il.* 23.80–81), the shade of Patroclus informs Achilles that it is his fate to die beneath the walls of Troy.
42. Lycoph. *Alex.* 584; see also Aesch. *Agam.* 126–28.
43. Stat. *Theb.* 1.632.
44. Xen. *Mem.* 1.1.1–20.
45. Hdt. 1.91.

46. For a discussion of how Herodotus may have woven many Homeric literary tropes into his narrative history of the Greco-Persian Wars, see Gainsford, 2013.
47. Hdt. 5.92d.
48. Hdt. 5.33.
49. For example, see Hdt. 2.133, 3.16.
50. For Herodotus' use of oracles as literary markers to signify importance, see Griffin, 2006, 51–52.
51. Thuc. 2.11, 4.40.
52. For example, see *Anab.* 3.1.22–23, where Xenophon states that the Greeks believed that victory in an impending battle against the Persians was certain as the Persians had broken oaths and offended the gods. Thus the Greeks would have felt that the divine were on their side. Later (*Anab.* 3.2.11), Xenophon specifically states that men fight bravely if they believe that the gods are favouring them.
53. Xen. *Anab.* 3.2.7.
54. Xen. *Hell.* 2.4.18.
55. Xen. *Hell.* 2.4.19.
56. Xen. *Hell.* 6.4.3.
57. Storey and Allan, in their examination of Greek drama (2005, 108) state that, 'the modern reader or spectator often finds curses a convenient way to explain what happens to characters in Greek drama, especially those who see the pre-destined workings of gods or 'Fate' ('Fate' is a word best avoided in the study of Greek tragedy. The Greek *moira* means really one's lot or portion in life, while Fate has strong overtones of the gods as puppeteers controlling every aspect of one's life and destroying any form of free will).' Such claims seem incorrect when passages such as Homer's description of Apollo turning Patroclus back from the walls of Troy because it is not his fate are considered. In such passages, the gods are clearly acting as puppeteers (as Storey and Allan call them) to ensure that one's lot or portion in life comes to pass in the correct manner. Thus, in such instances, the fate of a person and the intervention of the gods are one and the same – both working behind the scenes of a person's life to ensure that what has been predetermined occurs at the allotted time.
58. Ar. *Peace* 939–40.
59. Ar. *Peace* 365–68.
60. Ar. *Peace* 369–70; Hermes then informs Trygaeus that, due to the penalties implemented by Zeus, his death will occur immediately.
61. Eur. *Med.* 1416–19.
62. Aesch. *Pers.* 343–47.
63. Aesch. *Pers.* 803–08.
64. Corinth: Paus. 2.4.7; Sicyon: Paus. 2.11.3–4; Sparta: Paus. 3.11.8–10; Olympia: Paus. 5.15.4–5; Thebes: Paus. 9.2.4–5; Akakesion: Paus. 8.37.1; Delphi: Paus. 10.24.4.
65. Ap. Rhod. *Argon.* 4.1216; for the size of Corcyra's fleet during the Peloponnesian War, see Thuc. 1.33.
66. Holmes, 1989, 287.
67. Regan, 1996, 3; similarly, du Picq (1921, 18) states that courage is the domination of will over the instinct for self-preservation and that this can then lead to either victory or defeat. In their examination of combat veterans, Stouffer *et al.* (1949, 201–02) found that, out of a test sample of 277 soldiers, 65 per cent of them admitted to having at least one instance in combat where they were unable to perform due to intense fear.

68. du Picq, 1921, 94.

69. The Gospel of Matthew (24:42–44), for example, decrees that mortals should be alert, 'for you do not know what hour your Lord is coming', and further outlines how, if people were aware of what was to come, they would more adequately prepare for it. There are numerous other biblical passages (both Old and New Testament) which outline how God is responsible for everything that happens and/or refer to a divine plan – especially in relation to conflict. For example, see: Isaiah 45:7–12 – 'I form the light and create darkness, I bring prosperity and create disaster'; 2 Kings 19:25 – 'Long ago I ordained it. In days of old I planned it; now I have brought it to pass, that you have turned fortified cities into piles of stone'; Lamentations 3:38 – 'Is it not from the mouth of the Most High that both calamities and good things come?'; Amos 3:6 – 'When a trumpet sounds in a city, do not the people tremble? When disaster comes to a city, has not the LORD caused it?'; Psalm 144 – 'Blessed be the Lord my Rock, who trains my hands for war, and my fingers for battle.' The Book of Job also tells the tale of human despair and suffering as part of an unknown divine plan. Following such sentiments, in the fifth century AD, Augustine of Hippo wrote (*City of God* 5.22–23) how he believed that the duration and outcome of a conflict was determined by God and that faith in Christianity could bring about a speedy victory against pagan enemies – potentially victories where none of the Christian faithful suffer any wounds or fatalities.

70. US Army, 1994, 3.6 – Increased Religious Faith.

71. Stouffer *et al.*, 1949, 185.

72. Stouffer *et al.*, 1949, 88; in a similar study, Wansink and Wansink (2013, 768–79) determined that as combat became more frightening for the individual, the number of US soldiers in the Second World War who resorted to prayer as a coping mechanism rose from 42 per cent to 72 per cent. Based upon such figures, it seems that there are at least some atheists in foxholes – although, as combat intensity increases, they seem to be a distinct minority.

73. Stouffer *et al.*, 1949, 136, 173–89; for officers the responses were reversed – with not wanting to let their men down scoring higher (85 per cent for the Pacific theatre and 81 per cent for the Mediterranean) compared to prayer (62 per cent for the Pacific and 57 per cent for the Mediterranean) – possibly due to the responsibilities inherent in being an officer. Similarly, soldiers employed in non-combat roles also ranked not wanting to let comrades down higher than prayer (Stouffer *et al.*, 1949, 173–75, 177–86).

74. Stouffer *et al.*, 1949, 188; see also: Shalit, 1988, 5; soldiers in the German Wehrmacht in the Second World War wore belts with the phrase '*Gott Mit Uns*' ('God is with Us') inscribed on the buckle. However, belief in the workings of Fate and the divine was not limited to combat troops and just rank and file soldiers. For example, General Meindl, commander of the II German paratroop corps in Normandy in 1944, stated that 'he belonged to the set of toy soldiers into whose hands Fate had placed our [i.e. Germany's] fortune' (see Beevor, 2012, 399).

75. Shalit 1988: 93–94.

76. Stouffer *et al.*, 1949, 188; see also Holmes, 1989, 240–42.

77. Stouffer *et al.*, 1949, 188; see also Holmes, 1989, 240–42.

78. The belief in Fate and/or religious principles seems to be very much dependent upon the individual in the modern, increasingly secular world. In his autobiographical account of the recent war in Iraq, Nathaniel Fick (2005, 265–66) states that, 'it is a simple fact of human nature that people will more willingly go into danger

when they have a say in the crafting of their fate.' Similarly, in Moore's *Will They Ever Trust Us Again? Letters from the War Zone* (2004, 23), an American soldier in Iraq states in a letter, 'My life is left to chance at this point. I just hope I come home alive.' Another soldier says in another letter (p.62), 'who knows if I will make it back at all to see my family!' It is uncertain whether these sentiments reflect a belief in the possible intervention of a higher power (i.e. Chance [rather than chance], and God being the 'who' in the second letter), or whether they are merely descriptions of the randomness of war. Regardless, while a faith in oneself may be more prevalent for some in the modern, more secular world, it seems likely that aspects of religion – such as a belief in the Fates and divine intervention – would have had a strong influence on more religiously minded warriors, either modern or ancient.

79. Stouffer *et al.*, 1949, 182–83.
80. Shay, 1994, 146–48.
81. Holmes, 1989, 288.
82. Rom. 8.31.
83. This concern is less of an issue when forces adhering to two different faiths are in conflict with each other.
84. Gorg. *Hel.* 17; similarly, Aristotle (*Prob.* 887a) states that 'when recollection occurs, the part of the body concerned is stimulated. In men … when they see something, stimulation and recollection occur simultaneously.'
85. Tritle, 2013, 281.
86. Thuc. 2.87; for a quote from an anonymous American combat veteran from the Second World War which states almost exactly the same thing, see Kennett, 1987, 168.
87. Eur. *Heracl.* 821–1162; see also Matsakis, 2007, 196–97, 215–18.
88. Hdt. 6.117.
89. Worcester, 1919, 230.
90. For fear-induced visual impairment, see: Grossman and Siddle, 1999; Gabriel, 1988, 69; Godnig, 2003, 95–97; similar to the account of Epizelus, an inscription from Epidaurus (*IG* iv² 1.122) tells of how a warrior by the name of Anticrates came to the temple of Asklepios to be healed. It is recorded that Anticrates had suffered a spear wound to the face and was blind as a result of it (it is also said that the tip of the spear was still lodged in his face!). After spending a night in the temple, he emerged the next day with his sight restored: *IG* iv² 1.122.63–68 (*iama* xxxii); see also Edelstein and Edelstein, 1945, 235 *iama* xxxii. Tritle (2013, 281) associates Anticrates' condition with hysterical blindness. However, it is uncertain whether treatment of the wound itself (possibly involving the removal of the embedded head) reduced facial swelling and restored Anticrates' sight, or whether the comfort he received in the temple alleviated any psychological condition which may have caused hysterical blindness (or possibly a combination of both). For war-wounds and Asklepios, see also Matthew Gonzales in this volume.
91. Ar. *Peace* 237, 1173.
92. Grossman and Siddle, 1999, 142; Grossman, 1994, 70–71.
93. Plut. *Cleom.* 8–9. As Marshall, 2000, 65, states: 'simply to release [a] man from the fear of death does not ensure that he will act as if he were immortal.'
94. Phobos was the son of Ares, the god of war (Hom. *Il.* 13.299; Hes. *Theog.* 934). Pritchett (1979, 162–63) details how the cult of Phobos was exclusively military in nature. For example, according to Plutarch *Cleom.* 9, in Sparta the doors to the

temple of Phobos were closed only in times of peace. In Aeschylus' *Seven Against Thebes* (line 42), the Seven swear an oath to Ares, Enyo (Ares' lover and a goddess of war and destruction) and Phobos. For discussions on the nature of Fear in Spartan culture, see Wide, 1893, 275–76; Epps, 1933, 12–29.

95. Stouffer *et al.*, 1949, 190. Marshall (2000, 116) states that 'there is no system of safeguards known to man which can fully eliminate the consequences of accident and mischance in battle.' Such a sentiment would then account for the use of multiple means of attempting to protect oneself on both ancient and modern battlefields.

96. Daddis, 2004, 24–26; see also Holmes, 1989, 42; Shalit, 1988, 117.

97. Hom. *Il.* 24.45–49.

98. Spartan women of the Classical period were the exception to this rule, as they actually celebrated if their sons were killed in battle because the greatest honour in Spartan society was to give one's life in the service of the state. Others killed or admonished sons and husbands who returned from battle and were seen as cowards (Plut. *Mor.* 240c–241c, 242a–b). These principles are no more clearly illustrated than in the advice (Plut. *Mor.* 241f) that a Spartan mother gave to her son as she handed his shield to him as he was departing for war to either come back with his shield (i.e. carrying it in victory) or on it (often interpreted as meaning being carried back upon it dead) – although, somewhat interestingly, most Spartan dead were buried where they fell and were not carried back to Sparta. This may offer an alternative reading of the passage as meaning either carrying it home in victory, being carried back upon it wounded (suggesting that you have done your best only to survive the encounter regardless of victory or defeat) or do not come home at all in the event of defeat and be buried where you fell.

99. For example, see Iakovidis, 1966, 43–50; Finkenstaedt, 1973, 39–43; Hoffman, 2002, 525–50; Stears, 2008, 139–55.

100. Thuc. 2.34–35, 2.41–45; in another funerary speech for war dead recounted by Plato (*Menex.* 248a–c), the families of the fallen, whose fate is seen as having been predestined (*Menex.* 236d), are encouraged neither to rejoice nor grieve excessively, as this will upset the dead, but rather to bear the loss lightly and with temperance. Restrictions on funerary practices, especially those of women, are reported to have been initiated in Athens by Solon in the sixth century BC (Plut. *Sol.* 21), in which it became unlawful to speak ill of the dead at the funeral, and women were prohibited from lacerating themselves or reciting set dirges as part of their display of grief as this was seen as 'weak and unmanly behaviour, and ... carrying their mourning to extravagant lengths'. For other ancient Greek funerary laws, see: Cic. *Leg.* 2.25.62–64, 2.26.64–66, 2.27.67–68; Plat. *Laws* 12.958d–e. See Garland, 1989; Alexiou, 2002, 14–23. Some cultures, even into modern times, have similar practices where warriors quietly or contemplatively mourn lost comrades rather than through overt displays of grief. For the account of a Native American combat veteran, the sole survivor of his platoon in Vietnam, and how he dealt with the loss of his comrades, see Matsakis, 2007, 214.

101. Anacreon: *Pal. Anth.* 7.160, 7.226; Simonides: *Pal. Anth.* 7.248, 7.249, 7.677; anonymous epitaphs: *Pal. Anth.* 7.346; the anonymous epitaph to Tettichos (Friedlander, 1948, n.135) describes the deceased as 'a man of valour cut down in action, robbed of youth on the battlefield', and goes on to advise the reader to mourn him for only a moment and then go off and do something just. The epitaph for the famous playwright Aeschylus (Page, 1981, 131) interestingly makes

no mention of Aeschylus' ability or success as a writer of plays, but instead only comments on his martial prowess at the Battle of Marathon.

102. Wolfe, 2013, 4, 49. Conversely, overt displays of grief could also influence popular politics. For example, according to Diodorus 13.101.6–7, following the naval Battle of Arginusae in 406 BC, mourning relatives of the deceased were instrumental in securing a conviction against the Athenian admirals who, it was claimed, negligently failed to rescue those whose ships had been wrecked; see also Xen. *Hell.* 1.7.8.

103. For the grief of Achilles, see Hom. *Il.* 18.22–38; Achilles is also overcome with grief during a period of communal lamentation for Patroclus and at his funeral. However, at all times, his anger and fury quickly return; see Hom. *Il.* 19.1–11, 24.1–18, 24.120–33.

104. Hom. *Il.* 18.77–93: this is only thirty-nine lines of the *Iliad* after Achilles' period of grief, so the transformation is very quick and the fury stays with him for most of the rest of the story.

105. Hom. *Il.* 18.322–23.

106. Hom. *Il.* 18.335–36, 23.22–23, 23.75–76.

107. Hom. *Il.* 23.17–21 (author's emphasis); it is interesting to note that it is the divine Thetis who actually causes the grief in the hearts of the Greeks. This was all part of the Greek belief that everything about their lives was controlled by the gods.

108. Hom. *Il.* 23.37–46 (author's emphasis); this passage is often translated as saying 'no second grief'. The Greek word used (ἄχος), however, means 'pain' or 'distress' rather than 'grief', and none of the Greek words for 'grief' (λύπη, ἄλγος or πένθος) are used. Thus the interpretation of Achilles' 'pain' is dependent upon the context of the passage within the wider narrative of the poem. Is it the 'pain' of 'grief'? Is it the 'pain' of 'guilt' and/or of Achilles' 'anger'? Based upon how the earlier passages of the *Iliad* read, these last two interpretations (either singularly or in combination) make more sense within the context of the poem.

109. Hom. *Il.* 19.16–17 (author's emphasis).

110. Hom. *Il.* 22.6–20.

111. Hom. *Il.* 22.271–73.

112. Hom. *Il.* 22.328–34.

113. Hom. *Il.* 22.346–51.

114. Anger is often seen as a part of grief – especially in the modern world. Yet for the Greeks there seems to be a great disparity between the feminine expression of grief through public and animated displays of anguish, and the masculine transformation of grief and/or guilt into violence, particularly on the battlefield. Like many cultures today which have different customs for the mourning of lost comrades, the use of violence as a means of dealing with loss may have been the Greek warrior's method for engaging with their emotions while preserving their manliness (*aretê*). Whether the ancient Greeks actually saw this battlefield anger as simply one manifestation of grief or not is unknown. However, the way in which the feminine and masculine methods for dealing with loss are so distinctly separated from each other in literature and art suggests that the Greeks saw them as separate characteristics.

115. Hom. *Il.* 18.78–135.

116. Hom. *Il.* 16.1–154.

117. Shay, 1994, 69–72; see also Minchin, 2006, 11–16.

118. Hom. *Il.* 23.79.

119. Wansink and Wansink, 2013, 769–70, suggest that extrinsic religiousness 'relates to practicing religion in order to form a relationship with God, accepting the limits of personal control' and that 'one reason why some soldiers might use either religious or non-religious coping strategies may relate to the extent they believed they were able to control the outcome of their combat experience'.

Bibliography

Alexiou, M., 2002, *The Ritual Lament in Greek Tradition*, Lanham.

Beevor, A., 2012, *D-Day: The Battle for Normandy*, London.

Bertosa, B., 2003, 'The Supply of Hoplite Equipment by the Athenian State Down to the Lamian War', *JMH* 67.2, 361–79.

Bowra, C.M., 1958, 'A Prayer to the Fates', *CQ* 8.3/4, 231–40.

Clausewitz, C. Von, 1968 (1832), *On War*, London.

Crowley, J., 2012, *The Psychology of the Athenian Hoplite*, Cambridge.

Daddis, G.A., 2004, 'Understanding Fear's Effect on Unit Effectiveness', *Military Review*, July–August 2004, 22–27.

Edelstein, E.J., and Edelstein, L., 1945, *Asclepius. A Collection and Interpretation of the Testimonies*, 2 vols, Baltimore.

Epps, P.H., 1933, 'Fear in Spartan Character', *CPh* 28.1, 12–29.

Fick, N., 2005, *One Bullet Away – The Making of a Marine Officer*, London.

Finkenstaedt, E., 1973, 'Mycenaean Mourning Customs in Greek Painting', *The Bulletin of the Cleveland Museum of Art* 60.2, 39–43.

Friedlander, P., 1948, *Epigrammata: Greek Inscriptions in Verse from the Beginnings to the Persian Wars*, Berkeley.

Gabriel, R., 1988, *The Painful Field: The Psychiatric Dimension of Modern War*, New York.

—— 2013, *Between Flesh and Steel – A History of Military Medicine from the Middle Ages to the War in Afghanistan*, Washington.

Gainsford, P., 2013, 'Herodotus' Homer: Troy, Thermopylae and the Dorians', in Matthew, C., and Trundle, M. (eds), 2013, *Beyond the Gates of Fire – New Perspectives on the Battle of Thermopylae*, Barnsley, 117–37.

Garland, R., 1989, 'The Well-Ordered Corpse: An Investigation into the Motives Behind Greek Funerary Legislation', *BICS* 36, 1–15.

Godnig, E.C., 2003, 'Tunnel Vision: Its Causes and Treatment Strategies', *Journal of Behavioral Optometry* 14.4, 95–99.

Graves, R., 1992, *The Greek Myths*, London.

Griffin, J., 2006, 'Herodotus and Tragedy', in Dewald, C., and Marincola, J. (eds), *The Cambridge Companion to Herodotus*, Cambridge, 46–59.

Grossman, D., 1994, *On Killing: The Psychological Cost of Learning to Kill in War and Society*, New York.

Grossman, D., and Siddle, B., 1999, 'Psychological Effects of Combat', in Kutz, L.R. (ed.), *Encyclopedia of Violence, Peace and Conflict*, Orlando, 139–49.

Hansen, O., 1990, 'The So-Called Prayer to the Fates and Timotheus' *Persae*', *RhM* 133.2, 190–92.

Hanson, V.D., 1989, *The Western Way of War*, Berkeley.

—— (ed.), 2004, *Hoplites: The Classical Greek Battle Experience*, London.

Harris, S.L., and Platzner, G., 2008, *Classical Mythology: Images and Insights*, New York.

Hoffman, G.L., 2002, 'Painted Ladies: Early Cycladic II Mourning Figures?', *AJA* 106.4, 525–50.

Holmes, R., 1989, *Acts of War: The Behaviour of Men in Battle*, New York.

Iakovidis, S.E., 1966, 'A Mycenaean Mourning Custom', *AJA* 70.1, 43–50.

Kagan, D., and Viggiano, G. (eds), 2013, *Men of Bronze: Hoplite Warfare in Ancient Greece*, Princeton.

Kennett, L., 1987, *GI: The American Soldier in World War II*, New York.

Krentz, P., 1985, 'Casualties in Hoplite Battles', *GRBS* 26, 13–20.

Marshall, S.L.A., 2000, *Men Against Fire: The Problem of Battle Command*, Norman.

Matsakis, A., 2007, 'Three Faces of Post Traumatic Stress: Ares, Hercules and Hephaestus', in Cosmopoulos, M.B. (ed.), *Experiencing War: Trauma and Society in Ancient Greece and Today*, Chicago, 195–224.

Matthew, C., 2012, *A Storm of Spears: Understanding the Greek Hoplite at War*, Barnsley.

Minchin, E., 2006, 'Can One Ever Forget? Homer on the Persistence of Painful Memories', *Scholia* 15, 2–16.

Moore, M., 2004, *Will They Ever Trust Us Again? Letters from the War Zone*, New York.

Page, D.L., 1981, *Further Greek Epigrams*, Cambridge.

Picq, A. Du, 1921, *Battle Studies: Ancient and Modern Battle*, trans. Greely, J.N., and Cotton, R.C., New York.

Powell, B.B., 2010, *Classical Myth*, New York.

Pritchett, W.K., 1979, *The Greek State at War. Part III: Religion*, Berkeley.

Ray, F.E., 2009, *Land Battles in 5th Century B.C. Greece*, Jefferson.

Regan, G., 1996, *Fight or Flight*, New York.

Rhodes, P.J., and Osborne, R., 2003, *Greek Historical Inscriptions 404–432 BC*, Oxford.

Shalit, B., 1988, *The Psychology of Conflict and Combat*, New York.

Shay, J., 1994, *Achilles in Vietnam: Combat Trauma and the Undoing of Character*, New York.

Siewert, P., 1977, 'The Ephebic Oath in Fifth-Century Athens', *JHS* 97, 102–11.

Stears, E., 2008, 'Death Becomes Her: Gender and Athenian Death Ritual', in Suter, A. (ed.), *Lament: Studies in the Ancient Mediterranean and Beyond*, Oxford, 139–55.

Storey, I.C., and Allan, A., 2005, *A Guide to Greek Drama*, Oxford.

Stouffer, S.A., Lumsdaine, A.A., Lumsdaine, M.A., Williams, R.M., Brewster Smith, M., Janis, I.L., Star, S.A., and Cottrell, L.S., 1949, *The American Soldier: Combat and its Aftermath*, vol. ii, Princeton.

Tritle, L.A., 2013, 'Men at War', in Campbell, B., and Tritle, L.A. (eds), *The Oxford Handbook of Warfare in the Classical World*, Oxford, 279–93.

U.S. Army, 1994, *FM22-51 Leader's Manual for Combat Stress Control*, Washington.

Wansink, B., and Wansink, C.S., 2013, 'Are There Atheists in Foxholes? Combat Intensity and Religious Behavior', *Journal of Religion and Health* 55, 768–79.

Wees, H. van, 2004, *Greek Warfare – Myths and Realities*, London.

—— (ed.), 2009, *War and Violence in Ancient Greece*, Swansea.

Wide, S., 1893, *Lakonische Kulte*, Leipzig.

Wolfe, M., 2013, *Cut These Words into My Stone – Ancient Greek Epitaphs*, Baltimore.

Worcester, D.A., 1919, 'Shell-Shock in the Battle of Marathon', *Science* 58.1288, 230.

Chapter 9

Thanking the Gods and Declaring Victory: Trophies and Dedications in Classical Greek Warfare

Michael Schmitz

Victory trophies and monuments served important profane and sacred purposes in Greek warfare, their most obvious purpose being to serve as a material claim to victory after the completion of a battle. The other equally important purpose was to thank the gods for their victory, as the Greeks believed they had to express their gratitude to the gods for their assistance in a physical, material way. That the gods were involved in all aspects of Greek life and took an active part in the endeavours of humans was a crucial tenet of Greek religious belief, and as war was considered one of the most important of mortal pursuits, the gods were therefore believed to participate actively in warfare and directly affect its outcomes.[1] Interactions with the gods were believed to function on a reciprocal basis, and as such, if a god or gods had granted their assistance to an army in battle, that god would naturally expect something in return: something material and substantial. In Homeric and Archaic warfare, the pre-eminent manner in which reciprocation was manifested was through the offering of a dedication (*anathema*, plural *anathemata*) at temples or sanctuaries. In the Classical period of Greek warfare, however, this changed, as is evidenced by the reduction in warfare-related dedications, and the move towards a preference for the erection of the *tropaion* (plural: *tropaia*)[2] or trophy.[3]

Trophies – *tropaia* – only emerged in the Classical period of Greek warfare, with no evidence for their erection before the Persian Wars (490 BC, 480–479 BC).[4] The use of the trophy as a thanks-offering to the gods was a continuation and evolution of the *anathema*, the dedication of battle spoils offered in Panhellenic sanctuaries by individuals in the Homeric and Archaic periods.[5] There were two distinct forms of *tropaia*: the perishable and hence temporary primary trophy,[6] which consisted of despoiled armour nailed (or otherwise mounted) to a tree stump or solid wooden stake in the case of a land battle, or often to the prow of a ship or a ship's ram in the case of a

Figure 9.1: Silver *tetradrachma* of Seleukos I Nikator, showing the goddess Nikê (Victory), crowning a *tropaion* of armour taken from the defeated enemy in an unknown battle, dating to about 305–295 BC, minted at Susa and weighing 17 grams with a diameter of 26mm. (*Private collection. Courtesy CNG*)

naval battle;[7] and the secondary permanent trophy, which was rarely used until late in the fifth century and into the fourth century. Secondary trophies differed from their primary counterparts in that they were manufactured from either stone or bronze and were intended to be permanent, thereby providing a lasting commemoration of the victory being celebrated.

An example of a primary, 'temporary' *tropaion* is shown on an extremely fine silver *tetradrachma* of Seleukos I Nikator (who reigned from 312–281 BC), struck about 305–295 BC, showing on its obverse a helmeted head, with the ear and horn of a bull, and wearing a panther skin: presumably Seleukos himself, or perhaps Alexander the Great, whom he served under. On the reverse, the Greek legend gives his name: King Seleukos (Figure 9.1). A béwinged Nikê, goddess of Victory, stands to the left of a *tropaion* and is putting the finishing touches to it, crowning it with the wreath of victory. The *tropaion* has been erected on a tree stump, on which a few leaves are shown on its right. Seleukos attributes the victory to the goddess, and the coin commemorates the divine assistance granted to him in some unknown battle, and hence thanks the goddess and the gods generally for this. Moreover, the circulation of this coin amongst his subjects conveyed the message that the gods were on his side in his military undertakings, and publicized his gratitude for the divine assistance given to him.

Dedications: Despoilment as a Materialization of Victory

From the earliest recorded periods of Greek history, dedications to thank the gods were one of the main ways that the Greeks sought the favour of the divine.[8] Dedications were physical objects deposited in a sacred place to thank a god for some perceived favour, reflecting the contractual nature of Greek offerings in general. There was an expectation that a portion of any wealth would be dedicated to a god,[9] and Demosthenes' fourth-century BC oration against Timocrates even indicates that there were Athenian laws formalizing this expectation:

> Neither can he deny that the men for whose protection he has invented his law are thieves and temple-robbers; for they have robbed the temples of the ten per cent due to Athena and of the two per cent due to the other gods; they keep the money in their own pockets instead of making restitution, and they have stolen the public share, which belonged to you.[10]

Dedications differed from vows in that dedications were thanks for an act the god or gods had already performed, unlike vows, which were generally conditional, making an offering or promising to do so to a god in order to enlist their assistance to achieve a desirable outcome in some future event or undertaking.[11] Such dedications were offered to the gods for a wide variety of reasons, including successful childbirth,[12] as relating to prosperity in a trade,[13] an athletic victory[14] and victory in war.[15] Objects to be dedicated generally fell into one of two categories, the first being a literal portion of the spoils or wealth such as the 120 shields captured from the Spartans in the Battle of Sphakteria dedicated in the Stoa Poikile ('Painted Stoa') in 425 BC, one of which still survives, bearing the inscription: 'The Athenians (captured this shield) from the Spartans at Pylos (and dedicated this)'; in this case, all the shields from the 120 captured Spartan officers were dedicated.[16] Another example comes from just the year before, when 300 panoplies of enemy armour were dedicated by Demosthenes after the defeat of the Ambraciots at Olpae in 426 BC.[17] Similarly, Alexander the Great dedicated 300 panoplies to Athena at Athens for his defeat of the Persians at Granicus in 334 BC.[18] Capturing an enemy soldier's shield was the ultimate expression of his defeat; its display by the enemy was a public commemoration of that defeat. In the case of naval warfare, the bronze ram of a defeated enemy ship could be dedicated, such as a bronze ship ram from an Athenian trireme which was dedicated by the Megarians after defeating the Athenians at Salamis,[19] or in fact an entire ship could be.[20]

Alternatively, an object paid for by the sale of the spoils or wealth could be dedicated, such as the statues that stood in front of the tripod at Delphi which were paid for by the spoils captured by the Phocians after their defeat of the Thessalians,[21] or the 10-cubit high bronze figure of Zeus at Olympia paid for from the spoils of the Battle of Plataea.[22] Dedications could and often did bear an inscription that would identify the giver, although this was not a requirement, but the individuals and cities responsible for the dedication were generally keen to have their names recorded on the object to ensure their connection to the dedication was clear.[23] Therefore, inscribed dedications served the dual purposes of acting as an expression of piety thanking a god for a favour (and making a public statement of that fact), and at the same time presenting the giver with an opportunity to promote themselves and their deeds. Being a physical object, the dedication had a lifespan longer than the act for which the dedication was being offered, thereby benefitting the giver, who could commemorate the act, as well as reminding the intended divine recipient that appropriate thanks had been made.

Very common in this genre of material dedications were helmets, of which hundreds were dedicated at Olympia in the Archaic Age, but for some reason, not in the Classical. In this sense, they were very much like the shield dedications of the Classical period. Well-known examples of inscribed dedications include that of the Athenian Miltiades himself, general in charge at Marathon in 490 BC. A Corinthian helmet excavated at Olympia is inscribed: 'Miltiades dedicated (this helmet) to Zeus', thus dedicating to this god his helmet as a public commemoration in Zeus' sanctuary of his thanks to this god in repelling the Persians.[24] Athens itself as a polity would, a few decades later, commemorate and thank the gods at Marathon with the erection of a marble *tropaion* there (see below).

Similarly, Hieron, as tyrant of Syracuse, dedicated at least three captured Etruscan helmets to Zeus at Olympia after his victorious naval battle against the Etruscans at Cumae in 474 BC, and there could have been many more apart from these three which have been discovered to date. These three helmets are all inscribed, and are dedicated to Zeus, from 'Hieron … and the Syracusans'; both Hieron (as general and ruler) and the polity of the Syracusans as a community render their gratitude to Zeus, and do so at his main sanctuary.[25] One of these, found in the Alpheios River at Olympia in 1959, has a particularly fine inscription (Figure 9.2).[26] Hieron in fact sent the usual tithe (*dekatē*), the booty of the victory, to Delphi and Olympia, but an inscription records that the boat carrying them was shipwrecked.[27]

Figure 9.2: One of the three bronze helmets, bearing an inscription, dedicated by Hieron to Zeus for defeating the Etruscans. The left cheek of the helmet reads: 'Hieron, the son of Deinomenos, and the Syracusans (dedicated this helmet) to Zeus, (captured) from the Etruscans at Kyme.' (*Olympia Museum. Courtesy of Alamy*)

Soldiers prided themselves on the quality of their armour, and the Greeks went to war wearing the most costly armour that they could afford,[28] and as such the spoiled armour of the fallen became an important representation of victory and often formed the core of a dedication after the successful conclusion of a battle. This eagerness and desire to seize the armour of the fallen during war is compared in the *Iliad* to the conflict between wild animals over food:

> Two lions have snatched a goat from snarling dogs
> And are carrying it off through thick underbrush,
> Holding it in their jaws high above the ground.[29]

This clearly illustrates the desire of combatants to carry away the richest spoils. Furthermore, on at least one occasion, combatants had to be warned to restrain themselves from immediately gathering the spoils from their fallen enemies for fear of damaging their chances of success in the battle:[30]

> Soldiers of Greece, no lagging behind
> To strip off armour from the enemy corpses
> To see who comes back to the ships with the most.
> Now we kill men! You will have plenty of time later
> To despoil the Trojan dead on the plain.[31]

Objects in the ancient world were believed to possess an almost talismanic power, and this belief applied to the arms and armour of the fallen.[32] Therefore, in warfare, dedicating a portion of the despoiled arms and armour of the defeated was a way in which the victor could thank the gods for his success at war whilst also demonstrating and commemorating their own victory over the fallen. Conflating despoilment and victory is an important topos in Homeric epic and occurs repeatedly in the battle scenes in the *Iliad*, with the following as an example of these:[33]

> When he returns from war, bearing bloody spoils,
> Having killed his man. And may his mother rejoice.[34]

In Homeric epic, the despoilment of armour was clearly a way of materializing victory.[35] Hector, when speaking to both the Trojans and the Greeks, describes how, if he were victorious, he would dedicate the captured armour of his foe in Apollo's temple as an *anathema*.[36] An Athenian black-figure amphora dating to about 520 BC illustrates the theme of despoilment;

Figure 9.3: Two warriors, the one on the right with a Boeotian style shield, fight over a fallen hoplite, contesting possession of the body and its armour. Two women watch: presumably they are divine figures, probably Eos and Thetis watching their sons Memnon and Achilles respectively fight over the body of the Greek warrior Antilochos. Athenian black-figure amphora, Painter of Munich 1410, dating to about 520 BC. Munich Antikensammlungen 1410 (J328). (*Courtesy of Alamy*)

two warriors fight over a body: if the winner is the enemy of the fallen, he will strip off his armour (Figure 9.3).[37]

Tradition would have it that the gods receive a tithe after the victorious conclusion to a battle.[38] Some ancient sources suggest that 10 per cent of the spoils received or captured by a hero would normally be dedicated to thank the gods for a favourable outcome to the battle.[39] Archaeological evidence indicates that throughout the Archaic period, dedications would occur at Panhellenic sanctuaries and local temples. At least 350 helmets, 280 shields, 225 greaves and thirty-three cuirasses dating to the Archaic period have been found in excavations at the sanctuary at Olympia, illustrating the deposition of despoiled military equipment. Interestingly, the practice seemed to have ceased in the Hellenistic period.[40]

Victors could also sell the despoiled arms and armour and use a share of the monies raised to have a suitable dedication manufactured to offer to the gods:

> As for Xenophon, he caused a votive offering to be made out of Apollo's share of his portion and dedicated it in the treasury of the Athenians at Delphi.[41]

These manufactured dedications often retained the form of traditional dedications such as shields or armour, but were generally smaller and made of precious metals. There is some suggestion that temples could become overcrowded with spoils, and this could have been one way of reducing this issue.[42]

Dedication of the spoils was about more than just honouring or thanking the gods for their assistance; it also served as a permanent commemoration of the human achievement, such as military victory.[43] In Homeric battle, with its emphasis on individual heroes, the despoilment of the fallen enemy specifically signified the victory of one hero over another. Homer presents the act of despoiling the armour of the fallen dead as an expectation and an individual warrior's duty in battle, and this was intricately linked with the requirement or duty to return the corpses of the fallen after despoilment.[44] Hector's challenge to the Greeks in Book 7 of the *Iliad* clearly illustrates this connection:

> I declare these terms, with Zeus as my witness:
> If your champion cuts me down with bronze,
> He can strip my armour and take it back to your ships.
> My body, though, he will return to my home
> To be burned in honour by Trojans and their wives.
> If I kill him, if Apollo gives me that glory,
> I will take his armour to holy Ilion
> And hang it in the temple of the Archer God.
> The corpse I will send back to your hollow ships
> So you long-haired Achaeans can give it burial.[45]

That is not to suggest that the allies of the fallen hero would allow the victor uninterrupted access to the corpse in order to despoil their armour. Numerous passages in the *Iliad* describe warriors interrupting the despoilment of their fallen comrades, suggesting the normality of the act and the dangers associated with it;[46] even the goddess Athena interrupts Ares in the act of despoilment in the *Iliad*:

> And Athena got in next to Diomedes,
> Who seemed to glow beside the eager goddess,
> And the solid-oak axle groaned under the load
> Of an awesome deity and a hero at his best.
> Pallas Athena handled the reins and whip
> And drove the horses directly at Ares,
> Who at that moment was stripping the armour
> From a warrior named Periphas, a huge man,
> Aetolia's finest and his father's glory.
> Ares was busy removing the dead man's armour
> And getting smeared with blood.[47]

Similarly, Glaukos convinces the Lycians, the Trojans, Polydamas, Agenor and Aeneas to fight for the body of Sarpedon before making a rousing speech to Hector:

> Sarpedon is down, our great warlord,
> Whose word in Lycia was Lycia's law,
> Killed by Patroclus under Ares' prodding.
> Show some pride and fight for his body,
> Or the Myrmidons will strip off the armour.[48]

Despoiling the fallen was critically important to the Homeric warrior, as without the dedication of armour, the duration of the act would also be the duration of the glory (*kleos*) associated with the act. In order to increase the duration of their *kleos*, Greek warriors would dedicate despoiled armour at a temple or Panhellenic sanctuary, thereby creating a durable physical commemoration of their victory; simultaneously, the dedication of the despoiled equipment acted as a gift of thanks to the gods for their assistance and support. Therefore, the ability to take armour from the dead provided a materialized representation of victory.

Introduction of Trophies

It has been argued that the first exemplar of a trophy can be found in the pages of the *Iliad*, which would illustrate a much earlier use of the *tropaion* than generally accepted.[49] Although the description presented by Homer closely resembles the physical appearance of trophies used in the Classical period, with despoiled armour mounted on a bush, it was clearly not intended as such. Instead, what appears in the *Iliad* is Odysseus temporarily mounting despoiled armour on a bush for safekeeping:

> They stripped the ferret-skin cap from his head
> And took the wolf's hide, the recurved bow,
> And the long spear. Odysseus held these up
> And prayed to Athena the Despoiler:
> 'Rejoice in these, Goddess, first of Olympians
> To receive our offerings. Guide us once more,
> Now to where the Thracians and their horses sleep.'
> With that, he hoisted the gear into a tamarisk
> And stashed it there, leaving as a marker
> A bundle of branches that they couldn't miss
> On their way back through the black rush of night.[50]

Odysseus' intention is to return to collect the spoils later: the intended outcome here was clearly not to create a true battlefield trophy the same as those evident in the Classical period. Rather, that he holds the spoils aloft and prays to Athena suggests he plans to use the armour as a victory *anathema* to Athena after the conclusion of a battle. Homer specifically mentions Odysseus carefully marking the location of the spoils, not wanting to miss the bush on the way back at night, suggesting that the hero's intent is to return later to claim the mounted spoils, presumably in order to dedicate them properly in a sanctuary or temple associated with Athena. This 'pre-dedication' (a dedication without a formal deposition in a suitable temple) is seen again in Book 10, where Odysseus finds a temporary home for the spoils of war until such time as they could be properly dedicated:

> And on the stern of his ship Odysseus placed
> The bloody spoils of Dolon, until such time
> As they could prepare a sacrifice for Athena.[51]

Substantive changes in the way the Greeks fought their wars provided the stimulus for and coincided with the introduction of trophies proper, suggesting a potential causal relationship between these changes and the adoption of trophies to replace dedications. A number of important changes in the conduct of war occurred at about the time that trophies started to be used as symbols of victory, and these changes contributed to the changing nature of declarations of victory. Some sources, written well after the fact, suggest that trophies had been erected and used to declare victory in the period before the Persian Wars, such as Plutarch ascribing the erection of a trophy to the Spartan Othryades after his defeat of the Argives in 550 BC;[52] Herodotus, however, being the earliest source for this particular conflict, at no time mentions the erection of a trophy, but does discuss the collection of arms and armour most likely to be distributed and dedicated.[53] Consequently, there is no evidence for the use of trophies prior to the end of the Persian Wars.[54]

The evolution and introduction of Classical hoplite warfare coincided with the introduction and use of trophies as thank-offerings to the gods and material symbols of victory, and was therefore a prerequisite to the introduction of trophies, as it is only through this evolution that the conditions necessary for the adoption of trophies came into being. In order to understand the introduction of trophies and its correlation to the changes in Greek warfare, the changing nature of Greek warfare will be discussed in relation to the introduction of trophies. This evolution saw the focus of battle shift from the individual, who had been the focal point of Homeric warfare, to the group, which formed the core of hoplite warfare. A prerequisite to trophy use, therefore, is the tight formation combat not seen on the battlefield until the Classical period. Hoplite warfare and the development of the *tropaion* were contemporaneous: the dedication of helmets at the Panhellenic sanctuary of Olympia by individual combatants in the Archaic period gave way to battlefield *tropaia* which symbolized the collective achievement of the hoplite phalanx of the citizen body on land, or at sea, of the battleship crews operating as a corporeal embodiment of the *polis*.

There are three important phases in the evolution of Greek warfare, two of which pre-date trophy use and are lacking in the prerequisites for trophy use when warriors would individually dedicate despoiled armour in Panhellenic sanctuaries. The first phase, best described in the Homeric epics, is characterized by a very fluid heroic form of warfare that was focused on individual heroics. The *promachoi* (the men fighting in the front line warriors) were heroes who would engage in individual contests with enemy heroes in the so-called 'danger zone' between the two lines of combatants before withdrawing back to the safety of their own line. This is not to suggest that the other warriors stayed out of the fighting, but rather that victory did not depend on the actions of the close-packed formations that become evident later. Battle consisted of lines ebbing and flowing,[55] moving forward and retreating before re-engaging. Warriors were able to and often did engage and disengage from the fighting multiple times in any particular battle; heroes in the *Iliad* even regularly used chariots to move around the battlefield or to flee when the battle was not going their way. Unlike the Classical period, success in heroic warfare did not depend on the maintenance of a formation which once broken spelled the end of the battle for the broken side. There are instances in the *Iliad* in which warriors formed tight formations which have been used to suggest the existence of hoplite-like warfare even at this early period, but these are the exceptions rather than the rule. When warriors are described as having grouped together into a tight formation, it was not close-packed like the later periods, but small groups generally fighting over the corpse of a fallen comrade in an effort to prevent it being despoiled by the enemy, or a larger group when circumstances became desperate. One example of a situation desperate enough to force the Greeks into a tight formation was when Homer describes the Achaeans being forced back to the sea with nowhere else to go.[56]

When close-order combat was called for during this period, a telling feature which illustrates that the formations were not yet as tightly packed as they were to become in the Classical period is the continuing exchange of missiles. In order to be able to throw a spear effectively, the warrior required at least sufficient room to be able to step and rotate at the torso, which would not been possible in the Classical hoplite formation. Therefore, the exchange of missiles indicates that the lines (what there was of them) were not as tightly packed, or as dependent on tightly packed formations, as Classical warfare and were able to provide sufficient room to manoeuvre. The fluidity of movement evident during battle at this time meant that there was not a single decisive point at which the enemy force was routed or turned. With no single point able to be identified as where the battle had been decided or superiority illustrated, as would become the case later, heroic warfare was more focused on the individual hero than the group, and as such did not meet the preconditions necessary for the establishment of a trophy at the point where the battle turned.

The second phase in the evolution of Greek warfare, which is commonly referred to as Archaic warfare, shares elements with both the Heroic era that preceded it and the Classical period that would follow. There is some debate about the nature of Archaic warfare, with some authors suggesting that the hoplite phalanx style of war, utilizing and dependent upon close-packed formations, was already being employed by this period; there is little evidence, however, of anything other than a proto-phalanx before the Persian Wars.[57] That the heavy shield (the *hoplon*) and armour that accompanied the emergence of phalanx warfare were available and being used at this time would seem to support the argument that Classical hoplite tactics were being employed, and although Archaic warfare can be characterized as discussed earlier by a tendency to see more tightly packed formations used on the battlefield than those of the Heroic period, the formations used were clearly not yet as tightly packed or formation-dependent as those of Classical warfare. Sixth-century BC Athenian art clearly illustrates that warriors of this period were still being equipped to engage in missile combat, and as discussed above, the use of missiles by the hoplites required a certain amount of space within the formation so that missile weapons could be discharged effectively, which is not in keeping with the close-packed formation of the Classical hoplite phalanx. Furthermore, while the *promachoi* (front line) which had acted as individual heroes in Homeric epic no longer acted as such in the Archaic period, some of the ebb and flow evident in the earlier form of warfare remained. Therefore, although the Classical hoplite's equipment was beginning to emerge onto the battlefield, the tactics had not yet fully evolved to those evident in the Classical period. Additionally, although the emergence of the *hoplon*, the classical hoplite's iconic shield, can be seen, it was not yet used exclusively by the hoplite, as there is evidence of the continued use of Boeotian-style shields throughout this period. By dint of its weight (which has been suggested to average approximately 7kg) and its 90cm diameter, the *hoplon* significantly limited the manoeuvrability of the hoplite, contributing to the use of close formations.[58] Unlike the *hoplon*, the Boeotian-style shield (held by the warrior on the right in Figure 9.3) continued to allow the Greek warrior to retain a certain amount of manoeuvrability, and its use suggests that the continuation of some of the individual tactics and open formations seen during Heroic era warfare continued until the fifth century BC, again lacking the preconditions for the establishment of a trophy.[59]

During these periods, evidence for the continuation of dedications can be seen in the handling of the spoils of battle after the engagement was over; these were used to pay the victorious warriors, with a dedication of 10 per cent of those spoils by the individual considered typical.[60] The thank-offerings to the gods in the form of dedications thanking them for victory in Archaic warfare therefore continue to be focused on the individual, who would dedicate despoiled armour, or a dedication purchased from the profits of the sale of spoils, at a Panhellenic temple to celebrate their individual victory.

New Military Protocols Developed After 480 BC

By the fifth century BC, the period of Classical Greek warfare where the iconic hoplite versus hoplite lines had emerged, non-hoplite arms, lightly armed troops and throwing weapons all began to be excluded from the phalanx proper.[61] The hoplite versus hoplite style of warfare was completely reliant on teamwork; it was focused on the group as a whole and not the individual, and in this form of warfare individualism could only hurt the outcome of the contest – the group would succeed or fail together. This style of warfare then was about the collective, and the 'mob-like' pressure of the *othismus* (the shove). The victors would be the group that could exert its collective will over another group by breaking their formation, at which point the battle was to all intents and purposes over, so much so that the Spartans made a habit of not spending a lot of time pursuing their broken enemy.[62] The change from a Heroic, individual fighting system to one where success or failure depended on the unity of the forces is critical to the introduction of the *tropaion*, as it created the precedents required for the introduction of war trophies.

Classical warfare (479–323 BC) was a significant departure from the preceding styles of war. Firstly, it was now possible to determine the decisive point of the battle, where the enemy army 'broke', which as discussed was not viable in the more fluid forms of combat used in pre-Classical warfare. With the focus of the victory shifting from the efforts of the individual to those of the group, it follows that the group would make the thank-offering to the god(s) as a collective. Trophy erection is generally referred to in the sources as a group event, reflecting the new style of warfare and illustrating that the responsibility for thank-offerings has shifted from the individual to the collective led by the general.[63]

Another factor that likely contributed to the introduction of the trophy is the change in the way Greek warriors were paid for their military service to the state. In Homeric and Archaic warfare, Greek warriors were paid for their service in accordance with their status and merit directly from the spoils taken from the dead.[64] This remained the case during the Persian Wars, where hoplites would be paid from the spoils captured according to the status and merit of the individual warrior,[65] as is demonstrated by the payment given to the Spartan general Pausanias after the Battle of Plataea. Herodotus relates that 'tenfold of every kind, women, horses, talents, camels, and all other things also, was set apart and given to Pausanias'.[66] Sometime in the twenty years after the conclusion of the Persian Wars, Pericles is credited with changing the way combatants were paid by introducing formal pay for hoplites which,[67] importantly, saw the state retain possession of the booty captured during a victory; this system appears to have become the standard across all of Greece for the payment of soldiers.[68] After the implementation of this change, Athens no longer paid its hoplites directly by using the spoils of victory; these were now kept by the state, deposited into the state treasury and utilized to fund the payment of soldiers or dedicated, as in the case of the Pylos shields (see above). Each hoplite was now paid a set amount (one *drachma* for him and one for his servant) by the state, apparently intended to ensure that the hoplites could support themselves on campaign whilst away from their regular source of income.[69] Although the available evidence of these changes is only detailed in the case of Athens, it is clear that the Spartans also began to retain control of the booty at approximately the same time.[70]

These changes not only had a significant effect on the Greek ability to maintain wars, allowing them to transcend previous limitations, but more importantly for the focus of this work, also ensured that the warrior would no longer be in possession of despoiled armour as it was instead claimed by the state. This of course meant that the individual no longer had a personal collection of spoils from which they could derive a dedication to the gods to be deposited at the Panhellenic temples, as had been the common practice previously.[71] This is not to suggest that individuals were not able to pay for an object that could be dedicated, but it seems that warfare was no longer the potentially profitable endeavour that it had been in previous periods. The payment of a single *drachma* per day for the hoplite and another for his servant seems to be a subsistence payment rather than a way of generating wealth, and as such it seems unlikely that the warrior would feel it necessary to tithe a tenth of these earnings to the gods, which helps to explain the decrease of offerings seen at the Panhellenic sanctuaries at this time. Of course there would remain the implied obligation that the warriors thank the gods for their success and survival, and it seems that a communal thanks-offering consisting of the now state-owned despoiled armour was now undertaken in order to thank the gods and, perhaps just as importantly, appease the warriors' need to participate in the thanks-offering. This communal act of thanking the gods in addition to meeting these needs also served to further strengthen the esprit-de-corps and sense of unity within the group and emphasize the collective over the individual, a vital element in this era of warfare.

Although never codified, it seems that the Greeks generally believed in a common set of principles governing the construction of *tropaia*. These become clear in the sources when one of these rules is broken. Perhaps the most important of these rules regarded the materials used in the construction of battlefield trophies. Trophies were expected to be non-permanent in nature. They were to be constructed using perishable materials such as wood because, as Diodorus Siculus points out, the celebration of victory over other Greeks should be short-lived so that the hatred between the warring factions could fade as the trophy itself deteriorated:

> For hatred between Greeks should only last until the moment of victory, and punishment only until the enemy is subdued ... So the ancestors of the Greeks ordained that trophies for victory in war should be constructed of whatever wood was available and not in stone. Was this not done so that these trophies should last but a short time and that these memorials to enmity should then disappear?[72]

Dedications at temples during the Heroic and Archaic periods could be made by individuals or the state. These differed from trophies in that they were located in a temple or sanctuary and not on the battlefield, where their presence would help to continue the animosity between the warring factions; that said, Plato has Socrates criticizing the dedication of Greek spoils by other Greeks in religious sanctuaries.[73] Dedications by individuals were in essence symbolic of one individual's victory over another individual and were unlikely to elicit prolonged enmity between states. By the fifth century, a primary trophy made up of despoiled armour located at the site of a battle came to symbolize the victory of one city-state over another, which corresponding with the change in the nature of warfare victory was now dependent on a collective effort, and the trophy celebrated the victory of one collective over another. The appearance of apparently generally accepted unwritten rules regarding trophies seems to have come into being at the same time to prevent the prolonged continuation of hostility and ill-will between the communities involved. As a result, trophies celebrating victory over other Greeks were only to be manufactured from non-permanent materials, primarily dependent on a wooden stump, so that the animosity between the combatants could rot and fade as the trophy rotted.[74] This was a measure designed to ameliorate warfare,[75] which would have been less of an issue with dedications housed in a sacred location often close to the victor's home.

Erecting the battlefield *tropaion* can therefore be seen as a continuation and evolution of the Homeric tradition of capturing the arms and armour of the fallen, and as an evolution of the system of dedication previously used rather than a wholescale change. The trophy becomes the indisputable measure of success for the Greek army of the fifth century, all but eliminating the confusion sometimes evident in the sixth century BC when there was no commonly agreed method of determining or claiming victory. Prior to the use of trophies, examples where both sides claimed victory are evident, with some instances based on differing criteria: for some it was holding the field, for others it was having killed more of the enemy. With the introduction of the use of the trophy, the criteria for victory became clearer – ownership of the battle site and control over the bodies of the dead was universally seen as the determinant of victory; but even this did not eliminate all confusion. There are three occasions mentioned in Thucydides where both sides set up trophies or claimed victory, with these situations presenting unusual circumstances that allowed both sides to assert they had reasonable grounds for claiming victory.

Of the three disputed results, only one was a land battle, and it can be argued that in general the results of land battles were more difficult to dispute as possession of the corpses and the battlefield were clear signifiers of victory. Conversely, corpse retrieval could be very difficult after a naval battle because of the vagaries of the tides and corpses disappearing beneath the waves. The one disputed land battle came about as a result of it coming to a premature conclusion due to nightfall: the battle which took place at Laodoceum between the Mantineians and the Tegeans had seen both sides rout an opposing wing before night fell and prevented the continuation of the clash. The Tegeans decided to camp on the field of the battle itself and immediately set up a trophy, whilst the Mantineians left for Bucolion and afterwards set up a rival trophy.[76]

Thucydides in Book I provides the first naval example where both sides, the Corinthians and Corcyraeans, set up trophies and claimed victory after a naval conflict that had occurred the day before. The Corinthians felt they had won as a result of the fact that they had destroyed more Corcyraean ships and carried off more of the corpses and captives. Yet the Corcyraeans also believed themselves victorious because they too had sunk a number of enemy vessels and carried away corpses, but primarily because their opponents had left the site of the battle when the Athenians had arrived to support the Corcyraeans. As a result, both the Corcyreans and Corinthians set up trophies on nearby Sybota and claimed the victory.[77] The second naval example occurred when the Corinthians and their allies faced an Athenian fleet apparently attempting to land soldiers in Corinthian territory. This engagement saw the Corinthians cripple seven of the Athenian vessels, and the Athenians for their part managed to sink four of the Corinthian ships before leaving for open waters. On the basis that the Athenians left the scene of battle, the Corinthians claimed victory, while the Athenians themselves claimed victory because the Corinthians did not pursue them, and they were able to recover more of the wrecked vessels as they were pushed out to sea by the tides.[78]

Perishable Anthropomorphic Trophies

Perishable anthropomorphic trophies, more commonly referred to by modern historians as primary trophies, were in most cases created by hanging or nailing despoiled armour to a tree trunk or wooden stake on the battlefield. As they were constructed of perishable materials, there are no recognizable extant examples of this type of trophy in the archaeological record. Greek coinage from the fourth century BC on provides visual evidence. An Athenian red-figure *pelikê* depicts a Greek *tropaion*: Nikê is shown fastening a Corinthian helmet to a post. In addition to the helmet, the *tropaion* consists of a *linothorax* (upper body armour), *xiphos* (sword) and *hoplon* (shield, here with an eye device) leaning against the post (Figure 9.4).[79]

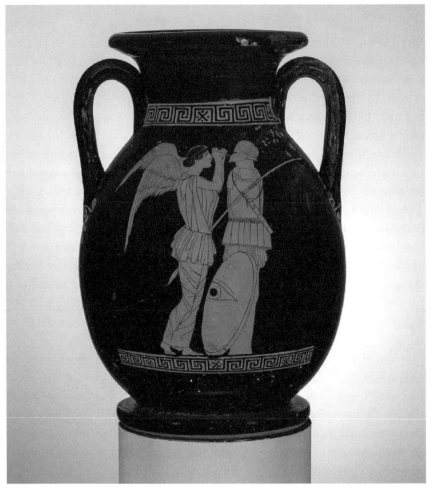

Figure 9.4: The goddess Nikê assembles a *tropaion*; the warrior's *linothorax*, spear, Corinthian helmet and shield (with eye device) are shown. The rectangular marked area beneath the neck indicates where the *linothorax* has gone over the wooden support for the *tropaion*. Athenian red-figure *pelike*, by the Trophy Painter, dating to about 450 BC. (*Boston Museum of Fine Arts 20.187*)

Perhaps the best literary description of the primary trophy is provided by the Roman poet Virgil; although he is not describing a Greek victory trophy specifically, Virgil accurately describes the appearance of a primary trophy:

> A mighty oak shorn of its limbs he sets upon a hill and clothes it over with glittering arms, the spoil of King Mezentius, and a trophy proud to thee, great lord of war. The hero's plumes bedewed with blood are there, and splintered spears; there hangs the corselet, by the thrusting steel twelve times gored through; upon the left he binds the brazen shield, and from the neck suspends the ivory-hilted sword.[80]

Virgil's description not only describes the physical appearance of the trophy but also the manner in which trophies were manufactured. It is possible that archaeological evidence for the construction methods used to make primary trophies might be seen in what have previously been described as 'sauroter holes' in armour finds. These pieces of armour have been used in recent times to suggest that warriors that had fallen under the weight of the *othismus* ('shove') but who were not yet dead might have been dispatched by their enemies as they were marching over them using the butt-spike of their spear (the sauroter) which, it is argued, left a distinctive square hole. These distinctive holes have more recently been attributed to the square cross-sectioned nails that would have been used to fasten the armour to a stump, a post or a wall in a sanctuary.[81] Another type of trophy which is less commonly mentioned in literature differed slightly in appearance from the standard design described above; this variant consisted of a pile of weapons and armour on top of which the pole bearing enemy spoils is placed.[82]

The Erection of the Trophy

The earliest Greek literary reference for the erection of a trophy is found in the first book of Thucydides where the author discusses the Corcyraean erection of a trophy on Leukimme, a Corcyran headland overlooking the site of their naval victory over the Corinthians in 435 BC.[83] There was clearly no minimum size of conflict required before a trophy could be erected, with even small raids celebrated and victory declared through the erection of a trophy:[84]

> There was a trifling affair at Phrygia between a squadron of the Athenian horse with the Thessalians and the Boeotian cavalry; in which the former had rather the best of it, until the heavy infantry advanced

to the support of the Boeotians, when the Thessalians and Athenians were routed and lost a few men, whose bodies, however, were recovered the same day without a truce. The next day the Peloponnesians set up a trophy.[85]

By the act of setting up the trophy, one side demonstrated that they had undisputed control of the battlefield and the corpses on it. Simply because one side felt that they had achieved victory, however, in no way prevented the other side from disputing this claim by attacking during the erection of the trophy. This is demonstrated by the Athenian attack on the Corinthians when the latter decided to construct a trophy because they had been shamed into it by the elders of Corinth twelve days after the conclusion of a battle. The Athenians, having already set up a trophy and declared victory immediately after the conclusion of the original conflict, emerged from Megara and routed the Corinthian forces engaged in building their trophy.[86] There is at least one recorded case in the sources that illustrates the erection of a trophy as a means of testing the opponent's desire to continue the conflict. Plutarch describes the Spartan general Agesilaus ordering the erection of a trophy, not because he felt that he had won a clear victory but to test the willingness of his opponents to engage in further conflict, thus contesting his somewhat furtive claims to victory:

> Early next morning, Agesilaus, wishing to try the Thebans and see whether they would give him battle, ordered his soldiers to wreath their heads and his pipers to play their pipes, while a trophy was set up and adorned in token of their victory.[87]

It is highly unlikely that this was the only time the erection of the trophy was used to determine the enemy's disposition. This example suggests that in instances where the outcome of the battle was uncertain, the erection of a trophy would have been a very nerve-wracking time for those involved in its construction and dedication, waiting during the ceremony whilst the warriors had their heads wreathed and pipers played their pipes to see whether or not the enemy would accept a declaration of victory or attack to prevent the erection of the trophy and continue the conflict until a more decisive conclusion was reached.[88]

Control of the battlefield was an extremely important element of Greek warfare, as the owners had the ability to determine what happened to the remains of the dead. Retrieval of the dead was considered a normal part of the post-battle activity,[89] and an important obligation owed to the deceased by other Greeks whether or not they fought on the same side:

I think it right to bury the fallen dead, not injuring any state nor yet introducing murderous strife, but preserving the law of all Hellas. What is not well in this? If you suffered anything from the Argives, they are dead; you took a splendid vengeance on your foes and covered them with shame, and now your right is at an end. Let the dead now be buried in the earth, and each element return to the place from where it came to the body.[90]

There are very few instances where the dead are not retrieved after battle, and failure to deal appropriately with the dead was considered a crime against both gods and mortals, leading to serious repercussions.[91] Antigone addressed Creon about this:

I would not tell you to do it, and even if you were willing to act after all I would not be content for you to act with me! Do you be the kind of person you have decided to be, but I shall bury him! It is honourable for me to do this and die. I am his own and I shall lie with him who is my own, having committed a crime that is holy, for there will be a longer span of time for me to please those below than there will be to please those here; for there I shall lie forever. As for you, if it is your pleasure, dishonour what the gods honour![92]

This could be a particularly difficult obligation to fulfil after a naval battle.[93] Generally, the defeated could not mount a search for their dead for at least a day or so after the conclusion of the battle, by which time many bodies would have been irretrievable; it is unlikely that even the victor would always be able immediately to retrieve their lost dead. These difficulties must have been well-known and understood; however, six Athenian generals who failed to retrieve all of the Athenian dead after their victory in the naval Battle of Arginusae in 406 BC were put on trial and eventually executed for their failure in this regard, even though they had won an unlikely victory.[94]

After about 460 BC, there were differing traditions regarding the correct disposal of the fallen between city-states, but in all cases the retrieval of the dead was intimately connected to the declaration of victory and the erection of the *tropaion*. In many cases the victor would not set up a trophy until the enemy had sent an envoy and requested the return of their dead, which was a clear admission of defeat. There were a very few instances where the use of force was considered in retrieving the dead in order to avoid the humiliation of admitting defeat.[95]

Like those of the majority of Greek states, the Spartan war dead were generally buried at or near the site of the battle which cost them their lives.[96]

After the Battle of Mantineia in 418 BC, the Spartans chose to transport their dead to nearby Tegea for burial, rather than bury them on the battlefield.[97] One critical exception was the disposition of a Spartan king killed on campaign, who would have his body packed in honey to prevent the decomposition of the corpse whilst it was in transit back to Sparta. The Athenian dead were, after about 460 BC,[98] generally cremated before having their bones and teeth gathered and returned to Athens, where they were given a public burial during an annual ceremony at home. The Athenian burial of the war dead elevated them to the status of heroes,[99] and as Thucydides describes, the remains would be divided into tribal groupings and placed in a tribal coffin before being deposited into a public tomb for the Athenian war dead in the Kerameikos.[100] That this had become accepted practice is demonstrated by the fact that Thucydides felt it unusual and noteworthy that the Athenians buried their dead at the battle site at Marathon and Plataea.[101]

The significance of the possession of the battle dead should therefore not be underestimated, particularly in cases where the battle itself concluded in an ambiguous fashion; the possession of the dead would become the determining factor in a technical victory. Often the erection of the trophy would only occur after an enemy herald had come and asked for the return of the dead, which was seen as a clear admission of defeat.[102] The few instances where confusion still existed over which side was victorious were the result of neither side waiting for the retrieval of the dead before erecting trophies. There was even at least one instance where the Athenians, although they had achieved a victory over the Corinthians at Solygeia in 425 BC, had failed to retrieve two of their dead, forcing them to send a herald to retrieve those bodies, and thereby were forced to concede defeat. Plutarch specifically states that in this instance:

> Nicias endured rather to abandon the honour and reputation of his victory than to leave unburied two of his fellow citizens.[103]

Choice of location was important in the erection of trophies. In land battles, the primary trophy would be set up at the point that the battle turned, which would in hoplite battle equate to where the *othismus* broke the enemy formation.[104] Naval victories would also be celebrated and claimed through the erection of a trophy,[105] often using the prow of a wrecked enemy vessel, instead of the arms and armour used in trophies celebrating land battles. However, necessity required that the trophy be erected on a nearby promontory often overlooking the site of the battle, as it would have been impossible for a trophy to be erected on the site of the battle itself.

Thucydides Book 2 provides an excellent example where the engagement took place some distance from either shoreline between the Athenians and the Corinthians, and after the Athenian victory they set up the trophy on the nearby promontory of Rhium.[106] Apparently another acceptable choice of location for a trophy to be erected was at the location that the fleet had set out from immediately before the battle.[107]

Trophy inscriptions generally seem to have followed a relatively set formula: the inscription would present the name of battle and its location (for example in the plain, on the hill or on the river bank), name the combatants involved and finally provide a dedication to a god (most often Zeus Tropaios, 'Zeus of the Trophy').[108] Generally, primary trophies were considered to possess a transitional sacredness, as once they were dedicated to a god they were considered the god's property and as such sacred. As objects sacred to a god, they were treated in the same way as dedications in temples and left unmolested, even in enemy territory.[109] They were considered transitional because in time the elements would wear them down and destroy them. Trophies could, however, sometimes be deemed unjustified, in which case they could be torn down.[110] For example, the Mylesians tore down an Athenian trophy because it was argued that the Athenians had not actually managed to take control of the area;[111] otherwise, primary trophies would be left alone to decay over time.[112]

Secondary Trophies and the Evolution of Permanence of Commemoration

Secondary trophies were a later development than primary trophies. Secondary trophies differed in two important ways, the first being a physical one as they were manufactured using 'permanent' materials like stone or bronze, giving them much more durability than the trophies mounted on wood. The second distinction is that they served a different purpose: rather than being declarations of victory, secondary trophies functioned as commemorations of victory. Although neither Thucydides nor Xenophon mention the use of stone or bronze in the construction of any trophies celebrating victory over fellow Greeks,[113] permanent trophies existed as early as the 460s BC commemorating the victories of the Persian Wars, as demonstrated by the three-headed Serpent Column, dedicated, as Thucydides relates, from the tithe of 10 per cent (*dekatē*) of the booty taken from the Persians (Figure 9.5). This consisted of three intertwined bronze serpents, originally standing at 6 metres high, surmounted by a golden tripod, and dedicated at Delphi. Thirty-one Greek cities which opposed the

Persians in 480–479 BC were inscribed on the serpents' coils.[114] Pausanias, regent for the Greeks, inscribed a couplet of verse on the golden tripod: 'Since as leader of the Greeks he destroyed the Persian army, Pausanias dedicated this memorial to Phoebus [Apollo],' which the Spartans immediately had erased when they learned of it. Constantine the Great removed the sculpture to the hippodrome in Constantinople, where it can be seen today. Herodotus notes that there were three dedications to the gods for their role in saving Greece from the Persians: the Serpent Column at Delphi, a statue of Zeus at Olympia and of Poseidon at the Isthmus.[115]

Figure 9.5: The Serpent column: three intertwined bronze serpents, on which the names of the thirty-one cities that fought against Persia in 480–479 BC were inscribed, and dedicated to Apollo at Delphi, in gratitude for divine assistance in defeating them. Now at the site of the ancient hippodrome of Constantinople. (*Courtesy of Alamy*)

These aforementioned permanent trophies were constructed to commemorate victory over a foreign enemy, however, and not victories over fellow Greeks. It is very likely that the permanent monuments placed at the battlegrounds of Marathon, Salamis and later Plataea were constructed well after the conclusion of the victories they reference, and were placed on the spots where the previous primary trophies had originally stood. Considering their much later date, these permanent monuments must have served a different purpose to the primary trophies they replaced. Where the primary trophies stood as symbols of the enemy's defeat and the Greek victory,[116] the permanent secondary monument stood specifically to commemorate that victory well into the future, and is mentioned several times in the ancient sources as inspiration to achieve great deeds. Permanent trophies were, according to Cicero, not meant to be established for victories over fellow Greeks, and the debate about the permanent trophy celebrating Leuktra,[117] which is discussed in detail below, demonstrates that this remained the case until at least the fourth century BC.

Towards the end of the fifth century BC, there is, for the first time, evidence for the emergence of the use of permanent trophies commemorating victory over fellow Greeks. Secondary trophies differed from primary trophies in a number of ways. As permanent versions of primary trophies, secondary trophies required specialist tradesmen for their construction and undoubtedly required significantly longer to build. Therefore they could not have been erected immediately following the conclusion of a battle and as such could not have functioned as declarations of victory; rather, their purpose appears to have been to act as permanent commemorations of important victories.

There are several references in the ancient sources to a permanent *tropaion* at Marathon, and Pausanias describes it as being made of white marble.[118] Several large marble fragments found at Marathon must certainly belong to this monument. Significantly, these fragments date to somewhere in the 460s BC, several years after the battle itself.[119] The trophy was clearly constructed to replace the rotten primary trophy that had been erected immediately after the victory over the Persians. There is also from Marathon, discovered in AD 2000 and awaiting publication, a casualty list originally from the *soros* at Marathon for the tribe Erechtheis, with twenty-two names, with a couplet referring to their bravery in dying fighting against the Medes (Persians). This stele is presumably one of ten such stelai at the *soros* listing the names of the dead from each of the ten Athenian tribes, for the stele has cuttings for clamps to attach it to other stonework: Pausanias refers to there being a pillar listing the names of the Athenian dead, according to tribe.[120]

The earliest secondary trophies appear to have been constructed in imitation of primary trophies, simulating the armour-bearing trunk motif of the primary trophies, the one distinction being that they were manufactured from permanent materials such as marble or bronze.[121] Designs could differ from the basic form provided by the primary trophy, some being significantly more complex, such as that of the Nikê of Samothrace (Figure 9.6).[122] Various dates have been suggested for this, in particular that the monument commemorated the naval victory of the Rhodians in 190 BC, but Stewart,[123] particularly on the basis of the ship type, suggests that it in fact dates to a naval victory in 154 BC. Nikê, larger than life at 2.75 metres high, carved from marble from Paros, has her wings outstretched as if the wind blows against her: her right foot is just landing on the deck while the left is in the air, poised to land. She stands at the prow of a warship (probably a quadrireme, and 2.82 metres high) made from blocks of grey marble from Rhodes. Her monument stood in a fountain at the sanctuary of the Great Gods on the island of Samothrace, looking out over the Aegean Sea, presumably to the site of the sea-battle.

Due to the materials used to construct secondary trophies, several examples, in varying states of repair, are evident in the archaeological record. The Leuktra trophy which was constructed by the Thebans to celebrate their victory over the Spartans in 371 BC is one example that, although incomplete, has in part survived in the archaeological record. It is considered one of the first examples of a permanent trophy erected to celebrate the victory of one group of Greeks over another.[124] Cicero, while discussing judicial inquiry, uses the example of the Leuktra trophy. His discussion illustrates that the shift to permanent trophies did not occur spontaneously and that there was a transitional period where the creation of permanent trophies over fellow Greeks was not widely accepted by all members of the Greek community. Furthermore, Cicero's treatment of the topic supports the argument that the purpose of the trophy had changed, with the Thebans challenged for building a permanent trophy to commemorate their victory over the Spartans, contrary to the Greek traditions.[125] Thebes justified its breach of protocol to the Amphyctions, who regulated and controlled the Delphic sanctuary, by arguing that their army had beaten the Spartans through valour, and felt it appropriate to erect a permanent commemoration to that valour for their descendants.[126] Cicero's clear implication is that it was not yet considered acceptable to erect a permanent trophy over other Greeks, but the lack of discussion regarding the permanent trophy erected at Marathon indicates that if it was erected over barbarians, a permanent commemoration was deemed acceptable.

Figure 9.6: Wingéd Nikê (Victory) lands on the prow of a ship to signify victory in a naval engagement. The monument commemorates her role in the battle and serves to acknowledge her role, and that of all the gods, in the victory. From the island of Samothrace. Louvre MA 2369. (*Courtesy of Alamy*)

The permanence of secondary trophies is clearly contrary to the ideal seen in the unwritten laws discussed earlier, that trophies should be allowed to rot over time and allow the enmity between the combatants to fade. That the purpose of the trophy had changed from a declaration of victory to be placed on the battlefield to a permanent commemoration of victory is illustrated by Thucydides in Pericles' funeral oration:

> Rather, the admiration of the present and succeeding ages will be ours, since we have not left our power without witness, but have shown it by mighty proofs; and far from needing a Homer for our panegyrist, or other of his craft whose verses might charm for the moment only for the impression which they gave to melt at the touch of fact, we have forced every sea and land to be the highway of our daring, and everywhere, whether for evil or for good, have left imperishable monuments behind us.[127]

It is unclear what the decision-making process that the Greeks followed was in choosing a location for secondary trophies, with some erected in a prominent location near the site of the battle likely replacing a primary trophy erected immediately after the battle, and others erected far from the site of the battle and even possibly in the victor's city.[128] West suggests that the famous permanent Athenian trophy set up after the Battle of Marathon in 490 BC was probably constructed decades later, in the 460s BC, and replaced the original primary trophy erected by Miltiades immediately after the battle.[129] Secondary trophies, like their primary counterparts, continued to be considered sacred as they were dedicated to the gods and were considered inviolable. After having their city captured and a permanent victory monument erected in their city celebrating its fall, the Rhodians were unable to demolish the sacred trophy and came up with a unique way of mitigating their humiliation:

> Artemisia, after taking Rhodes and killing its leading men, put up in the city of Rhodes a trophy of her victory, including two bronze statues, one representing the state of the Rhodians, the other herself. Herself she fashioned in the act of branding the state of the Rhodians. In later times the Rhodians, labouring under the religious scruple which makes it a sin to remove trophies once they are dedicated, constructed a building to surround the place, and thus by the erection of the 'Grecian Station' covered it so that nobody could see it, and ordered that the building be called Abaton [unapproachable].[130]

Conclusion

Thanking the gods for success in battle was an important element of Greek warfare. In the Homeric and Archaic periods, this was primarily achieved through the offering of dedications, usually taken from the spoils of the battle or bought with monies from the sale of said spoils. These dedications were commonly deposited in Panhellenic sanctuaries or temples. As the nature of Greek warfare changed, so did the manner in which the Greeks thanked the gods for their successes, and in the Classical period the *tropaion* emerges as the primary method used to thank the gods for the military success of the state. Erecting a *tropaion* came to serve several important roles in Greek warfare, foremost as a way of thanking the gods for victory by offering them the finest of the despoiled armour and weapons. Being located on the site of the battle where the enemy had turned, the primary trophy also served as a material declaration of victory, and was intended to prolong the honour associated with the act beyond the immediacy of the act itself. It is not until the introduction of secondary trophies that the purpose again shifts and the trophy becomes a permanent commemoration of victory. The trophy was created for the same reasons as dedications of despoiled armour were offered by Homeric heroes, as a materialization of victory. The emergence of trophies, which would largely replace the dedication of despoiled armour at Panhellenic sanctuaries, coincided with important changes in Greek society and reflect the changing nature of Greek warfare. The evolution of the *polis* and the introduction of hoplite warfare, heavily reliant on communal effort, are two key factors that influenced the move away from dedications offered in temples to the trophy set upon the battlefield, which was a group and collective offering, clearly complementing the shift of focus from the individual to the collective citizen body in classical Greece.

Notes

1. See in this volume the essays by Matthew Dillon, Sonya Nevin and Lara O'Sullivan.
2. *Tropaion:* a derivation of the Greek noun *tropé*, meaning turning point, indicating the point at which the enemy turned and fled, from the verb *trepô*: *LSJ*9 p.1826; Suid. *sv tropaia*. Servius' late fourth-century AD Latin commentary on the *Aeneid* at Book 10, line 775, quotes the Greek derivation for the Latin form, *tropaeum: apo tou trepesthai*, the point at which the enemy turned and fled.
3. For the *tropaion*, see esp. Rouse, 1902, 98–100; Lammert, 1939; Pritchett, 1974, 246–75; Lonis, 1979, 129–46, 265–84; Camp *et al.*, 1992, 448–49; Stroszeck, 2004; Rabe, 2007; Wheeler and Strauss, 2008, 173–75; Trundle, 2013; Vivo, 2013, 250–54, Vivo, 2014, 174–80.
4. Stroszeck, 2004, 309.
5. Vivo, 2013, 255–56.

6. Temporary trophies are mentioned no less than forty times in Thucydides: 1.30, 1.54, 1.63, 2.22, 2.79, 2.82, 2.84, 2.92, 3.91, 3.109, 3.112, 4.12, 4.14, 4.25, 4.38, 4.44, 4.56, 4.67, 4.72, 4.97, 4.101, 4.124, 4.131, 4.134, 5.10, 5.12, 5.74, 6.70, 6.94, 6.97, 6.98, 6.100, 6.103, 7.5, 7.23, 7.34, 7.54, 7.72, 8.24, 8.25, 8.42, 8.95.

7. Paus. 1.40.5; Hdt. 3.59. Naval *tropaia* could also, however, be erected on land near the battle-site, as was the case with the first *tropaion* mentioned by Thucydides: 1.30.1 (at Leukimme, see further below).

8. There is evidence of dedication in relation to military success recorded in both Thucydides and Herodotus, as well as both of Homer's epics.

9. Pritchett, 1974, 241.

10. Dem. 24.120, trans. Witt and Witt, 1949.

11. For vows in military contexts, see Pritchett, 1979, 230–39.

12. For example, *ThesCRA* i: 297 no. 118, pl. 76.

13. *ThesCRA* i: 308–11, nos 175–92.

14. *ThesCRA* i: 313, nos 200–06.

15. Paus. 1.15.4, 1.40.5; Thuc. 3.113–14.

16. Paus 1.15.4; Ar. *Knights* 846–49 mentions the captured shields, indicating their importance to the Athenian psyche of victory; see also Dio Chrys. *Or.* 2.36. Surviving shield with inscription: *Agora Museum* B262; see Camp, 1986, 71–72, figs 45–46; *ThesCRA* i: 302 no. 150; Wees, 2009, 237. For a detailed discussion of the evidence and the Ar. *Knights* passage, see Lippman, Scahill and Schultz, 2006.

17. Thuc. 3.113–14; Pritchett, 1979, 287; Hornblower, 1991, 534 (300 panoplies might be worth between three and five talents: a substantial amount).

18. Arr. *Anab.* 1.16.7; Plut. *Alex.* 16.8; *FGrH* 151 Anonymous F1. For dedications of armour captured in battle, see Pritchett, 1979, 240–76; Jackson, 1991, esp. 229–32.

19. Paus. 1.40.5.

20. See n.122 below.

21. Hdt. 8.27.5.

22. Hdt. 9.81.1.

23. *ThesCRA* i: 274.

24. The helmet is in the Olympia museum: Olympia inv. B2600 (Mallwitz and Herrmann, 1980, 95–96, no. 57; inscription: *IG* i³ 1472; *SEG* 14.351 bis; Meiggs and Lewis, no. 19).

25. Hiero's three helmets: *GHI* i no. 22; Meiggs and Lewis, no. 29; *LSAG* 266, 275 no. 7, pl. 51.7 (the helmet in the British Museum); *SEG* 11.1206, 23.253; 33.328 *et al.*; Harrell, 2002, 452–53; for the battle, see Diod. 11.51. Gelon as tyrant of Syracuse dedicated a tripod at Delphi, for which the inscribed limestone base survives, for his victory at Himera in 480 BC (*GHI* i: no. 17; Meiggs and Lewis, 28).

26. *SEG* 23.253.

27. Shipwrecked: *SIG³* 35 Bb.

28. Pritchett, 1974, 242, 269.

29. Hom. *Il.* 13.209–11, trans. Lombardo, 1997.

30. Plato *Rep.* 469d decries the stripping of corpses as a method used by some combatants to avoid battle.

31. Hom. *Il.* 6.67–72, trans. Lombardo, 1997.

32. As illustrated by Hector glorying in wearing Achilles' 'immortal armour': Hom. *Il.* 17.192–214.

33. Hom. *Il.* 5.185, 5.56, 5.469, 5.667, 6.70–73, 7.146–59, 7.146, 8.543, 10.547, 11.117, 11.268, 11.351, 11.389, 13.205–15, 13.647, 15.351, 16.533–35, 16.821, 17.57, 17.65–70, 17.82, 17.323, 18.87, 18.98, 21.192, 22.285, 22.408, 22.443.

34. Hom *Il*. 6.505–06, trans. Lombardo, 1997. At *Il*. 17.207–08 Zeus comments that while Hector is currently glorifying in Achilles' armour, he will never return from battle to give it to his wife Andromache.
35. Vivo, 2013, 184.
36. Hom. *Il*. 7.84–86. For the stripping of armour off an opponent one has just killed, in Homer, see Allan, 2005, esp. 7–11, with emphasis on Hector stripping Patroclus' armour – which was Achilles' – and wearing it himself in battle.
37. Figure 9.3: Munich Antikensammlungen 1410 (J328) (*ABV* 311.1). The incident occurred after the period of the war covered by Homer's *Iliad*.
38. Hdt. 9.81.1.
39. Dem. 24.120.
40. Jackson, 1991, 230, 244; Schwartz, 2009, 96; Wees, 2009, 50; Vivo, 2014, 164–65.
41. Xen. *Anab*. 5.3.5, trans. Brownson and Dillery. For the dedications in the Athenian Treasury at Delphi, see Neer 2004.
42. The melting down of dedications at the Asklepieion on the slopes of the Athenian acropolis provides a case in point.
43. Mikalson, 2010, 285.
44. As in the case of the body of Hector: Hom. *Il*. Book 24.
45. Hom *Il*. 7.79–88, trans. Lombardo, 1997.
46. Hom. *Il*. 4.500–11, 577–80, 5.672–75, 11.603–19, 13.530–35, 13.570–79, 15.439–43, 540–50, 609–14; cf. Allan, 2005, 6–7.
47. Hom. *Il*. 5.890–900, trans. Lombardo, 1997.
48. Hom. *Il*. 16.574–78, trans. Lombardo, 1997.
49. Pritchett, 1974, 249.
50. Hom. *Il*. 10.465–68, trans. Lombardo, 1997.
51. Hom. *Il*. 10.570–71, trans. Lombardo, 1997. This is how Eustathius understood these lines in his commentary; Rouse, 1902, 101; Ready, 2007, 16–17, 36–37.
52. Plut. *Mor*. 306b.
53. Hdt. 1.82.
54. Krentz, 2002, 32; Stroszeck, 2004, 309.
55. Wees, 2009, 183.
56. Hom. *Il*. 13.126–48.
57. Roalings, 2007, 58.
58. Wees, 2009, 48.
59. Wees, 2009, 51–52.
60. Schwartz, 2009, 95.
61. Wees, 2009, 50.
62. Thuc. 5.73.3.
63. Stroszeck, 2004, 310.
64. Hdt. 8.121, 8.123.1; Hom *Il*. 9.140, 9.280. Although Thersites complains about Agamemnon's hoarding of the spoils, it is clear from the response that he receives that this was not a concern for the majority of the Greeks, and later in Book 9 it is made clear on two occasions that there would be a division of spoils after a successful completion to the war.
65. Wees, 2009, 236.
66. Hdt. 9.81.2.
67. Dem. *Or*. 13.
68. Wees, 2009, 236.
69. Thuc. 3.17.3; [Arist.] *Ath. Pol*. 27.2; Dem. 13.11; Pritchett, 1971, 49–51; Ridley, 1979, 519–22; Hornblower, 1991, 402; Rhodes, 1993, 337; Rawlings, 2007, 170.

70. Wees, 2009, 237.
71. Schwartz, 2009, 96.
72. Diod. 13.24.3–6; trans. Oldfather, 1939.
73. Plat. *Rep*. 470a.
74. Diod. 13.24.5; Trundle, 2013, 124.
75. Diod. 13.24.5; Cic. *Inv.* 2.23.69.
76. Thuc. 4.134.
77. Thuc. 1.54; Gomme, 1945, 195.
78. Thuc. 7.34.
79. Boston Museum of Fine Arts 20.187 (*ARV²* 857.2; *LIMC* vi Nikê 159a; *ThesCRA* viii: pl. 16.3a).
80. Virg. *Aen*. 11.4–11; trans. Gransden, 1976. See Servius' commentary on the *Aeneid*, on 11.6–7, and also on *Aen*. 10.775: see above, n.2.
81. Schwartz, 2009, 184.
82. Xen. *Anab*. 4.7.25–26.
83. Thuc. 1.30.1.
84. Thuc. 2.22.2–3, 6.94.2; cf. Gomme, 1956, 78.
85. Thuc. 2.22.2–3; trans. Warner, 1954.
86. Thuc. 1.105; Trundle, 2013, 128.
87. Plut. *Ages*. 19.2; trans. Perrin, 1917.
88. Plut. *Ages*. 19.2.
89. Thuc. 1.63, 2.82, 2.92, 4.38, 4.72, 5.74.
90. Eur. *Suppl*. 524–34; trans. Braun, 1973.
91. Soph. *Ant*. 21–38, 42–47, 69–77.
92. Soph. *Ant*. 69–77; trans. Braun, 1973. For this issue of burying the dead in Sophocles, and in Greek belief as a whole, see Rosivach, 1983, esp. 207–11 for Antigone.
93. Wees, 2009, 225–26.
94. Ar. *Frogs* 687–99; [Arist.] *Ath. Pol.* 34.1; Xen. *Hell*. 1.7; Diod. 13.101.
95. Xen. *Hell*. 4.14–15, 6.4.8–15.
96. Hdt. 5.63, 6.58.3, 7.228, 9.85; Xen. *Hell*. 2.4.33.
97. Thuc. 5.74.
98. For a more detailed discussion on the likely starting date for this practice, see Gomme, 1956, 94–96; Travlos, 1971, 300, with plates; Hornblower, 1991, 292–94.
99. Hornblower, 1991, 294.
100. Thuc. 2.34.1–5; Gomme, 1956, 94–103; Travlos, 1971, 300, with plates.
101. Thuc. 2.34.5 with Paus. 1.29.4, 1.32.3; Pritchett, 1985, 166–67; Hornblower, 1991, 294; Fromherz, 2011, 388–91; Trundle, 2013, 127–28.
102. Thuc. 2.79.7, 5.10.6.
103. Plut. *Nic*. 6.5–6; trans. Perrin, 1916; see Wheeler and Strauss, 2008, 212.
104. Thuc. 4.67.5.
105. Diod. 13.51.7.
106. Thuc. 2.84, 8.106.
107. Thuc. 2.92; Hornblower, 1991, 370.
108. *IG* vii 2462, line 5 (see Tuplin, 1987, 94–98, who raises the possibility that this does not in fact, against previous interpretations, belong to the Battle of Leuktra in 371 BC). Zeus Tropaios had a shrine at Sparta: Paus. 3.12.9; see for Zeus Tropaios: Lonis, 1979, 136–38; Tuplin, 1987, 106 n.104 (listing occurrences of this epithet of Zeus, to which add a dedication of 145 BC: *SEG* 37.603); Stroszeck, 2004, 318;

Zeus Tropaiouchos also occurs: Tuplin, 1987, 106 n.104. See Paus. 4.32.5–6 for the curious story that the Thebans erected a victory monument before the Battle at Leuktra took place in order to unnerve the Spartans.

109. Mikalson, 2010, 45.
110. Stroszeck, 2004, 319; Xen. *Hell.* 4.5.10.
111. Thuc. 8.24.1–2. This instance is the only example of a trophy being torn down as recorded by Thucydides; cf. Stroszeck, 2004, 319; Hornblower, 2008, 814.
112. Plut. *Mor.* 273 c–d.
113. West, 1969, 9–10.
114. Meiggs and Lewis, no. 27 (Tod *GHI* i: no. 19); Hdt. 8.82.1, 9.81.1; Thuc. 1.132.2–3; Paus. 10.13.9. Couplet: Thuc. 1.132.2–3 (ascribed to Simomides, no. 17); Harrell, 2002, 458–59; Petrovic, 2010, 202–05 (but Thucydides explicitly states that Pausanias had the dedication to Apollo inscribed on the tripod, not the statue base, of the serpent column). He made a similar dedication when he was at Byzantium, as a 'memorial of his (own) prowess', to Poseidon (*FGrH* 432 Nymphis F9).
115. Hdt. 9.81.1.
116. Diod. 16.12.5.
117. Diod. 13.24.5; Cic. *Inv.* 2.23.69.
118. Ar. *Wasps* 711, *Knights* 1334; Plut. *Arist.* 16.5; Paus. 1.32.5.
119. Vanderpool, 1966 (first publication of the finds); West, 1969, 7–19; Stroszeck, 2004, 307–09; Fromherz, 2011, 394–95.
120. *SEG* 51.425, 53.534, 59.370; Paus. 1.32.3.
121. Stroszeck, 2004, 303.
122. *LIMC* vi Nikê 382 (compare Nikê 137). For dedications of captured enemy ships, either of the actual ships incorporated into monuments, or as worked in stone, see esp. Rice, 1993, 243–47 (247 for the Samothracian Nikê); also Pritchett, 1979, 283–85; *ThesCRA* i 300–01, nos 138–39.
123. Stewart, 2016.
124. West, 1969, 8; Tuplin, 1987, 94–103; Markle, 1999, 241; Stroszeck, 2004, 305–06, 321–22.
125. Cic. *Inv.* 2.23.69–70.
126. It is interesting to note here that there is no mention of the trophy acting as a declaration of victory.
127. Thuc. 2.41.4; trans. Warner, 1954.
128. Stroszeck, 2004, 315.
129. West, 1969, 8. See also Pritchett, 1985, 166–68; Matthaiou, 2003, 197–200.
130. Vitruv. 2.8.15; trans. Morgan, 1914; Pritchett, 1974, 258.

Bibliography

Allan, W., 2005, 'Arms and the Man: Euphorbus, Hector, and the Death of Patroclus', *CQ* 55, 1–16.
Babbitt, F.C., 1959, *Plutarch Moralia*, Cambridge MA.
Braun, R.E., 1973, *Sophocles Antigone*, New York.
Brownson, C.L., 1921, *Xenophon: Hellenica*, vol. ii, Cambridge MA.
Brownson, C.L., and Dillery, J., 1998, *Xenophon: Anabasis*, Cambridge MA.
Burkert, W., 1985, *Greek Religion. Archaic and Classical*, Oxford.
Camp, J.M., 1986, *The Athenian Agora: Excavations in the Heart of Classical Athens*, London.

Camp, J.M., Ierardi, M., McInerney, J., Morgan, K., and Umholtz, G., 1992, 'A Trophy From the Battle of Chaironeia of 86 B.C.', *AJA* 96, 443–55.

Cartledge, P., 1997, *Agesilaus and the Crisis of Sparta*, Baltimore.

Fromherz, P., 2011, 'The Battlefield of Marathon: the Tropaion, Herodotos, and E. Curtius', *Historia* 60, 383–412.

Gomme, A.W. 1945, *A Historical Commentary on Thucydides*, vol. i, Oxford.

—— 1956, *A Historical Commentary on Thucydides*, vol. ii, Oxford.

Gransden, K.W., 1976, *Virgil: Aeneid*, Cambridge.

Harrell, S.E., 2002, 'King or Private Citizen: Fifth-Century Sicilian Tyrants at Olympia and Delphi', *Mnemosyne* 55, 439–64.

Herodotus, *Histories*, trans. Flower, M.A., and Marincola, J., 2002, Cambridge.

Hornblower, S., 1991, *A Commentary on Thucydides. Volume i: Books i–iii*, Oxford.

—— 1996, *A Commentary on Thucydides. Volume ii: Books iv–v.24*, Oxford.

—— 2008, *A Commentary on Thucydides. Volume iii: Books v.25–viii*, Oxford.

Hubbell, H.M., 1949, *Cicero De Inventione; De Optimo Genere Oratorum; Topica*, Cambridge MA.

Jackson, A.H., 1991, 'Hoplites and the Gods: The Dedication of Captured Arms and Armour', in Rich, J., and Shipley, G. (eds), *War and Society in the Greek World*, London, 228–49.

Kovaks, D., 1998, *Euripides*, vol. iii, Harvard.

Krentz, P., 2002, 'Fighting by the Rules: The Invention of the Hoplite Agon', *Hesperia* 71, 23–39.

Lammert, F., 1939, *Tropaion*, in *RE* vii A.1.

Lanni, A., 2008, 'The Laws of War in Ancient Greece', *LHR* 26.3, 469–89.

Lippman, M., Scahill, D., and Schultz, P., 2006, '*Knights* 843–59, the Nike Temple Bastion, and Cleon's Shields from Pylos', *AJA* 110, 551–63.

Lombardo, S. 1997, *Iliad*, Indianapolis.

Lonis, R., 1979, *Guerre et religion en Grece a l'epoque classique. Recherches sur les rites, les dieux, l'ideologie de la victoire*, Paris.

Mallwitz, A., and Herrmann, H.V., 1980, *Die Funde aus Olympia*, Athens.

Markle, M.M., 1999, 'A Shield Monument from Veria and the Chronology of Macedonian Shield Types', *Hesperia* 68, 219–54.

Matthaiou, A.P., 2003, 'Athênaioisi tetagmenoisi en temenei Hêrakleos', in Derow, P., and Parker, R. (eds), *Herodotus and His World*, Oxford, 190–202.

Mikalson, J., 2003, *Herodotus and Religion in the Persian Wars*, Chapel Hill.

—— 2010, *Ancient Greek Religion*, 2nd edn, Malden MA.

Morgan, M.H., 1914, *Vitruvius. The Ten Books on Architecture*, Harvard.

Murray, A.T., and Wyatt, W.F., 1999, *Homer: Iliad*, Cambridge MA.

Neer, R., 2004, 'The Athenian Treasury at Delphi and the Material of Politics', *ClAnt* 23, 63–93.

Oldfather, C.H., 1939, Diodorus Siculus, Library of History, Cambridge MA.

Perrin, B., 1913, *Plutarch: Lives iii*, Cambridge MA.

—— 1917, *Plutarch: Lives v*, Cambridge MA.

Petrovic, A., 2010, 'True Lies of Athenian Public Epigrams', in Baumbach, M., Petrovic, A., and Petrovic, I. (eds), *Archaic and Classical Greek Epigram. An Introduction*, Cambridge, 202–15.

Pritchett, W.K., 1971, *The Greek State at War, Part i*, Berkeley.

—— 1974, *The Greek State at War, Part ii*, Berkeley.

—— 1979, *The Greek State at War, Part iii: Religion*, Berkeley.

—— 1985, *The Greek State at War, Part iv*, Berkeley.

Rabe, B., 2007, *Tropaia. τϱοπή und σϰυλα – Entstehung, Funktion und Bedeutung des griechischen Tropaions*, Tübingen.

Rawlings, L., 2007, *The Ancient Greeks at War*, Manchester.

Ready, J.L., 2007, 'Toil and Trouble: The Acquisition of Spoils in the *Iliad*', *TAPhA* 137, 3–43.

Rhodes, P.J., 1993, A Commentary on the Aristotelian Athenaion Politeia, revised edn, Oxford.

Rice, E., 1993, 'The Glorious Dead: Commemoration of the Fallen and Portrayal of Victory in the Late Classical and Hellenistic World', in Rich, J., and Shipley, G. (eds), *War and Society in the Greek World*, London, 224–57.

Ridley, R.T., 1979, 'The Hoplite as Citizen: Athenian Military Institutions', *AC* 48, 508–48.

Rosivach, V.J., 1983, 'On Creon, "Antigone" and Not Burying the Dead', *RhM* 126, 193–211.

Rouse, W.H.D., 1902, *Greek Votive Offerings. An Essay in the History of Greek Religion*, Cambridge.

Schwartz, A., 2009, *Reinstating the Hoplite: Arms, Armour and Phalanx Fighting in Archaic and Classical Greece*, Stuttgart.

Stewart, A., 2016, 'The Nike of Samothrace: Another View', *AJA* 120, 399–410.

Stroszeck, J., 2004, 'Greek Trophy Monuments', in Bouvrie, S. des (ed.), *Myth and Symbol ii: Symbolic Phenomena in Ancient Greek Culture*, Bergen.

Travlos, J., 1971, *Pictorial Dictionary of Ancient Athens*, London.

Trundle, M. 2013, 'Commemorating Victory in Classical Greece: Why Greek Tropaia?', in Spalinger, A., and Armstrong, J. (eds), *Rituals of Triumph in the Mediterranean World*, Leiden, 123–38.

Tuplin, C.J., 1987, 'The Leuktra Campaign. Some Outstanding Problems', *Klio* 69, 72–107.

Vanderpool, E., 1966, 'A Monument to the Battle of Marathon', *Hesperia* 35, 93–106.

Vivo, J.S. de, 2013, *The Memory of Battle in Ancient Greece: Warfare, Identity, and Materiality*, unpublished thesis.

—— 2014, 'The Memory of Greek Battle: Material Culture and/as Narrative of Combat', in Meineck, P., and Konstan, D. (eds), *Combat Trauma and the Ancient Greeks*, New York, 163–84.

Warner, R., 1954, *Thucydides, History of the Peloponnesian War*, Harmondsworth.

Wees, H. van, 2009, *Greek Warfare Myths and Realities*, London.

West, W.C., 1969, 'Trophies of the Persian Wars', *CPh* 64, 7–19.

Wheeler, E.L., and Strauss, B., 2008, 'Battle', in Sabin, P., Wees, H. van, and Whitby, M. (eds), 2008, *The Cambridge History of Greek and Roman Warfare, vol.1. Greece the Hellenistic World and the Rise of Rome*, Cambridge, 186–247.

Witt, N.W. de, and Witt, N.J. de, 1949, *Demosthenes Orations*, Cambridge MA.

Chapter 10

Magic and Religion in Military Medicine of Classical Greece

Matthew Gonzales

Introduction

> Indeed as many of them as came with naturally-occurring sores or wounded in their limbs by grey bronze or far-cast stone ... he released and led each away from their various pains, tending to some with gentle incantations, providing others with potions, or wrapping poultices all round their limbs, while others he set upright with surgery.[1]

Pindar's description in the *Pythian Ode* of the medical skills Apollo had the young Asklepios learn from the centaur Chiron immediately reminds modern readers that the ancient Greek practice of military medicine, indeed the practice of medicine in general, was never completely divorced from the realms of magic and religious practice. As the literary and epigraphic records make clear, magical spells and potions, as well as sacrifice and other religious rituals, all sat comfortably alongside traditional remedies and more 'rational' technical procedures throughout Greek history.[2] Pindar, writing in the mid-fifth century BC, shares the same basic view and expectations in this regard as the Hippocratic corpus and philosophers who touch upon medical matters, taking for granted recourse to sacrifice and purifications by the afflicted in the hope of effecting a cure. Many of these authors also freely admit divine causation in medical matters; all diseases are 'divine', as they all arise from physical phenomena themselves suffused with the divine: 'I myself also consider these diseases to be divine, as are all the others, none being more divine or human than the others; but they are all alike and all divine.'[3] Thus even texts from the height of the development of 'rational' medicine have much in common with both our earliest literary sources and the documentary inscriptions that detail the care of war-wounds both on and off the field of battle in the Classical and early Hellenistic periods. As will be seen, there is no area of early ancient Greek military medicine completely divorced from magical and religious practice and sentiment.

A brief orientation on the relationship of magic and religion and the main lines of scholarly interpretation seems in order.[4] Frazer's mammoth *The Golden Bough* stands as a distillation of the nineteenth-century approach, bringing together an impressive mass of anthropological comparanda to support his thesis that man had passed through three stages of 'belief': 1) the stage of magic, in which humans sought through arcane knowledge and power to compel, shape and explore the natural world; 2) the stage of religion, in which man sought through supplication, devotion and cultivation of otherworldly powers or energies to ameliorate their condition; 3) the stage of science, in which man sought to reveal and shape the natural order through the scientific method and its products. This relatively straightforward evolutionary schema did not long stand unchallenged. The functionalist reaction to Frazer's extreme positivism stressed the social context of magic and the expected results, seeking to understand rituals in the terms of the society under study. In view of the dizzying variety of human experience across cultures, the functionalist approach tends to blend magic and religion into a continuum of human behaviour and cognition. Some functionalists establish a dubious universal distinction between the two in the opposed realms of illegality and social acceptance; magic is practised illicitly by individuals for another end or goal, whilst religion is practised for its own sake, openly, with the approval of the group.[5] Alternatively, structuralist and semiotic approaches, which interpret magic and religious ritual as arbitrary complexes of signs and symbols that articulate social meaning and power, are particularly unhelpful for the current investigation, as they 'overemphasize the sociological aspect of ritual and ignore what the participants themselves think they are doing – trying to achieve some substantive goal'.[6] More can be said for the admittedly nebulous view that 'one can think of many common characteristics of magic, not all of which need be present, some of which might turn up in religion, but which combine in different ways to create unmistakable members of a family.'[7]

Religion and magic suffuse the practice of warfare in the ancient Greek world,[8] so it should come as little surprise that gods, prayers, spells and potions all find their place in ancient Greek military medicine. In the course of our investigation below, we will begin with the influence that deities were held to have over armies' and warriors' health, safety and survival. We will then proceed to a consideration of the magico-religious practices and outlook of human practitioners of early Greek battlefield medicine before considering the interplay of religious sentiment and Hippocratic medicine that culminates with the probable melding of some 'rational' Hippocratic medical practices and procedures with the cult of Asklepios at Epidauros and elsewhere.

Divinities and Greek Military Medicine

In the *Iliad*, Apollo appears as a deity who could affect or cure disease and wounds among humans. Chryses, the god's priest dishonoured by Agamemnon, calls upon this god as his tutelary deity and invokes him as *Smintheus*, an epithet probably connected to the Archaic Greek word *sminthos* – mouse. Rodents were recognized as agents of disease in the ancient world,[9] and the god's title here no doubt alludes to a time when the mouse was the totem of the god who could both use them as the instrument of his wrath or protect men from them.[10] As he visits the devastating plague upon the Achaeans, the poet's words eerily and accurately trace a plausible course for the development of a camp epidemic, while also making clear that the effects of the plague upon the Greek camp were conceived of as the deadly darts of the archer-god:

> He set himself apart from the ships and he let fly his arrow.
> And there was a terrible clang from the silver bow.
> First he visited the mules and the swift dogs,
> but then, releasing his pointed darts at the men themselves
> he kept shooting … and the close-packed and frequent funeral pyres
>   flared.[11]

As so often, Homer attests the normative cultural belief, and throughout antiquity illness and sickness were regularly attributed to the action of a deity, named or not.[12]

Burial pyres, normal for the heroic funeral in Homer, do not imply any awareness of contagion from buried corpses and in any event did not slow its spread, as the plague raged for ten days. Indeed, burning of infected corpses could have spread any infectious disease further, as happened in the Swine Flu outbreak in the United States during the First World War. But piety and religious decorum demanded prompt and appropriate burial for the dead Achaean heroes. This is not to imply that the ancient Greeks were unaware of the need for what would be termed camp sanitation, which they certainly were, merely that here the demands of conventional religious piety and practice prescribed funeral pyres, not sanitary concerns.

This opening scene of Homer's *Iliad* reinforces the predominance of religious thought when it came to illness and its remedies, even in an overtly military context. Somewhat surprisingly to the modern mind, when Agamemnon and Achilles seek a cure for the plague ravaging the Achaean camp, they consult not a physician or doctor, which as will be seen, were definitely present in the Achaean army, but the seer Calchas, who informs them in no uncertain terms that the plague stems from the wrath of Apollo.[13] The treatment for the plague is likewise thoroughly religious in nature, consisting of ritual purification of the army by the seaside and a lavish sacrifice to Apollo both on the seaside and at his sanctuary:

> But the son of Atreus bade the army to purify themselves.
> And they purified themselves and cast the unclean filth into the sea.
> And to Apollo they offered blemish-less sacrifices
> of bulls and goats beside the shore of the barren salt-sea.
> And fatty essence, twisting about with the smoke, reached up to
> heaven.[14]

The practical and symbolic aspects of the purification merge seamlessly, as so often – ritual pollution and the filth and grime of camp-life during the plague are simultaneously cleansed. The god is placated and the plague lifts. Just as the anger of the gods could cause disease, propitiation of the correct deity was believed to alleviate illness. The same basic outlook appears in the inscriptions recording health inquiries to the oracle of Zeus at Dodona: 'Nikokrateia asks to know to what deity should she sacrifice so that she might feel better and so that her illness cease'; 'Leontios asks to know concerning his son whether the cure of the disease … which has hold of him will happen.'[15]

As with disease and illness during war, the divine could also determine who was wounded in battle and whether the wounded survived or perished. Many times in the *Iliad*, deities turn aside their favourites' serious or fatal blows, as when Aphrodite directly intervened to protect her son, the Trojan champion Aeneas, his hip crushed by Diomedes, and Apollo delivered him into the curing arms of Artemis and Leto.[16] More illustrative of mortal Greek religious practice are the open prayers for divine assistance addressed to tutelary deities. Diomedes, seriously wounded and slowed by an arrow, prays to his ancestral divine patroness Athena, who immediately returns him to fighting form:

> Hear me, child of Aegis-bearing Zeus … if ever you had good feeling
> for my father and stood beside him in dire war, now then be a friend to
> me, Athena. Grant that I catch the man and that he comes into the range
> of my spear, that man who slipped up on me and shot me, boasting that
> I will not long see the bright light of the sun. Thus he spoke in prayer,
> and Pallas Athena heard him and made his limbs light, his feet and his
> hands above.[17]

And later Apollo, in response to Glaukos' desperate prayer, caused his haemorrhaging to cease:

'Hear me, Lord, whether you are in the rich land of Lycia or in Troy, for you are everywhere able to hear a man when he has trouble as has now come to me. For I bear this mighty wound and my hand is wracked with sharp pains, and my blood can't dry up, and my shoulder is heavy because of it; I can't hold my spear steady, nor go to fight with the enemy ... But you Lord, can heal this mighty wound for me, and soften my pains, and give me might, so that I may command and urge on my Lycian comrades ...' Thus he spoke praying, and Phoebus Apollo heard him. And straightway he stopped the pains and dried up the black blood from the grievous wound and cast strength into Glaukos' spirit. And Glaukos knew it in his heart and he rejoiced, since the great god had swiftly heard him when he prayed.[18]

The forms of supplication here employed were common to the experience of ancient Greeks in peace and warfare alike. The Greek nouns *euchê* and *ara*, with their corresponding verbs *euchomai* and *araomai*, both cover the wider semantic range of the English 'prayer'. *Euchê/euchomai*, probably originally used of public and/or vaunting speech in a profane (or at least not explicitly sacral) context, had already by the time of the Homeric epics, perhaps in fact because of the formulaic language of the epic, become associated and tied to the word for 'curse or sacred vow', *ara/araomai*.[19] The efficacy of such battlefield appeals for divine assistance constitutes, in the mind of the bard, an index of the heroes' piety that has earned divine patronage. Given the astonishingly high rates of mortality on the Homeric battlefield, with a wound resulting in death more than three-quarters of the time,[20] recourse to divine succour seems perfectly natural and understandable.

Indeed, the carnage of these heroic battles was such that even the gods themselves had need of battlefield ministrations. Hades, wounded by Heracles,[21] and Ares, run-through by an Athena-inspired Diomedes, both receive formulaic treatment from the healer-god Paieon:

And upon it [Paieon] sprinkled pain-relieving herbs ... and as when fig-juice quickly condenses white milk when it is liquid but makes it congeal quickly for him who stirs it, so swiftly did he heal raging Ares.[22]

Paieon applies a treatment against haemorrhage known and recommended by the Hippocratic corpus,[23] fig juice, which does in fact coagulate milk but actually retards the clotting of human blood.[24] Regardless of the efficacy of the treatment, its presence in one of the traditional Homeric formulae – fixed lines and phrases deployed in similar contexts by the bard – lent the practice deep antiquity even in 'Homer's' day, as well as an unimpeachable authority that even the medical rationalists of the Hippocratic corpus could not resist: *ab Homero principium*. In fact, Paieon's very early association with things military and perhaps 'military medicine' is suggested by documentary evidence even older than Homer, as well as later battlefield ritual.

From the remains of the Bronze Age palace at Knossos come a series of clay tablets, administrative documents, inscribed in a syllabary known as Linear B, used to write an Archaic form of ancient Greek.[25] These inscribed tablets, fired in the destruction of the Bronze Age Achaean palaces at Mycenae, Knossos, Pylos and elsewhere, served as palatial administrative records, documenting the centrally organized, redistributive economy of the era. Among these archival caches at Knossos was the group of documents that gave name to the so-called 'Room of the Chariot Tablets', archival records of the storage, repair and outfitting of the palace's formidable corps of chariotry.[26] A single tablet records the names of a cluster of military deities: Poseidon, Athena, Enyalios and Paieon, rendered in the Bronze Age dialect as Pa-ja-wo-ne, Paiawon.[27] The presence of Athena, the warrior-goddess par-excellence and mythical tamer of horses, makes sense, as does Poseidon, the creator of horses. Enyalios, a martial deity distinct from Ares,[28] who may also be attested at the mainland palace of Pylos,[29] makes sense in an archive dedicated to war paraphernalia, but the association of Paiawon, a Homeric god of healing, seems at first incongruous. But later Greek battlefield ritual can perhaps illuminate the connection.

In later times, Paieon or Paian became syncretized with Apollo, the main Greek deity of health, healing and medicine, and it was to this deity that hoplites of the Greek phalanx sung their initial battlefield cry, the *paean*, raised to Apollo as the averter of present evils as the phalanx began to advance.[30] The war-cry proper, the *alalagmos*, raised upon final closing with the enemy, invoked the Greek god of battle-fury, Enyalios.[31] The invocations to Enyalios and Paiawon thus reveal themselves as the two sides of a soldier's aspiration in war: to inflict pain and death upon the enemy while avoiding or surviving the same. The fury of Enyalios saw to the former while the divine protection of Paieon assured the latter. Likewise, Apollo Epikourios, venerated on his mountain-top shrine at Bassai, attracted the dedications of Arkadian mercenaries seeking the god's protection in their deadly trade.[32] Divine favour was clearly understood to be the best prophylaxis against wounds on the field of battle.

Doctors, Magic and Religion in Greek Military Field Medicine

But what of the battlefield ministrations of mere mortals? The *Iliad* and *Odyssey* include several vivid, if somewhat curious, scenes of wound-care, and in several cases religious belief and magic practice melding freely with 'rational' medical care can be seen. The first wound of the *Iliad* is that treacherously suffered by Menelaos. Stricken by an arrow that did not completely pierce his corselet, the hero is carried to the rear by his comrades, who immediately seek out and summon the aid of Machaon, one of the two sons of Asklepios who accompanied the expedition and served as its 'two good doctors', 'worth many men in battle':[33]

> But when they arrived at the place where red-haired Menelaos lay stricken … [Machaon] pulled the arrow out of the fitted belt, and as he dragged it out, the pointed barbs were broken back … but when he saw the wound where the bitter arrow had entered he sucked out the blood and knowingly spread healing herbs that once upon a time kindly Chiron gave to his father.[34]

The Homeric usage is the earliest literary evidence for the term 'doctor', *iater*, an old Ionic form related to the later *iator* and the Attic/*koine iatros*, indicating that the term could designate a doctor or surgeon by 800 BC at least and likely much earlier. The military context has led to suggestions of an original military genesis for the term, as an 'extractor of arrows',[35] a view for which no ancient evidence exists. *Iatros* derives from the verb *iaomai*, 'I heal'.[36]

But Homer is in fact not the earliest attestation for *iater*, which first appears in the Linear B archives of Bronze Age Pylos, where an *iater*, rendered in the syllabary as *i-ja-te*, is the recipient of a single grain ration as 'a benefit', alongside other craftsmen like bronze-smiths, presumably in partial recompense for services rendered.[37] The passing reference leaves completely opaque the precise nature of the medical care provided and to what extent it intertwined with magical and religious practice, but there is little reason to believe that Mycenaean doctors differed substantially from their Bronze-Age contemporaries, whose care and treatments developed within a religious context and were replete with folk-remedies that often contained a significant magico-religious component. This also accords well with the status of doctors as craftsmen working among the general population (*demioergoi*), reflected in Homer and implied in the Linear B record.

The numerous serious wounds, often to the limbs and head, found on the excavated bones of Mycenaean males attest both to the deadly reality of their warrior culture and the technical and practical skill of Mycenaean doctors and field surgeons. The presence of healed breaks and fractures, also often clearly from battlefield wounds, strongly suggests an effective and thoroughly practical knowledge of setting, binding and immobilizing the wounded limb, suggesting skilled post-trauma care as well. Males from the Bronze Age settlements at Lerna, Asine and Mycenae show evidence of battlefield trauma.[38] From the latter cemetery came the remains of a man in his 30s, who had, as an adolescent, survived a serious frontal cranial puncture, likely from an arrow. Likewise, many of the long-bones of other burials show healed breaks and fractures, also often clearly from battlefield wounds, that would have had to have been re-set and bound, again suggesting skilled post-trauma care.[39] The practice of trephination, well attested in Mycenaean pathology and apparently practised from the Stone Age as a therapy for a variety of maladies, ranging from headaches to fainting and battlefield head trauma, was nevertheless no doubt conceived of and practised primarily in terms more familiar to prehistoric shamans than modern trauma specialists, in the belief that evil spirits or 'bad energy' must be released from the victim's skull.[40] The Mycenaean *iater* might have been aided in his ministration to the wounded on the battlefield by opiate elixirs.[41] The opium poppy was widely cultivated in the Aegean basin during the Bronze Age and had strong associations with the Great Goddess of Minoan and Mycenaean religion, often adorning her statuettes. A potent narcotic is perhaps hinted at in Homer's later description of Helen's miraculous potion, *nepenthe*, composed of wine mixed with a drug:

> Then did Helen, born of Zeus, have a different notion:
> Straightway she threw a drug into the wine they were drinking;
> a drug to chase away grief and strife and to make them forget all
>   their ills.[42]

The weight of modern interpretation inclines toward opium,[43] and with good reason, as the *Iliad* also depicts the heavy-fruited head of the opium poppy, which tends to lean to one side in season when ripe and slit for harvesting:

> As a poppy leans its head to one side, swelling with its fruit and the
> spring rain in a garden, so did his head tilt to one side, weighed down
> by his helmet.[44]

The plant actually seems to have originated in Asia Minor,[45] so there seems little doubt that both the Mycenaeans and the Ionian bards of the epic tradition would have been intimately familiar with the analgesic properties of opium.[46]

How widely it would have been employed on the battlefield is another question, however, for none of the Homeric *iatroi* employ it, while the Hippocratic corpus is definitively ambivalent as to the wisdom of using opiate preparations for pain or wounds and shows a curious indifference to painkilling medicines or procedures in general.[47] There seems little doubt, however, that for more serious procedures involving deep cutting, trepanation or the setting of badly shattered limbs, a sedative stronger than alcohol offered advantages. Still, in the *Iliad*, wine stands forth as the analgesic of choice.[48]

The substances applied to wounds in the *Iliad* and *Odyssey* have attracted a wide range of reactions, from the general and enthusiastic modern approval of washing the wound with water, to the general curiosity and condemnation, ancient and modern, of treatment by a potion (*kykeon*) of cheese and barley mixed in Pramnian wine.[49] 'Surely inflammatory!' is the incredulous reaction of Plato.[50] Curiously, it is Asklepios' son Machaon, who ostensibly disposed of more or at least other equally potent measures, who receives the potion as his treatment. Patroclus, by contrast, when his time as care-giver arrives, makes good use of the herb-lore that Chiron taught Achilles, first washing the wound with water and then applying a 'bitter root' to Eurypylos' wound:

> And stretching him out, [Patroclus] cut out from his thigh the sharp, barbed arrow and he washed the black blood from it with bright water and grinding up a bitter root with his hand, cast it upon the wound, a pain-killer which stopped all his pains.[51]

Later,[52] he continues his care of the wound with more unspecified herbal preparations. That the root is specified as 'bitter' (*pikre*) surely signifies its power to heal and combat the wound of the arrow, which is often described in Homer with the very same adjective.[53] Here is encountered the magical logic of 'like has power over like', i.e. the bitter root will stop the possibly poisoned (see below) wound caused by the bitter arrow.[54] An Athenian red-figure cup shows Achilles tenderly bandaging Patroclus. An arrow, its head slightly bent by either the initial impact or Achilles' extraction, lies to the left of Patroclus. Achilles ensures a lightly bound dressing by having Patroclus hold a strip of the binding to his arm: Achilles, like Machaon, learned his medical craft from the centaur Chiron.

All these substances, and more, were subsumed under the rubric of what the Greeks termed *pharmaka* ('drugs' or 'potions').[55] As others have noted recently, the actual efficacy of any particular *pharmakon* is not an appropriate path of historical inquiry.[56] What matters is which *pharmaka* and/or treatments were applied and why, the latter question necessarily raising the question of how, precisely, the practitioner thought the substance or procedure to be efficacious. Given the nature of the ancient sources, this is often a very difficult question to answer with great certainty in any particular instance. As already seen above, in the discussion of Paieon's treatment of Ares and the use of fig-juice as a blood coagulant, widespread belief and practice does not ensure empirical efficacy. In the case of many *pharmaka*, the duality articulated above in the plague scene sent by Apollo and ritual purification of the Achaean camp and veneration of the deity is clearly seen: the same substances were often held to have the power to both harm and heal, and in the latter case, spiritual impurity and physical corruption are held to be simultaneously cleansed by the application of *pharmaka*. While it seems certain that some of the substances commonly applied to battlefield wounds would have been salutary and soothing – for example, the washing

Figure 10.1: Achilles bandages the wounds of Patroclus. The Greek letters adjacent to each figure are their names. Tondo (interior) of an Athenian red-figure cup, by the Sosias Painter, dating to about 500 BC. Altes Museum Berlin 2278. (*Courtesy of Alamy*)

of wounds with wine and/or vinegar – the harvesting, preparation and application of *pharmaka* in antiquity all nevertheless reveal a basis in the type of magico-religious thinking generally termed theurgy, i.e. the ritual practice of invoking divine power, in this case that held to be within the *pharmaka* themselves.[57]

'Drugs are in the hands of the gods,' intoned Herophilus, one of the most famous Hellenistic medical researchers attached to the Ptolemaic Mouseion, cited by Galen approvingly in his own treatment of drugs.[58] The early evidence of the Homeric epics suggests this view of *pharmaka* held sway from the beginning. In the *Odyssey*, Hermes provides Odysseus with the protective *pharmakon* moly to protect him from the baleful *pharmaka* of Circe.[59] Hermes notes, tellingly, that 'moly' is the name given to the plant by the gods themselves, but that the root is difficult for mortals to dig up, an indication of its affinity with the divine. Surprised by the failure of her potion to transform Odysseus, Circe is later forced to change his men back into human form with 'another *pharmakon*'. Thus the same duality was expressed with *pharmaka* as in divine intervention: the power to heal is the power to hurt, and vice-versa. We should note that the precise function of moly is not specified by the bard; Odysseus does not seem to consume it, but its mere presence acts as a phylactery against Circe's evil *pharmaka*.[60] This 'amuletic' prophylacitc power of *pharmaka* was reinforced by the power of incantations (see below) and other rituals in the harvesting, preparation and application of *pharmaka*.[61]

The trove of ancient pharmacological lore was the demesne of the so-called 'Root-cutters' (*rhizotomoi*), localized practitioners (*demioergoi*) and dispensers of traditional herbal medicine and lore. The distillation of their knowledge has been preserved by Theophrastus in his *Inquiry into Plants* (*Historia Plantarum*), particularly in Book 9, which relates not only the pharmacological properties of various herbs, but also, rather embarrassingly for those seeking a purely rational basis for Greek pharmacology, a wide range of theurgic proscriptions for the harvesting and preparation of herbal *pharmaka*. In this they followed the lead of mythical sorceresses such as Medea, who harvested her *pharmaka* by the light of the moon with a bronze sickle.[62] *Rhizotomoi* apparently believed that certain *pharmaka*, because of their powers and properties (*dunameis*), should be harvested with certain ritual precautions: to protect him or herself, the cutter should harvest *Thapsia garnica* and rose hips while standing to the windward side; one should chew garlic and quaff neat wine while harvesting hellebore. Even more curiously, peonies should be dug up at night, to avoid being seen by woodpeckers, lest the digger go blind, while the harvester should watch out for buzzards while cutting feverwort. More transparent and conventional is the prescribed offering of fruit and bread to Asklepios after harvesting his sacred plant, 'All-Heal' (*panakes*). Theophrastus dutifully records all this and more, and while clearly sceptical of some practices, still feels obliged to opine that 'praying while cutting is perhaps reasonable'.[63] Indeed, the doctrines of the late Classical/early Hellenistic *rhizotomoi* seem to have much in common with the later and more explicitly magical herb-harvesting rituals attested in the *Greek Magical Papyri*, where spells such as this are recorded:

> Spell for picking a plant: Use it before sunrise. The spell is to be spoken: I am picking you, such and such plant, with my five fingered hand, I (name of picker), and I am bringing you home so that you may work for me for a certain purpose. I adjure you by the undefiled name of the god … fulfill for me the perfect charm.[64]

In sum, the lore of the *rhizotomoi* preserve an important glimpse into the views and knowledge of *pharmaka* current among such *demioergoi* and their clientele, clearly revealing a worldview in which the divine powers of *pharmaka* were to be treated like all divine things: with circumspection, respect and due ritual precaution.

As seen above with Circe, *pharmaka* could be deployed for healing as well as baneful ends, and returning to Book 4 of the *Iliad* and the wounded Menelaos, he is to be found wounded by the most feared weapon of the ancient battlefield: the bow and arrow. While the physical effects of his wound are not serious, the thorough treatment he receives from Machaon clearly hints at the real danger of arrow-wounds: poison.[65] From the Greek word for 'bow', *toxon*, derives all Greek terminology for poisons of all sorts – and ultimately the English 'toxic', telling testimony to the ubiquity of poisoned projectiles in antiquity. Despite the fear, revulsion and ideological denigration these weapons engendered, their pedigree is enshrined in the earliest Greek myths. Both Heracles and Odysseus seek and employ poison to make their darts more certainly deadly. Heracles envenomed his arrows with the venom of the Hydra, a great, multi-headed serpent, perhaps an early aetiology for the invention and use of arrows tipped with snake venom.[66] The Greek hero Philoctetes, either bitten by a snake or accidentally wounded by one of Heracles' arrows, suffered a foul, festering wound for years:[67] a 'best-case scenario', while the ugly reality of an envenomed arrow wound, as described in the later medical treatises, was far grimmer: 'necrosis … haemorrhages, swelling limbs, vomiting, wracking pains, freezing pain around the heart, culminating in convulsions, shock, and death'.[68] The power of toxic weapons was enough to lure the great hero Odysseus far north of his homeland, to the kingdom of Ephyra, on the edge of civilization, in search of a 'man-killing' *pharmakon* derived from local plants. The king of the land, loathe to share his deadly power with Odysseus, refused to supply it, leaving the hero to his own, ultimately successful, devices.[69]

The painful lingering death from poison arrows so horrified the heroic ethos of the Greek warrior that, despite the use of poison arrows by their heroic ancestors, poison darts became identified with the cruelty of the Greeks' 'barbarian' opponents. The Scythians, wild nomads of the Eurasian steppe, were especially notorious for poisoning their arrows, and their recipe for arrow toxin reveals why their shafts were so invariably lethal: the Scythian toxin (*skythikon*) derived from the venom of an adder, but the processing involved both putrefaction of the snakes' flesh as well as a likewise rotten admixture of human blood serum and animal dung. When the components were finally mixed together, the product was a reeking toxin of multivalent potency: haemotoxic and riddled with the bacteria that cause tetanus and gangrene. Few of those wounded with such weapons would have survived, and even those who did would have suffered a crippling and long-festering wound.[70] Small wonder that poisons were viewed as magical substances, with even their delivery systems, the shaft of the arrows themselves, marked with malevolent symbols to empower the poison tips.[71]

Against such dire weapons, even the shrewdest *iatros*, Machaon himself, had recourse to arcane counter-measures. The sucking of the blood from Menelaus' wound, while perhaps somewhat effective at evacuating contaminants and any possible arrow toxin from the wound, derives from the realm of folk-medicine and magic. On a basic level, blood was itself believed to be both an agent and vessel of contamination, able to absorb malign spiritual influences and transmit them to the body.[72] Three tribes in the ancient world – the Italic Marsi, the Numidian Psylli and the more obscure Ophiogenes – were particularly renowned and even sought-out as wound-suckers for ancient armies.[73] Significantly, in the case of the better-documented Marsi and Psylli, the ancient sources make clear that the ability of these peoples to heal snake-bite and poisoned arrow wounds derived not from practical medical knowledge, but was an innate ability or skill, deriving either from the *terrior* of their native land or inherited from a mythical ancestor or founder.[74] In the case of Machaon, his descent from Asklepios and ultimately Apollo, as well as his teaching by the mystical centaur Chiron, no doubt assured that his wound-sucking was efficacious. The Psylli became notorious purveyors of poisons of all sorts, selling their knowledge and wares in Rome, finely illustrating in the realm of *pharmaka* the now familiar duality: those with the power to heal also hold the power to harm, and vice-versa.

Beyond the battlefield ministrations of the *Iliad*, the *Odyssey* also preserves the earliest literary depiction of a clearly magical ritual, an *epaoide* – a spell or sung charm, deployed to care for the wound of a youthful Odysseus, badly gored by a wild boar:

> But his relatives, the sons of Autolycus, busied themselves round about him, and they knowingly bound the wound of noble, godlike Odysseus, and stopped the black blood with an incantation.[75]

While not inflicted by a human weapon, the gash on Odysseus' thigh would resemble in general terms the punctures and lacerations suffered on the battlefield and treated by doctors in the field. The Greek term *epaiedein*, from the term *epaiedein*, 'to sing over', encompassed all such medically efficacious chants and songs,[76] so common that Plato casually includes them, alongside pharmaceuticals and surgery, among the expected methods of a doctor.[77] In fact, the practice of chanting to stop haemorrhage appears across the family of Indo-European cultures, attested as well in Old Irish, German, Russian and Vedic sources.[78] In each instance, the chant accompanies a simultaneous tying or bandaging of the wound. Some point to this as a separation of a purely practical measure, the bandaging, from the magical power of the incantation.[79] The matter is, however, not so clear-cut.

The verb deployed by Homer to indicate tying, *deein*, is also regularly employed for magical bindings, and the close association of binding/bandaging with the singing itself strongly suggests that it is part of the same ritual treatment. In the Vedic ritual, a poultice of dust, sand and mud is applied simultaneously with the singing charm. But an Old Irish comparandum is the most telling: 'all they could do for them was to apply spells and incantations and charms to them to staunch the bleeding and haemorrhage *and to keep the dressings in place.*' Here, the power of the chanted spell reinforces the efficacy of the bindings themselves and this sympathy of speech and action is repeatedly seen in such rituals.[80] Pliny records a groin-cure involving a thread from a spider's web, knotted seven or nine times and then tied to the groin, but to make the cure work one must utter the name of a widow as each knot was tied.[81] Likewise, a Scottish charm for curing a sprained leg required a similarly knotted black thread to be fastened around the limb while uttering an invocation to the divinity.[82] When it is considered that knots and tying were themselves seen to be suffused with magical power to impede or hinder for good or evil,[83] the distinction between a 'practical' field-tourniquet and a magically potent binding of the artery or injury falls to the ground.[84] As seen above and will be seen again, the ancients made no firm distinction between the 'rational' and the 'magical' elements of a medical treatment. That the bandaging of wounds and, indeed, concern for haemorrhage, were relatively uncommon or at least not emphasized in Homeric medicinal practice,[85] further reinforces the view that the binding of Odysseus' wound derives from the special magical knowledge of his paternal uncles, sons of Autolycus, who, like the centaur who taught Patroclus and Asklepios, crackle with arcane power.[86]

Care of War-Wounds at the Greek Asklepieia

Unfortunately for some casualties, the prospectus was not simply death or natural healing and a return to physical health. There remained the unpleasant third outcome of the lingering, unhealed wound, constantly weeping and suppurating, a constant source of misery. And in at least four ancient documented cases, when 'conventional' medical treatment could not heal wounded warriors, they turned in extremis to the mercy and skill of the medical god par excellence: Asklepios.

The Asklepieia, sanctuaries of Asklepios, god of health and medicine – attested at Epidaurus, Athens, Pergamon, Cos and elsewhere – had become, by the fourth century BC, centres of pilgrimage for the ill and injured from all around the Aegean.[87] The afflicted pious would make their journey to the sanctuary of the god and, after initial sacrifices and other ritual preparations, enter a special building within the sanctuary, the *enkoimeterion*, literally 'the sleepery', where they would lie down for treatment of their illnesses and injuries by the god himself, a process known as *enkoimesis*, or *incubation* in Latin. Not infrequently, the patients would have a vision or dream that the god had attended to their various needs. They would then awaken in the morning, their illness cured or their wound healed.

These cures have been memorialized by numerous inscribed thanks-dedications from the various shrines, but by far the most remarkable documents are the so-called *iamata* (healings) inscriptions from the great sanctuary of Asklepios at Epidaurus.[88] Originally inscribed on six tablets attested by the second-century AD traveller Pausanias, three complete stelai and fragments of a fourth were discovered in the modern excavation of the sanctuary. Each begins with the heading 'The healings of Apollo and Asklepios', and go on to record extraordinary, miraculous cures and healings and other wonders accomplished by the gods for those who visited his sanctuary. A good many of the *iamata* are clearly impossible: Cleo, pregnant for five years, who gave birth to a walking, talking young boy; Aristagora of Troizen, whose head was detached and body split open before being stitched back up by the god.[89] It seems beyond doubt that the inscribed record of these and other miracles performed by the god served a didactic purpose, attesting the power of the deity and thus teaching the audience proper reverence and awe (*aidos*) in approaching his sanctuary for help.[90] To assume that all of the *iamata* were fantastic, whole-cloth fabrications, genuine miracle-cures or marvellous cures of psychosomatic illnesses, however, paints with too broad a brush a variegated group of experiences. While some were, no doubt, miraculous, inexplicable cures of previously intractable diseases or conditions, others seem to reflect a more 'hands-on' and practical basis in the battlefield trauma-care attested in the Hippocratic corpus.

Of particular interest in this regard are four individuals healed of chronic wounds received in battle: Euhippos, Gorgias of Herakleia, Timon, and Antikrates of Knidos. The first three cases all differ from the last in explicitly involving the removal of a weapon-tip from the patient's body:

> Euhippos carried around a lance-head in his jaw for six years. When he laid down in the sanctuary for treatment the god drew out the lance-head and gave it to him in his hands. When day came, he awoke healed holding the lance-head in his hands.[91]

Edelstein has suggested that these three cases of removed weapon-points are best understood as ejections of the intrusive mass by the body:[92] purgations that would have naturally happened in any event, but which serendipitously accompanied the patients' pilgrimage to Epidaurus. Needless to say, such repeated coincidence strains credulity. The unlucky Euhippos was nevertheless fortunate to have avoided the tetanus or sepsis so often attested as the result of penetrating wounds in the Hippocratic corpus.[93] Regardless, it is noteworthy that Euhippos' treatment is not explicitly characterized by a vision or dream. The *iama* tells only that he laid down and the god removed the lance-head from his jaw. The removal of an externally exposed weapon-tip would not have been an overly-complicated procedure, involving merely forceps and perhaps a probe, especially if, as Edelstein suggests, the body was well along the path of ejecting the point anyway. In fact, an entire Hippocratic work survives from antiquity on the procedures for the removal of weapon-tips from a wound,[94] with detailed techniques for both the removal of arrowheads and care of suppurating penetrating wounds. Such works were, in fact, didactic, so it is certainly not beyond the realm of possibility that the literate, among whom would number the priests and attendants of the god, could learn and teach basic wound care, especially shallow wounds like that suffered by Euhippos.

The second case, that of Gorgias, however, is more complicated:

> Gorgias of Herakleia, of pus: this man, wounded by an arrow in his lung in some battle, for a year and a half produced so much pus that he filled sixty-seven basins with pus. When he lay down in the sanctuary for treatment, he saw a vision – the god seemed to him to draw the arrowhead out of his lung. When day came, he came out healed, carrying the arrowhead in his hands.[95]

Unlike the shallower jaw-wound of Euhippos, Gorgias' was a deep, penetrating arrow-wound to the chest. Successful extraction of arrowhead and patient survival were not unheard of; the Hippocratic corpus preserves two instances: 'Billos had been wounded in the back; much air came out of the wound, with noise; he bled; he was treated with *enhaimes*,[96] and healed. The same happened to Dyslatas.'[97] Gorgias was not so lucky and the chronic nature of his suppuration accounts for the impressive volume of pus, but how was the evacuation accomplished? Remarkably, there is a detailed description from the Hippocratic corpus describing the treatment for chronic suppuration in the chest, often the result of penetrating injuries from 'spears, daggers, and arrows':[98]

> Cut as low as possible so that the pus may flow out more easily. Cut between the ribs, the skin first, using a sharp knife with a rounded blade. Then take a round-pointed knife, wrap its blade in a cloth so that only the point will protrude as much as the length of a thumb's nail, and cut through [to the pleural cavity]. Let out as much pus as you think best, then put in a tent of raw linen attached to a thread [to aid in retrieval of the linen strip, should it slip within]. Let out the pus once a day … When [after several days' treatment] the pus becomes thin as water, slippery to the finger, and scanty, put into the wound a hollow tin drain. When the pleural cavity becomes dry [i.e. ceases to produce fluid] cut the drain shorter little by little, and allow the incision to heal as you retrieve the drain.[99]

The unhappy Gorgias had likely undergone an initial treatment as described above, yet his suppuration would not cease, no doubt due to the continued presence of the arrowhead in his lung. Given the likely presence of an open incision and stint, removal of the arrowhead would have likely involved perhaps a slight widening of the incision for the drain and then careful work with forceps and probe. Again, nothing is encountered here beyond the established capacity of Hippocratic surgeons. The deeper nature of the work could perhaps have been facilitated by administration of an opiate to dull the pain and senses, perhaps also contributing to the 'vision' in which the god seems to draw the arrow out of his lung directly.

In both of these two instances, the healed veteran is given the point as a token of his cure, likely meant to be dedicated in the sanctuary as a thanks-offering to the god, a tangible testimony to the healing skill of the deity. It should be noted that patients were not the only dedicators in the Asklepieia; doctors too dedicated their instruments to the deity as thanks-offerings.[100]

The next case, involving Antikrates of Knidos, is the most problematic in its interpretation:

> Antikrates of Knidos, his eyes: This man became blind after being stricken 'between his eyes on either side'/'through both his eyes' by a spear in some battle and he carried the spear-head sticking in his face. When he lay down for healing in the sanctuary he saw a vision – it seemed to him that the god drew the missile out and then fitted his so-called pupils back into his eyelids again. When day came, he went out healed.[101]

The nature and extent of the wound itself is unclear. At issue is how the preposition *dia* with the genitive case is to be understood. Is it the common usage found in Homer, when a spear penetrates through a body part?[102] Such a wound would obviously have severely damaged the eyes beyond any normal hope of repair. But *dia* can also mean 'between', a usage found in the medical texts.[103] In such a case, the blindness could then be attributed to pressure on the optic nerve that was relieved by the removal of the projecting weapon-tip. But the vision of the god replacing Antikrates' pupils would suggest that the former meaning is preferred: without the surgical skill of the god, his shattered pupils could not have been repaired and replaced. Adding to the likelihood of this interpretation is the observation that the miraculous healing of wounded eyes appears to be a folkloric motif still found in the early modern Balkans.[104] Antikrates' wound, then, ranks alongside the most miraculous of Asklepios' impossible miracle-cures. Note that unlike the first two instances, both of which also involved weapon points, the spear-point is not given to Antikrates as a token of his healing to be dedicated to the god.

After the remarkable extractions of weapon points from the wounds of Euhippos, Gorgias and Antikrates, our last case seems relatively tame:

> Timon ... wounded by a spear-head beneath his eye: this man, having lay down in the sanctuary for treatment saw a vision – the god seemed to him to have rubbed and poured an herb somehow into his eye and he was healed.[105]

No weapon extraction was necessary in this instance. Timon suffered only from a serious battle-wound beneath one of his eyes. The precise nature of the wound and its effects is not even related: did it make him blind in that eye? Was it slow to heal and/or producing pus? How old was the wound? Treatment of such a wound, presumably an infected or weeping penetrating wound, would, like the first two cases, have been a fairly simple surgery involving opening access to the affected area, drainage of any pus, cleansing of the wound and as the vision attests, treatment with any number of *pharmaka*. We should note that two of these cases involve eye-injuries and that images of eyes are among the most common of the *typoi*, small metal punched images, dedicated to the god at his Athenian sanctuary, perhaps indicating a 'specialization' of the god there.[106]

Of these four cases, only one can easily be dismissed as a miraculous healing along the lines of Aristagora of Troizen or Cleo. The other three were all well within the ability of a skilled surgeon of the fourth century. But how likely was it that the priests of Asklepios were also physicians or that the temple availed itself of the services of medical professionals? Most, following the lead of Edelstein,[107] have been loathe to accept the possibility, attributing the often rational procedures followed by the god to general familiarity with medical practice that was transferred to the visions. It is true that there is little hard evidence for direct association of physicians with the Asklepieia. Not even the Asklepiadai, or sons of Asklepios, a medical association at Cos, are directly tied to the Asklepieion there. On the other hand, there is some evidence from Athens that cult staff, in particular the *zakoroi*, could have been involved in medical treatment of visitors to the sanctuary,[108] and some slim evidence for doctors being involved with the Athenian cult, although the precise nature of the tie is unclear.[109] We are, in fact, remarkably ignorant as to what exactly transpired once the pilgrim entered the *enkoimeterion*.

On the whole, I am less ready than Edelstein and his followers to dismiss ancient testimony suggesting that the cult attendants of the Asklepieia dressed up to impersonate the god.[110] To what end? The obvious answer is that in some instances, those attending the sick and injured impersonated the deity while effecting his treatments and cures.[111] Archaeological finds of medical instruments both on Cos and at Epidaurus certainly suggest that at least some of them were used in the shrines themselves.[112] The fact that the attending god appeared differently to different patients, now looking like an old man, now like a youth, to my mind, only increases the likelihood of involvement of multiple cult-staff in the treatment of the afflicted. Far from the work of charlatans, such theatrics were not alien to Greek religious, or even political, ritual.[113]

Conclusion

In the course of this exploration from the world of myth and Homer to the late Classical period, it has emerged how freely the practice of magic and religion mixed with the empirical practice of medicine in the Greek world. The ancient Greeks clearly made no hard and fast demarcation between the two realms, either in theory or practice. To some extent, this is the expected result of a Greek medical practice that derived much of its methods and knowledge from the body of folk-belief and practice. The thorough amalgamation of theurgy into Greek medical practice, especially pharmacology, in some ways provides a more comfortable setting for the integration of Hippocratic methods into the miraculous cures of Asklepios at his healing shrines. If the ancients believed that the gods and their power were a 'normal' part of the natural world, as Edelstein has persuasively argued, why should not the healing power of the god become manifest in his sanctuaries, just as the divine power of the other gods and the natural world manifested itself in divine intervention on the battlefield and the miraculous healing and protective power of *pharmaka*.

Notes

1. Pin. *Pyth.* 3.47–53.
2. Dodds, 1968, 102–78.
3. Hippoc. *Aer.* 22, *Morb. sacr.* 18; Longrigg, 1998, 40–61, contains a convenient compilation of Hippocratic source material; Plat. *Laws* 899b; Arist. *Cael.* 288a 4–5; the classic treatment of Edelstein, 1937, still retains much of its cogency.
4. Fowler, 2005, 283–86; Fowler, 2000, 317–43.
5. Mauss, 1902–1903; Durkheim, 1912.
6. Fowler, 2000, 335. He incisively continues, 'Instinctively we recoil from taking *that* seriously; to do so might imply that we actually believe, for instance, that the crops will grow better if we chop up a pig. Yet it is the attitude of people who do believe that we must see from the inside.' The emphasis is in the original.
7. Goode, 1949; Versnel, 1991; Fowler, 2005, 285.
8. A general treatment is available in Lonis, 1979, who, unfortunately, does not touch upon military medicine *per se*.
9. I Samuel 6: 4–5.
10. Willcock, 1978, 187; Kirk, 1985, 57.

11. Hom. *Il.* 1.48–52.
12. Cf. Hom. *Od.* 5.394–97, 9.411.
13. Hom. *Il.* 1.10–317.
14. Hom. *Il.* 1.313–17.
15. Parke, 1967, 268–78.
16. Hom. *Il.* 5.305–17, 447–50.
17. Hom. *Il.* 5.115–22.
18. Hom. *Il.* 16.514–31.
19. Jakov and Voutiras, 2005, 108–09.
20. Santos, 2000; Frölich, 1879. See Salazar, 2000, 126–58, for the ideological and literary patterns behind wounding and dying in Homer.
21. Hom. *Il.* 5.401.
22. Hom. *Il.* 5.900–04.
23. Hippoc. *Morb. sacr.* 4.52.
24. Majno, 1975, 151–52.
25. Chadwick, 1976; Chadwick and Ventris, 1973.
26. Driessen, 2000.
27. KnV 52+; Chadwick and Ventris, 1973, 311–12; Gulizio, Pluta and Palaima, 2001.
28. Gonzales, 2008, 131–32.
29. PY An 656; Palmer, 1963, 239.
30. Fairbanks, 1900; Pritchett, 1971, 105; Gonzales, 2004, 54–55.
31. Gonzales, 2008.
32. Cooper, 1996, 75–79.
33. Hom. *Il.* 2.729–33, 4.192–219.
34. Hom. *Il.* 4.210–19.
35. Gabriel and Metz, 1992, 142, following Garrison, 1970, 37.
36. Chantraine, 1980, 453.
37. PY Eq 146+; Duhoux and Morgpuro Davies, 208, 139.
38. Lerna, 181 and 182 Ler., see Angel, 1971, 58–59; Asine, 59 As., see Angel, 1982, 111; Mycenae, 51 Myc., see Angel, 1972, 380.
39. As Arnott, 1999, 502, notes, studies of bone-breaks in wild animals make clear that serious breaks will not simply heal over time without setting.
40. Arnott, 1999, 501–03; see more generally the series of essays in Arnott *et al.*, 2003.
41. Arnott, 1999, 501 (see below for Helen's potion, *nepenthê*).
42. Hom. *Od.* 4.219–21.
42. See for example, Stanford, 1959, 275; Scarborough, 1991, 139–40; cf. Heubeck *et al.*, 1988, 206–07.
43. Kirk, 1990, 323–24; Scarborough, 1991, 140.
44. Hom. *Il.* 8.306–08.
45. Trease and Evans, 1978, 569; Tyler *et al.*, 1981, 225–26.
46. Scarborough, 1991, 140; Arnott, 1999, 501.
47. Salazar, 2000, 60–65.
48. See Hom. *Il.* 11.638, discussed below.
49. Hom. *Il.* 11.638; cf. *Od.* 10.234–36, where Circe prepares an identical potage, to which she adds a 'destructive *pharmakon*', for Odysseus' unfortunate companions.
50. Plat. *Pol.* 405e; cf. Porph. *Abst.* 1.167.11.
51. Hom. *Il.* 11.844–48.
52. Hom. *Il.* 15.390–94.

53. See for example, Hom. *Il.* 4.217, above.
54. The bitter root of Homer may be the bulb of squill (*Drimia Maritima*) which, in part because of its acrid pungency, had several magico-religious prescriptions. See Scarborough, 1991, 146–47.
55. Salazar, 2000, 54–67, and Scarborough, 1991, provide sound introductions to military and sacred pharmacology respectively.
56. Salazar, 2000, 66.
57. Scarborough, 1991, 142.
58. Marcellus *Letter of Cornelius Celsus on Remedies* (Herophilus F248b), in Longrigg, 1998, xiii.14.
59. Hom. *Od.* 10.391–94.
60. Scarborough, 1991, 139.
61. See for example, Plat. *Charm.* 155e–156e for a plant (*phyllon*) used as an amulet in conjunction with a sung charm or spell.
62. Macrob. *Sat.* 5.19.10; Scarborough, 1991, 144, discusses Medea's presentation in Sophocles' lost tragedy the *Rhizotomoi* (*TrGF* 4 FF534–36).
63. Theophr. *Hist. Pl.* 9.18.3–11; see also Scarborough, 1991, 14–50.
64. *PGM* iv.286–95, trans. O'Neil, 1986.
65. See Salazar, 2000, 28–30, for a concise discussion of the treatment of poisoned wounds in the medical writers.
66. In the fight against the Centaurs, Heracles accidentally struck his ally Telephus, who suffered for years until cured by Achilles at Troy: Ovid *Met.* 9.62–75; Apollod. *Bibl.* 2.5.2, 2.5.4, *Epit.* 3.17–20; Diod. 4.11; Pliny *Nat. Hist.* 34.152–54; 25.33, etc. Heracles himself ultimately succumbed to Hydra venom: Ovid *Met.* 9.170–204. See Mayor, 2009, 1–62.
67. Soph. *Phil. passim*, esp. 685–700; Apollod. *Epit.* 3.26–27, 5.8–10; Quint. Smyrn. 9.334–480.
68. Mayor, 2009, 65; Majno, 1975, 193, 198–99.
69. *Od.* 1.252–66; 2.325–30; Heubeck *et al.*, 1988, 107–08; Mayor, 2009, 56–58, 266.
70. Ovid *Tr.* 3.1.55–65, 4.1.77, 5.10.21. The recipe is preserved in [Arist.] *Mir. ausc.* 845. See also Ael. *Nat. An.* 9.15; Diosc. 1.106, 2.79; Mayor, 2009, 80–82; Rolle, 1980, 65.
71. Mayor, 2009, 85–85 with Figure 11.
72. Ackerknecht, 1970, 5; Majno, 1975, 145.
73. Pliny *Nat. Hist.* 7.13–15; Plut. *Cat. Min.* 56.3.
74. Pliny *Nat. Hist.* 28.30; Aul. Gell. 16.1–7. Significantly, according to Gellius, the Marsi were descended from the son of the Homeric archetypal sorceress Circe.
75. Hom. *Od.* 19.455–58.
76. Pfister, 1924, 325.
77. Plat. *Pol.* 426b.
78. Renehan, 1992, 3–4; Ehrismann, 1954, 107–09; Stanford, 1959, 334 with references; Sigerist, 1961, 23, 159.
79. Renehan, 1992, 3.
80. Frazer, 2002 (1913–1915), 5.303–05.
81. Pliny *Nat. Hist.* 28.48; Frazer, 2002 (1913–1915), 5.303.
82. Frazer, 2002 (1913–1915), 5.304–05.
83. Frazer, 2002 (1913–1915), 5.293–317.
84. Frazer, 2002 (1913–1915), 5.303–05; Kotansky, 1991, 108.

85. Majno, 1975, 143.

86. Burkert, 1983, 120, 131.

87. See the massive collocation of evidence in Reithmüller, 2005.

88. Edelstein and Edelstein, 1945, 220–40, has conveniently collated and translated the *iamata* and dedicatory inscriptions; see also the fuller collection of LiDonnici, 1995.

89. Cleô: *iama* i of *IG* iv² 1.122 (Edelstein and Edelstein, 1945, 229); Aristagora: *iama* xxiii of *IG* iv² 1.122 (Edelstein and Edelstein, 234).

90. Dillon, 1994, 239–60.

91. *IG* iv² 1.121.95–97 (*iama* xii).

92. Edelstein and Edelstein, 1945, 168.

93. Majno, 1975, 192–200; Salazar, 2000, 30–34.

94. See for example, the work entitled *On Wounds and Arrows*. Other, more generalized, treatments in the Hippocratic corpus, such as *On Wounds*, *Epidemics* and *On Diseases*, also contain details on wound-care, battlefield surgery and case histories. See Salazar, 2000, 1–5.

95. *IG* iv² 1.122.55–60 (*iama* xxx).

96. *Enhaimon* or *enhaimes* was a drug for wounds still 'in blood', i.e. fresh. It was compounded from equal parts of copper acetate, copper oxide, lead oxide, alum, myrrh, frankincense, gall nuts, vine flowers and wool-grease diluted in wine; Majno, 1975, 154.

97. Hippoc. *Epidemics* 5, no. 98 (*Epidemics* 7.29).

98. Hippoc. *Morb. sacr.* 1.21; Salazar, 2000, 15–16.

99. *On Diseases* II, no. 47 (trans. of Majno, 1975, 157).

100. Herzog, 1931, 148; Vlastos, 1949, 278 with no. 36.

101. *IG* iv² 1.122.63–68 (*iama* xxxii).

102. See for example, Hom. *Il.* 4.481.

103. Hippoc. *Morb. sacr.* 2.61.

104. Maric, 1954, 90–92.

105. *IG* iv² 1.122.119–22 (*iama* xl).

106. Straten, 1981, 149–50; Rouse, 1902, 212; cf. Aleshire, 1989, 42.

107. Edelstein and Edelstein, 1945, 139–80; Dillon, 1994; Reithmüller, 2005, 382–88.

108. Aleshire, 1989, 87.

109. Aleshire, 1989, 65–66, 87–88, 94–95.

110. The priest of Asklepios in Aristophanes' *Plutus*, acting in the guise of the god, disposes of both a medicine chest and sacred snakes, as does Asklepios at Epidaurus and the healing hero Amphiaraos from Aristophanes' homonymous lost play (*Amphiaraos*: *PCG* iii.2 F28). Aristid. *Or.* 49.21–23, where the neokoros provides the stricken orator with a salve, shows fairly clearly that some temple staff could and did in fact provide attention.

111. Vlastos, 1949, 276–80.

112. Herzog, 1931, 148.

113. During the Dionysiac festival of the Anthesterion in Athens, the *archon basileus*, the magistrate overseeing religious matters in Athens, probably dressed as the deity to consummate a sacred union (*hieros gamos*) of the god with his Athenian consort, in this case the archon's wife, presumably also suitably attired: [Arist.] *Ath. Pol.* 3.5; Kerényi, 1976, 307–13; Burkert, 1983, 230–38. For the intersection of politics and similar theatrics, see the story of Peisistratos and Phye in Hdt. 1.50–51.

Connor, 1987, argues that such episodes are not simply instances of clever rulers manipulating a credulous public, but complex and subtle encounters in which the audiences empathetically participate, reinforcing communal bonds, goals and values.

Bibliography

Ackerknecht, E.H., 1970: *Therapie – von den Primitiven bis zum 20. Jahrhundert.*, Stuttgart.

Aleshire, S., 1989, *The Athenian Asklepieion*, Gieben.

Angel, J.L., 1971, *The People of Lerna: Analysis of a Prehistoric Aegean Population* II, Princeton.

—— 1972, 'Human Skeletons from Grave Circles at Mycenae', in Mylonas, G. (ed.), *Grave Circle B of Mycenae*, Athens.

—— 1982, 'Ancient Skeletons from Asine', in Styrenius, C.-G., and Dietz, S. (eds), *Asine* II, Stockholm.

Arnott, R. 1999, 'War Wounds and their Treatment in the Aegean Bronze Age', in Laffineur, R. (ed.), *Polemos: le context guerrier en Égée à l'âge du bronze*, vol. 2, 499–505.

—— et. al. 2003, *Trepination: History, Discovery Theory*, Lisse.

Burkert, W., 1983, *Homo Necans: The Anthropology of Ancient Greek Sacrificial Ritual and Myth*, Berkeley.

Chadwick, J., 1976, *The Mycenaean World*, Cambridge.

—— and Ventris, M., 1973, *Documents in Mycenaean Greek*, 2nd edn, Cambridge.

Chantraine, P., 1980, *Dictionnaire etymologique de la langue grecque*, Paris.

Connor, W.R., 1987, 'Tribes, Festivals and Processions: Civic Ceremonial and Political Manipulation in Archaic Greece', *JHS* 107, 40–50.

Cooper, F., 1996, *The Temple of Apollo Bassitas, vol. i: The Architecture*, Princeton.

Dillon, M., 1994, 'The Didactic Nature of the Epidaurian Iamata', *ZPE* 101, 239–60.

Dodds, E.R., 1968, *The Greeks and the Irrational*, Berkeley.

Driessen, I., 2000, *The Scribes of the Room of the Chariot Tablets at Knossos*, Minos Supplement 15, Salamanca.

Duhoux, Y., and Morgpuro Davies, A. (eds), 2008, *A Companion to Linear B Studies*, vol. 1, Louvain.

Durkheim, E., 1912, *Les forms élémentaires de la vie religieuse*, Paris.

Edelstein, L., 1937, 'Greek Medicine in its Relation to Religion and Magic', *Bulletin of the Institute of the History of Medicine* 5, 201–46.

—— and Edelstein, E., 1945, *Asclepius. A Collection and Interpretation of the Testimonies*, 2 vols, Baltimore.

Ehrismann, G., 1954, *Geschichte der deutschen Literatur bis zum Ausgang des Mittelalters, Erster Teil. Die Althochdeutsche Literatur*, Munich.

Fairbanks, A., 1900, 'A Study of the Greek Paean', *CSCPh* 12, 19–24.

Fowler, R.L., 2000, 'Greek Magic, Greek Religion', in *idem* (ed.), *Greek Religion*, Oxford, 317–43.

—— 2005, 'The Concept of Magic', in J. Paul Getty Museum, *Thesaurus Cultus et Rituum Antiquorum*, vol. iii, Los Angeles, 283–87.

Frazer, J., 2002 (1913–1915), *The Golden Bough: A Study in Magic and Religion*, 15 vols, New York.

Frölich, H., 1879, *Die Militärmedicin Homers*, Stuttgart.

Gabriel, R., and Metz, K., 1992, *A History of Military Medicine*, vol. i, London.

Garrison, F.H., 1970, *Notes on the History of Military Medicine*, Darmstadt.

Gonzales, M., 2004, *Cults and Sanctuaries of Ares and Enyalios* (Diss.), Berkeley.

—— 2008, 'New Observations on the Lindian Cult-Tax for Enyalios', *ZPE* 166, 121–34.

Goode, W.J., 1949, 'Magic and Religion: A Continuum', *Ethnos* 14, 172–82.

Gulizio, J., Pluta, K., and Palaima, T., 2001, 'Religion in the Room of the Chariot Tablets', in Laffineur, R., and Hägg, R. (eds), *Potnia: Deities and Religion in the Bronze Age, Aegaeum* 22, Liege.

Herzog, R., 1931, *Die Wunderheilungen von Epidauros: ein Beitrag zur Geschichte der Medizin und der Religion*, Leipzig.

Heubeck, A., West, S., and Hainsworth, J.B. (eds), 1988, *A Commentary on Homer's Odyssey*, vol. 1, Oxford.

Jakov, D., and Voutiras, E., 2005, 'Gebet, Gebärden und Handlungen des Gebetes', in *ThesCRA* iii, 105–41.

Kerényi, C., 1976, *Dionysos: Archetypal Image of Indestructible Life*, Princeton.

Kirk, G.S. (ed.), 1985–1993, *The Iliad: A Commentary*, 6 vols, Cambridge.

Kotansky, R., 1991, 'Incantations and Prayers for Salvation on Inscribed Greek Amulets', in Faraone, C., and Obbink, D. (eds), *Magika Hiera: Ancient Greek Magic and Religion*, New York, 107–37.

LiDonnici, L., 1995, *The Epidaurian Miracle Inscriptions*, Atlanta.

Longrigg, J., 1998, *Greek Medicine from the Heroic to the Hellenistic Age: A Source Book*, New York.

Lonis, R., 1979, *Guerre et religion en Grèce a l'époque classique: Recherches sur les rites, les dieux, l'idéologie de la victoire*, Paris.

Majno, G., 1975, *The Healing Hand: Man and Wound in the Ancient World*, Cambridge.

Maric, R., 1954, 'Ein Märchenmotiv in den Inschriften aus Epidauros', *ZA* 4, 90–92.

Marot, K., 1961, 'Autolykos', in Georghiev, V., and Irmscher, J. (eds), *Minoica und Homer*, Berlin, 24–30.

Mauss, M., 1902–1903, 'Esquisse d'une théorie générale de la magie', *L'Année sociologique* 7, 1–146.

Mayor, A., 2009, *Greek Fire, Poison Arrows and Scorpion Bombs: Biological and Chemical Warfare in the Ancient World*, London.

O'Neil, E.N., in Betz, H.D. (ed.), 1986, *The Greek Magical Papyri in Translation*, Chicago.

Palmer, L., 1963, *The Interpretation of Mycenaean Greek Texts*, Oxford.

Parke, H.W., 1967, *Oracles of Zeus: Dodona, Olympia, Ammon*, Cambridge.

Pfister, F., 1924, 'Epode', in *RE* Supplementband IV, Stuttgart.

Pollak, K., 1993, 'Frühe Medizin in Griechenland', in Pollak, K. (ed.), *Wissen und Weisheit der alten Ärzte*, Düsseldorf, 5–83.

Pritchett, W.K., 1971, *The Greek Sate at War. Part i*, Berkeley.

Reithmüller, J.W., 2005, *Asklepios: Heiligtümer und Kulte*, 2 vols, Heidelberg.

Renehan, R., 1992, 'The Staunching of Odysseus' Blood: The Healing Power of Magic', *AJPh* 113, 1–4.

Rolle, R., 1980, *Die Welt Der Skythen: Stutenmelker und Pferdebogner: ein antikes Reitervolk in neuer Sicht*, Munich.

Rouse, W.H.D., 1902, *Greek Votive Offerings*, Cambridge.

Salazar, C., 2000, *The Treatment of War Wounds in Graeco-Roman Antiquity*, Leiden.

Santos, G.H., 2000, 'Chest Trauma During the Battle of Troy', *Annals of Thoracic Surgery* 69, 1285–87.

Scarborough, J., 1991, 'The Pharmacology of Sacred Plants, Herbs, and Roots', in Faraone, C., and Obbink, D. (eds), *Magika Hiera: Ancient Greek Magic and Religion*, New York, 138–74.

Sigerist, H., 1961, *A History of Medicine, vol. ii: Early Greek, Hindu, and Persian Medicine*, Oxford.

Stanford, W.B., 1959, *The Odyssey of Homer*, 2 vols, London.

Straten, F.T. van, 1981, 'Gifts for the Gods', in Versnel, H.S. (ed.), *Faith, Hope and Worship*, Leiden.

Trease, G.E., and Evans, W.C., 1978, *Pharmacognosy*, 11th edn, London.

Tyler, V.E., Brady, L.R., and Robbers, J.E., 1981, *Pharmacognosy*, Philadelphia.

Versnel, H.S., 1991, 'Some Reflections on the Relationship Magic-Religion', *Numen* 38, 177–97.

Vlastos, G., 1949, 'Religion and Medicine in the Cult of Asklepios: A Review Article', *Review of Religion* 13, 269–90.

Willcock, M.M., 1978, *Homer: Iliad I–XII*, London.

—— 1984, *Homer: Iliad XIII–XXIV*, London.

Index